Praise for *Henry Hudson*
and the Algonquins of
New York

"Henry Hudson and the Algonquins of New York is without a doubt the most interesting and thorough exploration of Hudson's legendary journey up th waterway our ancestors called the River of Tides. It's rich with details abou Native American coastal life in the early 17th Century and should spark se rious discussion about the dramatic events that unfolded in the New Yorl region four centuries ago."

—JOSEPH BRUCHAC, author of *Our Stories Remember*

"Pritchard uses investigative techniques to explore how an originally peaceful encounter with Native Americans ended in distrust and ultimately violence. He constructs plausible vignettes to enhance the understanding of readers, many of whom will be learning new information in his book's pages."

—BONNIE LANGSTON, *Kingston Daily Freeman*

No one but Evan Pritchard could have written this book with its nuanced, intricate look at what happens when great cultures collide and their dreams are destroyed—or fulfilled in ways their peoples never could imagine. I find something of inestimable value, which Pritchard, of both Amerindian (Algonquin Micmac) and western origins, seems to understand implicitly: *Discovery is a two-way process.*

Pritchard's scholarship, first maturing in full splendor in *Native New Yorkers* (2001) now moves comfortably from European histories, including ship's logs and captain's journals, to something heretofore (apparently) unthinkable: Ethnography from the other side: *How the many and varied indigenous peoples of Eastern America might have perceived the coming of Europeans among them.* Pritchard is eminently qualified for this difficult task by two things: his ancestry and his love for the language and worldview of the original peoples.

Evan Pritchard is both an historian and a poet. His ability to tell a story well prevents this book from being dry in its accuracy of detail, as he navigates the seas skillfully with Hudson and his treacherous mate Juett, destined to become Hudson's nemesis. Great deeds, and equally great misdeeds, vie dramatically in its pages, and Pritchard is able to show how skill and generosity can coexist in the same person, along with immense egotism and bad judgment. I found myself sharing Pritchard's infectious fascination with the details of Amerindian life, their harmonious and sustainable lifestyles, the details of their language, their diets, dress, their commerce, their politics. It is this fascinating juxtaposition of factual minutiae, good anthropology, history and geography, along with an intuitive grasp of the mythology and spirituality of both cultures that makes the book such a worthwhile read.

Like Joseph Campbell, a self-described "maverick scholar," Evan Pritchard could be accused of "reveling" in his subject matter. It is, in fact, that sheer love of what he is describing, that should communicate to every intelligent reader of this book. He does in fact get caught up in the excitement of describing what happens when mythologies collide and the ancient god Chaos reigns.

Let this book stand as enduring testament that historical and ethnographic scholarship need not be tedious—if the details are woven into the texture of a fascinating story of worldviews in collision.

— STEPHEN LARSEN, co-author, *Joseph Campbell: A Fire in the Mind*

"Evan Prichard deftly navigates the uncharted waters of Henry Hudson's exploration of the river that bears his name, intuitively recreating, when documentation fails, the discovery we celebrate this Quadricentennial year. His is a brilliant solution to the puzzle of missing pieces that was the Half Moon's voyage; a solution not without controversy. Much of what little is known about Hudson's journey was written by the man ultimately responsible for his death.

"Prichard combines the oral history of the Algonquian Peoples with the facts as we know them to tell the compelling story of discovery, betrayal and death.

— RICHARD FRISBIE, editor of *Ruttenber's Indian Tribes of Hudson's River, 1700-1850*

Praise for *Native New Yorkers*

"The book is a tour of Indian landmarks and historical sites, with descriptions of the cultures, history, languages and lore of the Native American inhabitants. Drawing on archival material as well as interviews with present-day leaders of the Algonquin nations, Pritchard offers a wealth of information that doesn't make it into many New York City histories or guidebooks."

—*Publishers Weekly*

"I suspect that many American Indians will feel as I do, that this is a book we've been wanting for many generations. Every New Yorker should read it."

—JOSEPH BRUCHAC, author of *Lasting Echoes* and *Sacajawea*

"Evan Pritchard, a Micmac scholar, has produced a miracle: a scholarly, informative book that is fun to read and full of surprises."

—PETE SEEGER

HENRY HUDSON
AND THE ALGONQUINS
OF NEW YORK

HENRY HUDSON
AND THE ALGONQUINS
OF NEW YORK

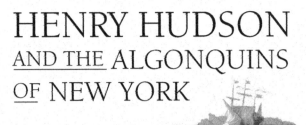

Native American Prophecy
& European Discovery

1609

EVAN T. PRITCHARD

COUNCIL OAK BOOKS

Chicago

Published by Council Oak Books, LLC
An imprint of Chicago Review Press Incorporated
814 North Franklin Street
Chicago, Illinois 60610

First edition

Cover art: Henry Hudson, The Granger Collection, New York.
Mandush, a Shinnecock Sachem circa 1640 by Shinnecock
and apache artist David Martine. Used by permission of the
artist. Half Moon, Library of Congress

Cover and book design: Carl Brune

ISBN 978-1-57178-222-9

Library of Congress Cataloging-in-Publication Data

Pritchard, Evan T., 1955-
Henry Hudson and the Algonquins of New York : native
American prophecy and European discovery, 1609 / Evan T.
Pritchard.
    p. cm.
Includes bibliographical references and index.
ISBN 978-1-57178-222-9 (trade pbk. : alk. paper)
1. Hudson, Henry, d. 1611. 2. Algonquin Indians--New
York (State)--New York--First contact with Europeans.
3. Algonquin Indians--New York (State)--New York--
History--17th century. 4. Hudson River Valley (N.Y. and
N.J.)--Discovery and exploration--Dutch. I. Title.

E129.H8P75 2009
910.92--dc22
                                            2009024411

CONTENTS

List of Illustrations

August 29   – Delaware Bay

August 30   – Jersey Shore

August 31   – out at sea

September 1 – out at sea

September 2 – see fire, enter Barnegat Bay, exit via Cranberry Inlet

September 3 – "three rivers" at 40 degrees

September 4 – "further up, good harbor," two cables in, many people, tall oaks, Wolfe's Pond Park.

September 5 – three fathoms hard by southern shore, Princes Bay

September 6 – Half Moon still, row boat with John Colman to Harlem River, Long Island Sound, then returning to Clasons Point, mouth of Bronx River, battle, Colman killed, boat returns

September 7 – Tottenville, Wards Point burial

September 8 – Tottenville

September 9 – Tottenville to Arthur Kill, both captives escape

September 10 – Arthur Kill

September 11 – lower Manhattan

September 12 – same location

September 13 – to Yonkers (take two more prisoners)

September 14 – Yonkers to Cornwall

September 15 – Cornwall, two prisoners escape, to "place of loving people," Saugerties

September 16 – 4.4 miles to Catskill/Mud Flats

September 17 – to Lower Schodack

September 18 – sailed ashore with old chief, saw pit of stored corn

September 19 – to Port of Albany 4.4 miles Upper Schodack

September 20 – 4 miles in row boat to Troy, round trip

September 21 – no travel, carpenter on land, Upper Schodack

September 22 – tour same location, meanwhile row boat to Cohoes and back

Return Trip

September 23 – South to Bear Island then south to tip of Lower Schodack, 130 feet deep

September 24 – mud flats, Athens-Hudson, Catskill

September 25 – Catskill, corn and slate

September 26 – "loving people" visit from 4.4 miles south. HH stays in Catskill

September 27 – south, pass "loving people" at Saugerties at 5 miles, then 8 miles more to Kingston/Rhinecliff. Fishing, Van Horen taken (?)

September 28 – travel 4.4 miles to Staatsberg, then 6.6 to Poughkeepsie

September 29 – Poughkeepsie to Cornwall

September 30 – Cornwall no movement

October 1 – travel 15.4 miles to Indian Point, (2 captives return) cook's sword, then 4.4 miles to Croton Bay

October 2 – travel 15.4 miles to Yonkers, battle with falcons firing six muskets, then 4.4 to cliffs

October 3 – No movement; does Hudson go alone onto Manhattan Island with a Quaick cup and a keg of rum?

October 4 – out to sea via either shallow river or "northwest river," no distances

There are a number of cross-references in Juet's log. This overview, or summary, of my reconstruction of Juet's log will explain how these can be worked out logically.

GREAT FLOATING BIRD

he story behind New York State's quadricentennial, at least for most, is the saga of Henry Hudson, brave explorer, nice guy, crossing the sea on the Half Moon, charting the length of the river that now bears his name, and then returning home safely, alerting all Europe to the great fur trade that awaited them north of the narrows.

But here is the story behind that one, and the other one behind that: Hudson's ill-fated relationships with his son; his strong-as-an-ox friend John Colman; his body guard, scribe, and personal Judas, Robert Juet; plus various Dutch crew members, some of them probably former pirates, most of whom he could not understand. Then there he is, caught in legal limbo between his Dutch employer and his English King, unable to complete his mission, but stumbling upon a golden opportunity that he grasped boldly, resulting in a century of war between England and Holland and a promotion that brought his doom. There is even the harrowing tale of how this information has come to us today, not really intact, but rather molested, mostly through the convoluted mind of a certain Robert Juet and other exigencies of fate.

But this book is not really about Henry Hudson, first European to explore New York's Hudson Valley, nor his crew. This is about the land that discovered him, the people who encountered him, and the river that flowed beneath him, both ways, upstream and down. The land is Turtle Island, the river is the Mohicanituck (spelled various ways, most notably Muhheakunnuk "Great Waters Constantly In Motion, as interpreted by DeLaet) and the people are the Eastern Algonquin people. It is their story.

In Juet's log, the Algonquins are merely part of the backdrop, stock characters in the story of his ship. He doesn't report their names or the names of their villages, or their names for plants and animals. With research, much of the setting of the story can be reconstructed. Once we have the setting, the story begins to unfold, and it is a dramatic one—filled with both affection and distrust between two great navigators, Hudson and Juet, and two great cultures, the European and the Native American.

In order to test and complete the account that Juet records, to "tell both sides of the story," we need to take the same facts and create a mirror image of the events, as seen through the eyes of the "others," both as individuals with feelings and human needs, and as representatives of what we know about Algonquin society at that time. We cannot know the full range of what happened, but we can explore what probably happened without too much trouble. The story that emerges is a clash between two well-established cultures, long separated by distance, resulting in violence between the two, which, with a few notable exceptions, was unprecedented in North America. When we look into the whys behind the story, yet another tale slowly takes shape, one that brings us into the realm of dreamtime, where "Creation is happening now," in which giant manta rays, wild deer, great rivers, and tall trees have rights, just as people do, and their wishes must be acknowledged or a price must be paid.

The people Hudson met were members of a great civilization of Algonquian-speaking nations stretching across North America and called by various names, Anishinabi, Algonquin, Ooskidjinabi, but all praying to Manitou (and variations on Kitchi Manitou, translated as "The Great Spirit"). At the time of Henry Hudson, there were dozens of nations within the Algonoquian "hoop,"[1] generally organized as confederacies or "leagues." We can see how closely related linguistically these many nations really are by carefully examining this list of words for "bear" among the many far-flung peoples of the Algonquin culture: *Mukwa* in Ojibway, *Mko* in Potowatomi, *Mahk(w)* in Shawnee, *Mok(w)* in Munsee, *Muhk* in Unami, *Mahkwa* in Mohican and *Mak* in Cree, to name a few examples.[2] The word Manitou is spoken among these nations with similar consistency. It has been acknowledged by countless experts and by the people themselves that these nations are also closely related culturally and spiritually. These similarities persist in spite of the wide variety of environments they may find themselves in, today as in the past.

The people Hudson encountered, as far as it can be determined, were all Algonquian-speaking people (I will use the –ian ending to refer to the linguistic family, but Algonquin otherwise; some use the ending -kin). Other possibilities will be acknowledged as the narrative continues. Although it is utterly impossible to present the world view of the individuals Henry encountered with complete accuracy today, I hope at least to present clues as to their cultural inclinations, practices and beliefs, using my own inbred Algonquian instincts, plus every scholarly means at my disposal, using historical records, linguistics, archaeology, anthropology, and the oral tradition in combination, and interpreted through logic to reconstruct a reasonable picture of what was going on around Mr. Hudson at the time — a kind of historical triangulation similar to navigational techniques used by Henry Hudson himself.

Hudson was not the only navigator on the ship the Half Moon in 1609. His "first mate" (as some refer to him, probably incorrectly) was a certain Robert Juet, meticulous navigator and log keeper. We will take a look at the portion of the text of Robert Juet's Journal that applies to New York and New Jersey, just as it appears in the collections of the New York Historical Society, Second Series, 1841.[3] The reader is welcomed to check this against Samuel Purchas' version, from *Purchas, His Pilgrimes*, which uses Juet's spellings[4] utilizing each day's observations on the people and geography of the Hudson River's shores as a reference point for gaining a better understanding about what the actual Native American political and cultural landscape might have been.

We will consider the significance of everything Hudson and crew saw and some things they didn't see as well. In this way I hope to offer the reader a much more meaningful account of the journey now, four hundred years later, than would have been possible even at the time of the publication of Juet's journal in 1625. To accomplish this we will first need to reconstruct Juet's actual position each day, which is somewhat controversial. Over the course of the book, I will occasionally compare geographic interpretations by Edgar Bacon, Donald Johnson, Paul Huey (northern portions), Ian Chadwick, Edward Hagaman Hall, and Michael Sullivan Smith (Hope Farm Press 2008), among others. They are strikingly different as the reader will see, and yet each has its merits. Part of the reason for doing this is to remind readers that they, like Hudson, are charting a "sea of darkness" (to quote Donald Johnson) into historically and culturally uncharted waters.

Creating a synthesis of all the evidence that has come to my attention was only a first step towards approaching what I feel is a reasonable account of the voyage. My next task was to describe the geo-political significance of those locations, objects and events, and what they say about the people the Europeans meet—their self-identification, political alliances, population centers, roads and waterways, and so forth. This opened up the possibility of reconstructing some of the more important cultural landmarks just beyond the periphery—the richer cultural heritage Hudson might have absorbed had he more time to wander and reflect. Finally, this opened me to the hearts and minds of the people who greeted Hudson, in the form of plausible, though fictionalized, characters.

The larger part of this book objectively annotates the well-known but little understood diaries of Juet and Hudson, revealing often-forgotten aspects of the daily lives of native coastal people in New York at contact. But there must have been much more to the story; in fact we can be certain of it. Juet's journal in particular holds back more than it includes, and as most of Hudson's diary disappeared, that leaves us very little in terms of inarguable fact. There are also two or three Native American accounts of first contact with Hudson that do not match Juet's accounts, nor those of later European colonists. And yet these accounts restore to us the feeling of these dramatic moments, regardless of the facts, feelings that Juet does not disclose. It is a fascinating cultural comparison.

Even after assembling all these parts, the story of the Half Moon still does not add up to a whole. Neither Juet nor Hudson record the names of the native people, the names of their villages, their customs, or their beliefs. For the most part they do not share with us their own reactions to what is happening. In order to fill this gap, I have interspersed this somewhat scientific study with what I will call "dramatizations." These will be clearly defined and separated from the rest of the text, as they are historical fiction, rather than history. They should not be quoted out of context as fact. These dramatizations will use dialogue and action to help the reader experience the moments of drama in the story where many of the details are either known or can be surmised. I think the reader will agree that they do not stray far from the course of known history.

For the most part, the story of this world-changing contact between the people of the Algonquin nations and the people of Europe is a joyful story. Sadly, most of the languages Hudson and Juet heard, many of the species of fish they ate, some of the minerals they examined, some of the birds they saw hunted, many of the animals whose skins they saw in abundance, and some of the plants they describe, are now either extirpated from the Hudson Valley, endangered worldwide, or are extinct. Also vanished from the Hudson Valley are the villages of the mostly peaceful people that these journals describe, as well as the fine ecological balance in which they apparently lived and worked. The "Great Floating Bird," the Half Moon, was not long for this world either. It was wrecked and abandoned during a voyage to the East Indies, on the Island of Mauritius in 1615, not long after Hudson himself vanished into a bank of fog and rain somewhere near the Arctic Circle in what is now called *in memoriam* Hudson's Bay. Some change is healthy, some is not, and Hudson brought both kinds to this remarkable river valley of steep hills, their effects rapid and irreversible. Reconstructing a picture of this lost balance between humans and the rest of what we call nature is important to today's ecologists, as it represents a reference point for our region in terms of what words like "healthy" and "sustainable" really mean. It is our own case history. Native American scientist and author of *Gathering Moss,* Robin Kimmerer, calls this "the reference ecosystem"; perhaps the one truly meaningful benchmark we will seek in our long journey back to a sustainable society.

The title "Great Floating Bird" reflects the nature of the Algonquins' first impressions of the Half Moon as they gazed out from shore.[5] They called it "a great waterfowl, floating..." "a great floating house..." "a serpent..." and even *a visit from Manitou Itself.* This title acknowledges all of these impressions at once and yet is not limited to one. A poignant sub-theme of the book is one of disillusionment, of unmet expectations, even betrayal, and a growing sense of realization that these powerful transcontinental traders and their flamboyant leader were not divine and that the Half Moon was not a magical bird but only an overstuffed canoe. We can read these feelings between the lines of Juet's journal as he describes actions on the part of their Algonquin guests aboard ship, actions which cannot otherwise be explained.

As Henry and crew went plowing up the river and back down again, seeing everything and yet nothing, they brushed past some remarkable people and places, unawares. From reading Robert Juet's journals and what little is left of Henry Hudson's, we don't know much at all—postcards from an unknown paradise—but through this same process of triangulation between stone, bone, and paper, we can also reconstruct some of what was just beyond the captain's line of vision, just out of reach of his row boats and scouts, to give us a much deeper understanding of the world he entered and yet saw not, but dimly. I will use these occasional dramatizations to connect the Half Moon to the villages and pathways on shore via the people who trod both. Nonetheless, I feel there is no better way to introduce the modern reader to the almost completely unfamiliar world of the old Algonquins than show from Hudson's point of view (as reported by his assistant) his rather limited encounters with these traditional ancestors.

The log of frustrated poet Robert Juet, scribbled from the deck rails of the Half Moon as a sort of backup to Henry's journal, has puzzled scholars for four hundred years. Juet's job was to keep records of tides, fathoms, and navigational problems. Although he faithfully attempts to be precise and consistent in his chronicle of their adventures encountering an unfamiliar culture, he is more concerned with the running of the ship and keeping good nautical records. There was too much that was unlabelled, too much that was totally unfamiliar, and some of which was alien to him and his shipmates, and this makes it a challenge to determine exactly where they were on many a given day.[6]

Hudson's diary was lost about 1821, either thrown away as trash accidentally, burned in a fire, stolen, or sold to someone, perhaps someone who didn't want the secrets of New York City's rebirth as New Netherlands to be known. Accounts from the oral tradition of the Native American side of the story have been elusive few and do not correspond closely with the European side. All we have left of the Half Moon's records are three days of diary entries from Henry Hudson's journal, copied over into Dutch before 1821, and a mostly-complete version of the ship's log, written by Juet. Robert Juet was an old but not-to-be-trusted friend of Hudson's, and his log is strangely journalistic for a ship's log but disappointingly terse and technical for a travelogue. Bacon writes, "Juet's approach to keeping a log book … owed its origin and development to the Muscovy Company,"[7] a powerful international trade cartel that Hudson's grandfather may have been involved in, and for which he and Juet had worked in the past.

As a rule of thumb, I will presume everything that Juet and Hudson wrote in their respective logs was accurate unless it can be shown otherwise. Without this rule as a hypothesis, there can be no basis for rational discussion. This does not mean that they were in fact accurate. We can be sure that all humans, thrown into unfamiliar circumstances, will be imperfect and make mistakes. But we should be able to detect those mistakes or take Juet and Hudson at their word. Once we do, the journals then become solvable historical puzzles. Some of Juet's observations open up possibilities not often brought to mind. For example, the use of wampum as medicine, the lack of drumming references, (although William Penn saw "drumming" in 1680) the popularity of metal smoking pipes, especially yellow copper, the hunting of passenger pigeons, and the abundance of pumpkins and grapes may be surprising to those relatively new to "the old ways."

Readers want to know both the European and the Native American side of the story, and so I have made every effort to be bi-partisan, with an emphasis on that which is not well known. There are unusual challenges facing anyone who wishes to reconstruct Hudson's journey of 1609 or the geopolitical landscape of the Algonquin people of the Hudson Valley region at that time. Both are the subjects of endless controversy. I welcome experts, scholars and tribal historians to write in and present better interpretations than what is found here. If convincing, these can become incorporated into future editions. The address is: Resonance Communications, P.O. Box 1028, Woodstock, NY 12498.

Many of my "scenarios" and conclusions are not to be found in other books or studies but are the results of original scholarship. Long-argued questions will be answered, such as, "Where did the Half Moon first land when arriving in New York harbor? How long was Juet's 'league?' His 'fathom?' His 'cable?' His 'shot?' Who killed John Colman? Where was he killed and why? Where he was buried? What were the native views about the manta rays that Hudson's men were eating, and how might that have affected the voyage? Where was the watch fire they saw from the sea? Where is 'a pleasant land to see?' How did Hudson get out of Barnegat Bay while moving north? Who were the "very loving people?" Did Hudson's men discover the Mohawk River? Where was Hudson's ship when it was attacked? Where did the natives acquire so many copper smoking pipes, some made from European copper? Whether my answers will convince all readers or not remains to be seen, but at least they are reasonable answers, based on known facts, and presented straightforwardly.

I present this volume as a celebration of New York State's joyful quadricentennial. I have made a heartfelt effort to consider both Dutch and Algonquin viewpoints equally in the creation of this narrative. My intention is to show how, even under duress, the proud Algonquins and the equally proud men of the Half Moon quite nearly experienced lasting racial harmony in spite of their fear, mistrust, and other human foibles of emotion. Their failures were similar to our own. The natives wanted to be left unmolested, their dignity in place, and Hudson was "just doing his job." I hope I have treated the Dutch and their likable English captain and scurrilous ship's mate justly, as well as the various Algonquins Hudson met in 1609, for whom it is difficult to do justice to today.

In concluding, it should be stated that the origins of New York's multi-racial history and its successes and failures over the years can be traced back to the first encounters between Europeans and natives in the Hudson Valley, none of which is better known or less understood than the mysterious voyage of the Half Moon, the "Great Floating Bird."

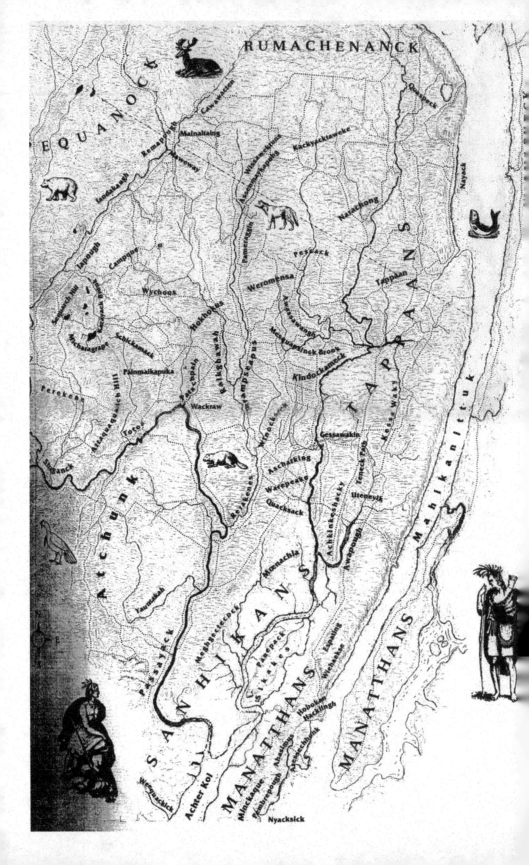

Chapter One

THE SAGA OF THE HALF MOON, A SYNOPSIS
The Untold Story of Henry Hudson's Voyage of 1609
from a Native American Perspective

*T*o reconstruct the tale of Henry Hudson's trip of 1609 has not been easy. In fact it has become for me a long and somewhat arduous voyage of discovery. I admit, the story I am about to tell is not the one that you expect to hear, and not at all the one I first set out to tell.

There are a dozen possible reconstructions of Robert Juet's cryptic logbook, and each author who tries to chart this "sea of darkness" seems to end up somewhere new. Yet I see it now as vividly as if I was onboard ship, or in the lodges of the First Peoples who ran to greet that colorful craft. In this first installment, I will tell it as I would tell any mystery story, without apologies or explanations. I will leave aside for now the dozens of interviews with native elders and experts, the hundred or so books I read in search of clues, the endless background work in verifying facts, the fitting together of a million puzzle pieces of information to make this mosaic laid before you. I beg the reader's pardon only for a chapter. Please bear with me if you find this story hard to believe; I am asking you to suspend old realities and enter into the numinous space between the Native American dreamtime world and that of seventeenth century seafarers. In spite of appearances, there is nothing in this chapter that can't be defended by known facts and the opinions of noted scholars. In the remaining chapters, there will be plenty of time to go through step by step and explain how logic and reason led me to these conclusions and inspired me to write down this strange saga of the arrival of the "Great Floating Bird."

It should not be surprising to learn that the Algonquin perspective concerning Henry Hudson's historic visit would be different than that told in most English history books. I for one firmly believe that the saga of the Half Moon of 1609 began 392 years before, on a tiny island in the Bay of Fundy still called Fire Island by the Mi'kmaq people who live nearby and who consider it a sacred shrine. It was there in what would become St. Johns, New Brunswick, Canada, that a series of eight prophets arrived, according to the Red Sky Scrolls. They brought warnings for the future and teachings for the ages. They brought these to the Algonquian-speaking people, and, so some believe, for all humankind. They spoke of "medicine wheels," and hoops within hoops of what we'd call ecosystems, and hoops within hoops of what we'd call "time," though there still today is no such word in the local language of the Mi'kmaq people.

In order to warn the people of certain moments far into the future at which time they would have to make decisions that might affect the future of the planet, the prophets provided a calendar of sorts. There was already a cycle of the day and the positions of the sun and moon; already a cycle of the month, which went from new moon to new moon; and there was a solar "year" and a lunar "year" marked out on the backs of "moon turtles." The prophets also taught of a "life walk" cycle, of 56 years, 14 years per each of the four directions, which each of us walks in our own way. I was taught by Wabanaki elders (the late Irvin Polchis among others) that this wheel or hoop took 56 years to complete, 14 years per each of the directions. It was said that in the time of Creation, we were each granted two cycles, which I assume to be 112 years, but as an approximation, as the universe is constantly in flux. Those who reach the age of 56 today are often considered elders by native people, though one's actions speak louder than the gray hairs that appear. Even then, foolishness and angry ways had cut that time in half for many native people. The prophets said that each lifespan-length was to be called a "fire," and that seven of these fires laid end to end would be the length of the era of the great prophecy that was about to begin, the era of "the seven fires." This was the largest of hoops, a single round of which would take 784 years to "walk." The important highlights would be preceded (or in some cases, followed) by solar eclipses, rings of fire visible from the Bay of Fundy's Fire Island, and would roughly coincide with the newness or the fullness of that cycle. Wherever these "prophets" came from, they were evidently people who understood something about eclipses and Saros cycles.[8]

These prophets foretold of seven cycles to come and what would happen in each fire. The prediction about each "fire" was presented by one prophet. However the fourth and central "fire" (the one directly opposite the starting point on the wheel) was so important it was represented by two prophets. It was a teaching in duality, a morality play on a grand scale.

According to accounts still preserved by the Midewiwin lodges (mostly now in the Great Lakes region) a prophet of the fourth fire told the people of visitors from the eastern direction who would come in brotherhood to teach them new things they never knew. Then another prophet of the fourth fire came and told them of visitors from the eastern direction who would be filled with hatred, bringing weapons of war. They were told that if these the eastern visitors did indeed come in brotherhood, all would be well and a new "rainbow" race would emerge on Turtle Island (their name for North America), a mingling of the four colors of humanity, which the elders say was known because of the four colors of the birches, red, brown, white, and yellow. However, if the visitors came with weapons of war, their arrival could lead to disaster at the end of the seven fires, unless the fears and misunderstandings could be worked out. If both types of visitors came together, well, that was a different story. It would bring a series of difficult tests for the native people of Turtle Island.

The Algonquin spiritual leadership must therefore have been primed for the arrival of visitors in September 1609, the central year of the central "fire" of the seven, the furthermost point on the wheel from the beginning/ending, in their cyclical view of time. At that time they made a special wampum belt to record these prophecies. The belt is of purple and white, with a diamond representing each "fire" or cycle of time. This magnificent work of art features a double diamond in the fourth position at the center, where the belt buckle would be if fastened behind as a sash or belt. There are many layers of meaning imbedded into that magical weave; however, one that all agree on is that it represents the passage of time, measured by the sun and moon. Therefore, the center of this diamond would have included, through a complex system of lunar and solar calendars, August 28, September 11 and October 1, 1609, as we shall see.

The leadership had studied the skies and consulted with the seers and prophets, and had prepared songs, stories, and special gifts for the visitors. In the minds of the less informed, the visitors might be prophets themselves, from a highly advanced race of beings living across the water. It was incredibly important for the future of the earth that things go well for the predicted visitors and for their hosts. The Munsee remembered this in 1849 and mentioned it in their letter to Zachary Taylor:

> Previous to your arrival into our vast Continent, our Ancient Prophets and wise men had a Vision and Revelation in regard to your coming, though they did not understand fully the meaning of it, whether it was to be the Almighty himself or our fellow men, this was a matter of deep consideration for a while with our forefathers until you did arrive.
>
> Our ancient men, without any delay made a Song concerning their expectation of your coming. Likewise a Drum was made for the purpose, out of the shell of a Sea Turtle. The drumming and their singing of the song were connected together and were performed jointly together, and also dancing which was performed with great solemnity in honor of your coming.

The lodge leaders and uninitiated alike were bracing themselves for this spiritual test. Thus the stage was set for the arrival of the unsuspecting Henry Hudson, a compassionate man for the most part, a free spirit who felt a sense of fondness for Native Americans, probably more than for his crew. They were also prepared for the arrival of Officer Robert Juet, a treacherous man who would later have his own captain killed in a mutiny that he apparently had planned for years. Ironically, except for three pages from Hudson's diary, Officer Juet's ship's log is all that has survived to record the journey from the Europeans' perspective. On the other hand, the "seven fires" wampum belt is in pristine condition, in the hands of William Commanda, an Algonquin Nation elder of Quebec who has been highly decorated by the Canadian Government for his spiritual leadership and work for social equality. He himself is only 17 winters short of a "fire" and has walked the earth to spread the message of the prophets.

Both Juet's log and the wampum belt are four hundred years old. While the meaning of Juet's narrative has been lost to most until now, the teachings of that belt have been carefully preserved as they have been passed down for four hundred years to elders like Eddie Benton Banaise, the Medicine Chief of the Three Fires lodge and author of *The Mishomis Book*.

The Europeans came in search of a navigable passage through North America to the Far East. Henry Hudson's ship, the 85-foot long Half Moon, attempted to pass through the icy waters of northern Canada, but they found the waterway crowded with icebergs and the ship's crew nearly mutinied. (Juet leaves this out of his diary.) Hudson turned south to seek other passages west, hoping to find one at 40 degrees latitude. Earlier in the trip, the Half Moon had visited Nova Scotia not far from St. John's, New Brunswick, and there was conflict there with the natives. Juet explains away his violent acts, "They would have done the same to us," implying that the natives didn't get a chance to do anything first.

Unable to fulfill his duties as described in writing by the Dutch East India Company's corporate directors, Hudson went south to warm the hearts of his "frozen" crew of mutineers and also to search for the fabled places his hero Giovanni di Verrazzano described in his diary of 1524. Suddenly finding himself with no schedule, a "free spirit," Hudson somehow slipped into the Algonquin equivalent of dreamtime. On August 28, by the dark of the moon (which signified to the elders of the secret lodges the end of the first lunar year since the eclipse of the fourth fire) Hudson entered and explored the gateway to the river of the Lenape, or "ordinary people." For the people on shore, the prophecies had been fulfilled, and nothing short of disaster could convince them otherwise. Henry Hudson, the ever-punctual Londoner, had arrived precisely on time.

Needless to say, the people of the bay were overjoyed. This large bay, which Verrazzano had glimpsed and called Vandome, is now called Delaware Bay, and Hudson is given credit for its true discovery. But the intrepid Hudson could not enjoy his success for long—his ship got stuck in the mud and he had to turn around after only a few hours.

He then sailed the Half Moon along the barrier reefs of New Jersey headed north, looking for a fabled "interior passage" to China at the fortieth parallel, a latitude that ancient sailors knew to be, for a variety of reasons, favorable to great civilizations and magnificent cities. A few hours past midnight, they saw a fire on a hill in the distance, the first reported sign of human habitation in the region. They came closer. At dawn of September 2, they found the fire on a hill and at the foot of the hill was an entrance through the barrier reef, and it was at 40 degrees north latitude exactly. This is now called Barnegat Inlet. There were natives tending the fire on the hill. Were they lighting a lamp to welcome strangers from the east, Hudson and his crew? Were they lighting a beacon to guide their own boats through the narrow inlet as Barnegat Light does today? Or were they lighting a council fire to discuss the arrival of messengers from another civilization? We don't know. The Half Moon sailed right by. There was strange tidal activity before the fire, as the lake or channel behind the islands would fill at high tide and empty at low tide.

The Half Moon turned north and explored Barnegat Bay up to Tom's River. They soon determined Tom's River was not a passageway to China and headed out of the bay via Cranberry Inlet and back into the Atlantic. It was lucky for them that the inlet was open. Cranberry Inlet seems to have been appearing and disappearing on an eighty-year cycle at that time, and has reappeared twice since then. If it had been closed, they would have had to backtrack over twenty miles and then come back up along the seaward side, losing a day in the process. (This unpredictable channel is now blocked by a patch of sand, and the town of Seaside Park, New Jersey, sits on top of that patch.)

They then sailed around Sandy Hook to Great Kills Harbor, Staten Island, and on Thursday, September 3, they saw "three great rivers," which were the "Great Kills" of Great Kills Harbor, which exist now in name only. They tried to navigate inside the point, and approached the largest of the kills, which was right inside the peninsula, but found it too shallow for the Half Moon and exited the harbor.

The next day, on Friday, September 4, Hudson sent a rowboat to measure the depths of the harbor, and then went in again, using a different approach. Hudson sent a fishing crew into the shallows of the harbor to fish and found a large manta ray "as great as four men could haul into the ship." Officer Juet writes, ". . . many great rays." These were the giant manta rays, a sacred fish to the Canarsie and other Long Island natives. They call it the "eagle ray," because of its ability to leap and then glide in the air, and the "Guardian of the Sea," while the Europeans call it the "devil ray." They are no longer found in the area, which may be due to a change in temperature and water quality as well as over-hunting.

Not satisfied with the many other fish they found in great size and abundance, the fishermen were obsessed with capturing the colossal manta as a kind of trophy and beat it to death. The muscular sailors then strained to carry the strange-looking being onto the deck of the main ship.

Meanwhile, Hudson went ashore to greet the people. The moment Hudson stepped onshore, the natives all stood around and sang to welcome him. The Europeans were given many gifts, mostly of tobacco, and they traded with the native people, at least some of whom seemed to live on the beach in temporary shelters, while a great number came from a few miles away in every direction. Some were allowed onto the ship. The men traded extensively in furs and food with the native people. The people had smoking pipes made of yellow copper from 85 miles away (near what is today Ellenville, New York) which they wore as pendants.

As the cook began to cut the manta up with his sword, (more about the sword later) we can assume the Canarsie were horrified, possibly tearful. The hungry men ignored the pleas and warnings of the Canarsie and began to eat it Friday night, probably in front of the Canarsie. One can imagine the Canarsie women on board, singing the manta songs as they knelt to pray for the alien-looking creature.

Saturday, September 5, Hudson then sailed west two miles to Prince's Bay, passing Wolfe's Pond, where they were amazed at the towering oaks. Canarsie-speaking natives brought them tobacco and corn of various levels of cultivation from what is now Old Town, Staten Island, part of the Arrochar Region that is still marked on maps of Staten Island. John Colman and the other members of the crew feasted on the manta, oblivious to the taboos of the territory in which they were guests.

On Sunday, the morning of September 6, now fortified with a big meal, the crew's English strongman, John Colman, led a small crew of six in a rowboat to explore Muscouten, now called the East River. They rowed up the Kikeshika (Harlem River), and then back down, smelling sweet scents in the air. They went east as far as Long Island Sound and then turned around. As the fog lowered and rain began to fall, they unwittingly headed straight towards the mouth of the Bronx River and for the heavily guarded Snakapins Wampum Factory, where much of the wampum for the Iroquois (Hodenosuannee) Confederacy and for the various nations of the "River Indians" was cut and stored. It was like barging into Fort Knox unannounced. Two large canoes filled with 26 heavily armed warriors approached them, shouting at them to turn around. Colman's crew shouted back, not understanding. Colman was shot with an arrow through the throat and died on the return trip. It was such an uncanny shot, one wonders who unleashed it; the father of the famed Wampage perhaps? The remainder of the crew tried to get away but paddled right into the Hellgate and some of the most treacherous cross-currents on the east coast. Finally, they managed to get to a shore, and exhausted, spent a few hours hiding and caring for Colman. At dawn they continued south and at 10 AM finally found the ship and told their tragic story. By this time John, a beloved senior officer, had died. Was it bad luck? Or the curse of the manta ray, as Long Island natives would have presumed?

Some time around high noon on Monday, September 7, Hudson took the ship to Wards Point, where the deep channel (now the Ambrose Channel) comes closest to the land, to bury Colman's body there. It is just below the bluff where lay the famous Native American burial grounds of Tottenville and a Raritan Unami village. The rowboat arrived quickly at the shore, they dragged Colman's body from the boat, frantically dug a hole, and then dragged his body into the hole, and just as quickly covered it up. They put up waist-boards on both sides of the rowboat, fearful of an attack from above, and then were hauled safely back to the Half Moon. They declared the point of land, now the southernmost tip of New York State, "Colman's Point," and named the river that emptied into Raritan Bay at that spot, "der Rivierten achter Kol," which is Dutch for "The River Named After Kolman." A later generation of sailors mispronounced this as the Arthur Kill in bungled memoriam, but the previous name stood on maps of the New World for a hundred years.

The Half Moon then traded with the Canarsie again and on Wednesday September 9 tried to capture some of them, possibly as slaves, and dressed them in red uniforms; but after a while the Canarsie men escaped, quite angry. The Half Moon made its getaway, probably up the "Rivierten achter Kol," and then eastward through the Kill Van Kull, which pointed them towards lower Manhattan, visible in the distance.

On September 11, 1609, the Half Moon anchored at the far landing of the great crossing place of the Tulpehoken (Turtle Island) Trail, where they were greeted by a great throng eager to trade. Hudson and others rowed to shore in their small boat and stepped onto Manhattan opposite Kamunipaw, which itself means "on the opposite side." It was apparently an important spot for greeting and exchanging trading goods with foreigners. This was the site of the future World Trade Center, which fell exactly 392 years later, on the same day of the year of omens after the end of the seven fire cycles. In 1609 it presented the people of Turtle Island with a crossroads, a time of decision, as had been predicted so many centuries before.

Those who knew of the prophecies greeted the Half Moon voyagers royally. Although the native people of New York did not generally share their prophecies with whites, some of them relating to Hudson were revealed in a letter from Munsee descendants to Zachary Taylor in 1849. In addition, many links have been revealed over the years between the Midewiwin holders of the Seven Fires prophecies and the Lenape, and there is reason to believe the Delaware (ie. Lenape) were leading proponents of that tradition.

The men of the Half Moon ate oysters of the finest variety, later to become famous worldwide until tainted by pollution in the early twentieth century. They then went north to about 96th Street. Henry Hudson spent September 12, his fortieth birthday, on or near Manhattan. At Inwood Hill, near Spuyten Duyvel, they were approached by over 200 natives, women and children, in canoes, and were offered a wide variety of goods. Officer Juet saw the women and children, thought it a trap to kill them and contemplated attacking first, but was obviously talked out of it. The crew saw the full moon rise dramatically over Spuyten Duyvel Hill and were drawn to it, until they found themselves coming to a stop at the opposite shore across from Nappekemak Village, now called Yonkers, New York.

The next morning, September 14, they captured two natives, intending to bring them back to Europe. This angered the natives, and the Half Moon sped up the Mohicanituck, (the Hudson River) zigzagging northeast, northwest, northeast, northwest, following the course of the river, and landed at the southern end of Cornwall Bay, near Newburgh.

At Cornwall, on the morning of September 15, the two captives escaped, calling out in anger to the crew of the Half Moon, who had somehow mistreated them. Juet blames the natives, calling them "savages." He never tells what was done to them, and we suspect he had a major part to play in their abuse. Nonetheless, trading continued, and the ship proceeded another forty miles upriver to "The Place of the Loving People," which I have come to believe is Saugerties. When Hudson wanted to leave, the natives broke their arrow shafts and threw them into the fire in the universal sign of "ah-kink" (unworthy) to show that they didn't want him to fear them. It was a sign of great friendship, but Hudson left anyway.

The next day of travel, September 16, the Half Moon moored on a "mud flat," which many believe is the one still present between Athens and Hudson, New York. Then when the tide came in, they caught a good wind and made it all the way to the Mohican capital, an "island of fire" called Schodack. They anchored at Lower Schodack Island on September 17.

Hudson here managed to keep Juet out of the way and his men under control while he met with various sub-chiefs and finally with the grand sachem. Hudson was treated like visiting royalty, given feasts and guided tours all around. The natives went out and found several passenger pigeons for him to eat, and then butchered a dog and also a deer as part of the feast. Hudson sent a rowboat north to explore for a northwest passage, and in fact it seems probable that the rowers found the mouth of the Mohawk River then turned around and made it back to Schodack in a single day with much to report.

Hudson took a Mohican family onto the ship and gave them much "aqua vita" to drink. This might have been ethanol or distilled Cognac; we don't know. The natives became drunk for the first time. One man in particular showed the effects of the drink, and his friends brought him strings of wampum to hold, as medicine to cure him of bad spirits. This was the original purpose of wampum belts, according to some traditions. (If it was ethanol that Hudson gave them, they were right about the bad spirits!)

The Europeans then began the return trip home on September 23, stopping at the bottom of lower Schodack where there were rich planting fields and a narrow passage between Bear Island and Mull Island. They anchored in deep water just past that point. They were visited by the Grand Sachem of the Esopus Munsee from "the Loving People" south of them, apparently. The elder returned home, thinking Hudson had promised a visit, but Hudson got stuck on that same mud flat a second time (right near the town that glorifies his name, and near a trail crossing, now Route 23) and so passed by the Loving People, missing a great feast in his honor, which the Munsee had scheduled for September 27.

The Half Moon stopped near Kingston/Rhinebeck (near a native trail crossing for the Minisink Trail / Sepasco Trail) and the men went on a fishing trip. According to legend, one of the crew, Jacobus Van Hooren, was captured by the natives during such a fishing trip and eventually married a Wappingers woman named Manteo. Years later, he saw a passing Dutch ship and swam out to be rescued. His abandoned wife, according to some versions of the legend, jumped from Indian Brook Falls to her death in her grief. In other versions, her body is found near the falls, dead of a broken heart. There is no mention of this in Juet's journal and no real evidence, but it is a famous story.

On September 28, they stopped briefly at Poughkeepsie, (a native trail crossing, now Route 44) then proceeded south. The ship arrived at Cornwall Bay again, (another native trail crossing, now Route 52) and again found many willing to trade. They left Cornwall on the morning of October 1, one lunar year since the midpoint of the Great Cycle, or first cresent, and headed south to Indian Point (another native trail crossing, the crossing place of the Sagamore Trail, or what we now call Route 6) where they were greeted by an angry mob. One man climbed the rudder of the ship and into the window of the captain's cabin. He was apparently angry at Officer Juet. He climbed out of the window again carrying two of Juet's shirts, Juet's pillow, and a bandolier, a shoulder belt used to carry ammunition and in some cases, a musket. He was probably trying to stage a protest against something Juet had done, but was shot dead on the spot. Hudson seems nowhere to be found in Juet's account of the incident.

The protester (not the last one to be found at Indian Point) dropped the pillow and the shirts and the bandolier in the water as he fell to his death. Juet and his friend the cook went out in a rowboat amid the angry mob to retrieve the items. A friend or brother of the dead "prankster" tried to overturn the rowboat, but it was too heavy. The cook chopped off the man's hand with a sword, and he fell into the water and drowned. The mob ran away in fear.

The Half Moon found a safe haven for the evening at Croton Point, then on the morning of October 2, proceeded to Yonkers again, but ran into another angry mob, led by one of the escaped captives. They were just a few miles below a trail crossing now called Dobbs Ferry. The warriors came about in canoes and fired at the stern of the ship, shooting dozens of arrows at the same window where the other man was killed, a non-verbal protest of the Half Moon's actions, or of Juet himself, both for the incident with the cook's sword, and for whatever it was that happened inside that window earlier in the trip.

In retaliation for the harmless show of arrows bouncing off the stern and the window, Juet and the crew opened fire with six muskets blazing. Then Juet climbed down to the interior of the ship and began firing the "Falcons," the port-hole cannons usually used for battle against attacking pirates. He blasted some of the canoes to bits, killing several natives. Then, from the top of Spuyten Duyvel Hill, probably on a signal whistle, came a hundred warriors from Fort Nipnischen, letting loose arrows upon the ship. Juet ran across the deck to the other side of the ship and with considerable aim, fired the Falcon cannons into the heart of the band of warriors. Surprised by the cannons, the like of which they had not seen before, they fled into the woods.

The Half Moon sailed southward to a point near Hoboken to anchor for the night. While Juet excused himself for giving the savages what they deserved, Henry Hudson was filled with remorse that he didn't keep a tighter rein on his men, lamenting the loss of so many Native American lives, with whom he felt a heart-connection, and who were also his only source of peltries.

Their last day on the river, October 3, 1609, Hudson decided to make one last effort to restore the confidence of the Native Americans in him. All alone he rowed out to Manhattan, to that same spot where he had landed before, at the great crossing, armed only with a bottle or possibly keg of his best Portuguese rum and a Scottish Drinking Cup called a quaike. Like most sailors of the time, he was very fond of rum, and presumably rewarded his men after a successful day by passing the bottle, or perhaps the quaike itself, as a legion of captains had done before him. He also noticed that the native people at the north end of the river seemed to enjoy the taste very much. Again the natives stood around him in song, and he drank from the cup of rum and then offered it to the circle of men. They sniffed it and passed it on, afraid to drink. If Henry sensed there was tension and mistrust building, he was apparently right. Finally, "The Bender of the Pine Bow,"[9] the last one, decided if he didn't drink it there would be more attacks. He drank from the cup, blinked several times, his eyes watered, and then he fell to the ground as if dead.

Hudson, drawing on his long experience as ship captain, gestured to the other native men to remain calm and wait for him to revive. When he did come back to life, he reported that he had had a pleasant dream and wanted more, so they all drank the rum and became very merry. Hudson was hailed as a great friend, and he returned to the ship before the party got out of control. The Half Moon headed back to England with Hudson aboard and apparently unaware of the scourge of alcoholism he had visited upon the Native Americans; trade in rum for furs would continue for decades, to the utter destruction of the People of the River and their fur-bearing brothers and sisters.

The natives, so the story goes, were left wondering about the Seven Fires Prophecies. Did the visitors come in friendship, bearing gifts, or in hatred, carrying weapons of war? No one could decide, and it was vital for them to know for the sake of the planet and the future of humankind. They knew the story of the two brothers, one wise brother and one foolish (every tribe and nation calls them by different names), and had teachings that wisdom and folly would always be in conflict amongst their people until they all let go of their own selfish side. Now it seemed that the white-skinned people from across the water, the visitors that were foretold in the prophecies, also had their twin brothers of light and darkness benevolent and malevolent beings, and were also in conflict amongst themselves about right and wrong. Who could have guessed?

In the much-talked-about Mayan prophecies of Chalam Balam, as found in the Dresden Codex, also based on long-count calendars, eclipses, and repeating cycles of human events (52 year cycles instead of 56), we also hear about twins, the "hero-twin" sons of the First Father. The end of that calendar on December 21, 2012, coincides somewhat with the eclipse of May 20, 2012, over Mexico and the passage of Venus across the sun on June 6, 2012. The degree of free will we have concerning those drastic events that Chalam Balam predicted depends on who is telling the story. The stories of the Algonquins emphasize free will, symbolized by the twins, the one brother who chooses creativity and truth and the other who chooses destruction and lying. It is a teaching of acceptance and non-duality, since to kill the spiteful one would wound the heart of the good brother who is filled with compassion for him. We learn instead to heal the harmful one of his terrible ways as best we can.

If a survivor of the battle of Indian Point, and of the battle at Nipnischen, somewhat shaken by this sad turn of events, had gone tearfully to his elder for instruction and comfort, he might have learned that Manhattan is a vortex of creative and destructive energy, and that over the coming centuries the best and worst of humanity would come and live there. The greatest spiritual and political leaders would visit there, live there, and teach there, but also the greatest villains, scoundrels and cheats. While great evil would be done, the greatest of heroes would appear to rescue the helpless and innocent. The warrior was one such hero. The opposites that would tend to appear simultaneously here would provide a test for the people of each age. Hearing all this, the young warrior, consumed with worry, would wonder, "which side will win? The invaders or the heroes?" The elder would then answer wisely: "Whichever one you let get to you!"

The elder, if a member of a teaching lodge associated with the prophecies, would also speak of the emergence of a new "rainbow" race, led by those born of the four colors of the world, red, yellow, black, and white, here on Turtle Island, with Manhattan in the forefront. If all the people of Turtle Island could embrace racial and cultural diversity and the process of negotiation through loving communication that brings peace, it will be a sign of great hope for the lighting of the eighth fire, and will help bring peace to all the world. Thus say the Seven Fires Prophecies.

Hudson, the European story goes, returned to England where he was immediately arrested,[10] treated first as a criminal and then as a hero. The following year he was given the good ship Discovery, to find a passage across the top of Canada for real this time, and again he brought Robert Juet with him, his shadowy alter-ego. When the ship went off course and got in trouble in what is now Hudson's Bay, Juet masterminded a mutiny and was caught in the act. On September 10, 1610, there was an on-board trial and the crew members accused him to his face and under oath of being a villain. Hudson, with a remarkable show of compassion, forgave him and the other men of their crimes and assured them he knew the way back to an island full of birds just waiting to become a feast. They spent the winter in Hudson's Bay, and later, in June of 1611, Hudson was attacked from behind, bound in ropes and lowered to a small open boat with his son and some sick crew members. Hudson cried out, "Juet has done this! He will overthrow ye all!"

Juet, in his last words to his captain, lied, "It's not me but that villain Mr. Greene!" However, Henry Greene, inveterate gambler that he was, had nonetheless comforted Hudson the night before on his misfortune, so Hudson's suspicions about his "fraternity brother" from Limehouse maritime community in London Robert Juet were confirmed. Juet betrayed his friend of all these years, and, trying to cover up his crime, betrayed Greene as well. The news of this evil was soon to shock the western world.

The ship's carpenter, a courageous soul of considerable virtue, was so outraged, he jumped from the ship to rescue Hudson, saying he'd rather die with Hudson than live on a ship with such scoundrels. He untied Hudson and son, and yet now found himself in the same boat, doomed to a horrible death in that sub-arctic clime. Juet hoisted all sails and beat a hasty retreat, leaving his captain to freeze to death and die of exhaustion and starvation, with his son and his carpenter and some dying sailors. The year was 1611. The date was June 21, the longest day, the most sacred day in the Algonquian "year" of the solar calendar. Like Tujiskeha and Tawiskarong in the Huron teaching tales, the good and the harmful brothers had finally parted company, thus making way for the time of mortals to follow. The episode characterized much of what was to occur during the second half of the era of the Seven Fires Prophecy. The next 390 years were to be packed with significant events both on earth and in the heavens for the Algonquian-speaking people, filled with tests of the spirit and real-life teaching tales of duality—what the missionaries would later call "the struggle between good and evil."

In one version of the tale, the hard-headed brother says to the sweet-hearted one, "O, honest brother who tells no lies, how can I kill you?" The honest brother answers, "Beat me with a bag of seeds and I might die." The hard-headed one then persues his compassionate sibling all over Turtle Island, beating him with a bag of seeds until he stumbles and lies as if dead. In their footsteps, millions of plants are now growing from those seeds. But the good brother is immortal, and awakened by the Grandmother of all Life he rises again, but wisely remains in hiding from his murderous sibling to this day.

How does this relate to Henry Hudson and his first mate Robert Juet? Recently, a stone was found in the Province of Ontario, marked "HH 1612, Captive." It seems possible that Hudson was captured, some say by Inuit hunters, and perhaps rescued by (or traded to) the Mistassini East Main Cree, where Hudson would have lived for the rest of his life in hiding—from Juet, the VOC, his disappointed King, and his creditors, hunting and fishing and telling stories, the life of freedom he had always wanted. Juet, realizing he would probably be hanged for his crime, died suddenly of health complications just as he (with help from a man named Robert Bylot) had navigated the Discovery to within sight of the British Isles. He was posthumously found guilty of murder in a famous trial, his name dishonored in England forever. Hudson, in many ways Juet's sweet-hearted "brother," on the other hand, has found immortality in the hearts of New Yorkers, and is reckoned among the greatest explorers of the age of discovery.

New York has indeed witnessed a great struggle between forces of light and of darkness ever since. We are now at the period beyond the era of the seven fires, and everything, according to the modern-day teachers of the Native prophecy, is up to us. We can make anything happen. It is a test of the spirit. We can let the darkness take over, or bring about the lighting of the eighth fire, an era of peace and harmony. It is understood that if the conflict between harmony and hatred was not resolved by the end of the seventh fire, that the people of Turtle Island would have to undergo a period of purification, either by sheer will power or through the power of Great Spirit, G'tchee Manitou, to resolve the conflict. The purification is happening now. On Manhattan we can see it on Wall Street, whose NYSE head-quarters stand right next to the Kapsee Village whose children ran up the trails that were to become "Greenwich Street" and "Broadway" to greet Henry Hudson. We see it in the "Fur Market" where natives used to prepare and trade their pelts along the trail, at City Hall where the Werpoes Village and their beautiful lake once stood, and we see it in the publishing houses of the great white way.

This great test is for us all, and we are waiting to see how it will turn out.

Chapter Two

THEIR DESTINIES LINKED BY WATER

Truth and Consequences

*H*enry Hudson was born an Englishman and resided in London. His birthday is thought to have been September 12, 1569, though he left no paper trail to prove it. He had a wife named Katherine and three sons named Oliver, John, and Richard. He was a descendant of Henry Hudson the Elder, an alderman in the City of London in 1555, and some say his father was named Christopher. He had relatives in England's exclusive Muskovy Company, who engaged in privateering (legal piracy) for Queen Elizabeth while searching for a northern sea route to China.[11] He would have been surprised to know that many school children around the world today believe he was a Dutchman.

Washington Irving, a bastion of pro-Dutch sentiment, added greatly to that erroneous impression in his book *Knickerbocker's History of New York* if only by referring to Hudson by the Dutch name Hendrick. In that delightful narrative Dietrich Knickerbocker, the humorous fictional character, claims that his great-great grandfather was cabin boy aboard the Half Moon and passed down the intimate details of the voyage that have been otherwise lost to history.

He writes, "It has been traditionary in our family, that when the great navigator was first blessed with a view of this enchanting island, he was observed, for the first and only time in his life, to exhibit strong symptoms of astonishment and admiration. He is said to have turned to master Juet, and uttered these remarkable words, while he pointed towards this paradise of the new world, —see! There! — and thereupon, as was always his way when he was uncommonly pleased, he did puff out such clouds of dense tobacco-smoke, that in one minute the vessel was out of sight of land, and master Jeut was fain to wait until the winds dispersed this impenetrable fog."[12]

Although pictures show Henry sporting a Dutch pikeman's helmet, the kind developed a year after his voyage[13] for foot soldiers fighting English with nine-foot-long spears, but useless against Native Americans, Hudson was an Englishman of some education, commanding a ship called the Half Moon by the English, The Halve Maen by the Dutch, a hybrid merchant ship and jaght (yacht, this hybrid also called a "Galliot") of somewhere between 16 and 20 crewmen,[14] most of whom spoke Dutch and at least three of whom spoke English. Hudson chose long time friend, though one that he could not always trust, Robert Juet, (also spelled Juitt, Juit, Jeutt etc.) to be his first mate, but there is no evidence to prove that Juet spoke any Dutch. Hudson needed a translator while in Holland, and used a man named William Stere for the purpose,[15] but Stere was not onboard the ship. Who would have translated for him on the ship? One way or another, we imagine that they could understand each other fairly well,[16] if perhaps only in the language of sailors. Whatever their bloodlines, it mattered little now—their destinies were linked by water.

Hudson was a likeable but eccentric optimist off-duty; though under pressure he could be completely unreasonable. He was a boastful dreamer who occasionally realized his dream, as much by luck as by breaking every rule in his way. Juet was his right-hand man, his cold, calculating advisor and scribe, only telling Hudson what he wanted the captain to hear. Intensely quiet, he controlled everything that happened on the ship like a mute chess player using the Dutch sailors as pawns. If the Half Moon's voyage were a game of Clue, Juet would be the meticulous butler of many years' faithful service in the Cabin Room with a musket and perhaps a broad axe.

The following year Juet would mastermind the mutiny that sent Henry, his son John, the ship's carpenter and seven others to a horrible death (so we assume) out in a shallop (a small open boat) on an ice-packed sea, because Hudson wouldn't lie for him.[17]

Hudson, at one point, removed Juet from duty because of insubordination, but Hudson himself was not exactly one to follow orders. According to the author of God's Mercies, Douglas Hunter, "The VOC's (Dutch East India Company) problems with Henry Hudson came to a head long before the Half Moon left the dock. After signing him to the contract, his Dutch backers quickly realized that Hudson was all but impossible to control. Hudson momentarily left the project in a huff in March 1609, after arguing with the VOC's chief boatswain, Dirck Gerritsz, about who knows what, and being dissatisfied with the wages offered to the select group of Englishmen he intended to take with him: his own son, John; John Colman, a veteran of his 1607 voyage; and Robert Juet, sometimes referred to as "the old man,"[18] a skilled navigator who had been with him in 1608. The Zeeland chamber of the VOC, writing their counterparts in Amsterdam, presciently stated, 'We are much surprised at Mr. Hudson's strange behavior and consider it inadvisable to let him undertake the voyage, for if he begins to rebel here under our eyes what will he do if he is away from us?'"[19] The Zeelanders go on to recommend that Petrus Plancious should find a "competent and sensible person" to replace Hudson, so that, in Hunter's words, "the voyage could proceed as planned."[20]

As one author, Reverend Dr. DeCosta, wrote, "The character of Hudson... judged by the age in which he lived, was tolerably fair; though of course hardly superior to ordinary examples."[21] Ian Chadwick describes him this way: "Hudson had not shown any qualities that would have endeared him to the natives in the past..."[22] Although Hudson comes across as cold and self-absorbed at times, and Juet as a "cynical, paranoid loner,"[23] the two Englishmen carved open a Dutch doorway into the heart of Algonquin territory, which the Munsee still refer to as "Wundjiyalkung,"[24] "Our Old Homeland Back East," that the rest of the world walked through. By sailing under a Dutch flag, they cleared the way for the establishment of a Dutch/Algonquin state in the Hudson Valley, one that was short-lived but which would take root almost invisibly throughout North America as its descendants were pushed further and further west, and in fact, all directions. Many, such as Fiske and others, have attributed to this durable population much of that which is progressive and community-minded in the United States. If they had only known.

Hudson arrived in the new world in 1609 over a hundred years after Columbus set foot on Hispaniola, but it was still a difficult journey into mostly unknown territory, and our present history books do not record the names of many of the Algonquin leaders living along the mid-Atlantic coast at that time, just a handful. The following names may not all be familiar to the casual reader. They stand at the very edge of what modern writers call "history," one foot planted in the "real" world as seen by Europeans, another one lost in the ghostly world of dream and story, myth and legend. Each of these leaders greatly impacted the fortunes of white European "founding fathers," mostly for the good. We should honor them by at least learning their names.

Although their ages are not certain, we can be fairly sure that all of these Algonquins were alive in 1609, and might have seen the Half Moon as it sailed up and down the coast of the Atlantic. Massasoit of the Wampanoag was approximately 29, Manteo of the Croatan was about 45, Powhatan of the Mataponi was at least 47 and probably much older, Membertou of the Mi'kmaq was said to be about 104 when the Half Moon sailed past Nova Scotia; (he outlived Hudson by almost three months![25]) Squanto or Tisquantum of the Wampanoag was about 24, Towaco II (or someone of a similar name) was probably Hudson's age, as was Myanis of the Siwanoy. The father of Chief Tamanend III would have been born around 1609.[26] Tackamack, sachem of the Weckweeskecks of Dobb's Ferry (Wyskwaqua village) was about ten years old around the time the Half Moon sailed by what is now Wickerscreek, Dobb's Ferry in 1609.[27] His name translates as, "He gives out much food."

The warrior Wampage (Siwanoy) may have been all of four years old in 1609. Oratam, (Oratamy or Oratamin) Turtle clan (Unami) sachem of the Hackensack, who had provided so much friendship and support to the Dutch at New Amsterdam, and who signed the peace treaty to end the Kieft War in 1643, was possibly thirty years old when Hudson arrived.[28] Chief Mamarranack was at least five years old in 1609. Probably named after the place we call Mamaroneck, he negotiated for peace at Stamford, Connecticut in 1644.[29]

Though even less famous, we should mention the names of Quesqakons, Quesquackous and Easanques, sachems of Manhattan in 1629 who deeded land to the Dutch, all of whom would have been alive in 1609 and probably saw the Half Moon, or at least heard about it. Aepjen, grand sachem of the Mohicans who also signed the treaty to end the Kieft War on August 30, 1645, must have been at least forty, according to custom, and probably fifty, in that year, so he must have been between four and fourteen years old in 1609. It is also likely that he was related to previous grand chiefs, though not a requirement, and probably grew up near Schodack Island. This means that he probably saw Henry Hudson, or at least his ship, with his own eyes, in 1609.

The people who helped the survivors of the crash of the Tyger in 1613 must have also seen "the Great Floating Bird" four years earlier. According to our history, during that winter the Indians supplied the survivors "with food and all kinds of necessaries,"[30] and quite possibly helped them build the ship, as there are certain repetitive aspects to the construction of a ship that require muscle and little training, such as sawing and hammering pegs. The fact that they obviously were working together peacefully gives us further reason to suppose this.[31] Back in Holland, the art of managing construction workers from other races and cultures who spoke other tongues was quite common, as the Netherlands had a small but highly educated population.[32]

There is no reason to believe that Hudson actually thought these people he encountered were "Indians" in the literal sense. He knew he wasn't in India or China. Columbus had coined that term, some say because he was confused about his location, and others say he meant "in dios," with God, because of their saintly air. There is no evidence, either, that Hudson ever used the word "Indian" in his journal, and it does not appear in Juet's journal (except for "Indian corn"). It has been suggested that Hudson probably already knew that he was not likely to find a northwest passage on this trip, but saw the Mohicanituck (Hudson River) as a possible route west in what appeared to be a tidal strait, at least until he got to Beacon or Poughkeepsie, where the presence of fresh water was more obvious.

I believe he knew that a northwest passage overtop of Canada was dangerous and impractical, if it even existed, but took the assignment because jobs were scarce in his field and he had bills to pay and three children to feed. Bacon writes, "Hudson found in 1609 no immediate chance of employment by his own countrymen."[33] In that he brought with him few objects suitable for trade with the Chinese, and no letter of introduction translated into Mandarin by scholars, the premise of his trip does seem shaky. Apparently, his crew threatened to mutiny as they approached Labrador, but we don't know why.

At the same time, it is clear that Hudson knew about the river some now call Hudson, and that he believed it might be a passage to a great ocean to the west. Edgar Bacon writing in 1907, says, "We believe that previous to 1609, geographers had some information concerning a stream that flowed southward and debouched into the ocean about the latitude of Manhattan Island. There is hardly room for a doubt on this subject."[34] According to Henry Murphy, author of *Henry Hudson in Holland*, "The idea thus entertained by Hudson was based upon information derived from Captain John Smith and the journals of Captain Weymouth, who had, one or other of them, visited the regions. . . . Captain Smith had explored the Chesapeake and run up its confluents, where he had doubtless heard from the natives of the existence of the great inland seas which debouch through the St. Lawrence. . . ."[35]

So the existence of such a river was known to Henry, but what of its use as a passage to China, or at least to a western sea? Did Hudson seriously think that such a thing was possible? Van Meteren is our best source for evidence on this subject. Again, Murphy writes, "Speaking of the plans of Hudson, when he encountered the ice, Van Meteren says: 'Master Hudson gave them (the crew) their choice between two things, the first was to go to the coast of America at the fortieth degree of latitude, mostly incited to this by letters and maps which a certain Captain Smith had sent him from Virginia, and on which he showed him a sea by which he might circumnavigate their Southern Colony from the North and from thence pass into a Western sea; the other proposition was, to seek the passage by Davis' Straits."[36] They did visit Davis Straits briefly, then headed south to the fortieth parallel.

It seems that Captain John Smith had written of this sea to the west only months before.[37] Henry Murphy writes, in a remarkably long, but interesting sentence, ". . . it is evident both from the account of Van Meteren, who says that letters and maps were sent by [Captain John] Smith to Hudson, and that a Western sea was marked on the map, and from Hudson's map in Plancius' possession, also showing this sea, that Hudson relied upon something more than the public statements of the renowned Captain, and was probably in actual correspondence with him: but the communications of Captain Smith related, it will be observed, to the existence of a Western sea behind the English colony, and to a Northerly opening to it from the Atlantic. Hudson however was led to think that the strait might be found as far South as latitude forty..."[38]

The fortieth parallel, as we reckon it today, runs through Seaside Park, New Jersey, where Hudson exited Barnegat Bay through a now non-existent passage that led to Tom's River. It also runs through Philadelphia on the Delaware River, further to the west. Further north lies Tottenville, Staten Island, NY, and the entrance to New York Harbor, which are at 40 degrees, 30 minutes. So the imagined entrance to the western sea might have been the Delaware or the Hudson Rivers, both of which were glimpsed by Verrazzano in 1524.

The fortieth north parallel has had a special inspirational significance to every world traveler since Marco Polo. Many of the great and ancient cities are built within one degree of this line, if calculated correctly of course. Here is a short list, flying or sailing east from the Greenwich line; Lisbon (39), Toledo (40), Madrid (40+), Sardinia (40), Rome (42), Salerno (40), Naples (41), Croton (39), Otranto, Brindisi and Bari (40-41), Corfu (40), The Isle of Lemnos (near Athens) (40), The Dardonelles (40), Constantinople (41), Angora (or Ankara) Turkey (40), Thessalonia (41), Mt. Arrarat (40), Peking (40), Philadelphia (at that time called Shackamaxon (40), Fort Nassau (est. 1623)(40), Staten Island and New York Harbor(40°.30'), Barnegat Inlet (40), and the Azores (39).[39] We can be certain that someone like Hudson who rubbed shoulders with Muskovy Company and Dutch East India Company navigators, knew the significance of the fortieth parallel in world history, as did Captain John Smith. The more ancient of these ports of call would have flowed from their lips eagerly had the question come up in their meeting in 1608. Not only is the northern fortieth parallel a most salubrious climate for human populations, it has over time become something of a mystical tradition among kings and architects to plan great cities at the mouths of estuaries near the fortieth parallel. If the thought dared to arise in Henry's mind that by discovering a passage at the fortieth parallel to Cathay, now Peking, (also at an estuary on the fortieth parallel) it might some day lead to the erecting of a great city on the banks of that water way, an ancient habit of civilization, he wasn't too far wrong. His crazy idea of finding a passageway to China at 40° led to the establishment of European-style cities at the Native American sites of Shackamaxon (Philadelphia), Manna-hattan (New York City) Schodack (Albany) not to mention Hoboken and Tom's River, New Jersey, plus others. If he dreamed even bigger and imagined a city on that waterway named "The City of Hudson," he wasn't far wrong there either. That city now stands on the east bank of the river that bears his name, in the

County of Columbia, named after you-know-who!

Another European who came merely to observe and ended up changing everything was Giovanni de Verrazzano. A true Renaissance man in every sense of the word, Verrazzano was a superb mathematician, botanist, astronomer, and much more. Born in Florence in 1480, he grew up breathing the heady vapors of that city towards the end of its Golden Age. He apparently had a great deal of impact on Hudson's life.

We know that Verrazzano discovered what is now New York Harbor in 1524, but ventured no further than a long stone's throw into the harbor, (Liberty Island) glimpsing Manhattan and Brooklyn from a distance, eighty-five years before Hudson's men got a closer look. We know that Verrazzano's men brought smallpox and other diseases that swiftly and drastically changed the quality of life for Native Americans for at least thirty miles upstream, decimating population figures in those areas and changing that which Hudson was to see later in 1609. Although Hudson's route took him through the narrows which Verrazzano also passed (and gave his name to posthumously), it is unlikely that any of the natives that hailed him from the shore were remembering Verrazzano's arrival. Those natives would have most likely been struck down by disease shortly afterwards, or been at least weakened enough by poxes to prevent them from living to see ninety-five winters and watch the Half Moon as it passed carefully through the precarious tides of the Kill Van Kull on its way back home. But there must have been stories still circulating amongst the people of that joyful earlier visit with Verrazzano, the fatherly figure bearing strange gifts, and there must have been talk of his return. And some native observer must have said, "So grandfather was right!"

What is surprising to consider is that one hundred and one years earlier, in 1508, a French ship, looking for a "Northwest passage" to China discovered the St. Lawrence Seaway (French spelling Laurence) instead. The ship traveled westward for quite a while along that passage, but turned around before finding China, or even Sudbury, Ontario. The name of one captain is given as Thomas Aubert, a Frenchman, "and that of the other as Jean Vérassen, a Frenchified form of an Italian name, Giovanni da Verrazzano."[40] Both the St. Laurence expedition and the one in 1524 left from the small town of Dieppe. Records say Verrrazzano had just moved to Dieppe the year before, in 1507. On August 10, 1508, two ships from Dieppe "entered a mighty river, they named after the patron saint of the day, St. Laurence."[41]

They went inland at least 80 leagues (at least 180 miles) to trade in pelts, and brought back with them seven "wild men" (I presume they were Algonquin speakers, but there were many Mohawk and Huron near Hatchalega Montreal in that time) to Rouen. They wrote of these "beardless men," "...of bread, wine, or money they have no knowledge."[42] These were the first-known Algonquins to visit Europe, but there is no record that they had abilities as translators or diplomats. It is not clear whether Cartier knew of this earlier sail, when he thought he discovered the mouth of the St. Laurence in 1535.

Rumor has it that Giovanni de Verrazzano believed that there was a "northwest passage," but that its mouth must be south of the St. Laurence River, as he and others had explored areas to the north. As Donald Johnson writes, "Into the second quarter of the 16th century... Giovanni de Verrazzano was convinced that the route to Cathay lay somewhere in the middle of the North American continent."[43] He himself tried to find that passage in 1524 to no avail, and then died two years later in the Caribbean. If he was sailing in 1508 under the alias Jean Vérassen, it is little wonder he was so sure the northwest passage did not lie near the St. Laurence. He had himself helped discover it!

Two years after Verrazzano's death in 1526, a Dutchman, Gemma Frisius, invented the technique of triangulation (1528) and in 1570, Abrahm Ortelius, another Dutchman, published what most would call the first atlas. This was followed in 1587 by a surprisingly accurate map of both North and South America by a Flemish man from Rupelmonde named Gerard Mercator, using a new mathematical projection of a globe onto flat paper.[44]

Henry Hudson may or may not have had Verrazzano's maps, we can't be sure, but his friend John Smith probably did. But in spite of great efforts by every major power in Europe to keep such data classified, the information literally under lock and key, the great mapmaking houses in Holland were doing a booming business in acquiring all that knowledge and blending it together to come up with the latest charts of the New World, culminating in the Blaeu Haus atlases of the mid 1600s. Working for the Dutch, Hudson most certainly carried one of the predecessors of those Blaeu Haus maps in his hands, perhaps one drawn by Plancius, who was Hudson's immediate superior in the Dutch East India Company, a man who quarreled with both Hudson and the Blaeu family as colleagues. Hudson's findings were soon to show up in Velasco's map of 1610, perhaps via Argall who returned to the region the following year.

Hudson also apparently inherited similar information from the deceased captain George Weymouth. Murphy writes, "Weymouth had made two voyages to America, one in 1602, and the other in 1605..." "Gosnold, who was on the coast of America in 1602, had, like Weymouth, gone south only to about 41° 30'; and the navigators to the Southern Colony of Virginia had, on the other hand, not sailed farther North than latitude thirty-eight or thereabouts, leaving two hundred miles of the intermediate coast unexplored."[45] This explains the magnetic pull on Hudson's inner compass for exploring New York Harbor: it was the last unopened box, the last coastal frontier, and perhaps the last undeveloped real estate at 40° latitude.

Hudson had told his Dutch superior, the cartographer Plancius, that he believed there was a passage west above Virginia, but Plancius assured him that was nonsense, and gave him specific instructions to stay well above New France, in other words, in international waters.[46] He was to focus only on reaching China by the shortest route, then returning to Holland without losing a man. Henry accomplished none of these objectives. Instead, he and his friends went on an all-expenses-paid vacation in the company yacht.

Not only that, for Henry it was apparently a theme vacation. I believe Hudson was somewhat of a Verrazzano fanatic, and was quite familiar with the writings and maps of his predecessor of eighty-five years. Not having the support of the crew to sail through icy and as yet unexplored waters must have been a factor; they were "blocked by ice and snow," as Hudson later told his superiors, truthfully or not. It is difficult for us, lounging in our heated drawing rooms with a book in our hands, to ascertain the dangers Hudson and his men recognized upon reaching those ice-clogged passages at the future Hudson Straits, "above New France." Perhaps they felt a mariner's twinge of intuition that this might be their last expedition if they plowed ahead any further. In any case, Hudson took the opportunity to visit most of the balmier ports of call his hero had visited, and, where possible, to outdo the great Florentine navigator, perhaps if only to prove to himself he was a seaman worthy of the favors of the somewhat judgmental and implacable King, James I, "the most learned fool in Christendom,"[47] who had not been hiring him recently. If Henry was skeptical about the northwest passage idea, he had a right to be. That northwest passage was not to be penetrated successfully for another 300 years. Roald Amundsen, finally achieved it in steel boats loaded down with better equipment, but it took him three years, from 1903 to 1906.

Hudson visited Labrador, Nova Scotia, Maine, and the Virginia Colony (he did not visit Cape Fear, North Carolina as Verrazzano did) in reverse order from his hero. Everyone knew that Verrazzano had seen the wide bay to "a river of steep mountains," New York Harbor, but had been driven back out to sea by a strange storm and was never able to return. Hudson was going to do him one better and explore that river himself. If it turned out to be a passage to China, as Verrazzano had hoped,[48] Hudson would be more than forgiven for his change of plans. If it turned out to be a dead end, well, Hudson would have to cross that bridge when he came to it.

As it turned out, the "river of steep mountains" was no passage to China, and Verrazzano's dreamed-of route to the Orient through the middle of the continent had other serious consequences for the crew of the Half Moon. As soon as they informed their employers back in Amsterdam, Holland would then claim that land as its own colony, according to the rules of international commerce.

There was one little problem. England, Hudson's own nation, had already claimed rights to that entire middle coast, however tentatively. By sailing up the Hudson River in a Dutch ship under a Dutch flag, he was committing an obvious act of treason. It was territory that the British claimed already thanks to Hudson's friend John Smith, who always made sure there was a Union Jack above his head whenever he was in British territory.[49]

Hudson's alternative caused the two rival sea powers a century of struggle, costing the English millions of pounds sterling. The English took the colony back twice by force, once in 1664 and then again in 1674, and lesser Dutch rebellions continued to the 1720s.[50] There is no proof that the Dutch ever wanted a colony "at 40 degrees latitude," prying its way inland from a "coast" (not including the islands) only 28 miles long,[51] surrounded by almost 3000 miles of British-controlled shoreline.

Under oppression from the British, after their successful invasion of 1664, Dutch communities quickly found themselves making alliance with Algonquian communities, also underground. By December 1675, the Dutch were accused of assisting King Philip of the Wampanoag in King Philip's War, in order to weaken England's hold on them. This may have been true, as the English had been interfering politically with their communities and Dutch Reformed Churches.[52] A new clergy was sent in during the 1680s that seemed more compliant with British rule, and were willingly trained to conduct services in English as well as Dutch.[53] One of these was Rudolphus Varick, who set out to create one of the first "Indian Schools," catering largely to Delaware students, in Manhattan, near the street that now bears his name, Varick Street. His mission school was a role model for the later Wheelock School in Connecticut, also ministering mainly to "Delaware Indian" students. His rectory stood on the street that also bears honor to him, Rector Street. Considering the political situation of the day, and the fact that the British were even less tolerant of Native Americans than Dutch, one has to wonder about how complacent Dominie Varick really was behind the closed doors of his rectory.

If we had been alive in 1664, walking along the smaller, uncobbled streets of Manhattan, we could easily have found at least one person, a Native American over the age of 55, blessed with long white locks perhaps, or with graying rash or cockscomb, who remembered what it was like to sail the Hudson before Henry, and who remembered the Hudson Valley as it was in the old days before the sound of gunfire echoed through the Highlands and the thumping sound of axes signaled the clearing of a forest to make way for wheat and clapboard-sided farmhouses. This period, this "day" of the Dutch, was in many ways a "great day in the morning," (*tchi-bun-geez*, a positive Munsee expression heralding new beginnings, which apparently migrated into folk speech before the Civil War). It was just long enough to solidify a complex blood relationship between the natives and the Dutch, evidence of which still exists in scattered remnants to this day. There is an Indian grave yard in the westernmost reaches of Ulster County filled with worked slate pieces for headstones, some of which bear Dutch hex signs. However, it was a reign so brief it was outlived by some of the children who, according to legend, greeted Henry's boat at a spot we still call "Kinderhook," the children's landing-place.

The "River Indians" were one with that waterway and with that lost landscape, and so the spirit of the terrain, untouched by the steel plow, lived on within them for a few more years, until their individual deaths, falling one by one like corn stalks in the fall, taking their memories with them until no one was left standing who could recall the Muhheakannuk, "the Greatest of Estuaries," or more commonly called, Mohicanituck, the "the greatest of estuaries, a river that ebbs and flows," as it was in its original innocence.

The last of those witnesses to the past survived into the time of the English, a very different time indeed, a time of industriousness, punctuality and properness, and yet their descendants continued, some holding firmly to their beliefs, some converting to Christianity, some losing their spiritual teachings but keeping the traditions alive in name only.

The English values of hard work, respect and consideration had parallels in Algonquin and Dutch culture, but the British enforced a rather different, and apparently one-sided and authoritarian type of respect, a respect for the crown and for the British Sterling Pound. We have to also keep in mind that the minority-rule British colonists were outnumbered by both Algonquian and Dutch-speaking rebels, determined to overthrow the yoke of empire at any moment, and the British used their authority to invoke a fear greater than their own, which ultimately cost them New York. The Algonquin/Dutch spirit of revolution did not go away in 1720, it merely underwent a metamorphosis into a more general sense of colonial independence which included less-fortunate English settlers as well, expressing itself through barbed words as much as weapons.

In 1775 New York was at the forefront of rebellion against British rule, and rebels (British subjects!) took over City Hall, which is now Federal Hall on Wall Street. In August of 1776, during the battle for Long Island, General Woodhull's troops deserted him as he awaited orders from a detained George Washington. That evening, he was captured by a party of English dragoons at an inn two miles east of Jamaica, Queens. Surrendering his sword, he was ordered by the Major simply to say, 'God save the King!' and he would be free. Instead he exclaimed, 'God save us all!' His wit and meaning were not lost on the officer, who attacked him viciously and would have killed him but the other officers intervened. He died from the wounds, after being held a prisoner in a Dutch Reformed Church of his own community,[54] the point being that Henry Hudson was in some sense Woodhull's predecessor, and the first English subject to rebel against the crown while on Terra Nova.

It was also New York, led by Poughkeepsie's diminutive Melanchton Smith, that rebelled against Alexander Hamilton's new Federalism and threatened to secede from the union and thereby divide the territory into two if a "Bill of Rights" were not guaranteed to the signers of the Constitution. Smith got his way, and New York got its IOU for a Bill of Rights and signed the document, thereby insuring that a hundred years of Dutch/Algonquin civil disobedience was not in vain. The irony is that Hamilton, who had been abused by his poor family and was therefore swayed towards the aristocracy in his youth, was both a New Yorker and part Native American.

Unknown to most readers of history, the Matouac (of Long Island) and other "River Indians" or at least their relatives on the western banks, may have had a sort of royal blood line of their own, the Amorgarikakan, which apparently was not prone to mutinies or rebellions. In fact the somewhat more self-governing Munsee[55] who "never had a king,"[56] seemed to welcome their help; at least there are no records of conflict between the two groups.[57]

The lives and deeds of these men are shrouded in mystery; our histories barely mention them. However there is a statue at the county fair grounds in Middletown, New York, over twenty feet tall, made from plaster of Paris, labeled Chief Towaco. Some call him "The Middletown Indian," but he may have been one of the greatest leaders of the forgotten Amorgarikakan lineage.[58]

There are many alternative translations of Towaco. It means the "land of the snake;" snake is *axk-kok*, but Julian Salomon translates it as "at the foothills." Towahgue means "ear" in Mohican, but this may be a coincidence.[59] Up until at least 1736 we have records of the town of Towaco, New Jersey, being called 'Waughaw'." It's a matter for further study.

It could be said that the time of Peter Minuit was a high tide of international prominence for the Matouac (and Wappingers). These Renneiu (R dialect coastal Algonquian) speakers had control of the harbor, with all its islands, the East River and the Lower Hudson during a time of intensive trade in furs, a worldwide phenomenon which Henry Hudson had started[60] simply by bringing back so many pelts, as we see him receiving in this narrative. It is ironic Juet describes few beaver pelts being traded, for it was the beaver that was to suffer the most during the fur wars, a creature that was extirpated from the Hudson Valley and much of the east coast for decades due to over-hunting. When Jacob Eelkins, an English-born trader, discovered the value of wampum, they had a good stake in that as well. But the Dutch traded guns to the Hodenosuannee (Iroquios) and not the Renneiu, and the strategy worked out beyond expectations. By the time Minuit was looking to buy property on Manhattan Island in 1626, the Renneiu were caught in a crosscurrent: they had become highly visible to Europeans and were sought after for trade, treaties and for council.

We can be sure that numerous intermarriages were beginning to happen on the frontier, but at the same time, the game animals were disappearing, the beaver already scarce, and the Mohawks were challenging the Algonquin political status quo with their Dutch supply of firepower. The Weckweeskecks were emerging as a powerful central group of the Wappingers Confederacy along the Hudson, even as their new-found power was slipping out of their fingers. They controlled upper Manhattan, the Bronx, and all of Westchester.

The family that was to produce Wyandanch, who was born in 1615, was emerging as the leading family of Long Island east of Canarsie territory, while the powerful Canarsie controlled Brooklyn and lower Manhattan. When Minuit was maneuvering to buy all of Manhattan, it seems that he may have started a turf war between its northern and southern administrators, who were separated by a large band of hunting land across the middle of the island. According to New York City oral tradition, the Weckweeskecks won out, and the final deal went down in November 1626 at Shorapapkock (Inwood Park) with a Weckweeskeck sachem present with authority to sell the whole island. It is possible that in order to sign that treaty he had quietly managed to conjoin the two great Renneiu speaking confederacies of New York, the Matouac of Long Island and the Wappingers of the East Bank. This however has never been proven, and the treaty for Manhattan is nowhere to be found. It would have been a powerful union, but in 1643, the Kieft War shattered this union and it would never recover.

It gives one pause to think that a great number of these Native Americans of the Mohicanituck, the river that somehow now bears Henry's last name, who were born before 1609, survived until after 1664, the year the English took over. This time period saw similar catastrophic changes in the psychological landscape of the Munsee, the Wappingers, the Matouac, the Mohican, and the Unami.

The Cosmopolitan Landscape in 1609

While readers are somewhat familiar with the European cultural leaders of 1609, a year marked by the decline of England and the upward climb of the Netherlands, few know the history of the Algonquin nations of that time, a people in the midst of a somewhat goldening age of their own. For the Algonquins it was not a gilded age; but a time of ripening within. As colors are verbs in Algonquin, it seems appropriate to honor the processes of nature that give us the ever-changing colors of nature's canvas, and describe the goldenness of that age as a process as well.

In the Hudson Valley region, the people had already been enjoying corn or maize for more than 500 years, and in central New York, for 1600 years. Squashes were introduced in the Early Woodland period; Beans apparently arrived in the area around AD 1300.[61] These and dozens of other foods we enjoy today (and which helped the European golden ages to flower by re-invigorating their nutrition) were first developed by Native Americans, mostly of Central America, mostly by women.[62] In fact, it seems they had only started using bows and arrows and the fishhook eight hundred years earlier, and copper trade was increasing. The Owasco-style pottery the Munsee started using only 600 years earlier[63] was reaching a high level of individual artistic expression among the Algonquin women. These ingredients and others were coming together to make life more enjoyable for all, amid a general communal effort to preserve and revere ancient traditions whenever possible.

The progressive Wappingers culture had only existed along the river for three hundred years or less and was just starting to form into a new confederacy, loosely structured like its two parent confederacies, the Matouac of Long Island and the earlier Mohican. Like the Florentine Renaissance, the local Algonquin golden age was broken in the middle by a black plague that probably had its origins in Florence, thanks to Giovanni de Verrazzano, but like the Italians of 170 years earlier, they made a strong comeback with a more centralized leadership with a smaller population to feed. In spite of the plague, the quality of life was rather high in 1609, and the Algonquins were anything but savage.[64]

American readers are probably much more familiar with the cultural landscape of Europe at the time of Henry Hudson's trip than that of the land they now stand upon. Queen Elizabeth had brilliantly contrived a "golden age" in England by favoring the most talented of her countrymen, including Bacon, Shakespeare, Raleigh, Drake, and Smith, all of whom played some role in popularizing the settlement of the Algonquin territory. Elizabeth, the first queen to choose a string of pearls from the New World to wear for her official portrait sitting, was succeeded in 1603 by the Catholic King James I, who continued the English renaissance, but on a less ambitious scale. He began one very ambitious project, the translation of the Bible into English,[65] so in 1609, the King James Bible would have been in its fifth year of translation, finished the year Hudson disappeared, in 1611, possibly written with Shakespeare's help.[66] James left the throne in 1625 and with his successor, Charles I, came chaos and civil war.

What did Hudson miss by being absent from London in that eventful year? Shakespeare registered his Sonnets in 1609, one of which included the line, "Shall I compare thee to a summer's day?" He wrote the plays Coriolanus and Pericles, and started Cymbeline in that year, but without Elizabeth on the throne, his plays became less ambitious in scope. Francis Bacon in 1609 wrote "The Wisdom of the Ancients," and was not only centrally involved in the governance of England, but involved in the settlement of the New Jerusalem as well.

On June 2 of that year, her Majesty's unfortunate ship the Seaventure launched from London. On July 23, while Hudson was somewhere off the coast of the Maritimes, she struggled to endure a terrible storm off the islands of Bermuda, one that lasted for days. The ship sunk, (some say the captain rammed it into the wharf to avoid sinking at sea) but all 150 passengers made it safely ashore. Among the passengers was the young John Rolfe, the young Robert Frobisher, whose elder Martin discovered Frobisher Bay in Canada, the young Thomas Gates, first governor of Virginia,[67] and the young Stephen Hopkins, who later became a prominent leader of the Mayflower crew in 1620 and a leader of the Massachusetts Bay Colony. Also on board was George Somers, future founder of the modern British state of Bermuda. All of their fates became entwined by water that day, and some by blood later on.

One of the major financiers of the trip was Francis Bacon. The play *The Tempest,* written in 1611, was attributed to Shakespeare. The play contains many details of the voyage Bacon would have had been privy to, however Strachey wrote a book about the wreck in Bermuda entitled, *True Reportory of the Wracke,* which may have been Shakespeare's source.

Unbeknownst to all, the wreck of the Seaventure was to play as significant a role in Native American history as it did in English Literature. The young John Rolfe and his wife were on that ship, and the wreck led to the death of his wife and child, leaving him a widower who spent many years in mourning. Two small ships, or "Pinnances," the Deliverance and the Patience, were constructed in nine months and arrived in Virginia on May 10, 1610, carrying a grieving John Rolfe with them. Pocahontas, whose real name was "Mataokah," may have been there to greet the ship as a young child.

Mataokah was the grand-daughter of Chief Powhatan whose personal name was Wahasunacook. Most agree that her famous tryst with Captain John Smith could never have happened, but Mataokah really did marry John Rolfe, went back to England with him and bore him children. She died in England of tuberculosis, adding greatly to his sorrow. He married a third time and had more children, all of whom ended up back in Virginia. The children of Pocahontas became known as the "Red Rolfes," (including Thomas, born in 1614) while the children of his third wife became known as the White Rolfes.

Thomas Jefferson, who always maintained an avid interest in Algonquin culture, spent much time trying to prove he was a "Red Rolfe," but his research was not conclusive. Geneologists today are still confused, but it is currently thought that he was a White Rolfe, and that there were some "frontier marriages" in his pedigree, crossing some of these same blood lines. Edith Galt Wilson, wife of Woodrow Wilson, believed herself to be a descendant of Pocahontas. She ran the United States as its first lady (Algonquin *sunksquaw*—top or chief woman) for eighteen months during her husband's illness in the White House, apparently without much trouble. Song interpreter Wayne Newton, who also considers himself a descendant, has recently raised a great deal of money to help locate the English grave of his reputed ancestor Pocahontas and bring her back to be repatriated in Algonquin (Powahatan) soil. The language of both the Munsee and Wappingers is related to that of those Powhatans.[68]

Stephen Hopkins went with the others to Jamestown, then made his way back across the Atlantic, to England. Although not a Puritan by faith, he signed on to the Mayflower[69] and signed the Mayflower Compact along with forty others. He was respected for his experience interacting with the Powhatan and was elected ambassador for native relations for the Massachusetts Bay Colony.[70]

Hopkins played a supporting role in history, but one that in the long run was probably as important as Hudson's starring role: Shortly after Hudson's trip, a Wampanoag named Tisquantum was taken by ship to England where he learned the English language and became known as Squanto.[71] When Squanto made it back to Patuxet, (via Spain, and many more ship berths) he was shocked to find his entire village destroyed and all his relatives either dead or missing. Most had died in a plague in 1617. Instead of his Wampanoag village he found the struggling Plymouth Colony.

Grief-stricken and angry, the young man wanted justice, and named himself Tisquantum, which means "rage of Manitou,"[72] but it seemed there was no justice possible. Stephen Hopkins was able to calm him down, and in any case convinced "Squanto" to reside with him and his family. Squanto was instrumental in getting the colony through the first winter of 1620. In 1621 Hopkins, Edward Winslow and William Bradford were delegated to engage in diplomatic relations with the Wampanoag and other natives in the Plymouth vicinity on behalf of the Pilgrims and succeeded in gaining the friendship of Chief Massasoit (1580-1661), concluding a peace treaty that was negotiated on March 22, 1621, in the Hopkins home, subject of at least one famous painting. Although that peace didn't last a generation, it bought enough time for the colonies to take root in such a way that King

Philip's War would not be able to extricate it from the soil, by mixing blood-lines with the leading Algonquin families. Many of Philip's own powerful relatives, such as Passaconaway and Wannalancet, had married white settlers and could not join in the fight. They escaped to Canada by canoe and land, linking water routes as they went north.

By Line of Sight

Just while Henry Hudson was opening up new avenues and passages for future exploration in New York, Galileo was opening up a pathway to space exploration. Late in 1608, two men from the town of Middleburg in the Netherlands named Hans Lipperhey and Sacharias Jansen[73] had unknowingly opened up a secret passage of their own. That passage was of light through a tube with lenses affixed to both ends, a "spyglass," (from the Dutch word spy=to see, which they called Hollandse Kijker) what we now know as a telescope. Galileo heard about the invention about the time Hudson was departing England, and was able to reproduce it by trial and error. By August of 1609 he had already created an eight-powered instrument, and presented it to the Venetian Senate who governed his hometown of Padua.

Rewarded with life tenure and a doubling of his salary, Galileo immediately created the first telescope to magnify images up to twenty times their size. As Hudson was arriving in what is now New York Harbor, opening a gateway to fur trade with the Algonquin world, Galileo began to turn his spyglass to the night sky.[74] Just as Cartier had pointed the way west for future Henry Hudsons in 1534, so Copernicus had pointed the way to the stars for future Galileos in that same year, 1534, with his yet-unproven theories about a heliocentric solar system.

In the fall of 1609, as Galileo was upsetting the old earth-centered world of the Catholic Church that would prove Copernicus right and have catastrophic effects on his private life,[75] so Hudson was upsetting the Algonquin world with his great floating bird; beads in exchange for furs, knives in exchange for tobacco, and cannon balls in exchange for arrows. We can only imagine how much more useful and meaningful his and Juet's logs would have been had he had possession of that first Hollandse Kijker, or something much more powerful furnished by Galileo. Perhaps he could have seen from the ship deck some of the council fire islands of the Wappingers, further inland; he could have peered further down the canyons to see the waterfalls of tributaries on each side of the main river. Perhaps he could have gotten a better view of the birds, plants and animals of Indian Brook Falls, which he passed on September 14 and again on October 1 without comment,[76] the place that John James Audubon later called home.

The following year, sailing again for the English, Henry Hudson departed for the arctic in possession of one of these first telescopes, presumably Dutch. Ironically, he became lost on that voyage by misestimating distances, a rare mistake for Hudson, one which eventually caused the crew to run short of food, "beating about for months 'in a labyrinth without end.'"[77]

Galileo's invention allowed us to see the moon much more clearly, including the seas later named after that sharp-eyed Genoan and it greatly increased the western fascination with space. Those seas whet the Western thirst for sending a man to the far reaches of the unknown, in this case to the moon. Those explorers during the 1960s, which some would label the golden age of American invention, became part of a tradition which Columbus, Verrazzano, Henry Hudson (and later Martin Frobisher, both controversial, larger than life figures with links to piracy) had already helped establish, for better or worse. The first major series of space rockets were named "Discovery," presumably named after the ship sailed by Waymouth, Argall, and finally Hudson, in 1610.

Heroes of a Golden Age

Hudson was not as consumed with ambition as was Columbus. Donald Johnson, author of *Charting the Sea of Darkness,* believes that Hudson most likely had a close encounter with mutiny early on in the journey across the Atlantic, the days that Juet judiciously left out of his diary, so that the salacious details might not discourage future financiers from backing their work. It was not the first, nor was it to be the last rebellion under Henry's command. The man who charted the Arctic seas and came within ten degrees of the North Pole centuries before down jackets and parkas were popular, was not a people-pleaser. But let us remember that eight years after his first landing at Hispaniola, Christopher and his two brothers were arrested and sent back to Spain in manacles for their cruelty to the Spanish as well as the natives.[78] Hudson can easily be placed among the more colorful and eccentric heroes of that golden age of exploration; but we must not place him at the extreme end of that ethically challenged spectrum with Frobisher, (who explored for gold in Canada in 1577 for the Muskovy Company, and brought back fool's gold) Columbus, and DeSoto.[79]

Most of us forget that in the 1560s there began several attempts to colonize the Atlantic coast, all of them short-lived, even when compared to the New Netherlands experiment. A group of Huguenots attempted to launch a chain of "French Florida colonies" in the 1560s, and in the 1580s Sir Walter Raleigh and his half brother Sir Humphrey Gilbert attempted to colonize the coast as well. Sir Gilbert died on one of his journeys, but in 1582, Richard Hakluyt the younger, a friend of Raleigh's, published a book, a collection of accounts of English and

French voyages to America.[80] In July of 1584, inspired in part by this book, which he probably helped to write, Sir Walter Raleigh found himself landing just north of Cape Hatteras among Algonquin-speaking people living on an island which the settlers called Roanoke. There he met Granganimeo, "the king's brother," a regal figure and later Wingina, the *werowance*, or chief.

Manchese and Manteo were two young men from the Island of Roanoke who agreed to go back to England as Algonquin interpreters.[81] Not including seven "wild men" who sailed back to Rouen, France in 1508 and were never seen again, Manchese and Manteo, as far as I know, were the first Algonquin speaking people to live in Europe, and they made many friends in England and must have heard many queries about their unfamiliar language. Even though Manchese turned against English culture a few years later, Manteo continued to find favor as the first Algonquin ambassador to what was to him a "new world." Manteo and his brother were linked by blood, but now Manteo was linked to England by water, and it proved stronger. Although no record survives of the Roanoke (Croatoan) language today, it is possible that certain basic concepts of pan-Algonquin language were available to the English-educated Henry Hudson, who was born around 1569.[82]

Manteo was preparing to take over the governorship of Roanoke, but as a representative of England. Then came Drake's arrival in June of 1586; Drake rescued most of the colonists as chaos broke loose on the ill-fated island. In 1587, three more ships set out from England with one hundred and fifty settlers to re-establish the lost colony. John White was with them but went back for supplies. In 1588, the Spanish Armada invaded the English Channel, and Drake and some bad weather helped defeat the Spanish. It took a year for England to restore safety on the seas, and so when White was finally safe to return to Roanoke in August of 1590, the inhabitants of Roanoke had disappeared into thin air, leaving only the sign carved into a tree, "CRO." The lost colony was never found. The Lumbee nation and the Malungeons are most likely their descendants.

Columbus was a hero of a golden age of Spanish exploration, an age which many now look upon with consternation. The English competed with Spain for supremacy of the waves until around 1588, when England's true golden age began with the defeat of the Spanish Armada. The Brits were inspired further by the publication in 1590 of Richard Hakluyt's *The Principle Navigations, Voyages and Discoveries of the English Nation*.[83] Hudson was a young man, probably 18, when the Armada made a gambit for the crown of England, and Chadwick believes emphatically that Hudson was aboard one of those ships that fought back the Armada.[84] His victory was to lead indirectly to the Dutch pact of independence from Spain, signed in 1609. Now the English and Dutch were linked by blood, which both had shed against Spain.

Hudson's explorations of the arctic and elsewhere during the next twenty years could have earned him a chapter in the revised edition of that book, as a hero of the golden age of British exploration. His friendly defection to the Dutch is significant as well: his new employers signed a treaty with their Spanish overlords only days after Hudson's departure which in many ways marked the beginning of the rather impressive era for the Dutch —especially in terms of sea power. In 1609, most of the great painters of the Dutch Renaissance were not even scribbling on their nursery walls yet; first would come shipping, then wealth, then great art. For the Dutch, prominence on the oceans had already become a part of their famously cosmopolitan image; now they would be the world's sea-going colonizers in competition with the British, whose success had slightly declined since the death of Elizabeth. Soon, Peter the Great of Russia would be apprenticing incognito with Holland's best shipwrights. The Algonquins of the Hudson Valley were very much caught in between the clashing ambitions of those two sea monsters.

Was there such an Algonquin golden age? From our English-speaking perspective, the Algonquin high water mark starts in 1584 with the arrival of Manteo in England. Although not well documented, his narratives, stories, songs, and philosophies of his native people must have had a tremendous impact on England, and possibly France. A number of such accidental tourists from the estuaries of Algonquin territory arriving in various states of array and disarray, some in shackles, some in top hats and coats, may have made it to England before him, but we don't know their names. The seven Algonquin "wild men" taken back to Rouen, France in 1508, were never heard from again. There may have been several more before the arrival of Hudson, but we don't know. What was said, and what explorers said on their return, spurred Jean Jacques Rousseau to write some of his most inspired political essays, including *Discourse on the Origins of Inequality*, and perhaps *The Social Contract*. If golden ages can be measured by their impact on igniting others, this was their moment in the sun.

It was not to last. Eastern Algonquin political influence in America was, for the most part, forced underground in 1811 with the fall of Tippecanoe and in the War of 1812, when the great fires of creation were buried or placed in hiding. For such a vast territory of people, a network of loosely organized confederacies spanning thousands of square miles, it is surprising that their undoing took only 227 years to complete. The western Algonquins were to fall 90 years later.[85] Their transformation into an underground movement within American society is a remarkable phenomenon, one which produced dozens of great American heroes whose Algonquin lineages cannot now be certain, figures such as Clara Barton the nurse, Andrew Jackson Davis the father of American Spiritualism, Edgar Allen Poe the writer, Jefferson Davis, one of the first heads of Indian Affairs and later a president of a republic, Black Beaver (not an underground figure, but certainly important) the scout, William Apes the religious leader, and many more.

From a political perspective, the day of the Dutch in the Hudson Valley lasted 55 years (1609-1664) less than the span of a man's life. It does seem (from Speck 1909) that a number of the natives who conversed in the pubs along Broadway (Breedwegh) with the residents of New Amsterdam during that tumultuous span of time claimed to have glimpsed Hudson's ship, the Halve Maen (or Half Moon) from the shoreline. It does seem more than likely that many such boasters actually did, if only from their mother's arms. It is therefore probable that some of those natives also lived to see the arrival of four British Man 'o' War ships in September of 1664, ships which filled the Dutch with the same wonder and awe that Hudson's Half Moon had inspired in the Algonquins fifty-five years earlier, and which urged the Dutch to give up control over their colony in the Hudson Valley. Oratamy was one such witness to history. Budke writes, "Oratamy's lifespan covered the entire period of the Dutch discovery and occupation of the country. His eyes, no doubt, saw the Half Moon exploring the river he knew so well..." Budke believes he died at an advanced old age in 1667, after three years of British rule in the colony.[86]

Trying to share this river with the somewhat agreeable Dutch was difficult enough at times for the Munsee and Renneiu speakers of the estuarial culture that was so filled with vitality those first years. On the surface, it seemed like a golden age was dawning for the native people, as they acquired new tastes, new ideas, and in two or three cases, got to see Europe, but the effect of disease, rum, money, guns, over-hunting and inter-cultural misunderstanding brought ruin to these same people, and in record time.

The "river Indians" as some called them, were largely dependent on the estuaries for transportation, food, fishing, and for drinking water. The Dutch too were dependant on that same water, but in a different, more indirect, and less shamanistic way. The Dutch were skilled mariners but did not see rivers as "veins of our mother," nor did they perform tobacco ceremonies before crossing rivers as the Algonquins did,[87] offering something in exchange in order to insure safe passage. Nevertheless, their destinies were now also linked by water.

The new colony was set up to resemble Holland, in fact New Haarlem was the same distance from New Amsterdam as Old Haarlem was from Old Amsterdam. Both pairs of cities were connected by a prominent pathway, and by water. In 1678, Jasper Dankers describes Harlem, walking north on Broadway; "Upon both sides of this way were many habitations of negroes, mulattoes, and whites. These negroes were formerly the proper slaves of the West India Company...situated about three hours' journey from New Amsterdam, like as old Harlem in Europe is situated about three hours distance from Old Amsterdam." (Dankers and Sluyters'

Journal 1678) There was also a waterway to the north that connected the two cites, similar and yet different than the East River, which led to the Harlem River. To see the water connection, you merely have to turn the map of Holland 90 degrees, so that north is east.

But no matter how hard it was under the Dutch, the first days under the English flag were infinitely more harsh for the natives. A hardy few, blessed with typical Algonkian longevity, the ones who survived various smallpox outbreaks, would have lived to cheer on the short-lived uprising of the Dutch in 1674 but these old grandfathers probably would not have survived much longer. Nor would such elders of the tribe have been very happy to see what had become of their beautiful valley since their childhood. In that short time, the pristine waterfall paradise they knew intimately had changed greatly. Signs of change were everywhere, and lower Manhattan had become despoiled, beginning a spiral of unnaturalness that is now irreversible.

The Munsee had known the less-than-characteristic cruelty of Petrus Stuyvesant, who captured twenty Munsee after the Second Esopus War and sent them off to Caracao knowing they'd end up as slaves there eventually. But the Amorgarikakan "moved at the breath of the people"[88] and Stuyvesant played the tyrant more like a Shakespearian actor would; trying to catch the sunlight with his eyes as he raised his sword, intoning important-sounding words, such was the extent of his tyranny most of the time. The British were different.

Although Governor Lovelace was kind and sympathetic to the Native American "problem," and the distant Governor Dongan was fair in his dealings, they and others were powerless puppets used by the Crown in London to expand a worldwide empire. Cruelty and exploitation were common and it was not saved exclusively for Native Americans; the British colonists themselves were also exploited, a habit which resulted in the taking of City Hall (later called Federal Hall) on Wall Street by rebels in 1775, and the American Revolution the following year.

Though Juet described "tall oaks" in the area of New York City, such forests were not to last. The fatal blow came when the British held control of Manhattan's multi-ethnic population through most of the Revolutionary War. Surrounded by American patriots, they were afraid to go off the island to barter for wood or water. They cut down almost every tree in Manhattan with the exception of Washington Heights. In August of 1781, George Washington and Rochambeau took a look at British military works on Manhattan from the Palisades across the Hudson. Washington wrote, "The island is completely stripped of trees, but low bushes… as high as a man's waist, appear in places where were once covered with wood in the year 1776."[89]

The great Dutch rebellion of August 7, 1673, which though instigated by captain Anthony Colve probably could not have lasted as long as it did without the underground support of Algonquins from Albany to Manhattan, was crushed the following year on February 9, 1674. At least a few elders of the Algonquins, who still held within their souls' vessels the untroubled waters of the Hudson as it was before Henry, may have looked "with straight eyes," at the retaking of New York by the crown in 1674, seen what was coming downstream, and decided to exit westward, possibly taking their half-Dutch grandchildren with them. In fact, some went eastward as well. Their Delaware Indian great-grandchildren were the first students to enroll at the Wheelock Indian School in Lebanon, in eastern Connecticut, which later moved to New Hampshire to become Dartmouth College, just before the Revolutionary War. For many years, this Ivy League college was for "Indians Only."[90]

Although no Native American of the Hudson Valley kept a diary during that time that we know of, it is nonetheless possible to reconstruct the Algonquin world of the Hudson before Henry, as they would have remembered it, its waterfalls and weirs, its roadways and boundaries, its farms and floodplains, its sacred sites, quarries, and capitols. The oral tradition of the east is still somewhat in existence, much of it still unwritten. If we use archaeological findings, colonial records, and linguistics, we can deduce quite a bit about that time just before contact, using the same kind of logic, reasoning and detective skills that has helped paleontologists reconstruct dinosaurs for the last hundred years. If we check that against the oral tradition, or visa versa, we have an avenue for discovering new insights about the past.

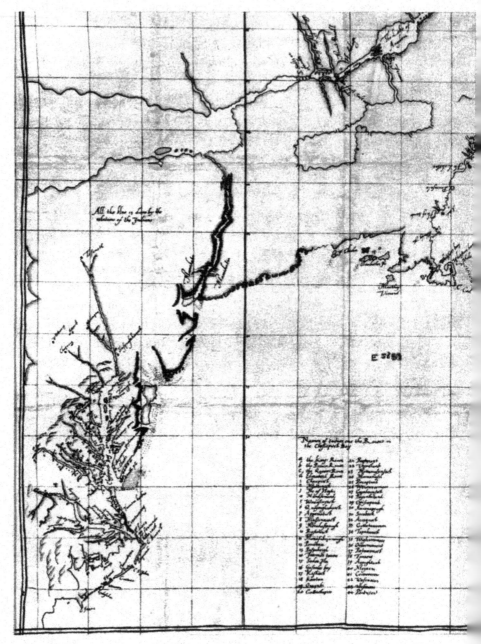

Part of the Velasco map of 1610
showing results of the exploration of Hudson.

Chapter Three

HUDSON OUT AT SEA

*T*he Half Moon's two diaries, Juet's and Hudson's, hold a unique fascination for New Yorkers, and for people around the world. While the rare scraps from Hudson's book shed a favorable light on Native Americans in the region and are easy to understand, Juet's cryptic logbook is filled with mutterings of mistrust and shadows of secrecy. His is a canvas filled with inanimate objects painted in vivid, hard-edged detail, floating against a vague background. Over time we begin to see order amid the chaos of events and objects flashing by, conveying sometimes surprising news. Places so familiar to us now slowly become recognizable, but the features are strangely different. These two diaries combined have tremendous meaning for our time, a record of life as it was in New York before the first white settler, a world so different from our own as citizens of this modern technotopia that many of the languages, nations, stones, birds, fish and villages, and even streams and hills, no longer exist in the area at all, or are in fact extinct.

Through Juet's cynical eyes, we glimpse an incredible innocence in the people he meets, a sense of trust in the universe which Algonquin people up and down the coast called, and still call, "Tchee Tchan Kwee Wee," Great Spirit is watching over me,"[91] a spontaneity and freedom that many feel missing today. In addition, we see an unmistakable description of what it was like to be totally connected to the land, completely "belonging to Mother Earth" as they say. Perhaps by claiming that natural heritage, we too can make a connection to the land beneath New York City, and the many other cities of the Hudson River Valley, and find a way to "belong to" this part of Mother Earth, as these people did then. That would be a spiritual awakening for all the races who live here, one that might be good for the environment as well.

Juet's journal begins back in England, and is interesting reading to say the least. For our purposes, we need start no earlier than the entry of August 28, the day Hudson discovered the Delaware Bay, and the day it discovered him.[92]

The Road Not Taken

JUET'S JOURNAL; FRIDAY, AUGUST 28 : *Fair and hot weather, the wind at south-south-west. In the morning at six o'clock we weighed, and steered away north twelve leagues till noon, and came to the point of the land; and being hard by the land in five fathoms, on a sudden we came into three fathoms; then we bore up and had but ten foot water, and joined to the point. Then as soon as we were over, we had five, six, seven, eight, nine, ten, twelve and thirteen fathoms. Then we found the land to trend away north-west, with a great bay and rivers. But the bay we found shoal; and in the offing we had ten fathoms, and had sight of breaches and dry sand. Then we were forced to stand back again; so we stood back south-east by south three leagues. And at seven o'clock we anchored in eight fathoms water; and found a tide set north-west, and north-north-west, and it rises one fathom and flows south-south-east. And he that will thoroughly discover this great bay must have a small pinnace, that must draw but four or five foot water, to sound before him. At five in the morning we weighed, and steered away to the eastward on many course, for the more norther land is full of shoals. We were among them, and once we struck, and we went away; and steered away to the south-east. So we had two, three, four, five, six, and seven fathoms, and so deeper and deeper.*

It was the dark of the moon the night that Henry Hudson left the waters of the Delaware and sailed back into open sea. But to Algonquin eyes, this was no ordinary dark sky. This night marked the end of thirteen moons since the great eclipse of August 10, 1608, an annular solar eclipse, but one so stunning to watch that Captain John Smith, exploring the Rappahannock that day with his Algonquin friend Mosco, wrote about it in his book "Relations..."

Its epicenter occurred in the Sargasso Sea, the latitude of Cape Hatteras, but its shadow fell over Delaware and Barnegat Bays as well. All solar eclipses happen at the new moon, the beginning of the lunar cycle, so it was easy for the natives, marking calendar turtle shells, also called "moon turtles," to map the lunar year, because there are thirteen central platelets on the turtle's back, and 28 small dorsal platelets around the edge called scutes. If a "moon" is measured by alternating 29 and 30 nights, (the synoptic month, measured from new moon to new moon, which the Nanticokes would have called *echtupananahenk*[93]) then 13 of those is 18.5 days longer than the solar year, 383.5 total days. The thirteenth moon, and lunar year, was therefore completed on the 28 of August, 1609, a day of great significance to these prophetic watchers of the skies.

The Seven Fires prophecies of the Algonquins simply state that important visitors from the east would arrive during the fourth of seven cycles of fires of 112 years. As the fourth was the central one of seven, it stood to reason that the halfway or balance point was the most important year. That fell around 1609. But in a great number of cases, the event that characterized the era, and the mathematical beginning or middle of that era, was preceded by a solar eclipse that signified change, destruction of the old, and birth of the new. The events of the next 13 moons after such markers in aboriginal time were always critical, to be regarded carefully, as portents of the future. Sometimes the event would come one or two moons later, but rarely more than thirteen complete moons after the eclipse. It was a time to watch for *kee-gay-no-lay-woa-gun*, or "signs." (Literally, "The universe is teaching you something wonderful.") Henry Hudson, who sometimes seemed to follow his whims like will-o'-the-wisps, surely believed that he was a free, autonomous agent, "master of his fate, captain of his ship," as he penetrated "Delaware" Indian waters for the first time, and could have proved it five ways past Tuesday. "No savage God controls my fate," he would have said. Nonetheless, to the Algonquins watching their turtle shell timepieces, such arguments were vain. Hudson had arrived, Englishman that he was, exactly on time.

Judging by the New Netherland Museum's replica, the ship even had a large carved crescent moon on the back of the ship, above the Captain's cabin window, brightly painted. No wonder native "astrologers" were so sure that Hudson was the Manitou that fell to earth. His ship bore signs of prophecy in terms that they could understand. He must have thought no eyes were watching him as he sailed around Delaware Bay but indeed there must have been a few, and some were probably wide, their owners running helter-skelter, looking for someone to tell the news to.

We don't often think about the so-called "Lenape" (as they are called today) as people who participated in the Midewiwin tradition, or who shared the seven fires prophecies, but they were, centuries ago. All Midewiwin history confirms it. As Joseph White Norwood writes, "This was his religion, philosophy and science taught in secret societies universally distributed and variously named, but essentially identical in principle. Among the Lenape, as among all Algonkin peoples, this society was known as the Mide-Wiwan or Priests House....The Mide were both priests, warriors and healers. They were the leaders of their clans. The respect in which they were held made every young warrior ambitious to become a Mide, as this increased his social, political and religious standing in every way. Early pioneers knew of this organization, though no white man was ever admitted and it is upon the information grudgingly furnished by its native members, coupled with the known customs of the various tribes, we must depend for what knowledge we possess of it. The pioneers called it "The Great Medicine Society" and referred to the Mides as "Medicine Men," because one of the things obviously taught the initiated was the art of healing with herbs and appeals to the *manitos* or spirits: a sort of combination medical and mental healing school....Every lodge was dedicated to The Great Spirit and from this Great Spirit flowed all good things, knowledge of herbs and incantations being merely one of them....The Algonkin legends indicate that the Midewiwan was established among them on the Atlantic Coast before their great flood. It was given them from the Great Spirit, through the Dzhemanito or Good Spirit, first to their culture hero Nanaboush, because he had fought the battles of mankind against the Makimani or Bad Spirit and his hosts. Both these Good and Bad Spirits had been made by the Great Spirit; in fact they are to be viewed as opposites of the same thing—The Great Spirit. Thus Winter and all hostile forces to man's comfort are opposed to Summer and those forces that make for man's comfort. All the *manitos*, good and bad, are but the natural powers derived by the individuals possessing them from the Great Spirit and are 'good' or 'bad' according to their use by the individual in relation to man as a child of the Great Spirit."[94]

Based on Juet's journal, there's little doubt the Half Moon reached the shoals of Delaware Bay. In 1854 the Historical Society of Delaware issued a statement that Henry Hudson was the first European to "discover" the state of Delaware, on the 28 of August, 1609.[95] It is true that Verrazzano did not clearly describe Delaware Bay in 1524, but his "Vandome" is thought to be that selfsame bay. Hudson is credited with "discovering" the bay for Holland in 1609, and Samuel Argall with rediscovering it (for England) and naming it after Lord de la Warr the following year. Others would argue that Hudson's friend John Smith should get the honors for discovering the Delaware, all of which should be taken with a grain of salt, since we all know who was there first — the people who became known as "Delaware Indians."

Chadwick writes: "The lookout reported sighting a large bay, (Delaware Bay). Hudson tried to navigate it, and sailed about nine miles, but it became too shallow and full of shoals. He found many shoals, and several times the Half Moon was stuck upon the sands; the current, moreover, set outward with such force as to assure him that he was at the mouth of a large and rapid river. This was not encouraging. After a day, he gave up, went back and headed north again."[96] Johnson comments, "Delaware Bay entered." John T. Cunningham writes, "The ship was apparently sailing in shoal waters of the Bay near Cape May."[97]

Hudson's choice to turn around and give up on exploring what we now call the Delaware River was of great historical importance. He would have encountered a much more centralized Unami Delaware political system at Philadelphia, and a slightly more centralized Munsee system at the fall line (the Falls of the Delaware, called Sunckheagan, or "she is head of the waters" now Trenton, New Jersey)[98] and the Delaware Water Gap where he would have met a large population of Shawnee on what is now Shawnee Island, and then Minisink Island, the Munsee council fire island.

At the head of that bay was Shackamaxon, now the Kensington section of Philadelphia, and Shackamaxon Island now Petty Island, which was a council fire island. Sakimaxing may mean "The Place of Kings, or Sachems."[99] Philadelphia was already associated with "brotherly love" in the minds of the Algonquins, years before Penn's Quakers arrived, thanks to the teachings of Tammanend, later granted sainthood by a church that knew him not, but who welcomed his message. If he had visited there he would not only get credit for discovering Pennsylvania, it is probable he would have met the grandfather of Tammanend III, "The Affable," (1628-1698). Tammanend III became a grand chief in 1683, and soon afterwards, wearing a "crown" of buck horns and accompanied by hundreds of warriors, he greeted William Penn (whom he called "Miquon," or "quill pen," a play on the last name Penn) and his Quakers near the place Independence Hall now stands. He gave Penn a wampum belt with two men holding hands, one with a top hat on. He said, "We will live in love with William Penn and his children as long as the creeks and rivers run, and while the sun, moon and stars endure."[100] A similar wording was later used by George Washington in a treaty with Cornplanter of the Seneca, promising not to encroach on a certain beautiful plot of land and its people—a town which now lies at the bottom of the Kinzua Reservoir,[101] and President Andrew Jackson used similar wording when promising the Cherokee their perpetual safety.

The name of Tammanend is probably derived from (and pronounced exactly the same as) Déminán, a mythological blue-faced Taino god of creation, who lands on a turtle's back (as does Sky Woman in the Lenape/Mohawk tale) as he falls from the constellation of Orion, a God whose widely celebrated birthday (at least in Central America) was the same as Henry's, September 12.[102] Tammanend was later known as Tammany (an Irish word) during the middle 1800s, for whom New York's famed Tammany Hall was named. With John Trumbull's help, Tammany was placed on the List of Saints, defiantly as "The Patron Saint of American Liberty" in 1771, five years before the Declaration of Independence was even signed, although His Holiness the Pope was not consulted.

The details of the lives of Tammanend and his line are somewhat established in a book called *The Tammany Legend* by Joseph White Norwood, published in 1938. According to this account, the descendants of Tammany were run out of Pennsylvania at the point of a matchlock musket by the disloyal sons of William

Penn during the Walking Purchase Wars. They fled with empty hands northwards towards their old enemies, the Oneidas, seeking refuge. When they arrived, old animosities were buried like so many hatchets, and they were welcomed with open arms. According to some, Tammany is buried near Doylestown, Pennsylvania, "close by the stream of the Neshaminy" where he had lived his life. According to others, he is buried in the Tammany Burial Grounds near Chalfort, Pennsylvania. Yet others say he is buried in Southampton, Pennsylvania, in Tamanend Park, where there are five boulders from 1683, with the names of five members of the Unami, and Tamanend is among those names. It is believed that his two sons were Yaqueekhon and Quenameckquid.

Why would the Taino have come to Philadelphia? The Taino whalers would have followed these highly seasonal mammals during the summer as they migrated north. Philadelphia, along with Hudson and Newburgh, New York, were major inland estuarine whaling ports during the eighteenth and early nineteenth centuries and Philadelphia was the closest to the Caribbean. Other whaling ports such as Boston, (Greenport, Long Island) Port Jefferson Long Island, Mystic, Connecticut, and Portland, Maine, were located on the sea, but at the mouths of estuarine rivers. These were possibly Algonquin whaling centers, and whale meat was an important part of the local diet.

Why do whales migrate such long distances? According to the authors of *Amerikanuak*, Douglass and Bilbao, whales are very intelligent, and avoid places where whalers tend to congregate, changing their habitual routes if necessary. The whalers themselves are then pushed to change their habits, wandering further out to sea, boldly (or fearfully in some cases, I'm sure) in pursuit of their prey.[103] It is believed that Basque whalers may have encountered the New World just before[104] or after Columbus while chasing whales who had seen the wisdom of leaving the Bay of Biscay where Basque whalers established their main port.[105] In a similar way, it seems that the Taino were among the best whalers of the Caribbean, and the whales in response moved further out to sea to evade capture. Highly seasonal animals, they move northward en masse during the summer months (depending on the species). One can easily see how the Taino might decide to follow the North Atlantic currents to Philadelphia and Long Island. [106]

The shallows presented a serious threat to the safety of the Half Moon. But if Hudson hadn't turned around, and if he had been extremely diplomatic (not his strong suit, as we shall see), he might have been able to make major diplomatic progress in establishing relations between the Dutch and the Unami and Munsee. Making a mistake such as taking captives at Shackamaxon, Sunckheagan, or Minisink, might have gotten Hudson and his crew members killed by overwhelming forces, and today's Hudson River would be known by another name, perhaps

Mohicanituck, the name it was known by for a thousand or more years by its original inhabitants. Tormenting Hudson with sandbars was history's way of telling the Dutch, "not yet."

JUET'S JOURNAL, SATURDAY, AUGUST 29 : *Fair weather, with some thunder and showers, the wind shifting between the south-south-west, and the north-north-west. In the morning we weighed at the break of day, and stood towards the northern land, which we found to be all islands to our sight, and great storms from them, and are shoal three leagues off. For we coming by them, had but seven, six, five, four, three, and two and a half fathoms, and struck the ground with our rudder, we steered off south-west one glass, and had five fathoms. Then we steered south-east three glasses, then we found seven fathoms, and steered north-east by east, four leagues, and came to twelve and thirteen fathoms. At one o'clock, I went to the top-mast head, and set the land, and the body of the islands did bear north-west by north. And at four o'clock, we had gone four leagues east-south-east, and north-east by east, and found but seven fathoms, and it was calm, so we anchored. Then I went again to the top-mast head, to see how far I could see land about us, and could see no more but the islands. And the southern point of them did bear north-west by west, eight leagues off. So we rode till midnight. Then the wind came to the north-north-west, so we weighed and set sail.*

"Glasses" here are hour glasses, sand clocks which take a half an hour to empty when turned over. A "watch" was usually eight "glasses" long, or four hours. There were also sand clocks which took thirty seconds to empty, used to measure speed in knots. These are literal knots, tied into a rope that is unraveling into the river.[107]

"*…. and stood towards the northern land, which we found to be all islands to our sight, and great storms from them, and are shoal three leagues off…*" The land to the north is lower New Jersey, where the Unalatchtigo were said to live, the people of the Turkey Totem.[108] The ship turned left around Cape May, and saw the many islands that are scattered there like bread crumbs left for seagulls along the lower Jersey shore. He indicates the ocean was so shallow they were hitting sand bars seven miles out at sea. It seems they moved back and forth several miles off shore. They may have had trouble with cross-winds.

"*Then I went again to the top-mast head, to see how far I could see land about us, and could see no more but the islands…*" They reached North Wildwood, which is all islands. The latitude there is 39 degrees and zero minutes. We can imagine the scrappy Robert Juet climbing thirty feet into the air up to the top-mast, braving blustery winds to get a good look at all the islands lying around them. At midnight, the wind finally reversed and blew to the north by north-west, so they pulled up anchor and let the wind pull them towards New York.

JUET'S JOURNAL, SUNDAY, AUGUST 30 : *In the morning between twelve and one, we weighed and stood to the eastward, the wind at north-north-west, we steered away and made our way east-south-east. From our weighing till noon, eleven leagues. Our soundings were eight, nine, ten, eleven, twelve and thirteen fathoms till day. Then we came to eighteen, nineteen, twenty, and to twenty-six fathoms by noon. Then I observed the sun, and found the height to be 39 degrees 5 minutes, and we saw no land. In the afternoon, the wind came to north by west; so we lay close by with our fore-sail, and our main sail, and it was little wind until twelve o'clock at midnight, then we had a gale a little while. Then I sounded, and all the night our soundings were thirty, and thirty-six fathoms, and we went little.*

"From our weighing till noon, eleven leagues." From midnight until this point, they had traveled about 24 miles, but much of that was out to sea. *"Then I observed the sun, and found the height to be 39 degrees 5 minutes, and we saw no land."* At noon on the equinoxes, you can measure the angle of the sun above the horizon [with an astrolabe, as the sun is a star] and subtract that from 90 degrees to determine the latitude, making seasonal adjustments the rest of the year. If it were September 21, at this location, the sun would be 50 degrees 55 minutes above the horizon at noon. This plus 39 degrees 5 minutes would equal 90. Autumnal equinox was three weeks away, so the adjustment wasn't too hard, however here it seems he may have made a mistake. 39 degrees, 5 minutes would be our present-day Avalon, New Jersey. Later he says he is at 38 degrees, 39 minutes, which is much further south. Yet later he says he has to readjust his compass.[109]

JUET'S JOURNAL, MONDAY, AUGUST 31, 2009 : *Fair weather and little wind. At six 'o'clock in the morning we cast about to the northward, the wind being at the north-east, little wind. At noon it fell calm, and I found the height to be 38 degrees 39 minutes. And the streams had deceived us, and our sounding was thirty-eight fathoms. In the afternoon I sounded again, and had but thirty fathoms. So that we found both by our observations and our depths. From noon till four o'clock in the afternoon, it was calm. At six o'clock we had a little gale southerly, and it continued all night, some times calm, and sometimes a gale; we went eight leagues from noon to noon, north by east.*

Wait a minute; 38 degrees, 39 minutes is Hereford Inlet. Something went wrong. Johnson comments: "Back and forth by deceitful tidal streams." Later, they travel north again, possibly 19 miles. I believe they ended up the day near Peck Beach.

JUET'S JOURNAL, TUESDAY, SEPTEMBER 1: *Fair weather, the wind variable between east and south, we steered away north-north-west. At noon we found our height to be 39 degrees 3 minutes. We had soundings thirty, twenty-seven, twenty-four, and twenty-two fathoms, as we went to the northward. At six o'clock we had twenty-one fathoms. And all the third watch till twelve o'clock at mid-night, we had soundings twenty-one, twenty-two, eighteen, twenty-two, twenty-one, eighteen, and twenty-two fathoms, and went six leagues near land north-north-west.*

"At noon we found our height to be 39 degrees 3 minutes." This is hardly possible. Either Hudson has made a navigational mistake, or Juet has made a mistake in locating his position. "...and went six leagues near land north-north-west." Cunningham writes, ""Currents had caused ship to be 2 minutes farther south than two days earlier." I believe they traveled at least 13.2 miles north, which would take them as far as Atlantic City. Chadwick comments, "As in the previous entry, the Half Moon is well east of the coast of New Jersey, heading north."

SONG OF MACH-QUOYUOKUS, (LITTLE BEARS) A NAVESINK INDIAN, SUNDAY AUGUST 29 THROUGH WEDNESDAY, SEPTEMBER 1(*a fictional dramatization based on known circumstances and customs*). (Native words are Sanhikan/ "Unalatchtigo" terms from Johannes DeLaet's list of 1633,[110] except where otherwise noted) : "*This morning I paddle my dugout alone, sailing towards the rising sun, along the inlet Manasquan and out into the sea. A beautiful morning, full of light. A beautiful morning full of light. Hey hey a no ha, Igato(n) Igato(n).* [111]

I toss out my nets on the sea and nacha syackameek [three eels] come to me. We will wait three days, three days! I see Peckamanna [Cranberry Inlet/inlet through the island[112]] to the west and as the tide is right, I ride the back of niska, [rushing wave of water] through the inlet and into the Lake: "The Long Shallow Lake Inside the Islands."[Barnegat Bay] Hey hey a no ha igato(n) igato(n). Hey hey a no ha igato(n) hey.

It's miles to the south where I go, so I land my canoe on duchke-hakee ["the upper arm of land"] above the inlet and make tinteywe [fire] from one of the embers in my tarope [turtle shell], to cook syackameek. I see many tareckak [cranes] which is a good sign, on this auspicious morning. I see woucous [fox], but he does not get away with my syackameek [eels]. I find a spring and drink ouret-empye [good water]. I eat and rest and make a prayer, offering my tobacco to the land, and then I climb back in my boat and head down to the meeting place. The mannus k'tchiwyeranou [The long-tongued island] always to my left. Always to my left. Hey hey a no ha igato(n) igato(n).

I arrive as night begins to fall, first of many men to follow, at the windswept end of long-tongued island, as go to the hitteockek [trees]I gather piles of wood. My friend arrives also by boat, and we carry the wood to the top of the hill, the towering hill of golden sand. The hill is so steep, the height of six men, six men standing end to end. From its summit one can see the Forked River burial grounds on the mainland, and the fires of Pygmy Forest too. Then I take the embers from my torope shell and saying prayers, I make a fire for the council. Its light will guide their boats to this most sacred spot. And tomorrow discuss the prophecies, the seven fires prophecies, the turning time of which is dawning now. Hey hey a no ha, igato(n) igaton(n); Hey hey a no ha igato(n) hey.

And here we stand, thirteen moons from when we saw the sun reveal its circle of fire. We see the union of sun and moon and see grandfather sun turn dark at mid-day, and then we wait one turning of the earth, we wait the thirteen moons and then it comes. The fulfillment of the prophecy. A messenger arrives; he says the strangers from the east are headed right this way. We build this fire in the dark of night to welcome them, visitors who come in brotherhood and peace, so that they might find their way to Turtle Island safely.

We wait three nights, according to the signs, and then they come. A crescent moon arises in the east at sunset. Not too long after the dawn there comes a great floating bird with wings unfurled, the tips of which are loftier than the hill on which we stand. It bears the sign of a crescent moon. It enters the Shallow Lake Behind the Islands, passes us by without a sound. It is a most amazing sight, fulfillment of our prophecy. Will they come with hearts of hate? Or will they come in peace? We hide behind the hill and let it pass, but we find much to say among our selves that day! Hey hey a no ha igato(n) igato(n) Hey hey a no ha, igato(n) hey.

JUET'S JOURNAL, WEDNESDAY, SEPTEMBER 2 : *In the morning close weather, the wind at south in the morning; from twelve until two o'clock we steered north-north-west, and had sounding twenty-one fathoms, and in running one glass we had but sixteen fathoms, then seventeen, and so shoaler and shoaler until it came to twelve fathoms. We saw a great fire, but could not see the land, then we came to ten fathoms, whereupon we brought our tacks aboard, and stood to the eastward east-south-east, four glasses. Then the sun arose, and we steered away north again, and saw land from the west by north, to the north-west by north, all like broken islands, and our soundings were eleven and ten fathoms. Then we luffed in for the shore, and fair by the shore we had seven fathoms. The course along the land we found to be north-east by north. From the land*

*which we first had sight of, until we came to a great lake of water, as we could
judge it to be, being drowned land, which made it rise like islands, which was
in length ten leagues. The mouth of the lake hath many shoals and the sea
breaks upon them as it is cast out of the mouth of it. And from that lake or bay,
the land lies north by east, and we had a great stream out of the bay; and from
thence our sounding was ten fathoms, two leagues from land. At five o'clock we
anchored being little wind, and rode in eight fathoms water, the night was fair.
This night I found the land to haul the compass 8 degrees. For to the northward
off us we saw high hills. For the day before we found not above two degrees of
variation. This is very good land to fall in with, and a pleasant land to see."*

"*In the morning close weather, the wind at south in the morning; from twelve until two
o'clock we steered north-north-west...*" The ship traveled for two hours, but we don't
know how fast. If it started near Atlantic City and was traveling ten miles an hour,
it would have gone north for twenty. There are many "broken islands" along this
stretch. This is obviously Egg Harbor, a rough translation, probably inspired by a
great nesting area they must have discovered.[113]

"*We saw a great fire, but could not see the land...*" This is Juet's first real glimpse
of human habitation, a haunting prelude to the Dutch East India Company's "First
Encounter." The moon was still too slight to offer help in seeing the land. The
question is, "where was the fire located?" It must have been at a high point of land,
and yet such peaks are rare in eastern New Jersey.

I travelled to the Ocean County Historical Society in Tom's River, New Jersey
to find an answer. There I discovered a number of experts in local history gathered
together in a basement library clustered around some ancient maps and documents. They were eager to help me find answers to my questions concerning their
county's illustrious history.

I was told that there is a twenty to thirty foot dune right behind Barnegat Inlet
lighthouse today. These Ocean County historians felt that the most likely location was at the top of this mound. The diary clearly indicates the men were just
south of Barnegat Inlet looking north. Perhaps they steered towards the light just
as sailors use the Barnegat Light to find the entrance to the bay in a fog. It must
have been dark or morning twilight when they spotted the fire, as he adds afterwards, "*...then the sun rose... .*" There are two reasons they couldn't see the land.
It was dark—on September 2, 1609; there was just a slim crescent of light upon
the moon's right shoulder, hardly enough to light the landscape for seafarers. The
second reason was that the mainland was too far away and they were looking
northward across the pointed end of the barrier reef.

The fire could have also been at the Indian Burial grounds at the mouth of

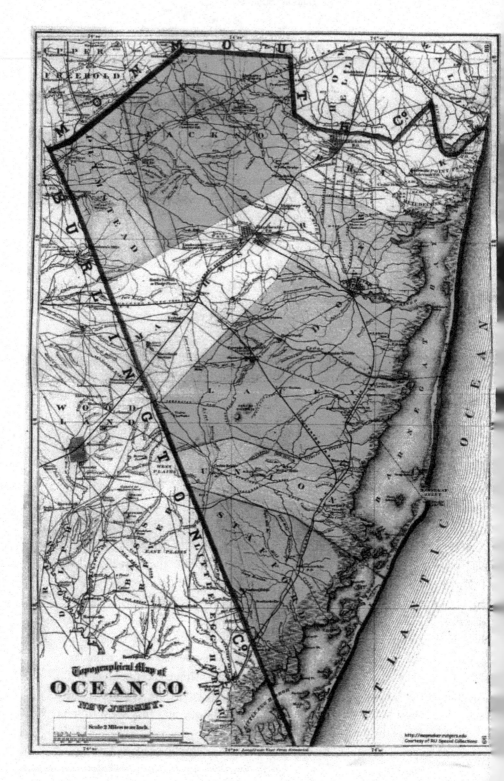

Topographical Map of
OCEAN CO.
NEW JERSEY.

Scale 2 Miles to an Inch.

Tom's River, at Island Heights, although it was not a funeral pyre as Lenape do not perform cremations. The fire could have been on top of the Forked River Mountains, which rise to between thirty and forty feet high, above the Pigmy Forest in Stamford Township, a few miles west of Barnegat Inlet and slightly north. All three are fairly close to one another and to the inlet, but the Navesink Highlands are over 45 miles away. The curvature of the earth and the principles of perspective would make the Highlands appear lower than these other hills. The north branch of the Forked River flows into Barnegat Bay just northwest of the Barnegat Light. On the other side of the reef is Manahawken, or Menahoking, "where the land slopes,"[114] (or from another source originally Manach'hen (island) hawken (place).[115] If Juet's chronology is correct (and he was writing things down as they happened, using a pencil or quill pen, not a word processor) he saw the fire before entering into Barnegat Bay, not after, so it must have been further south than Navesink, which is where so many writers have placed the mysterious fire.

"From the land which we first had sight of, until we came to a great lake of water, as we could judge it to be, being drowned land, which made it rise like islands, which was in length ten leagues..." Juet is describing Barnegat Bay—which is a unique 22 mile long (ten leagues) lake/bay inside the intracoastal waterway barrier reef—entering at the spot where Barnegat Light House now stands. The Ocean County historians heartily agreed that their beloved Barnegat was where the Half Moon sailed that day in August. Depending on the tide, it would be a bay at high tide, and a lake at low tide. When the tide came in, the waves would tumble into the lake again. The waters there are understandably turbulent.[116]

"Barnegat" is not your average word in Dutch, however a "gat" is a gate or a "hole" between two points of land that a ship must navigate through. This expressively describes the opening in the sand bar through which a mariner must pass to enter Barnegat Bay. The suffix "barre" in Dutch relates to the English word "barrens," which is appropriate for these sand dunes and barrier reefs.[117] It means an unproductive land spotted with shrub, brush, and featuring sandy soil. This meaning of Barnegat is confirmed by the book The *Origin of New Jersey Place Names*.[118] The loose translation: "Gateway to Nowhere," may have had a Native American precursor.

"The mouth of the lake hath many shoals and the sea breaks upon them as it is cast out of the mouth of it..." Cunningham writes, "Barnegat Inlet." If Hudson traveled ten leagues north in that lake or bay from that point, they would be at Point Pleasant Beach, at the Manasquan Inlet. Touching Leaves, Nora Thompson Dean, defined Manasquan in Unami to mean "a place to gather grass," however, if broken down syllabically, it seems to refer to many little islands in shallow water; mana=island, us=small=, k= plural, quan= shallow water. More than half the time, Algonquin

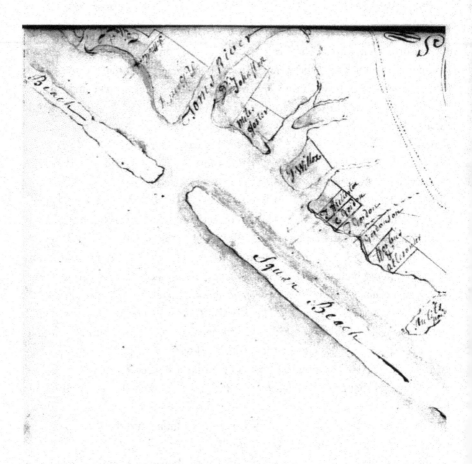

place names acquire secondary "translations," which are not literal renderings of the name used, but accurately describe the place. In addition to this is the translation or nickname, "where streams and paths meet," although the syllables don't seem to suggest this.[119]

"...drowned land which makes it rise like islands..." seems to describe perfectly the 22 mile long trough and the 22 mile long rise to the east which becomes an island at high tide. Juet said, "the land lies north by east," meaning the reef, we assume, as where else would the land be to the east?

"...and we had a great stream out of the bay;" There is a narrow canal today that flows northward out of the bay, into Manasquan Inlet in the area of Point Pleasant, but it is hardly a "great stream." Did it exist in 1609? Was "Poplar Stream" in that location before the canal? On the way to the Ocean County Historical Society I stopped by the site of the canal.

In fact, the question is moot. Both Velasco's map of 1610 and Adriaen Block's map of 1614 seem to show a significant "gat" or opening in the barrier reef at the *upper* end of Barnegat Bay, through which the Half Moon would have been able to pass and continue northward as described, an opening to the sea that no longer exists. Both maps also show the lower entrance, which does still exist.[120] According to Ocean County records, this northeast passage out of the bay was called Cranberry Inlet. The term Cranberry Inlet seems to be of native origin, probably a translation of Peckamannak, a typical Algonquin play on words. Peckamannak would mean "an inlet through the islands," whereas Peckaminak would mean "Cranberries."[121]

A storm filled it some time after 1609 (possibly around 1685) and then it opened up again in 1758, playing an important role in the American Revolution, but then closed up again during a terrific storm that occurred in the 1830's.[122] The Ocean County Historical Society has in its files a large hand-drawn English-language map labeled in cursive, which shows Cranberry Inlet opposite Tom's River, but unlabelled. The sand bar to the north is called Squan Beach. It seems to be from the time of George Washington.

This dangerous spot, so prone to appearing and disappearing in an eighty-or-so-year cycle, is known today as Seaside Heights, the site of a beach resort, complete with a boardwalk, hotels and arcades, across from the mouth of Tom's River to the west, and of similar width as its mouth. Apparently, these storms cause Tom's River to break through the barrier reef, creating Cranberry Inlet. Ortney Avenue at the north of town sits upon the former site of the notorious Cranberry Inlet. It seems that extensive building and civil engineering have put an end to Cranberry Inlet for good. Or has it?

> 1609 Cranberry inlet open
> 1685? Cranberry inlet closed
> 1758 Cranberry Inlet open
> 1830 Cranberry Inlet closed

Running into Barnegat Bay just north of the spot where Cranberry Inlet lay was the Metedeconk, which may mean *Meteu* or "Medicine Man," and *saconk*, "outlet of a stream."[123] Just south of the phantom inlet is a place on the barrier reef called Mantaloking, translated as *Mantua,* a subtribe, [actually the Matuas are "frog totem" Lenape] with *lekau* or sand plus *ink* or place;[124] however the current spelling of this town is Mantoloking, which could be translated as "the sandy land of Manitou."

"*...and from thence our sounding was ten fathoms, two leagues from land.* They must have headed out of the inlet and into the sea. "*Then we luffed in for the shore...*"

"*This is very good land to fall in with, and a pleasant land to see.*" Point Pleasant has made its fame by claiming to be Juet's "pleasant land to see." Everything in the journal indicates to me that all the boastful claims made by the Point Pleasant Chamber of Commerce are correct. Point Pleasant is ten miles south of Asbury Park Beach.

Ian Chadwick agrees the Half Moon was located off the coast of New Jersey at this time, but places the ship further north. He writes, "The lookout saw a "great fire" ashore on the highlands of Navesink. Hudson anchored near what is now Sandy Hook." The word Navesink means "A high promontory," in Unami and in fact it is. On the Adriaen Block map of 1614, written in cursive, in smudged pencil, (probably smudged by Block's own hand) on the eastern side of Sandy Hook, just below the marking Sand Hoek, are the words, *"Der Roodeberg,"* which means "The Red Mountain" in Dutch. Was there a red mountain near the beach a short walk south from Sandy Hook? What was it made of? This term also shows up in a later map to mark a spot in southeastern Connecticut.

Just inland from that spot, in what is generally thought of as the Navesink Indian tribal territory, Block wrote the word *Aquamachukes. Aqua* in this area generally means "a high bank." Mount Mitchell is 248 feet and the highest point in the "Highlands," is 260 feet. The Bolton map also shows the similar term *"Aquehonga"* meaning "high sandy banks" for all of Staten Island. *Mach(oo)kus* would indicate "the small bears."[125] The *ch* would be pronounced as in the German "buch." The same word appears on a map of 1616. Block also indicates the "Sangicans" situated on a river just to the northwest of Staten Island. This was the Raritan River. The Raritan is also called the Naraticong,[126] sometimes translated as "the river behind the island," but more likely "place at the point of land." Usually called the Sanhikans, they were referred to either as, "The Fire Makers," or "The People of the Fire Bow Drill," however the name Sinhikan implies, perhaps in a double layer of meaning, an estuarine river with many stones. North of this river were the Munsee territories, but the powerful Sanhikans also occupied this region. There is a place on Sandy Hook called "Henry Hudson Springs," still marked, but when did he arrive there?

Verrazzano saw a similar fire burning 85 years earlier, but that was at Block Island, [at the eastern end of Long Island, near Rhode Island, the name of which was based on Verrazzano's description of Block Island] although legend has it that Fire Island also got its name from Verrazzano, in reference to this fire. Such fires were used by coastal Algonquins as navigational points for sailors, similar to light houses today. Verrazzano had named the Navesink Highlands of New Jersey, " San Polo," after the count of San Polo. This earlier visit, which Hudson was certainly aware of, occurred on April 17, 1524. Verrazzano passed through the narrows between Grymes Hill on Staten Island and Bay Ridge in Brooklyn.

"...shoaler and shoaler..." meant "shallower and shallower." M. S. Smith's map

places Juet at Perth Amboy, just north of the Raritan. Perth Amboy is associated with some of the oldest artifacts associated with the Unami culture, as we find soapstone vases here of the highest quality of great age that are in the newer Unami style. (See William Richie.) Across the Arthur Kill, on the northwest corner of Staten Island, at a place called Bowman's Brook, famous for the archaeological digs there by Allanson Skinner, were early examples of artifacts of Munsee culture. Here we find the oldest of the Richmond incised pottery (named after Richmond County, another name for Staten Island) with its castled or four cornered rims, honoring the four directions. In strata above it, we find Unami and then the most recent of the three, the Clasons Point pottery, associated with Renneiu speakers, and with Wappingers settlements in particular. Although in 1609 the leadership of the Unami were at faraway Shackamaxon, the area of Perth Amboy hosted a highly artistic and somewhat cosmopolitan version of Unami culture, probably more like Manhattan today than any other region Hudson could have visited in his day.

If so, they are at the mouth of the Raritan River, a word which means, in the Renneiu language, "a sandy stream (*rari*, a misspelling of *rechi-*, the equivalent of the Unami *lechi-* or sandy) of fresh water that runs into salty (*tan*, a Renneiu variant on *wan*, *ran*, etc.) [127]

The Raritan River is widely considered to have been the southernmost border of the Munsee's vast territory. There were many subtribes of Munsee throughout New York and New Jersey, all associated with a totem symbol or phratry of the wolf, and in this area were the "Raritan Munsee." However the Sankihans were in this same area, and are sometimes called "Raritan Indians," a large Unami-speaking group.[128] To the south and west of the headwaters of the Raritan, located halfway into New Jersey, would have been the Unami, whose symbol on border markers was the turtle, a totem animal or phratry symbol. The turkey's footprint was the symbol of the Unalatchtigo (Unalachtgo, various spellings) and the turkey was their totem symbol or phratry. These terms were probably not used until 1721 when they were camped on the Susquehanna, which they called also Wyoming.[129] When they relocated in Ohio, they used the term Delaware, a unifying term, but the three animal groupings still camped separately.[130] Ultimately, the Unalatchtigo merged with the greater Unami.

The Unalatchtigo were the people of lower New Jersey, "nearest to the sea, between the coast and the high mountains,"[131] but many Nanticokes traveled through this area as well. According to Dr. Daniel Brinton, Unalachtigo, properly W'nalachtko, means "people who live near the ocean" from *wunalawat*, "to go towards," and *t'kow* or *t'kou*, "wave."[132] The people of this area were also apparently called Sijanoy, or "shell bead people."

The Unalatchtigo sub-tribe specific to the area of Peak Beach were the

Kechemeches, "The Very Great." The Unalatchtigo people associated with Point Pleasant were the Assomoches, possibly "muddy clams or oysters." Also in south-east New Jersey were the Klyne Siconese, and the Narraticons.[133] Narraticons is the same term as Naraticong, associated with the Raritan.

These three supposedly formed a Lenape Confederacy, although there is no mention of this Confederacy until 1793, and this by United States Government officials under George Washington. The word Lenape is first mentioned in 1721, in an English document, about the time when many "Lenape" were leaving New Jersey and New York, so it would appear that this term, too, was not the original term for "the people," any more than the term "Delaware." If Hudson had spent more time conversing and writing down what he heard, and if his diary had not been destroyed or lost, we might have a better answer to the question "who were the people of the harbor at that time?"

JUET'S JOURNAL, THURSDAY, SEPTEMBER 3 : *The morning misty until ten o'clock, then it cleared, and the wind came to the south-south-east, so we weighed and stood to the northward. The land is very pleasant and high, and bold to fall withal. At three o'clock in the afternoon, we came to three great rivers. So we stood along the northernmost, thinking to have gone into it, but we found it to have a very shoal bar before it, for we had but ten foot water. Then we cast about to the southward, and found two fathoms, three fathoms, and three and a quarter, till we came to the southern side of them, then we had five and six fathoms, and anchored. So we sent in our boat to sound, and they found no less water than four, five, six and seven fathoms, and returned in an hour and a half. So we weighed and went in, and rode in five fathoms, ooze ground, and saw many salmons, and mullets, and rays very great. The height is 40 degrees 30 minutes.*

"The land is very pleasant and high, and bold to fall withal." They may have been approaching Sandy Hook, looking west towards Mount Mitchell, a pleasant land. Here Juet tries out a little poetry, but one wonders if he is not stealing lines from some now-forgotten sea chanty and passing them off as his own. However, the Highlands of the Navesink really do drop off "boldly," into the sea. Nonetheless, I believe he may have been referring to Mount Loretto on Staten Island.

"...At three o'clock in the afternoon, we came to three great rivers..." They started at ten, so that's five hours of open sea travel. Even at 6 miles per hour, that would take them thirty miles north from Point Pleasant, which would bring them to Sandy Hook. The question that puzzles everyone is, where were these three rivers? He makes it sound as if their courses run parallel to each other, with their mouths in a series on a western shore, one in the south one in the middle and one in the north. There is no such place at 40 degrees 30 minutes. However, Great Kills Harbor is at about 40 degrees, 32 minutes—Juet's range of inaccuracy with an astrolabe was obviously greater than that—and Great Kills withholds many secrets from today's sailors and shore-side wanderers.

Juet is more cryptic than Nostradamus, who died in 1566, about the time Juet was born. (We can say with relative certainty that Hudson was born in 1569.) The phrase, "The height is 40 degrees," sounds like one of the great French Mystic's verses, translated into English, reminiscent of, "The sky will burn at forty-five degrees..." which is often interpreted as reference to Ground Zero in nearby Manhattan which is roughly at 40.5°. "The three rivers" is as mystifying as anything Nostradamus ever penned.

However, looking at ancient maps, we will see three "rivers" arranged just as Juet describes, inside Great Kills Harbor. Were they salt creeks or rivers? The Dutch called them "Great Kills," so they must have looked impressive from the bay. There were actually five, but the southernmost one, which served as a territorial border between the Canarsie and Unami, was small in size, and the uppermost two would have appeared to Juet as one "great kill" just inside Crookes Point. This is clearly documented on R. P. Bolton's map published in *New York City in Indian Possession*. There doesn't seem to be any other rational possibility, although later in the journey Juet will see other groupings of three rivers, on a grander scale.

As Edward Johnson, curator of the Staten Island Museum, points out, so much of the harbor area has been changed it is difficult to compare then and now. According to Smithsonian maps, there was an aboriginal trail where Winchester Street runs today, which reached the shore at the southern tip of Canarsie territory, where a small salt stream trickled out, although as I mentioned, the Canarsie claimed temporary possession of the beach extending south from there during the summer, like Canadians visiting the Maine coastline today, and these were the people Hudson first met in what is now New York. The mouths of the three rivers were arranged south to north as Juet describes, but they angled in from the northwest. Today's Nelson and Fairlawn Streets must cross the first two, while the third and greatest is underneath Great Kills Park.

Later in Juet's journal, there will be another three rivers. Of these three we will see that the "second river" is clearly the Muscouta, or "East River." That means (given that Juet is from a culture that reads the page left to right), that the "first river" is the Mohicanituck, or "Hudson," and therefore the third can only be Rockaway Inlet.

"So we stood along the northernmost, thinking to have gone into it, but we found it to have a very shoal bar before it, for we had but ten foot water. Then we cast about to the southward..." The "northernmost" was the great kill that flowed along the inside

of Crookes Point, fed by two tributaries now under the town of Oakwood. We get an idea of how powerful a stream it must have been for the cautious Hudson to try to explore it in the Half Moon. He must have thought the channel there would be deep, but as Juet describes, he was mistaken. They circled counterclockwise around the harbor (probably against unfavorable winds from the sea) and found only shallow water, but then found 15 to 18 feet of water probably at the mouth of the stream that emptied somewhere near today's Nelson Avenue, as they were exiting along the coast, and anchored; *"... till we came to the southern side of them, then we had five and six fathoms, and anchored."*

"...So we weighed and went in, and rode in five fathoms, ooze ground, and saw many salmons, and mullets, and rays very great. The height is 40 degrees 30 minutes..." 40 degrees, 30 minutes is the exact latitude of Sandy Hook Point, but also of South Amboy where the mouth of the Raritan would be just to the north of them. But their latitudes were not ours.

Mantas only like open sea, not closed spaces, and do not like fresh water or going up stream. They do not like steep sand banks but prefer flat sandy slopes under water. As Juet saw *"...rays very great"* in size, they are most certainly mantas, called "the great ray," and not stingrays, as any sailor who had sailed southern seas would know the difference. It is important to note that a giant female stingray, seven feet by seven feet, and weighing in at 771 pounds, was recently found in Thailand, but it was towed to shore, tagged, and then released. No one wanted to deal with its ten foot long stinger.[134] Such a large stingray is highly unusual, while mantas of that size are common. In addition, it is unlikely that these experienced fishermen would tangle with a stingray that large, therefore I believe the "great rays" were mantas, not stingrays. Donald Johnson writes, cryptically: "The south coast of Staten Island, three great rivers." The south coast of Staten Island is a good guess as far as the mantas are concerned, and the three great rivers can only be the Great Kills.

Chapter Four

THE PEOPLE OF THE HARBOR

*H*enry Hudson had entered the harbor and was about to encounter New York's Native Americans for the first time, face to face. The barrier of distance that had separated the European from the Algonquin civilization for millennia had been slowly dissolving over the centuries. In 996, the Vikings stayed several seasons in Labrador and Nova Scotia and some remained to intermarry and have children with the Skrayligs, as they called them. Then there were the Basques, some of whom also stayed and raised families. Verrazzano had made an appearance on two occasions, but no major settlements were built, no known marriages occurred. Now there were major breaches in that wall to the north, leading to the mixed blood Muis families of Port Royal; and to the south at Virginia, leading to the mixed blood families of the Rolfes.

Hudson's men did not stay and put down roots, but those immediately following them did, starting with Jan Rodriguez, who manned the lonely trading post after the wreck of the Tyger in 1613. He married a "Rockaway Indian" woman to ease his loneliness. This is significant to us today because Hudson's arrival four hundred years ago was a tipping point in the slow process of racial mixing in what we call America, (not a "melting pot" as Teddy Roosevelt once quipped) one that is becoming more evident than ever. Natives had learned of the coming of races from the four directions, red, white, black and yellow, according to the Seven Fires prophecies. They were told of a new race, a "rainbow race," and now knew those predictions were true. Colors are verbs in the Algonquin languages, they are active, ever-changing, as we observe in the colors of nature. Such is the case with the colors of humankind in North America, and in New York City especially.

In this chapter, we will look at the significant events in the life of Henry Hudson from September 4 through September 10 and discuss the cultural significance of the things he and his men were seeing and places they were visiting during this

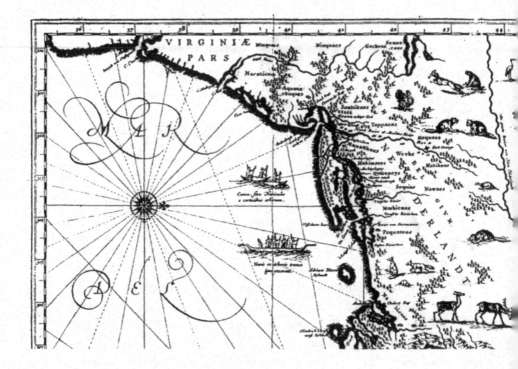

landmark week in the history of Euro-American relations. These details gain us purchase on the slippery banks of the Native American cultural, spiritual and political geography of that era as well, albeit a reconstruction subject to pratfalls and missteps at times. The resulting conclusions may be surprising.

First of all, here is a quote from the letter of March 29, 1849 to President Zachary Taylor from Munsee leaders of that time, first published in *Native New Yorkers*. This excerpt, generally considered to be about Hudson's first landing on Algonquin soil, is similar to a story from the oral tradition which appeared in Heckewelder. It gives us a Native American view, certainly, but does not match the Juet journal in a literal sense. It is of great importance to the Munsee oral tradition, a people who lived along the western shoreline of the Hudson River and south into New Jersey's Raritan Valley. Although Henry Hudson stepped on land on September 4, this story most probably did not occur on Staten Island, (most likely Manhattan) but it gives us a feeling for the heightened spiritual significance Hudson's journey must have had for the people of the shore.

"Previous to your arrival into our vast Continent, our Ancient Prophets and wise men had a Vision and Revelation in regard to your coming, though they did not understand fully the meaning of it, whether it was to be the Almighty himself or our fellow men, this was a matter of deep consideration for a while with our forefathers until you did arrive.

"Our ancient men, without any delay made a Song concerning their expectation of your coming. Likewise a Drum was made for the purpose, out of the shell of a Sea Turtle. The drumming and their singing of the song were connected together and were performed jointly together, and also dancing which was performed with great solemnity in honor of your coming.

"This foreknowledge of our forefathers of your coming was one year previous to your arrival;[135] our forefathers collected together frequently and preformed these celebrations until you did arrive, and when the vessel came at last into open sight to the eyes of our forefathers at the shore, the appearance of the vessel at sea was truly a great mystery to our forefathers, and immediately many wise men and counselors of high respectability among our ancient forefathers were called and collected together by the rumors and influential men of our Nation in order to ascertain what that mysterious sight could be, which was making progress toward the shore.

"By the distant appearance of the sails of the vessel, our forefathers first concluded that it was some great water fowl, and as the vessel came nearer to their open view, they concluded that it must be their God, coming to bring them some new kind of game. And when the vessel reached the shore, they saw the Captain of the Ship, and then concluded that he must be the Almighty himself, as he had blue eyes. This was another great wonder, and by it they further concluded that he must certainly be the Great God.

"Our forefathers highly respected the arrival of their Great Father, and did instantly spread white Beaver skins from the shore where the vessel landed to a certain tent where the wise men and counselors were assembled together, for the Captain to walk on. The kind disposition of the Captain induced him to tell our forefathers that he was not the almighty, but that he was their brother, that in ancient times he was with his brethren, and by the various changes that frequently occur in this life, he had somehow got separated from his brethren, but he expressed great joy, that he had now arrived and found his brethren again, and hoped that he would never be again separated from his brethren.

"He further told our forefathers that he had merely come in search of his red brethren and seeing that he had discovered his brethren he would then return to his people, and inform them how that he had discovered their brethren on the great Continent and which would cause great joy throughout the nations who were situated beyond the Deep Waters.

"He gave our forefathers many presents such as hoes and axes and tin buckets and the next year he came again in company with a large number of his people in order to come and reside among their red brethren, at which time they saw our forefathers wearing hoes and axes and covers to the tin buckets about their necks. He then showed our forefathers the design of the hoes and axes. Handles were put into them, and large trees were cut down before them, which created a general time of laughing, to think how greatly they had been mistaken in regard to the design of the present that he had given to them."[136]

In direct contrast to this lush, wonder-filled, somewhat metaphysical view of the meeting between Hudson and the Algonquin nations is Robert Juet's arid ledger-book account of what well may be the same events.

As the curtain rises on the events of September 4, it is difficult to tell, through the distance of history and the fog that is Robert Juet's journal, where they are located geographically. But in the light of existing evidence explained below, I believe they were tacking off Staten Island's southeastern shore, from today's Great Kills Harbor to Lemon Creek, Seguine Point, and beyond.

The previous entry mentions the latitude of Sandy Hook Point, and then speaks of three mysterious rivers that don't exist at that latitude. Typically, Hudson's journal does not mention travel distances, but Juet's does, and states that they sent the "boat" into the harbor. This would be the "tender" or by-boat, a rowboat, not the ship. These were often stored onboard in the form of "kits," that could be nailed together with relative haste.[137] The depths of the waters were then sounded by the crew of the rowboat, which needed very little draw and could pull off of almost any sand bar. If the water was deep enough for the Half Moon to sail safely, they would then scurry back to the main ship and re-board, towing the tender behind, or hoisting it on board with hoisting cables. In this case the depth of the outer harbor was adequate, about 4 to 5 fathoms. The prevailing wind would have helped a large ship enter the outer harbor, but also presented a danger of pushing a keeled ship into water too shallow to navigate. Dugout canoes would have been ideal for landing at Great Kills thanks to the depth, the wind, and the protection the harbor offered. Paddling outward, however, might have been another story.

The term fathom comes from the Dutch *vadem*, which means "to embrace," and is derived from the length of a man's outstretched arms, fingertip to fingertip. Although for years the fathom varied from man to man and from ship to ship, today it has become standardized to 1.6 meters, or 63 inches, or 5.25 feet.[138] Juet was telling us that the water was from 20 to 25 feet in depth.

This harbor was not New York Harbor, as many presume (the depths would not have been of any concern there), but a small harbor off Raritan Bay we now call Great Kills Harbor. Juet noted that the crew of the tender found a deep channel running "two cables from shore." A cable, as used on the rigging of a Dutch ship, is 180 meters long, so two cables would be 360 meters, and a meter is about 39.37 inches. They were then presumably 1,181 feet from shore, about a third of a nautical mile, which is 3,660 feet.[139] I presume the tender found the water much shallower inside the harbor beyond the channel. We still find this configuration today, with fairly shallow water inside Great Kills Harbor, at a length of about a thousand feet, and then the Ambrose Channel, which is renowned for its depth. Edward Johnson, curator at the Staten Island Museum, states that the shape of that area has been changed from how it was in 1609, in that Crooks Point has become an island intermittently throughout the last centuries. The term "Great Kills" makes no sense today, but Edward Johnson says there were "salt creeks" in 1609, running into the harbor, tiny estuaries where salty water entered and flowed upstream at high tide. However, I believe that this is where the Half Moon arrived on September 4, and that the underwater contours have not changed significantly.

Elsewhere, Juet states they found, at a nearby location, "three fathoms hard by the southern shore." There is only one place today where one can find a 15 foot deep channel right next to a southern shore, at least anywhere near New York Harbor, and that, according to Onrust reconstructor and Hudson River harbor navigator Will Van Dorp, is near the mouth of Lemon Creek, just a few miles west of Great Kills Harbor. In fact, today's Princes Bay, between Lemon Creek and Great Kills harbor, has a curving shore which faces due south, and it is from here to Seguine Point, and around Wards Point to Tottenville that the Ambrose Channel hugs the shoreline. I remember going out to Seguine with an old friend once to take pictures of ocean liners and freighters, waving to the huge boats as they chugged by just forty feet from shore.[140] Checking with nautical maps from 1778, 1867, and today, it seems that the channel has wandered just a few feet from its course over that expanse of time, so it is almost certain it was there in 1609, and is most likely what Juet describes in his diary of September 4.

A cable, by the way, is the line used on the rigging of a ship. They were hand made, with a number of layers of construction. The interior layer is of hemp rope, wrapped with strips of canvas and hand coated with pine tar to make it more waterproof (the word canvas comes from *kanevas* or cannibas, which is hemp, or flax).[141] The pine tar comes from the stumps of pine trees tossed in a pit and burned. The resins that drip as a black liquid from the stumps are collected and become usable as pine tar and then wrapped tightly with a thin coil of twine using a tool adapted from a mallet called a "mallet spool."[142] It is important for the reader to understand that the lifestyle of Hudson's mariners was similar in many surprising ways to their Native American counterparts: Not only were they barefoot much of the time, to gain traction on slippery ship's decks, they were also resourceful, self-reliant craftspeople using, at least in some cases, techniques similar to their Algonquin hosts, who also made sturdy rope out of hemp and other materials, and used similar techniques to make their materials more water resistant.

Did Henry Hudson name Staten Island? That is the prevailing wisdom, reported by numerous encyclopedias, and it may or may not be true. According to Nationmaster.com/encyclopedia/Staten-Island.com, "Henry Hudson named Staaten Eylandt after the Staaten-Generaal: The Dutch Parliament." But is this true? Juet does not mention it, and neither do the surviving pages of Hudson's journal. True, he spent quite a bit of time there, but if he named it during his trip in 1609, he would have written it on his map, and the name Staten Island does not show up immediately in the first maps that depict the island. When and how would he have passed along this information? He would not have been so foolish as to mention it to the British upon his return; he was in enough trouble with them. He never set foot in Holland again, so he would not have had a chance to tell Parliament himself of this great honor. Most of all, Hudson's Dutch was terrible. He was not a Dutchman by any means. Why would he have named the island after the Dutch Parliament? To imitate Verrazzano who named parts of our New York after his French backers? Hudson was supposed to be loyal to the British Parliament. It's possible he named the fifth borough, but these questions are not resolved. It makes more sense to suppose that Adriaen Block named Staten Island two years later. Block was a man who spoke Dutch and had a closer connection with the Staaten-Generaal.

JUET'S JOURNAL; FRIDAY, SEPTEMBER 4 : *In the morning as soon as the day was light, we saw that it was good riding farther up. So we sent our boat to sound, and found that it was a very good harbour; and four and five fathoms, two cables length from the shore. Then we weighed and went in with our ship. Then our boat went on land with our net to fish, and caught ten great mullets, of a foot and a half long a piece and a ray as great as four men could haul into the ship. So we trimmed our boat and rode still all day. At night the wind blew hard at the north-west, and our anchor came home, and we drove on shore, but took no hurt, thanked be God, for the ground is soft sand and ooze. This day the people of the country came aboard of us, seeming very glad of our coming, and brought green tobacco, and gave us of it for knives and beads. They go in deer skins loose, well dressed. They have yellow copper. They desire clothes, and are very civil. They have great store of maize or Indian wheat, whereof they made good bread. The country is full of great and tall oaks.*

*"In the morning as soon as the day was light, we saw that it was good riding far-
ther up. So we sent our boat to sound, and found that it was a very good harbour;"* The
"good harbour" seems to fit the description of Great Kills Harbor, (see below) so
if they *"saw that it was good riding farther up,"* that must mean that they saw that
section from further south, which means they spent the night near South Amboy,
or Tottenville, and rode northeastward along the coast of Staten Island. From this
direction, Great Kills marks the beginning of Canarsie territory to the north and
the end of the Eghquans to the south, thought to be a Unami-speaking territory,
although the explorers' descriptions convey to me that the Canarsee seasonally
"timeshared" the beachfront zone of the Eghquans territory, then retreated to Old
Town when the winter winds blew in off the ocean during the Freezing Moon
(November).

"... Then we weighed and went in with our ship." The only Coast Guard in New
York Harbor in those days was the fleet of large dugout canoes which the Canarsie
warriors commanded with great skill, but they were mainly trained to ward off
intruders, not help them, and Hudson's "Great Floating Bird" (which is a rough
translation of what the Munsee Delaware called the first sailing ships they saw[143])
at this point was an uninvited visitor which would have to prove its salt. To a vessel such as the Half Moon, thousands of miles from nautical assistance, one of the
worst things that could happen would be to become stranded on a sand bar. One
of the techniques they used in their battle against sand bars was to drop anchor in
deeper water, then navigate into the shoals. Then if they got stuck they could pull
the ship back out into deep water by heaving ho on the anchor cable, a clever tactic
they were prepared to use several times on this trip.

*"Then our boat went on land with our net to fish, and caught ten great mullets, of
a foot and a half long a piece and a ray as great as four men could haul into the ship."*
By "our boat" he means, "the men of our by-boat, or tender." He may have meant
"went inland," in other words to a stream.[144] But large rays do not swim in fresh
water and don't like streams or enclosed places, so this doesn't make sense.[145] He
must have meant they went to the shallow water near the shores of Great Kills
Harbor.

Rays prefer warm water, so it is likely that the currents off Staten Island were
warmer then than now. The Atlantic "trade current," or "sea stream" originates
with a hot undersea volcano or fissure near the island of Mona, northwest of
Puerto Rico, home of the Taino whalers. The fissure seems to have cooled a bit in
four hundred years, causing the sea stream to shift its course or become cooler as
well. The Ambrose Channel, which contains a branch of the sea stream, would be
warmer than surrounding waters, attracting manta rays.

Rays are of the taxonomic order Rajiformes,[146] and appear in many varieties of sub-species. According to Native American marine biologist Ray Rodriguez, each type of ray has its own level of intelligence, which he assesses based on his personal experience, and in the light of his familiarity with the oral tradition of the Nissequogue (a state-recognized nation of North Shore Long Island of which his uncle is currently chief, Raymond Wheeler). His assessments seem to be well in line with those of a number of Native Americans from coastal regions that I interviewed. The Atlantic Torpedo is an electric ray, which is the most primitive and, according to Rodriguez, least intelligent. Next is the skate ray, which is less primitive, and is sometimes two or three feet across. Next in apparent intelligence is the bat ray or the cownosed ray. Yet more intelligent is the stingray, and by far the most intelligent is the manta ray, *Manta birostris,* which travels in the open ocean, but comes into estuarine harbors in summer. The larger individuals may be 15-22 feet across and weigh 1,100 pounds, but some have been found that were 25 feet across, weighing 5,000 pounds![147] Although they are fish and not mammals, the natives of Long Island consider the manta ray as intelligent as dolphins and whales, even though it has long been known among natives, such as the Salish of the northwest (and recently proven by scientists), that dolphins have names, which are sounded out in clicks, and the Orcas have dialects that change from bay to bay.[148] The mantas are regarded by eastern Native Americans with an equal but markedly different intelligence. Some call them "eagle rays," because of their ability to jump out of the water and glide on their pectoral fins.[149] Mantas, like so many of the creatures that Juet described, are no longer found in the region. Worldwide, the manta's official conservation status is "near threatened," its IUCN (International Union for the Conservation of Nature) "endangered" rating a worrisome 3.1.

The "great ray" that Juet describes is definitely a manta, but not the largest of mantas. A ray that can challenge the muscle of four sailors is too large to be your typical sting ray and too small to be a full grown manta. They are good to eat and taste like their relatives, the shark. According to Ray Rodriguez, the Nissequogue of the time would not have hunted or eaten a manta because of cultural observances. It was considered good luck to see one, bad luck to eat one or even touch one. This is a Taino trait as well. It is said that the Matouac of Long Island considered the manta a "protector of mankind from the ocean."[150] The Chimu of Peru call it "sea lion."[151] By contrast, the white European colonists called it "the devil ray." Interestingly, Moon Hawk, a member of the Unquechaug, also a Matouac people, told me that although the manta was highly sacred to his people, they would, on special occasions, and in dire circumstances when starvation was imminent, make offerings, hunt them, and then feast on them according to the protocol of ceremony, thanking the manta for its generous offering of food. A member of at least one other tribal group said the same for his people. In all cases, for the indigenous people I interviewed, which included two indigenous Nyoongar from Australia, Troy Bennell, and Athol Farmer, (Nyoongar culture is very similar to Algonquin) the manta's sacred status is beyond question. The ancient Moche people of Peru worshipped the manta around AD 200. Paintings of manta rays appear on sacred clay vessels that have been preserved in the Larco Museum Collection in Lima, Peru.[152] This status did not apply to any other type of ray, such as the sting ray, which is considered highly expendable, or the electric ray.

In his article about the Boat People of Japan, *Sacred Fish,*[153] E.N. Anderson, Jr. of the University of California, Riverside, states, "...everyone agreed that the manta ray or at least some mantas, were powerful; a few thought that some could be sacred..." The sacred fish are normally consecrated to Tin Hau ("Sky Goddess"), patron and protector of fishermen. Failure to treat the fish properly, if they are caught, results in extremely bad luck—shipwreck, deaths in the family, loss of livelihood. Consecrating the fish at the temple reverses this and may even lead to good luck." If the Canarsie or other coastal Algonquin group were on the ship at the time and had become "superstitious," they were in good company. Coastal peoples around the world revere the manta and fear harming it, but with considerable variation as to degree, and as to the taboos involved.

In *The Gospel of the Red Man,* by Ernest Thompson Seaton, there are Twelve "Commandments," principles of conduct that Seaton compiled from an array of seven native writers and seven white scholars. Number four is as follows: "Thou shalt keep the feasts, learn the dances, respect the taboos, and observe the customs of your tribe, if you would be a good member of the community and prosper by its strength. For these things are the wisdom of the Ancients, and of your fathers in the long-ago."[154]

The Matouac, which includes the Canarsie, would have seen the butchered manta on the ship on Saturday, and would have been very concerned. Hudson's men caught the ray on Friday, they will devour it on Saturday, and on Sunday, their expedition will be struck by tragedy—their strong man, John Colman will become the first white homicide victim in New York City. The Canarsie will not be surprised about the tragic news.

Western science dismisess as superstition ancient stories about "animal powers" and taboos of every kind, yet aboriginal beliefs about God and nature are not wrong simply because they can't be explained by current scientific theories. As aboriginal people say, "Mother Earth makes the rules; we just live by her generosity."

Not all native belief is superstitious and supernatural; some of it is good science expressed in "dream time," in the language of Creation. In fact, these days the nation of Canada is investing a great deal of energy in collecting and preserving "TEK" — "Traditional Environmental Knowledge" — and comparing it to laboratory science to shed light on both. Obviously someone is starting to see a meaningful relationship between science and native belief.

The fact that they find a manta in September is further proof that they are near open ocean. Manta rays need shallow water, and like flat or gently sloped surfaces to rest upon. The Arthur Kill is very deep, sixty feet in some places, and the sides are too steep for a manta, so they are not inside the Arthur Kill at this time. Mantas also like the north Jersey Shore and Perth Amboy south of the Arthur Kill. Even the coastal Arrochar region of Staten Island, near the Verrazzano Narrows, might be unattractive to them due to the strong fresh water currents coming down from the Mohicanituck. However, the area of Great Kills Harbor would have been very attractive to manta rays as there is little fresh water there. The "two cables" (over a thousand feet) of presumably shallow shoals before the harbor would have been ideal for manta habitation. It was for them, as it was for the native canoers, a "Shancopshee," or "Shawcopoke," a "midway haven."[155] This was the Canarsie name for the spot.

The Canarsie language is also lost, except for a few fragments. It formed the core of Renneiu languages in the 1500 and 1600s. Algonquin linguist Blair Rudes describes it as a source of the Taconic Dialect of the "R" languages, which generally corresponds with Wappingers culture, although both would presumably have a Mohican base. David De Vries, in his travel journal, wrote down a phrase in Renneiu language before the year 1643. It was *"Rancontyn, mareuit,"* which means "Let us make a firm peace." Another expression, written in the margins of a treaty, was, *"Werite werite naytees naytees!"* "We are very good friends!"

It is certain that Canarsie was like Wappingers, and it is generally thought that Wappingers is closest to Naugatuck, a language of coastal western Connecticut, and a form of Quiripi. Unfortunately, all of these languages are poorly recorded and no longer spoken fluently. I communicated in the past with only two men who claimed to speak Renneiu fluently, Sagamore Mike D'Amico, now passed on, (he considered "Wappingers" a form of Mohican) and Iron Thunderhorse, who has spent much of his life in maximum security.

There are a handful of Naugutuck words listed in p. 491 of *History of the Indians of Connecticut,* by DeForest. (appendix i); man is *rinh*; woman is *wenih*; day is *kee-soop*; night is *toof-ku*; fire is *ru'uh-tah*; water is *nuppeh*; tree is *tookh*; bear is *awausu-so*; and river is *sepu*. We are led to believe that these words would be familiar to the Canarsie.

"So we trimmed our boat and rode still all day. At night the wind blew hard at the north-west, and our anchor came home, and we drove on shore, but took no hurt, thanked

be God, for the ground is soft sand and ooze." The sails were made of canvas, which is related to the word cannibas, and were indeed woven from hemp by hand. The process was almost as labor intensive for the Dutch as wampum making was for the Algonquins. Hendrick "Henk" DeBoer, of the Onrust project, a native of Holland, still weaves these giant sheets out of hemp in order to make the Dutch reconstructions of 17 century ships the most authentic in the world. The 2,400 square meter sail he wove for "The Amsterdam" took him ten years to complete, while the sail he wove for the Batavia, a mere 1300 square meters in size, took him only six years, working alone. It was no easier for the builders of the Half Moon. My great-grand-uncle George Washburn made sails by hand, and it took him a long time too. Many modern New Yorkers find it difficult to imagine such patience. We today tend not to live in one town (other than the great city of New York) longer than three years. Our attention span has grown shorter over four hundred years.

They took down their sails and floated in the same place for the entire day. But the wind at night was so strong it blew the hull of the ship to the other side of the anchor and into a sandbank. No one was injured, because the sandbank was all "ooze." Underwater sand often becomes oozey, which is to say it was extremely silty. I believe he means the wind was blowing towards the northwest, so with sails down they must have hit the sandbank to northwest. If this is so, they might have been at Princes Bay or anywhere along the southeast coast of Staten Island. Here, at the open ocean there are places in which the sand is very soft and rays would be in greater abundance than at the Arthur Kill.

"This day the people of the country came aboard of us, seeming very glad of our coming, and brought green tobacco, and gave us of it for knives and beads. The soil along Staten Island's south shore is loam, excellent for growing tobacco. Green tobacco is the local kind, not the "golden" or Iroquoian kind that is found in most cigars and cigarettes today. Iroquois tobacco is kakhi green on the top and golden on the underside. Green tobacco is associated with coastal Algonquin culture south of Cape Cod. It is kakhi colored on the upper side of the leaf, and green on the underside. The third kind is purple tobacco, with a somewhat grape-like color on its underside. This type is found among the Anishinabe (Algonquins as they are currently known in Canada) in the north, and along the coast to Cape Cod.[156] This does not give us proof positive as to their whereabouts, because green tobacco was found all along the entire coast. Another possibility is that all of it was acquired by trade. The Canarsie were constantly trading for goods as they traveled on their ships, and tobacco was a primary trade item. If the Eghquaons[157] were Raritan Indians, originally from the southern side of that river on the mainland, they were Unami speakers, and probably related closely to the Sapohannikan, Unami speakers who

settled a part of Manhattan now called "Greenwich Village." The word "*sapohanni-kan*" means "tobacco planting land." Again, this does not help us specify location.

But tobacco is a hungry plant, it requires rich soil, and depletes whatever soil it is planted in fairly quickly. As Virginia Colony settlers found out, you have to rotate tobacco with other crops such as beans, which restore the nitrogen, or let the land lay fallow. Such rich soil is not often found right next to a sandy beach area such as Juet describes. However its remarkable abundance in the hands of people who could not have had much warning or time to prepare, shows us that tobacco was nearby. Where could this location be? Staten Island's Old Town, (formerly Oude Dorp) is known for its rich planting soil and is a mile and a half from the beach, in the "ancient" Arrochar region. There is a train station there now, two stops from Grasmere Station.

SIRT's Grasmere Station is where the famous Grasmere Head was found in 1884 beneath a huckleberry bush at the edge of a swamp. This stone head is now on display at the Staten Island Museum. It is not a "Lenape" Maysingway (or M'singwe) mask by any means. It much more closely resembles Aztec art than Mayan or Taino, and in some ways resembles certain small Rappanui stone heads from Easter Island, but there are no perfect matches to be found between any of these and the Grasmere or "Concord" Head. There was one other such stone mask, nearly identical, that was found in Monmouth County, New Jersey, near to Staten Island, so though the Iroquois were much more inclined to stone portraiture, the origin of the Stone Head of Grasmere is probably Lenape.[158]

At the Staten Island Museum website, certain similarites with Iroquoian stone heads are noted. Although the Unami/Munsee/Wappingers, unlike their Mezzo-American cousins, have never been known for creating large stone head carvings, nonetheless the most striking aspect of the head is that the facial features are typically "old Algonquian," and highly typical of local Hudson River and New York Harbor native families.[159]

The location of its discovery was "just above the Fingerboard Road," just northeast of where the Native American trade route now approximated by Amboy Road split into Fingerboard Road, a trail which led eastward to the coastal village still called Arrochar today, and Grand, which led to the northwest. That branch led around the foot of Grymes Hill, past what is now Clove Lakes Park, across the trail now known as Victory Boulevard, and through the Hackensackee territory known as Matawuck. That trail connected to the one now called Richmond Terrace at an ancient burial site now called Sailors' Snug Harbor. That fork in the road would have been a hub of activity in AD 1300, and that head was found right next to one of the forks.

The terminal moraine of the Wisconsin Glacier runs just south of Todd Hill, and at the time of melting, a great deal of outwash was produced, leaving rich, loamy soil in this case. This lends itself to a great deal of corn and tobacco production, as well as "tall oaks." The first Dutch settlements on Staten Island were at Old Town, centrally located in this region. This was due to the fact that farming was so successful,[160] and corn and tobacco were cash crops. These flat, fertile fields extend from South Beach, near the narrows, southwest to Dongan Hills, and inland to Richmond Road/Korean War Veterans Parkway. Richmond Road is built on a land rise along an old fault line and the natives would not have farmed that area.[161] This leaves a large wedge of fertile planting land along the south shore, possibly 30 square miles. Old Town, Dongan Hills and New Dorp are well within the Canarsie language region of 1609. Today's Hudson Street and its continuation to the north, Henry Place, are in the Old Town region where these crops were probably grown.

The seasonal lifestyle of the native people at this place suggests they are at or near an ocean beach. This helps to further identify the region as Staten Island's south shore, as even now after much erosion, there is still a fifty-foot sandy beach front in this region from South Beach to Mount Loretto.[162] It also suggests that there were cultural influences other than Algonquin, who are not by tendency beach dwellers.[163]

Juet's journal is one of several colonial records that indicate that leaves of tobacco were used as currency by Algonquins in New York State and New Jersey. A number of colonial paper currencies, particularly those of early Maryland, depict tobacco leaves framing the borders of the paper.[164] These were not just to "advertise" the local export products, but formed a spiritual link for people of that time with the time period of their fathers, who traded with natives using green tobacco leaves as currency. The leaf-like designs on today's dollar bills are meant to suggest the shape of tobacco, and it can be said that those ambiguous leaves are direct descendants of earlier tobacco designs, and real tobacco before that. Iroquoian people from the north would have preferred the golden to the green. Therefore these people Hudson mentions were not Iroquoian. Green tobacco would not grow right at Great Kills Harbor, due to the sandy soil.

"They go in deer skins loose, well dressed." Juet did not mean that these citizens of what is now New York City were well dressed as in "they wore Brooks Brothers suits and Pierre Cardin ties." He was referring to the deer skin itself, commenting merely that the skins were well dressed. To dress a deer hide, one must quarter the deer, cut off the meat and scrape off the sinew from the inside, and if desired, scrape off the fur on the outside, and then tan the hide. The meat fibers must be removed quickly from the hide or it will give an unpleasant smell, and this must be done before tanning. In most cases, one would use tannic acid from hemlock

tree, or cook the brain of the deer, and then rub into the hide, called brain tanning. The Munsee Delaware would also cook the fat from the deer and "smoke" the skins in the greasy black smoke that would arise from the fat. This process would seal the skin and make it water resistant, something of great practical value to a people who lived outdoors most of the time.[165] Unless properly dressed, the skin of a deer will not last long, but will rot and fall to pieces in a short time. Due to the amount of labor and skill involved in this process, a single piece of deerskin, dressed in traditional Delaware style, can fetch over $700 in New York City today.[166]

The most interesting sentence here is, *"They have yellow copper."* Skinner (1909) indicates that there was not a great deal of copper found in Algonquin sites in lower New York. To solve this mystery, I interviewed New York State Museum's Curator of Geology, Marian Lupulescu, and asked him what yellow copper was, and he led me like an experienced trail guide through the maze of halls that make up the State Museum in Albany, and stood me before the largest mineral specimen in the house, a cluster of bright yellow stones surrounded by an array of clear, gleaming, terminated quartz crystals. This, he said, was chalcopyrite, or yellow copper, $CuFe$, plus quartz ($CuFeS2$) and that it was from Ellenville, New York. It was copper mixed with pyrite, which is iron plus sulphur 2. I was impressed. The service in Albany is excellent, if you're in search of yellow copper. Turkish wheat, who knows?

He said he had been to Ellenville many times to search through its tapped mines to find even an ounce of yellow copper but there was none to be found. It was mined out long ago and is now quite rare. He was not able to determine which one of the caves and mines that stretch in a line from Ellenville to Otisville, New York were the source of this specimen, but he knew it was from the collection of P. Edwin Clark of Ellenville. I thought it looked a lot like pyrite, a bright, tinny yellow. Marian thought I might find more specimens at the Yale School of Minerology at New Haven, Connecticut, as they were seeking it out at an earlier time before all known samples had disappeared.

Among Algonquins and other Eastern Woodlands people there was a "religious" rule against "piercing the skin of the mother," one which was well known to all. Any minerals that were found on the surface (of cave walls, for example) were considered "gifts"[167] and could be worked cold or hot. Yellow copper would have been carried down the Minisink Trail (209) from Ellenville to be traded at or near Minisink, the principle Island of Fire of the Munsee. From there it would have been carried down a trail closely following today's Route 23 to Bloomfield and then east, or more likely, down the well traveled Nanticoke Trail (206) and then east on the Raritan River trail (622).

"*They desire clothes . . .*" In fact, it is unlikely that they literally desired the sailor's clothes, and later did not enjoy being fitted out in red uniforms. They were merely curious. Juet's comment about their civility becomes important later because his experiences with other groups seems to change his view of these people as well. Hudson was much less apprehensive.

"*...and are very civil.*" This is an important observation for several reasons. One, it contradicts the conventional and unjust stereotypes of Native Americans as "savages," people who are unable to govern themselves or each other. Thomas Hobbes unintentionally promoted this misconception in his book *Leviathan*, making the point that men tend to be at a state of war when there is not strong a centralized government. These people Juet describes do have a government, but one based on communication among equals. There are no police force, prisons or courts on Staten Island in 1609, and yet Juet is struck by the people's civility. This word implies a kind of "civilization," an attribute that many scholars and historians deny Algonquins and indeed most Native Americans, because they have no writing. This would then have to apply to the Celts as well, who had no writing either. A better, more Hobbsian definition for civilization might be, "those who keep their covenants." Rousseau's "On the Origins of Inequality" and other philosophical works spring from this and countless other accounts of Algonquin and Iroquoian (Hodenosuannee) civility. In fact he mocks European ideas of civil society in the "Origins," as follows:

"The first man who, having fenced in a piece of land, said "This is mine," and found people naive enough to believe him, that man was the true founder of civil society. From how many crimes, wars, and murders, from how many horrors and misfortunes might not any one have saved mankind, by pulling up the stakes, or filling up the ditch, and crying to his fellows: Beware of listening to this impostor; you are undone if you once forget that the fruits of the earth belong to us all, and the earth itself to nobody."

— JEAN-JACQUES ROUSSEAU, *Discourse on Inequality*, 1754

It is likely that Rousseau, who initiated an intellectual foment throughout Europe based on his research on "noble savages" and their social structures, read Juet's journal, published in 1625, almost a hundred years before his own birth. The historians at the National Archives have suggested that Chief Seattle did not end his famous speech with the words, "The earth does not belong to us, we belong to the earth," that these words were inserted by the translator. But the statement stands as a cultural artifact of Native American culture, long predating Seattle. I believe that in Rousseau, we see proof of this, in that he is clearly referencing unspecified

Native American philosophers on this very point. This comment is also interesting because Juet soon becomes somewhat paranoid about their intentions, and begins to instigate conflict with his hosts.

"They have a great store of maize or Indian wheat, whereof they made good bread." The word *maize* is a Taino word which Henry Hudson would have known from his fellow explorers, such as his good friend Captain John Smith, who spent some time exploring the Caribbean. It is a translation from the Nahuatl word *teocentli*, possibly from a location in Central Mexico.[168] This word apparently refers to a "grassier" type of corn such as Turkish Wheat. It must have had a different name in its infancy further south, perhaps a word in Olmec, an extinct language.

The natives of the Hudson River valley roasted maize while it was young, but the dry, more mature kernels were ground into meal by stone pestels and mortars, and when this was moistened with water and baked upon heated stones, the product was called *nookhik*, from which have come 'nocake' and 'hoe-cake.'"[169] Corn bread, or Journeycake, later known as "Jonnycake" (spelling this with an h is incorrect north of Long Island) is of Native American origin, as is hasty pudding, fried mush, hominy, Suet Jonnycake, Cornmeal slappers, and green corn griddle cakes. [170] According to *The Yankee Cookbook*, "The first strawberry shortcake was probably made of corn meal," from strawberries introduced to the white men of the Plymouth Colony by Indians.[171] The use of shortening (hence "shortcake") probably developed out of the native use of suet that was skimmed off the top of meat stews.

"The country is full of great and tall oaks..." Juet would have mainly been familiar with French or Dutch oaks, but the lower harbor region provided many new variants he would not have seen. Nowhere to be found were the Old World oaks, the type the Dutch shipbuilders used to make ships, employing a burn-bending process in which they would soak the planks in the ocean and then burn them in a fire pit and then bend them for use in the hull.[172]

Where would there be extremely tall oaks right by a southern shore? The only other "southern shore" in the lower New York harbor region is at Coney Island. There are no oaks in the area of Coney Island today, but there were red and white oaks, the smaller variety, in times past.

As there are still many extremely tall oaks towering to over one hundred feet in height in the region of Wolf Pond Park, the presence of tall oaks suggests they are located on Staten Island's south shore. This stand of broad, healthy trees includes ancient red oaks, black oak, and white varieties. They are fairly near the water, so that a ship in the Ambrose Channel can easily see them. There seems to be something in the combination of loamy soil, southeastern exposure, and salt water that lends itself to exceptional oak growth, both now and in Hudson's time,

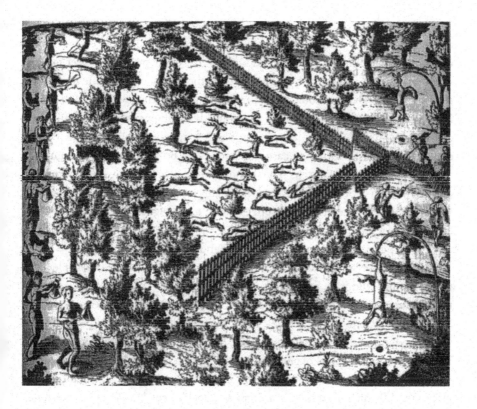

along the eight mile stretch of shoreline from Great Kills Harbor to Seguine Point and beyond.[173] Even today it is a natural landmark.

Oaks are very important in the history of New York's early human habitation. They appeared, along with pines, birches, chestnuts and hickories around 3500 BCE, during a warming period. Squirrels and deer eat the acorns, and bear and other big game feed on the deer. Before the advent of the bow and arrow, (and after 3500 BCE) humans had to rely on acorns and the animals that ate them to round out their diet.

That is not to say they were unable to hunt deer without bows and arrows. At Pound Ridge, New York, "... the English settlers found in good preservation ... an extensive trap which they called a pound...situated at the south end of the ridge ... built of logs held together by what the English called saddle-stones, was twelve or fourteen feet high, and enclosed an acre or more of ground."[174]

The "pound" had a narrow entrance, but with huge palisaded wings (walls) running up the hillsides. Large groups of natives would "beat the bushes" while yelling loud screams, goading the deer towards the entrance. Once a large number were inside, they would close the door of the entrance.[175] On one hand, this process does not support the idea that Eastern Woodland people "made offerings to the deer and asked them to voluntarily give up their lives so that the Delaware could live,"[176] before hunting them, although this would still be possible. On the other hand, the hunting weir method insures that every part of the deer is used economically and productively, as transporting the meat in a fresh state is always a major problem. The deer could live for many days inside the pound, possibly even in comfort, before being "put down" more quickly and humanely with a knife (and a lasso, most likely) than with an arrow, which generally results in a long pursuit and death by bleeding. In any case, the pound is a brilliant invention, requiring the close cooperation of dozens if not hundreds of native people over a long period of time, both in the constructing and in the continued use of it.

In Algonquin languages, the word Sagabun means "ground nuts" (acorns, but also hickory nuts, chestnuts, and others). Sag Harbor is derived from this word, as are several place names around Long Island and New York City.

What is surprising is that neither Hudson nor Juet mention the red maple until October 2. It could have been a late season, as they were in a cold, dry cycle, but it seems amiss here. The Iroquois of New York seem to have been the first to enjoy maple sugaring and the art of maple sugar tapping, which was soon picked up by the Algonquins and is now enjoyed around the world. The red maple thrives today in Staten Island, and it is thought to have been present in 1609, but the Sugar Maple of the north is the best for making syrup. The Munsee word for maple is *aa-sin-aa-mehn-shee*, [177] which means, "It is as hard as a rock to cut!" (*aasin* or *aasun*=stone; *aamsheew*=to cut and knock over)[178] Though not on the coast; it thrives in swampy areas. If Hudson had ventured further inland, he might have seen one or two, competing against old growth trees, in spots where slash and burn farming techniques had not turned them to ashes, as they are quite flammable.[179]

HENRY HUDSON'S JOURNAL FOR THAT SAME DAY, FRIDAY, SEPTEMBER 4 : *When I came on shore, the swarthy natives all stood around and sung in their fashion; their clothing consisted of the skins of foxes and other animals, which they dress and make the skins into garments of various sorts. Their food is Turkish wheat [maize or Indian corn], whey they cook by baking, and it is excellent eating. They all came on board [around], one after another, in their canoes, which are made of a single hollowed tree; their weapons are bows and arrows, pointed with sharp stones, which they fasten with hard resin. They had no houses, but slept under the blue heavens, sometimes on mats of bulrushes interwoven, and sometimes on the leaves of trees. They always carry with them all their goods, such as their food and green tobacco, which is strong and good for use. They appear to be a friendly people, but have a great propensity to steal, and are exceedingly adroit in carrying away whatever they take a fancy to.*[180]

"*When I came on shore, the swarthy natives all stood around and sung in their fashion.*"
It seems probable that the natives were not standing around Hudson and singing
"in their fashion" just for entertainment. It may have been a now-almost-forgotten
aspect of the peace-making and diplomatic branch of a large body of Algonquin
political practice called "The Way of the Heron." Giving a concert in honor of visiting royalty, especially a leader from a country you are trying to build trust with,
was occasionally a part of it, and this is still common practice in Europe. It softens
up the emotions, and opens up subconscious ties to the culture of the land. This
was Hudson's first time ashore in this region, and may have expressed that to them
in some way, so they greeted him with ceremonial song to acclimate him to the
spirit of the land. It was an important diplomatic moment.

Relatively little of Delaware music has been preserved, and no Canarsie music
that I know of still exists. The Smithsonian has a recording of one Delaware War
Dance. The Snake Song of the Unami Delaware of Hoboken was written down in
the 1600s by a school teacher named Caterina Post in standard music notation.
The words to the song, which is in ¾ time, are translated as "Hurry, hurry Brother
Snake [*axk-kok* in Munsee]. Return to the underworld and bring us rain."

I have heard the Washaniki Songs, "traveling songs," as performed by the late
Don Adanko of Oklahoma with solo voice and hand drum.[181] The rhythm is seemingly simple but follows the irregular rhythm of the words, which seem to be
vocables. The mode tends to be Aeolian, "the mode of the ancients." Although in
mixed meters, the downbeat of the drum is not stressed. I would say it is distinctly
Delaware.

In *Peoples of the River Valleys, The Odyssey of the Delaware Indian,* by Amy C.
Schutt,[182] the author begins with a story from Weslager, "One day in early January
1633, a Dutch crew of seven men on a whaling vessel called the *Squirrel* traveled
up the Delaware River. Along the way the crew traded with the Indian inhabitants of the area. The *Squirrel* anchored at the mouth of Newton Creek in the area
of present-day Gloucester City, New Jersey, where it was boarded by more than
forty Indians, with "a portion of them" commencing "to play tunes with reeds." A
sachem attempted to give "an armful of beaver-skins" to the Dutch, an offer that
would have signaled the construction of a relationship between allies and trading
partners. Suspecting the Indians of recently attacking an English crew, the Dutch
refused the gift, which their visitors may have interpreted as a call to war. Indeed,
the Dutch accompanied their refusal with a war-like pronouncement, commanding the Indians "to go ashore immediately," or else the sailors "would shoot them
all."[183]

Recently I saw a Delaware Stick Dance being performed, by Hodenosuannee
(Iroquois) and they were singing the original melodies as they knew them. It was

very enjoyable, and we were given a fine explanation of the history behind it.

In the 1740s, the lower Hudson Valley was in turmoil and warlike feelings rose up between English settlers and the Delaware, the Munsee, Unami, and Nanticokes. A large group of natives migrated north to live with the Hodenosuanee at Six Nations. In 1791, more Munsee moved in with the Seneca. They brought their Stick Dance with them and performed it as they had for hundreds of years. The Iroquois soon had their own version of the stick dance. Perhaps because the Six Nations were in a more defensible position, they were better able to preserve their own culture than the Delaware, and preserved those Delaware Stick Dance songs, making them their own. Algonquins of the region and the Iroquois apparently sung very similar sounding songs, irregular rhythms (one might call them syncopated) followed by a section of regular beats.

At Oswego there were for a time Oswegan Delawares, and a certain road was called, "The Delaware Line," along which many Delaware lived. The Allegheny people learned these dances from them and over years the songs were transformed into Allegheny songs. The Stick Dance is now being relearned by Delaware descendants thanks to the Six Nations people of today and a program at Cornell University. Delaware dances are still called "Cantico" dances, as they were at Hudson's time, and include round dances and short dances, and various others. I am sure that the Pocantico River along the Hudson acquired its name from the combination of pow or waterfall plus cantico, or dance, dancing waterfall. To find out why this waterfall may have been different, read chapter seven, "The People of the Waterfall."

It was also called the Skin Dance. What is perhaps most remarkable about the Stick or Skin Dance is its origins. Soon after the hunt, the skins would be cut and tanned. They would be double folded and stretched across a frame in some way, at a length of about 32 inches. Then a drum group would beat on the skins with drumsticks with ends carved in the shape of Maysingwe heads, the "Living Tree Masks" of the Delaware, depicting the red and black face of Maysingwe, whom some call "The Master of the Hunt," and some call a tree spirit. The dancers would dance accordingly, with the men leading the women.

How similar would music of the Canarsie be? If these are Canarsie people, there would possibly be a mixture of local and southern influences in the music. They too might "arrange and adapt" the stick dance as the Six Nations did 130 years later.[184] It seems that much of the music of the coastal Algonquins between the Powhatan and the Penobscot has been lost, although a CD of Penobscot traditional songs has just been released by Watie Akins, and Jesse Bruchac has recorded a collection of Abenaki songs. Robert Adams has released a recording, *Songs of Our Grandfathers: Music of the Unami Delaware Indians.*[185]

Neither Juet nor Hudson mention dancing, but it is common to see dancing in conjunction with festive songs. "Some of the songs have strange names, such as Stirrup Dance in which a man dances with a woman partner, and at a certain point in the song the man raises his foot and the woman places her foot on top of his, almost as if she was putting her foot in a stirrup, and they hop and dance. Another dance with a peculiar sounding name is the Go-Get-'Em Dance in which the women gather in front of the men singers and sing along with them. After about four songs the men come dancing in and they each get a woman to dance around the fire…. Frank Speck mentions that a Cayuga man from Canada made a trip to visit the Delaware while they were still in Kansas (prior to 1867), and he returned home with the Stirrup Dance. It has since been renamed Chicken Dance or One-Side Male Dance." (Speck: 154)[186]

"They appear to be a friendly people, but have a great propensity to steal, and are exceedingly adroit in carrying away whatever they take a fancy to."[187] They probably offered him some of those furs, and green tobacco, but it is possible he didn't understand this. He may have accepted them as gifts, but not understood the responsibility attached. They in return may not have been trying to "steal" the crew's possessions, but were probably showing them what items they found most attractive, in order to help them complete the trade of goods which establishes healthy diplomatic relationships. They were showing him how they made peaceful relations with other tribes. He may have appeared wavering and uncertain in that regard. Of course this is speculation, but it would fit the cultural pattern of the region, albeit in the extreme. Hudson does not seem hostile in his musings about their habits, however.

"…their clothing consisted of the skins of foxes and other animals, which they dress and make the skins into garments of various sorts." This comment is surprising, because most history books describe their clothing as being made predominantly from deerskin. Fox is used with fur intact as trim either for decoration or warmth, as the fur is very thick and good for insulation. According to one source, fox pelts were also used by hunters to cover their foreheads and noses while hunting, as the fox has a long snout. It also was believed to cover up the hunter's human scent.[188]

"Their food is Turkish wheat [maize or Indian corn], whey they cook by baking, and it is excellent eating." Chadwick writes, "Natives greeted Hudson and give him his first taste of American corn, which Hudson called 'Turkish wheat.'" The problem with that is, later in the journal, Juet writes with familiarity of "ears of Indian Corn." Why use the term Turkish Wheat and Indian Corn in the same diary?

According to native botanist James Flowers, "Indian Corn" is a highly complex breed of grass which requires human assistance to reproduce, a co-dependent species. It doesn't grow by itself. If you don't replant, a forty acre corn field may produce two or three stalks the following season. Indian corn has ears with substantial cores, which we call "cobs." Turkish Wheat refers to a kind of corn that is in a state of cultivation more akin to the grasses, either as a separate strain or as corn that has become feral. It is less dependent on humans. Turkish Wheat does not have ears or cores, its seeds are lined up in a row, in a simple construction, similar to foxtail.[189] The flavors of Turkish Wheat and Indian Corn may have been similar.

Although the Canarsie, like the Munsee, probably spoke about "The Three Sisters," corn, beans, and squash, recent discoveries in archaeology show that they arrived at different times, first squash, then corn, then the last born of the "sisters," beans.

The abundance of corn supports the theory that the Half Moon was either at Coney Island, or Staten Island. Further east of Coney Island, in the area now Brighton Beach, Hudson would have been just south of the great heart-shaped cornfield that fed first the Canarsie and later the Dutch. New Amsterdam's Governor Kieft was fond of capturing wagons-full of corn being shipped to places far and wide from the Canarsie "breadbasket," earning himself the name "Corn Stealer." To Hudson, on the other hand, it was offered as a gift. It would soon become a staple worldwide, and a gift to humanity.[190] Gandhi once said, "God comes to the hungry in the form of food." The line between feasting someone and giving them a gift is sometimes elusive in native culture, because food is the gift of life. Corn is one of the tastier gifts the Native American world gave to the European. On the other hand, there was a lot of corn grown on Staten Island in those times, which leads me to believe that the Half Moon may have been located there throughout these first critical days.

Plant cultivation was mainly performed by women in Algonquian societies.[191] Colin G. Calloway writes, "Indian women in the river valleys of eastern North America began domesticating indigenous plants such as sunflower, squash, marsh elder, chenopod, sumpweed, and goosefoot between about 2000 and 1000 BCE, but it took perhaps a thousand years for domesticated crops to become a substantial food source.... Corn was cultivated by AD 200 but it remained a minor crop for hundreds of years and only very gradually became the staple food of eastern farmers."[192]

"Between about AD 500 and 800, corn agriculture spread throughout Eastern North America. Then, over the next 200 years, the climate became warmer and moister, and corn production and consumption increased greatly.

"In the Northeastern United States and Great Lakes region some time before AD 900, a variety of corn appeared that required only a short growing season and was drought and frost resistant. This hardy Northern Flint corn opened the

Northeast to agriculture and sustained seven centuries of cultural development. Corn spread rapidly and widely toward the 120-day frost-free growing season limit of cultivation. Woodlands peoples continued to practice long-established patterns of hunting, fishing and foraging, but after AD 1000, corn became the major field crop."[193]

Corn apparently arrived in Brooklyn about 1100 AD and then spread throughout the area that is now New York City. It has been suggested that corn had to be bred to adapt to increasingly colder latitudes as it slowly moved north. The glacially slow trip eastward might have met similar challenges.

"They all came on board [around], one after another, in their canoes, which are made of a single hollowed tree;" the Algonquins used mainly tulip tree (a form of poplar) trunks for the dugouts, as these trees are particularly resilient in salt water.[194] These trees grow very large, however, if they are too big they are hard to work with. Dugouts are made in all sizes, from five or six passengers to more than twenty. They can last over a hundred years while in use. They rode low in the water, however, especially when fully occupied. Some were supplied with make-shift masts, and the pilot would use his clothing as a sail by draping it over the mast.

The other major type of canoe was made of birchbark, which dissolves more quickly in salt water than tulip tree wood, but is easier to maneuver in the ocean as well as inland.[195] A birchbark canoe has very little displacement, certainly compared to a dugout, and is better equipped to ride upstream in a shallow creek. Single pieces of birchbark thick enough to make a wrap-around canoe do not develop as well in the south, hence the old style canoe is a northern phenomenon. Air pollution is another factor that is preventing the white birchbark from developing. Hudson does not mean they brought their dugout canoes with them on board, in fact they are impossible to lift. Communities shared dugouts freely like shopping carts at a large supermarket. A passenger was rarely refused, and borrowing one was expected; the dugout had to come back eventually.

"...their weapons are bows and arrows, pointed with sharp stones, which they fasten with hard resin." Canarsie people are strongly associated with what is now called Clasons Point culture, an archaeological term describing their material culture. Most, though not all of their arrowheads would be in this style. It shows a great deal of influence from the Taino to the south.[196]

"They had no houses, but slept under the blue heavens, sometimes on mats of bulrushes interwoven, and sometimes on the leaves of trees..."[197] Staten Island's south coast had beaches directly facing the ocean. Algonquins of the region would migrate seasonally to the coast in summer, but they would tend to be more sensitive to the sun than their southern brothers and build makeshift wigwams or mat houses just past the beach under the trees. Most Algonquins would wear "suntan lotion" of

bear grease and almond oil when on the ocean. In southern regions it is very easy to live out on the sand of a beach such as at Coney Island or Staten Island because it is so soft and comfortable to sit or sleep on and seafood is readily available. We often see young people today in the Pacific Northwest living out on the beach, sometimes in the open. But Juet's description further indicates that the Canarsie people were not fully adapted in 1609 to the local environment, but were still living in the manner of Taino whaling people, accustomed to living on the beach, pulling fruit from the tree branches and eating fish baked over an open fire. It has also been suggested that it was part of the rigors of training young Matouac men to live outdoors.[198] These young men (the meaning of the word Matouac) were trying to prove how tough they were.

In Munsee Delaware culture, the mats were traditionally made by the women.[199] Native botanist (Nottaway/Meherrin) James Flowers suggests that some of the finer mats may have been made with dogbane, which is not a reed. Father Andrew White, who observed Algonquian peoples in what is now Maryland, noted how in that region they covered the wigwam frames with mats made from the reeds picked from nearby marshes.

In the book *1491*, Charles Mann describes Patuxet in a way that is very instructive to our understanding of this place that Hudson finds himself. "Unlike the upland hunters, the Indians on the rivers and coastline did not roam the land; instead, most seem to have moved between a summer place and a winter place, like affluent snowbirds alternating between Manhattan and Miami. The distances were

smaller, of course; shorelines families would move a fif-
teen-minute walk inland, to avoid direct exposure to winter storms and tides. Each village had its own distinct mix
of farming and foraging—this one here, adjacent to a rich
oyster bed, might plant maize purely for variety, whereas
that one there, just a few miles away, might subsist almost
entirely on its harvest, filling great underground storage
pits each fall."[200]

*They always carry with them all their goods, such as
their food and green tobacco, which is strong and good for
use.* The dugout canoes are convenient, in that you can
carry most of your heavy objects in the boat with you.
The great tradition of steatite soapstone pottery that grew
up around Long Island would never have taken off if it
were not for the use of dugout canoes and a habit of using water travel over foot travel. Soapstone jars can get
heavy. The Canarsie have always been described as sea-
going people, very adroit in the water. Sailors carry their
belongings with them in any culture, however at least one
descendant has commented that they wouldn't have had
all of their belongings with them, just some. They would have been well supplied
enough to be self sufficient in an emergency. Juet presumed that was all they had
as that was all he saw.

> JUET'S JOURNAL, SATURDAY, SEPTEMBER 5 : *In the morning as soon as the
> day was light, the wind ceased and the flood came. So we heaved off our ship
> again into five fathoms water, and sent our boat to sound the bay, and we
> found that there was three fathoms hard by the southern shore. Our men
> went on land there, and saw great store of men, women and children, who
> gave them tobacco at their coming on land. So they went up into the woods,
> and saw great store of very goodly oaks, and some currants. For one of them
> came aboard and brought some dried, and gave me some, which were sweet
> and good. This day many of the people came aboard, some in mantles of
> feathers, and some in skins of divers sorts of good furs. Some women also
> came to us with hemp. They had red copper tobacco pipes, and other things
> of copper they did wear about their necks. At night they went on land again,
> so we rode very quiet, but durst not trust them."*

Chadwick paraphrases as: "Most of the crew went ashore. Natives gave Hudson
gifts of tobacco. Hudson gave them knives and beads in return. He wrote they

were 'very civil' but Juet wasn't convinced they were friendly." He uses the original spellings from Juet's own hand:

"Our men went on Land there, and saw great store of Men, Women and Children, who gave them Tabacco at their coming on Land. So they went up into the Woods, and saw great store of goodly Oakes and some Currants. For one of them came aboord and brought some dryed, and gave me some, which were sweet and good. This day many of the people came aboord, some in Mantles of Feathers, and some in Skinnes of divers sorts of good Furres. Some women also came to us with Hempe. They had red Copper Tabacco pipes, and other things of Copper they did weare about their neckes. At night they went on Land againe, so wee rode very quiet, but durst not trust them." This is a sample of the spellings Juet used; I hope the reader will excuse me for using a more modern transliteration.

"In the morning as soon as the day was light, the wind ceased and the flood came. So we heaved off our ship again into five fathoms water, and sent our boat to sound the bay, and we found that there was three fathoms hard by the southern shore." What Juet is saying here is that his boat was still stuck in the ooze and soft sand when morning came. I asked experienced mariner Will Van Dorp where one would find a fifteen foot channel right next to shore, and he answered, "at the mouth of Lemon Creek, just past Princes Bay. The Ambrose Channel comes right up to the shore at that point." Further checking of nautical maps from 1778, 1867 and the present all confirm that this deep channel runs extremely close to shore at a point just a few miles west of Great Kills Harbor.

I interpret this to mean they were in Great Kills Harbor and got stranded when the tide was low, but that the tide rose up (hence the word "flood") and freed their boat. Then they went into the part of Raritan Bay which is just southwest of New York Harbor. Then they landed at the southern shore, past Wolfes' Pond Park, past Princes Bay, to the outlet of Lemon Creek, where there is a deep channel near land, as well as a lot of agricultural activity not too far to the west. This spot is only four miles west of Great Kills Harbor.

There is no "southern shore" of Brooklyn's Gravesend Bay today, but in Hudson's time there was because Coney Island was a small island then, fairly round, with a "sea gate" between it and the mainland. It was too sandy for agriculture. If they had somehow gotten into Sheepshead Bay, which is a narrow channel behind Brighton Beach, this scenario would make more sense, because the sand would be oozy, with a southern shore, and lots of rays. But there isn't much room on Brighton Beach for agriculture or people. If they were at Rockaway Inlet, there is a southern shore but it is just a sandbar, Rockaway Point, and not much agriculture. Therefore, their location must be Staten Island. Most of the north shore is Hackensack territory, eastward past the "point." The Canarsie-run Arrochar region begins from there as the shore curves southward.

"Our men went on land there, and saw great store of men, women and children..." It is interesting that Juet describes there being a "great store of men, women, and children," because historically there were never any large native villages on the southeast shore of Staten Island, and the archaeological record, according to Skinner, shows a similar lack of population, perhaps due to the scarcity of fresh water there, and it would have been poor for most agriculture near the shore line. This shore would have been prone to strong winds from the southeast, ideal for landing a boat, another reason for us to choose that site for our story, but terrible for Algonquin villages. Algonquins always chose to settle in spots with gentler winds, such as the well-sheltered Port Mobil site across the island. At the same time, it is interesting to note that Hudson seems to avoid landing at village sites and high population areas. Perhaps he feels that the size of the Half Moon and its sails would intimidate the people of the villages and might put them on the defensive.

Where did all these people come from? There are several major trail routes leading to the Lemon Creek site from more populated areas. Word must have gotten out from various scouts that a "great floating bird" had appeared on the water, and the people were eager to come out and take a look.

Perhaps the most important trail in Staten Island was the one that the Amboy Road now follows, also traced by the rustic rails of the Staten Island Rapid Transit. At Princes Bay, the trail is just over a mile inland and connects the point of land which is now Saint George, Staten Island, to Tottenville, both aboriginal village sites. There is another trail, marked on Smithsonian archaeological maps, that stretched from the Arthur Kill to Raritan Bay and hit the beach about a quarter mile southwest of Lemon Creek. Part of this trail is traced by today's Bloomingdale and Sharrot Avenues, but some of it is no longer visible, passing through the property of the former Mount Loretto Home for Children (still the site of a Catholic institution). The Mount Loretto Service Road may be a remnant of this trail which would bring ancient travelers to the precipice of this 30 to 40 foot high bluff that overlooks Raritan Bay to watch for invaders from the sea, invaders such as our friend Henry. There was yet another smaller trail parallel to that one, a quarter mile distant, both of which crossed the Amboy Road Trail and approached the beach,[201] making shoreline access a simple matter for those on foot. These three crisscrossing trails would have connected the shoreline to areas of tall oaks, beaches, good farming, and sandy beaches.

There was also a large population center at Tottenville, only two miles away, which would have been ice free during the Wisconsin glacier period, and which contains extensive shell middens which natives added to up until the contact period. There was also South Amboy, two more miles across the way from Tottenville, and the Rossville area on the banks of the Arthur Kill, about four miles on foot at the other end of the Bloomington Trail, also known as the Port Mobil site.

This Port Mobil site, written about by Herbert Kraft[202] and William Ritchie, had long been a great population center at least since 11,000–9,000 before the present and was still going strong in 1609. According to Kraft, the site, 3 to 16 meters (roughly 9 to 48 feet) above sea level, provided ideal hunting conditions for Paleo-Indian hunters. We can safely say the spot provided the same advantages for hunters of 1609 as well. He writes, "The topography of the Port Mobil Hill site is such as to provide an unrestricted view far to the south and north, and westward across the Arthur Kill and the lowlands of New Jersey. If indeed herds of caribou or isolated game animals were present, they could have easily been observed from this vantage point."[203] Kraft also notes the water levels 10,000 years ago might have been as much as 90 meters lower, and that the game would have included both mastodon and mammoth, as well as giant sloth (two forms), musk-ox, walrus, horse (Equus complicatus leidy and Equus fraternus leidy), caribou, giant beaver, moose-elk, and possibly bison. It was here that the first fluted point in the Eastern Jersey/Staten Island region was found, and at least 18 Clovis-style projectiles have been found there since.[204]

The forests of Port Mobil today are still predominantly deciduous. Kraft writes that "This pollen profile suggests that in the time period between 13,000–11,000 [before the present], pine, spruce, oak, and fir predominated."[205]

The words "...a great store of men and women..." is also interesting because Juet rarely mentions women in any way. We know from recent breakthroughs in anthropology that women played a highly significant role in Native American, and more specifically, Algonquin, history. In the book, Women in Ancient America, by Karen Olsen Bruhs, and Karen E. Stothert, "most standard treatments of the prehistory of the Americas have neglected aspects of human activity that, since the feminist revolution, are receiving more attention. These areas include childbearing and child rearing, family and household structure, food processing and other domestic technologies, and gender relations in all areas, including religion, art, politics, and economics."[206]

None should look with scorn at what "food processing and other domestic technologies" meant to Native American women in the millennium before contact: it apparently included an almost exclusive responsibility for breeding and cross-breeding plants and herbs to create countless new food staples and medicines. In terms of quantity, the lion's share of what is consumed today as food and

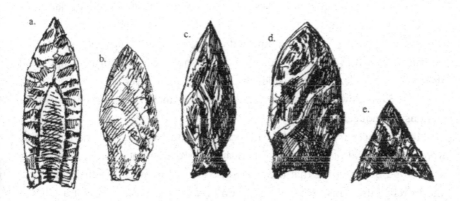

medicine worldwide can be traced back to Native American women, as their male companions rarely did this kind of time-consuming work until the time of Gregor Mendel.

According to Bruhns and Stothert, "In many ancient Native American societies, the interdependence of women and men was fostered, gender complementarity was promoted by ideologies, and collaboration was enforced by special division of labor. There existed many societies in which women did have the ability to achieve health, acquire wealth and privilege, and wield power."[207] Although not as pronounced in Eastern Algonquin societies as in Iroquoian (Hodenosuannee) ones, this statement certainly applies to Algonquin women such as Hudson must have met.

"...who gave them tobacco at their coming on land." Offering tobacco to someone as they arrive is a custom among most Algonquin people that is still observed today. Many other First Nations do the same, including some Lakota, some Hodenosuannee (Iroqouis), and some Cherokee. It is a gesture filled with spiritual importance.

Tobacco's principle role in Algonquin life is as a medium of exchange with spirit. It is an offering used for of communicating with Creator, Manitou or great mystery, and with the spirit of animals, rivers, plants, and people. It is used in prayer and in ceremonies of all kinds, including of course a fire ceremony. Smoking it in the pipe is yet another way of praying with it.

Tobacco is offered in giving thanks to Creator and to one's fellow man. It is often given to the fire, which is the mouth of the Creator, to be transformed into energy. The people they met may have been Canarsie speakers, as this territory was deeded in treaty by Canarsie chiefs a few years later,[208] and Canarsie language little known, (distinctly different from Munsee which is still spoken) but was similar to Unquechaug (both Matouac or "Long Island Indian" languages, however Unquechaug is a Y dialect, so in some words the Canarsie R would shift slightly towards Y). Several hundred words of Unquechaug were collected by Thomas Jefferson in the late 1700s. Although some of his word lists disappeared along with a trunk full of valuables during his lifetime, over one hundred of the words he wrote down survive today, and their pronunciation is passed on by generations of Unquechaugs.

My Penobscot friend, the late Eunice Baumann-Nelson, PhD, penned these words: "The world of the Native American, spiritual and otherwise, is not to be understood by assuming that it can be described easily in the English language, and in religious terms. What we now think of as spirituality was not a religion in the commonly accepted definition of the word. It was their way of life, which is to say that it permeated their lives to such an extent as to be inseparable from everyday living.... Manitou was not a supreme being, but rather a way of referring to the cosmic, mysterious power existing everywhere in nature."[209]

When you give tobacco to someone who is just arriving, you are asking Great Spirit to open up channels of communication between that person's spirit and your own. Diplomatically, however there is more to it.

In "The Way of the Heron," and other diplomatic and ceremonial traditions, there is protocol surrounding the tobacco. If you are offered tobacco, you should first ask "what this is for," before touching it. In the Great Lakes area, for example, many elders believe that accepting the tobacco may obligate you to do what the person asks, even if they haven't asked yet, because it is such a valuable medium of exchange between people and with spirit. On the other hand, even if the elder wishes to pray for that person, he or she must receive tobacco first before beginning the ceremony or prayer.

In the case of Hudson's men "receiving gifts of tobacco," they were probably meant as a blessing, and a peace offering, a way of connecting even as words were failing them.

In *Smoking and Culture*, by Sean Rafferty and Rob Mann, (page 74) we learn, "Most North American peoples had formal ceremonies for greeting strangers and incorporating them into the group so that interaction could take place. Most of this ritual involved nonmaterial or perishable components, such as singing, speechmaking, feasting, or the presentation of clothing, but nonperishable gifts were also included. Pipe smoking often was a part of these ceremonies."

De Soto's men encountered greeting rituals that involved smoking pipes, as did English settlers when greeted in Virginia by the Powhatan, including "stroking, oratory, feasting, dancing, and smoking." [210]

"When the French penetrated the western Great Lakes and upper Mississippi

Valley in the seventeenth century, they learned that calumet ceremonialism was an important validation for intertribal alliance and exchange. The calumet (wand or pipe stem) was 'very sacred and could be used as a safe-conduct pass when traveling through potentially hostile territory,' but it also figured importantly in greeting rituals that served as adoption ceremonies...used to establish fictions of kinship between prominent Indians in different villages or different tribes and... between welcome Europeans and the bands or villages they visited.... It could include presentation or exchange of pipe bowls or of the calumet alone."[211]

"...So they went up into the woods, and saw great store of very goodly oaks, and some currants. For one of them came aboard and brought some dried, and gave me some, which were sweet and good." The currants he is referring to are dried wild grapes. There are several varieties, however these were probably muscodyne, a grape that is similar to the concord grape but perhaps a third to a quarter of the size we see in the grocery store today. It may be a quarter inch in diameter. It is very tart, but when dried in the sun can taste sweet. It would have been used in making pemmican. As they used fire to render the fat for the pemmican they would smoke the just-picked wild grape to make it dry faster.[212] Samuel W. Eager on the other hand, believed they might be whortleberries.[213] Ed Johnson believes they could have been huckleberries or "fox" grapes.[214]

"Some women also came to us with hemp." Hemp is a hardy plant that can grow anywhere. The coastal Algonquins used it for rope and to make clothing. It was very common, and not used for smoking. The mantles of irridescent black feathers were ceremonial garb worn here to honor Hudson, just as they had been worn to honor Verrazzano. Unfortunately, they do not last long so there are no original capes remaining. As I am convinced Verrazzano was on Staten Island in 1524, the presence of these same cloaks supports the theory that Juet and Hudson were on Staten Island as well. It also follows that if Hudson had been given Verrazzano's notes and maps by his good friend Captain John Smith (a widely held notion), Staten Island would have been his main point of departure. In History of Westchester County, we find the following description, which is of unusual detail, but not sourced; "Their most elegant garments were mantles made of feathers, overlapping each other, as upon the birds themselves. Sometimes these were productions of real beauty."[215]

Verrazzano made similar descriptions of the native people of what is now St. George, Staten Island, whose landing faced Kapsee, the lower tip of Manhattan, about five miles to the north. He left his main ship below the narrows, and entered it in a smaller boat. He recounted that about thirty small native craft were shuttling back and forth across New York Harbor to come see them, presumably at St. George, traveling from the lower end of Manhattan. He wrote: "So we took the small boat up this river to land which we found densely populated. The people were almost the same as the others, dressed in bird's feathers of various colors, and they came toward us joyfully, uttering loud cries of wonderment and showing us the safest place to beach the boat. We went up this river for about a half a league, where we saw that it formed a beautiful lake, about three leagues in circumference. About (30) of their small boats ran to and fro across the lake with innumerable people aboard who were crossing from one side to the other to see us."

The presence of a red copper tobacco pipe in the vicinity of today's New York City in 1609 has been a hot topic of discussion for four hundred years. According to Marian Lupulescu, curator of geology at the New York State Museum, red copper can only exist as a copper oxide alloy, when copper is smelted with iron ore or other minerals. It does not occur in nature. European metallurgists created these alloys to make them stronger. Natural or "native" copper, is not red, but the color of a freshly minted penny, and Hudson would have known that. This native copper turns green when it is exposed to the air and weather. In its green state, it is expressed as $CuSO4$, or copper sulfate, noting the presence of sulfur and oxygen changing the surface of the copper. This is the kind found on the ground at the Michigan shores of Lake Superior in large green boulders.

French and English explorers found the source of this copper in 1650 on Michigan's Keweenaw Peninsula and on Isle Royale.[216] Natives would cut off pieces of this relatively soft rock and hammer it into copper ornaments or tools and trade them for thousands of miles. A gorget was found deep in the ground during the construction of the Brooklyn Bridge while creating the stantions, made from Lake Superior copper. This was probably the "other" copper that Hudson saw in the other ornaments, and as it was common he did not comment on its color. However, we now know that there was no local source for such native copper in any high quality or quantity. Herbert Kraft explored this lack in great depth in his book *The Old Mine Road, Pahaquarry, and the Quest for Copper*. Skinner in 1909 comments on the surprising lack of copper in the graves or in any archaeology in the east. It is a mystery that still puzzles archaeologists.

Marian Lupulescu noted that he believed it was possible that Algonquins could have invented copper metallurgy themselves before the arrival of the European. The "Highland Indians" (another name for the Wappingers, or Hoagland Indians) knew and showed the Dutch where the best iron ore deposits and veins were, and one cannot know that without actually digging, as the presence of reddish stone on the side of a hill is no guarantee of a good vein of iron ore within. Copper melts at 1200 degrees F, and using a two-man bellows system, they could have reached that temperature. But it seems to us that they didn't, overlooking one little red pipe to the contrary.

In *Indians Before Columbus,* Martin, Quimby and Collier, the authors, did an experiment reproducing high quality ornaments similar to those found in burial mounds, making them from native copper without smelting or metallury. Hammering, annealing, grinding, cutting, embossing, performating and polishing were all described as necessary steps. Hammering was done with stone hammers using a smooth stone as an anvil. As the copper nugget cracked at the edges, annealing was necessary. "Careful hammering and repeated annealing finally produced a thin sheet which was then ground down between two flat stones to a uniform thickness."

Annealing is done by heating the metal then plunging it into cold water. After grinding, circular pieces were cut, using sharp flints—cutting part-way then breaking off undesired pieces. The edges were filed with grinding stones. They made a mold out of driftwood by charring and scraping the wood with sharp flint. The copper was laid over the mold and then hammered lightly. It was also pressured into the mold with a bone tool. Annealing was necessary on several occasions. Preferations were made with flint, both as a drilling device and a reamer. Polishing was done with fine sand and wood ash. The final product was close enough to the original to satisfy them as to how it was made.

They went on to observe, "Some of the copper ornaments found in eastern and southern United States are so well made that investigators have thought that they had perhaps been made in Europe and traded to the Indians. Others who did not doubt that the ornaments were of Indian handiwork believed that the copper please from which they were made had been produced in Europe. There is now little if any grounds for holding either of these views."[217] By peering through microscopes at copper items excavated from Ohio burial mounds, scientists have concluded that some were hammered cold and some were hot-worked at temperatures between 500 and 800 degrees Celsius. This was probably the case with some of the pieces Hudson noticed.

Hudson did not mention any tools made with copper, only ornaments. It is curious to note that at contact, while copper was used in the northeast (and southeast) mainly as ornamentation, it was used in the Great Lakes region (Wisconsin, Illinois, and Michigan) almost exclusively for implements, including celts, picks, gouges, wedges, awls, fishhooks, knives, drills, and arrow, spear and harpoon heads.[218] This is perhaps why, according to the Munsee account of first contact, they wore the metal hoe heads they were given (by Henry Hudson, so they say) around their necks, until corrected by a second set of visitors a year later (probably Argoll in 1610). Several different oral traditions include this detail as part of the story.

In the days to come, Juet will record an enormous number of copper smoking

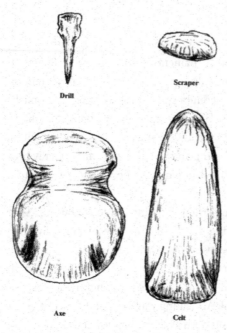

Drill

Scraper

Axe

Celt

pipes being brought to the ship, each made from different kinds of copper. The reddish copper varieties were most certainly made from European sources of metal, as this kind can only be produced by smelting, and they were appearing in surprisingly high quantities in the hands of natives throughout the area, eager to trade them, we assume. Where did this European copper come from in 1609?

As I looked through the records of various known explorers for signs that one might have landed on Staten Island a few years before Hudson, I could find nothing that would explain this weird phenomenon, the Munsee account of the "blue eyed God" in the red suit notwithstanding. For one thing, metal pipes are impractical, as they are likely to overheat. There are times when it is necessary to hold the bowl in one hand and tamp the tobacco with the other hand, and a copper bowl would be too hot to handle. They may have been wrapped in leather while being smoked. I was puzzled. Then I studied the history of the Basque whalers (which has been preserved at Boise State University) and their relationships with the natives, and there I reconstructed a scenario which seems entirely satisfying.

Around the year 1000, Basque fishermen followed schools of cod into the Atlantic. They fished as far west as Iceland in 1412. Between 1460 and 1510, the whales of the Bay of Biscay had been depleted, so the Basque ventured west. The Basque not only navigated some of Columbus' boats in 1492, the Nina was owned by Basque Captain Juan de la Cosa, and sailed by a Basque crew. They also piloted and crewed the second voyage of Columbus, and to a lesser degree, the third. It is believed that the first map of the new world, the Mari Galante, was first drawn in 1493 by Juan de la Cosa. By 1499, the Basque were exploring South America with great success. In 1520, Basque fishermen had followed the cod into Red Bay, Labrador, and found something more valuable; whales. They hunted right whales in June, and much more importantly, they hunted the bowhead whales in October, which were eventually hunted to extinction, so great was their value.

When Cartier landed on Labrador in 1534, he found Basque ports, but did not report them, as they were managed under the Spanish crown and would have added strength to Spain's claims for that region. They may have been there since about 1517. By 1550, the Basque were so deeply involved with Mi'kmaq culture that continental villages such as Oiartzun in Basque country, were adopting Mi'kmaq and other Algonquin ways, causing some social disruption.[219] It is at this point in history that we have to presume some considerable trading was going on between the two peoples, and in fact many Mi'kmaq families today in Nova Scotia bear the surname Basque. But there is more to the story.

There was a breakthrough that allowed the Basque to venture further west than any other sailors that history has had the inclination to tell us about. They developed a process of bringing whales caught at sea on board, stripping them of their blubber, and then boiling the blubber into whale oil right on the ship's deck, in reddish copper cauldrons. This type of copper was very common in the Bay of Biscay area, known for its copper mines. These cauldrons were suspended above large deck fires by the use of what were called "try-works," three to four feet high tripods, which were perhaps made of metal as well. The boiled whale oil was then cooled and used as fuel for fires, for light and heat, and may have been digested in some form. When they made camp in Labrador and other coastal points southward, they would set up a line of up to twenty copper cauldrons on try-works along the beach, boiling the blubber and creating large quantities of oil.

After the bowheads left at the end of October, the Basque would head back to Europe to trade the whale oil, leaving some of the tripods and reddish copper kettles behind. Usually, when they returned in the spring, the remaining copper kettles were gone. The Mi'kmaq often traded furs for these copper kettles, but the Beothuk (of Red Bay Labrador) were more likely to walk off with them in November, avoiding interaction or confrontation with whites. In either case, the kettles, nails, fish hooks, and other metal pieces[220] were immediately cut up and made into beautiful native jewelry, and in many cases, apparently, copper smoking pipes.[221]

Archaeologists comment that most of the smoking pipes and "Basque copper kettles" in their digs made of European metals seem to be from a narrow time frame: 1580 to 1600. "The kettles (often called "Basque kettles"), excavated from both Northern Algonquian sites in the Maritime Provinces and Iroquoian sites in Ontario and New York, were obtained from Basque fisherman in the lower St. Lawrence estuary starting around 1580 (Fitzgerald at al. 1993; Turgeon 1990, 1997) The spirals, manufactured indigenously from European metals, have been found almost exclusively at Iroquoian sites."[222]

According to records preserved in Newfoundland, the Basque were sending over at least 600 men each season in fifteen or more whaling ships, between 1530 and 1600. It was around 1600 that the Spanish empire began to crumble. In 1627, the Castillian economy collapsed and the Spanish could not afford to send any more Basque whalers westward. In the absence of any other explanation, and until another more likely scenario can be constructed, we have to assume that most if not all of that metal came from the Basque, and that the pipes were created by the aboriginals themselves.

"In 1643, while writing about his Narragansett neighbors, Roger Williams made a passing comment regarding their metalworking talents. In his words, 'They have an excellent art to cast our pewter and brass into neat and artificial pipes' (Williams 1936:45). Although archaeologists working on seventeenth-and eighteenth-century Native American sites in the Northeast have uncovered base-metal pipes made from pewter, lead, brass, copper, and iron, most scholars have logically assumed that these finds had a European origin (Trubowitz 2001:5)."[223] Perhaps a large number of them were crafted by Native Americans, using European scrap metal. The evidence for this conclusion seems to be growing.

Today there are less than 150 known "pewter pipes," formed by smelting lead and tin. The base material itself is associated with the Dutch, but all but two of the known specimens are associated with Native American sites, mostly burial sites, largely Iroquoian, and only one has been found in Holland. Veit and Bello state emphatically, "...our research generated no clear evidence that the Dutch made the pipes."[224] However Veit and Bello did not report finding any copper pipes.

Neither Juet nor Hudson (in the surviving entries) describe the construction of the pipes, however the Veit and Bello study includes photos of a number of pewter pipes, and all seem to be made of one continuous piece of metal, including bowl and stem alike. While in New England, Juet observed a pipe with a copper tube stem and a clay bowl, but this may have been an exception.

The most famous and historically significant story about Algonquins making pipes out of scrap metal is told by David Pietersen de Vries. "In 1632, he questioned a Native American regarding the massacre of some Dutch settlers at Swanendael, Delaware. During the questioning, he learned that the settlers had "set up a column, to which was fastened a piece of tin, whereon the arms of Holland were painted. One of the chiefs took this off for the purpose of making tobacco pipes, not knowing that he was doing amiss. (Myers 1912:16-17)"[225] The results were regrettable.

The Other Side of the Story

There are two sides to every story, and as we read Juet we occasionally have the distinct feeling we are only hearing one side. In the earlier transatlantic portion of the journey (not included here) we can be fairly sure he was involved in a failed mutiny attempt. His second attempt in Hudson's Bay in 1610 will be successful, resulting in the death of many men, presumably including Hudson himself. Those eventful days are merely left out of his journal. What else is he not telling us?

Readers should keep in mind that the name of the ship, "The Half Moon," was already one associated with piracy. The "good luck" medallions called "Half Moons" were worn by the Dutch "sea beggars," pirates who gained folk hero status in Holland by attacking and boarding Spanish freight ships. Their victims, however, were not always Spanish. Even if by coincidence, the name might attract a certain type of sailor, one who plays outside the rules and bows only to greater might.[226] Suddenly, we begin to understand how difficult Hudson's mid-level management position really was.

Our choices lie along two paths. To be satisfied with decoding a string of facts that are meant to distract us from what is going on, or to try to complete the story. Decoding Juet's references is challenging enough, and interesting as well, but it will not give us the whole picture. In order to complete that story, we must venture forth beyond Juet's cancrizan inscriptions. Each reader will have to imagine what is really going on, and what the Native Americans involved would be writing in their own diaries, if they had kept them. For educational purposes, I will offer, in the name of fairness, an entry from the fictitious "The Aquehong People's Daily Journal."

> THE AQUEHONG PEOPLE'S DAILY JOURNAL, YOUNG BEAR, SEPTEMBER 5, STATEN ISLAND (a dramatization based on known circumstances) : *At dawn, as soon as Father Sun rises in the east, the wind ceases and the tide comes in. So the Great Floating Bird, as we in our Arrochar Canarsie village call it, lifts its great white wings, and swims again out to sea. The salty-smelling ones send out a canoe into our bay which we call "Shancopshee," a "midway haven," or" Shawcopoke" which implies "a place in the south with shallow dark water." [Great Kills, Staten Island] The men of their canoe are trying to fish in our bay with a piece of metal on a string, and are not catching anything, and the disappointment is clear on their faces. We would offer to help them and show them how to fish, but it is not our way to condescend. They go back to the bird. We have observed that the Great Bird does not like shallow water, so it swims over to the deep place close to shore and lies still. Our scouts have been*

observing this big water fowl for several days, telling people to prepare, so it is not long before men, women, and children from all our villages arrive to greet them. Soon we are joined by our allies the Eghquaons Raritan Unami from Aquehong's western shore, and even a few Munsee from the Raritan valley itself. One or two Sanhikans arrive. Who invited them? There is a fairly direct path from the deep channel that lies between our island and the mainland to this spot. It is a two-hour hike. Some latecomers arrive who have ferried across from the Navesink and from "the Sandy Hook," or Rechtank across the lesser bay. As the white-skinned people come on land, we give them tobacco so that Manitou may connect our spirit and their spirit in love and friendship. It is an offering of peace. Our sunkskwa steps forward and says a prayer, in the Unquechaug dialect of our Matouac language, as she is from Poospatuck.

"Welcome, Brothers and Sisters! Peace! **Ha**-ka-me con-**tay**-uxk woch **kees**-sumsk! **Weeh**-sac!

Thank you Father Sky, Thank you, Mother Earth. Ta-**baugh**-na co-as **key**-ish, Ta-**baugh**-na **Cw**-ca As-**pa**-mu. *It is good to stand and walk on your back.* Wor-**ree**-ka-**nay**-oo co-**tok**-r woch **cop**-um-u-sah ki-**cup**-squan.

Thank you for the rain and thunder. Bi-**ney** ke-ya **suk**-e-run woch **Pa**-ta-**qua**-ha-moc.

Thank you Grandmother Moon and your sisters the stars. Bi-**ney** Nan-ax **Nee**-pa woch kee-**kees**-sumsk ar-**a**-qu-sac.

Thank you grandfather Sun, Bi-**ney** **Nump**-soonk Ha-**qua**-qua.

Thank you for the fire and the rainbow. Bi-**ney** ke-ya **yaht** woch pa-pu-**munc**-sunc.

Thank you for the blankets of white snow. Bi-**ney** ke-ya **quee**-wants sam-**pay**-o so-**ach**-po.

Thank you trees. Bi-**ney** Pee-**wy**-ek.

Manitou, you are great. Man-**to**, Kee Ma-sa-**keet**-mund.

Thank you, thank you for the whole world! Ta-**baugh**-na, ta-**baugh**-na, ke-ya **Wa**-a-me-pa-**nay**-oo.

It is good! It is very, very good!" Wor-**ree**, wor-ree-ka-**nay**-oo![227]

Manto is the Unquechaug word for Manitou; the pronunciation is similar throughout the Algonquin world, with one or two exceptions.

We take them on a little tour, to see the verdant growth here of which we are so proud. We have a stand of elder oaks nearby that are over a hundred feet tall, at which they show amazement. Although obviously hungry, they show no interest in our acorns, and do not seem to think of them as food. I come onto their giant canoe with a bowl full of dried whortleberries and meet more of their men. I meet an odd little creature called a "cat,"[228] and another very strange character they called "Joo-wit," paler than the rest and with a thing called a "logbook" with words that stay; onto which he inscribes, the way we inscribe on birchbark or sand. What a forlorn character! I durst not trust him! I give him the bowl of berries and he eats heartily. They have no women with them, so they must be some kind of hunting party, but I ask and they say they are "sellers!" And in fact they have many interesting items to trade.

Soon the rest of our people follow my example and climb onto the great canoe from below. The man dressed like some kind of featherless male cardinal in red is obviously some kind of grand sachem, to which his helpers show great fear and respect, so we think it best to wear our formal clothing, mantles of iridescent feathers, and of course otter fur and beaver. He must be the leader of some great nation, and may invite us to visit his people, so we show him the same respect we would like for ourselves. The Little Hawk sisters offer them hemp, as we see they use it in their "sails" and their ropes. We see these white people have discovered how to use metals, such as iron and copper. They have red copper just as we hammer into tobacco pipes, and other things of copper such as we wear about our necks as sacred medicines. However these whites do not seem to know their proper use.

While we are onboard, we see that they have hunted and killed a giant manta ray and are butchering it today to prepare for some horrible feast. To us the Great Manta is our Guardian from the Sea, it is our elder brother, which we call "the eagle ray," because of its ability to "fly" on its pointed fins as it leaps from the sea to greet us. For us this is cannibalism. If we eat manta meat, we will meet great misfortune, including death, drowning, fire, or shipwreck. This manta laying cut up on the deck of their ship looks to be all that four of our strongest men could carry. Our taboos forbid us from hunting even the smallest of these wise and intelligent creatures. My brother and I try to explain to them that what they are doing is wrong, but they laugh at us and make fun of us. They show us in mime and with their faces how happy they will be upon tasting its meat. We think they will not be so happy. My sister Red Hawk Sister kneels and embraces the "eagle ray" and shows her tears to the rough men. She speaks to the manta and sings to it, sobbing. Joo-wit leads the men in a loud "sea-chanty" about hunting and spearing whales to drown her out. We know they are not trying to be mean, but I'm sure my sister would rather it her that had died than our Great Leaping Friend from the Sea.

*At first my sister and I are terribly afraid for what might befall them,
now that they have killed the eagle ray. Then we become shocked at their
arrogance, and wonder at ourselves for not being sorry for the disaster we
know for sure will befall them if they refuse to listen to our pleas.*

*We know that the mean spirited cook will continue cutting up the manta
with his sword until all is butchered. Then some will be placed in buckets of
cold sea water and some will be cooked for the night's dinner, and then they
will begin to eat it. In our tribe, cooks should maintain a sweet disposition
when preparing food so as to not attract bad spirits, and man are not
allowed in our cooking areas at certain times. These people are savages.
They sit down around a table and begin to eat the manta. We leave in quiet
protest, as they continue to disrespect our taboos, but seem to be oblivious
to why we are leaving. That night we vote as a group to cancel the fire dance
ceremony, as the yelling might scare them, for we durst not trust them,
we durst not trust **any** of them."* RED LEAF MOON, FIRST LUNAR QUARTER
(WAXING), EIGHTH DORSAL PLATELET OF THE CALENDAR TURTLE.

Of course we don't have such journals, and don't know the names of the people
Hudson met. Young Bear and Red Hawk Sister are fictional constructs. However
we do know the names of six Native Americans who were definitely alive when
Hudson was there on Staten Island, surprisingly. They lived on the "west side
of Hamel's Neck," which is in the vicinity of the Verrazzano Narrows and Fort
Wadsworth. On August 10, 1630, these six people, plus two younger ones, sold
a parcel of their land to a Mr. Michael Paauw, and their names are recorded as
Krahorat, Tamekap, Tetemackwemama, Wieromies, Siearewach, Sackwewew, and
an underage Wissipeack, and Saheinsios, the younger one.[229] It is almost certain
that the six adults were alive 22 years earlier during the great eclipse and of course
when Hudson came ashore as well. Although the spellings are not reliable, their
names are not Mohican (at least as spoken by Hendrick Aupaumut), Munsee nor
Unami. These are Canarsie names (with their strange mix of Long Island Matouac,
Caribbean Taino, and Wappingers/ Taconic Renneiu syllables) and are almost un-
translatable today. Over time, their children's names would incorporate Dutch
and English syllables as well. These were the people of Arrochar, Nyack, and
Shawcopshee (the Great Kills Harbor), a defensively positioned colony of Canarsie.
The region to the west of the narrows continues to be called "Arrochar" today, and
may be the location of the deeded area. If all of Hamel's Neck and Arrochar were
Canarsie, it would extend their language territory well past Fort Wadsworth in
the north and near Richmond Avenue in the west. Speaking of their strange language, upon signing the treaty, these six Canarsie reportedly exclaimed, "Keene,

keene, keene, orit nietap!" "Thank you, thank you, thank you, good friend!"[230] *Orit* is clearly the Renneiu version of *woo-lit*, the closely related *werrite* or the Abenaki *oo-let* (good), and *nietap* is similar to *needap* ("friend" in Mi'kmaq).

> JUET'S JOURNAL: SUNDAY, SEPTEMBER 6 : *In the morning was fair weather, and our master sent John Colman, with four other men in our boat over to the north side to sound the other river, being four leagues from us. They found by the way shoal water two fathoms; but at the north of the river eighteen, and twenty fathoms, and very good riding for ships; and a narrow river to the westward between two islands. The lands they told us were as pleasant with grass and flowers, and goodly trees, as ever they had seen, and very sweet smells came from them. So they went in two leagues and saw an open sea, and returned; and as they came back, they were set upon by two canoes, the one have twelve, the other fourteen men. The night came on and it began to rain so that their match went out; and they had one man slain in the fight which was an Englishman, named John Colman, with an arrow shot into his throat, and two more hurt. It grew so dark that they could not find the ship that night, but laboured to and fro on their oars. They had so great a stream that their grapnel would not hold them.*

There is an urban legend that the exploration party was sent out from Coney Island, and returned the next day to bury John Colman. Colman Point, named after the slain crew-member, was supposedly near Gravesend Bay. Today's Gravesend is inland, behind Sheepshead Bay, named ostensibly after Gravesendt, in Holland. Gravesend Bay on the other hand, ends at Coney Island, which apparently was referred to by the natives as a point of land, hence the Canarsie name Narrioch, (or Nyack in Munsee). Another urban legend is that Colman is the sailor they named "snug harbor" after, in reference to the snugness of a sailor's grave who is buried on that gentle point of land. In fact, it was a Native American burial site centuries before that,[231] but not John Colman's. I believe that all of these are nothing more than urban legends. As we shall see, the evidence supporting the theory that the rowboat left not from Coney Island, nor Sandy Hook, but from Staten Island's windswept south shore, is going to accumulate as Juet's journal continues.

"*In the morning was fair weather, and our master sent John Colman, with four other men in our boat over to the north side to sound the other river, being four leagues from us. They found by the way shoal water two fathoms; but at the north of the river eighteen, and twenty fathoms, and very good riding for ships…*" According to Johnson, the smaller boat went "through the Verrazzano Narrows." This would be true if they left from Lemon Creek or Great Kills Harbor, or Coney Island, or possibly Sandy

Hook, and the "four leagues" measurement could apply in all three cases as well. They could only accomplish this as the tide was rising. When the tide is ebbing, it is impossible for a small boat to pass through the Narrows, due to the Hudson's powerful "plume."

"The second river" is the East River. This is really a channel or bay, and is not a river at all. In those days, it was shallow and filled with reeds, cattails and what we call weeds. The correct aboriginal term for the East River is Muskoota, a "duck blind," or marshy place of reeds.[232] To get a feeling for how the entire watery region between Long Island and Manhattan used to look, today's native New Yorker can travel to Flushing Bay, just east of Rikers Island, and to the mouth of Flushing Creek, next to LaGuardia Airport, and at low tide, gaze out over shallow, reedy waters, little changed since the death of John Colman.[233]

Four leagues is between eight and nine miles, which is the distance between Great Kills and the mouth of the East River, on a route through the Verrazzano Narrows. There are two islands there, Liberty and Governors' Island, but they are not the ones being mentioned. The East River was very shallow and swampy in those days in the southern portion, and ships had a great deal of trouble passing at times. One theory is that the natives built up oyster reefs across the bottom near what is now Pearl Street.[234] Further up, just below Roosevelt Island, it is much deeper.

"...and a narrow river to the westward between two islands. The "narrow river to the westward between two islands" must certainly be the Harlem River, which was an actual estuarine river in those days, though very little fresh water flowed out of it. It is unusually narrow. Further upstream, it was called the Kikeshika, or Elder River, (kee-kess=elder, shika from sheepu, river; the ka ending is puzzling, but presumably a variant on cook, cock, coke, or specific place of. The lack of a closing k may indicate it was not in reference to a specific spot on the river, but a long stretch. This name indicates to us that it was a place of early ancestral settlement. This is not surprising, because after the nomadic Clovis era of proto-Algonquin history came to a close as big game disappeared, it seems their descendants mostly lived along estuaries, and secondarily along inland waterways and near springs, or moving seasonally between the two. As the megafauna died out (the reasons are disputed) they shifted to smaller game and more reliance on fish and estuarial living, as they had no real agriculture. Hence the attraction to the Harlem River. It was at this point in history that ground nuts, the basis for a greater food chain, helped them survive.

The two islands were Ward's Island, east of 106 Street, and Randall's Island, which lies right in the mouth of the Harlem River, east of 125. They are now joined into one island. In fact, we can tell they rode through the West Channel between

Roosevelt Island and what is now the FDR Drive, because that course funnels you into the channel on the west side of Randall's Island, and then into the mouth of the Harlem River, which is otherwise hidden. This part of the Harlem River, at least to the Wading Place, has been called Muscoota by several sources, accurate or not. This clearly indicates this area was thought of as an extension of the East River. There is a muddled reference to a "great standing rock" near the Wading Place, but this is probably referring to somewhere else.

"The lands they told us were as pleasant with grass and flowers, and goodly trees, as ever they had seen, and very sweet smells came from them." The South Bronx, just to the right, was a place of sweetness in those days, yet further confirming this conclusion. They may have been smelling native wisteria, which smells very sweet. Or they could have been smelling the locust tree, or the American Linden, with its large flowers and leaves, which grows in the area and smells of sweet perfume. Its wood is known as basswood[235] and was often used by Native Americans for carving. Another highly aromatic indigenous plant that still maintains a strong presence in the area is the Beach Plum, a bush just under three feet in height, whose flowers in the spring are quite sweet to the smell,[236] however this was September, when the plums themselves were most delicious. There is a Native American legend that long ago, the birds were flocking to eat all the fruits in their season with such rapidity that the humans could enjoy none of it. So the Great Spirit created the beach plum especially for man. Now, in the autumn, when the beach plum bushes hang full of ripe fruit, no birds sit among the branches to feast, although they devour the bitter wild cherry, leaving to humans this fruit which combines aspects of the cherry, the plum, and the grape. The plant is somewhat supernatural because it grows in barren sand with no visible means of survival.[237]

"...So they went in two leagues and saw an open sea, and returned..." Juet had not been with them. Imagine the usually low-key Juet, hurriedly writing down what the blood-and-sea-soaked, badly injured passengers are telling him of their terrible ordeal as they struggle to haul John Colman's dying body from the row boat to the deck of the ship the following morning. It is a scene of utter pandemonium. A murder has occurred and all will be suspect upon their return to both England and Holland as no European magistrate will be able to examine the body. Juet must make a careful report, so he interviews them again within the hour for details. Meanwhile, all are concerned not only for the beloved senior crewman Colman whose great strength is waning before their eyes, but for the other crew members as well, whose injuries must not become infected. Either they forget to tell him they turned around and exited the Harlem River, or perhaps he skips the words "they turned around" as their words continue to gush forth, perhaps shouting overtop of one another in a tumult of Dutch and English. Imagine the ship's

medic shoving Juet aside to examine the injuries, thinking him an annoyance at this critical moment in his career.

It is left to us to figure out that they had not gone far inland along the Harlem River, but had returned towards Rikers Island. Once given this piece of information, we can easily unravel the rest of the narrative. To the north of the Harlem would have been the Renachqua (Shallow Sandy Stream People) who were friendly. Not ones to wage great battles against overwhelming odds, they treatied their land in friendship with the Dutch in 1639. To the west of the Harlem River's mouth were the Sachwranung and at Hunts' Point were the Quinnahung. These were related to the Renachqua, aligned with the relatively peaceful Wappingers, and ultimately the Mohicans, who were their elder nation. The speed and ease with which they rowed this distance through turbulent waters attests to the great strength of John Colman. As we shall see, without him, the team is unable to manage.

Then they traveled east, two leagues, or just over four miles, to where there is a small inland sea between Rikers, College Point and Hunts' Point. Some still consider it part of the East River, but it is very different from the section that runs along Manhattan. That sea is the beginning of Long Island Sound, which the Algonquian-speaking natives called Manunketesuc.[238] They had unwittingly now entered a rather different region, a territory of growing peril for the little crew.

"...and as they came back, they were set upon by two canoes, the one have twelve, the other fourteen men." They realize they are going into open water, so they turn around. They are probably tiring a bit. Then they see the two large canoes coming towards them, filled to the brim with warriors covered with war paint, and "loaded for bear." Although some dugouts are a foot and a half across,[239] these are some of the larger model dugouts attacking them, hewn and carved from very large tulip trees. The assailants are Siwanoy, known for their fierce fighting.

"....and they had one man slain in the fight which was an Englishman, named John Colman, with an arrow shot into his throat, and two more hurt. This is how I picture the ensuing moments: The canoes are still somewhat distant. It begins to rain, softly at first, then harder as the evening progresses. It is getting dark and a fog has rolled in. The tide is rough and both the rowboat and the two dugouts are bobbing up and down. Colman calls out in greeting. The Native Americans call back, telling them to "stop, go no further," but in Renneiu, a tongue that is completely unknown to them. A tall man at the front of one canoe lets loose a single arrow from his long bow and with remarkable precision it finds its mark and pierces John Colman's neck, wounding him mortally. Colman suddenly keels over, never to speak again.

Amid war hoops a shower of arrows befall the crew, wounding two more sailors. Some of the men fire matchlock rifles towards the canoes, but cannot tell if they are hitting their targets. One of the matchlock rifles becomes too wet and refuses to fire. Fortunately, the canoes back off and then disappear into the growing fog and darkness. The remaining two able-bodied men row furiously towards the south, trying to get away. Little do they know they are heading straight for Hell Gate, one of the most dangerous spots on the Eastern Seaboard to row a boat.

"*The night came on and it began to rain so that their match went out;*" The matchlock gun predated the flintlock, and was more difficult to use, especially in a rainstorm. The "match" of a matchlock was a wick or string of hemp, approximately six inches long, which burned very slowly. As the soldier pulled the trigger back, an upper arm with an eyehole through which the match had been threaded would move forward, lighting the charge of gun powder in the tray, which fired the gun. It was a cumbersome system by all accounts, but it must have been a hard rain to put the match out.[240]

"*It grew so dark that they could not find the ship that night, but laboured to and fro on their oars. They had so great a stream that their grapnel would not hold them.*" I picture them rowing to the opposite side of Randall's Island on their way back, the southeast side, the "wrong" side, which leads the little row boat into what is now appropriately called Hell Gate, less mysterious than the Bermuda Triangle, but in those days, perhaps as dangerous. There are very strong, swirling currents there. The current is so strong that their small anchor with several curving flukes, each with a sharp point at the end, cannot hold to the bottom of the East River. Hence they are tossed and turned in the tides while trying to rest. They feel as if a sea monster, at the bidding of some Siwanoy sorcerer, or even a giant manta ray seeking revenge, has risen from the depths to grasp their boat from the bottom, tossing it around like a toy. Any chance they have of saving John Colman's life is fading to nothing. Even his groans and moans cease to be heard.

Cowering near the shore, hiding under low hanging trees, their night is long and sad. Each of the crewmen fall asleep with exhaustion and are cast adrift as their small grapple anchor becomes loose and drags across the muddy bottom of the shallows at the Muscooten's shoreline. At dawn they begin to wake up, not knowing where they are. They row at a right angle to the sunrise and head south. At nine a.m. they see the ship the Half Moon in the distance and cheer. It looks beautiful to their eyes. They begin to shout for help. Juet's voice calls back. Their boat is hoisted aboard at 10 a.m.. All speaking at once, they begin to tell their tale and show their injuries, swearing in Dutch and English about the inhospitable Siwanoy, though they don't know what to call them. Robert Juet pulls out his pencil and ship's log and begins to write down the story. "One at a time! Slow down! Say it in English! I can't write in Dutch! What did you say?"

The Siwanoy Side of the Story

There are two sides to every story, and we only read Juet's side. But there is much that can be inferred about the Siwanoy. We don't know who killed John Colman, but we do know Wampage had already been born and was probably no older than four. Wampage is a short form of Wampumpeague, and sons often take shortened forms of their father's names, so it is reasonable to suppose that Wampage's father was named Wampumpeague, or "White Wampum."

Wampage was a well trained warrior who became chief at an early age, so it is not unlikely that his father was the warrior who trained him and that he was a chief as well, and leader of the war party. For the purposes of this story, we will suppose that the man who scored the first "shot heard round the world," just three miles from Coogan's Bluff,[241] was this Wampumpeague."[242] Wampage eventually became chief of his Siwanoy tribe and thirty-four years later, on August 20, 1643, in revenge for a massacre at Corlear's Hook and Pavonia, he led a raid on an English home at Split Rock within Siwanoy territory, built there apparently by mistake due to misinformation from Governor Kieft. Wampage personally killed Anne Hutchinson and the war party killed her family, but Wampage spared her daughter Susannah because of her red hair, the likes of which he had never seen.

According to legend and fairly reliable history, he named her Fall Leaf, named himself "Ann Hook," (or Enhoak)[243] and raised her as his daughter. When Stuyvesant negotiated for peace with various native nations at the end of the Kieft War, he asked for all prisoners to be returned, but Fall Leaf did not want to go back to white society. She now considered herself Siwanoy and spoke little English. Most of the Siwanoy were killed in retaliation for Anne Hutchinson's death but Wampage either escaped or was not present at the massacre which occurred in February of 1644, near Pound Ridge, during the maple sugar dance. Wampage later signed a treaty under the Treaty Oak near Bartow Pell Mansion with other Siwanoy chiefs, giving up 50,000 acres of land along the sound to a Mr. Thomas Pell, an ancestor of Claiborne Pell. We now call that land Pelham, New York. More importantly, he signed the treaty for Cross River in 1703, and there is no story of him living to an unusual age, so he could not have been born before 1603.

If Wampage were one hundred when he signed for Cross River, he was fifty-one when he signed the treaty in 1654, and forty when he killed Anne Hutchinson in 1643. Therefore, he would have been four at the time of John Colman's death, wide eyed and looking to his father as a role model, if indeed it were his father who fired the shot.

In 1609, the Siwanoy are the guardians of that bay and of the land we now call the Bronx, east of the Bronx River, which is called "Aquehung," a river with steep banks. They are not generally thought of as "Wappingers," although their language is the same. The other Wappingers, including the Weckweiskeck, Rechawanis, Neperhan, and Quarropus, live to the west of the Common Path, now Route 22, or White Plains Road in some sections. It is called this because they and the Siwanoy hold it in common, in equality, with mutual responsibility for its upkeep. It is their only common ground geographically. The Siwanoy live to the more prosperous side of that track, the eastern side. The other Wappingers are called "The River Indians," while the Siwanoy are called "The People of the Sea Breeze," or similar nicknames. It is their duty to guard the land and wampum against invaders.

Again, the relationship is defined by water. If rain falls on the Common Path (Route 22) half of it will roll to the east and end up in Long Island Sound, Manunketesuc, and half will roll to the west and end up in the Mohicannituck (Hudson) River. It's a matter of balance and flow. Symbolically, at least, there are only those two possibilities, though wind may draw up the waters back into the clouds. The Siwanoy are the people whose canoes float down to the sound, and thereafter the great waters, while the others are people whose canoes float downhill to the Greatest of Rivers, the Mohicanituck. Even at the Great Swamp, which is a huge bowl in the earth further north, this borderline or trail is maintained by both nations in 1609, with Siwanoy on one side, and various Wappingers on the other.

Some say the Tankitekes (pronounced Tengk-TAH-gees[244]) originally lived in this region to the east of the Common Path, in eastern Westchester and into Connecticut,[245] though some place them in southwest Connecticut, overlapping Siwanoy territory, probably in an earlier time.[246] Nonetheless, there was a Tankitekes village at Wampus Lake (named after Chief Wampus, who lived there) two miles east of Route 22, between Chappaqua and North Castle. There was also a village of Tankitekes just to the east, at Mount Pleasant, (yet further from 22) and another one in Bedford, New York, right near the trail.[247] The trail northward then entered territory that had never left the Mohicans before the arrival of Henry Hudson, and continued north. That trail is now 22, and extends to Montreal today.

Siwanoy means, on another level, "people who make wampum," as "seawan" is a word for wampum. They were known among natives for their prolific wampum production, and wampum was something of considerable material value, as the Dutch soon found out. The amount of work involved in creating wampum beads from quohog shells is almost unimaginable to modern people, but the end result is stunning. Once the beads are finished, the great artistry of weaving the beads into stropes one fathom long, and into belts with pictures that are considered by Native Americans to be a high form of writing, can begin. In some accounts, this artistry is performed by a different group of people, differently trained than those who work in these so-called "factories."

Many Sewanoy are great wampum weavers, an art form considered to be high-ly sacred to all Native Americans on the continent. The value of the resulting wampum belts cannot be measured. There is nothing in our society today to compare it with, but I often use as an analogy the precious illuminated manuscripts and Bibles of the 13th century, filled with original paintings bound to leather and brushed with gold. Riding into that territory unannounced is like breaking into New York's Pierpont Morgan Library, filled as it is with beautiful illuminated Bibles, to borrow a cup of sugar.

There is a large Snackapins[248] village there with sixty large lodges, and a "wampum factory" at the mouth of what is now Pugsley's Creek just to the east.[249] There are other Siwanoy "wampum factories" on the other side of Throg's Neck. Historians often speculate that John Colman must have done something offensive to inspire their wrath, or may have shot first. However, it is possible that he and the members of his crew accidentally entered some kind of 17th century "no-fly" zone and became a threat to the "siwanoy" or wampum production at Pugsley's Creek.

The mouth of the Aquehong (Bronx River) today is called Clasons Point. This is where the projectile points and other artifacts of the Canarsie, Wappingers, and Siwanoy were first identified as dramatically different than what had been seen before, and it was here that John Colman was killed.

THE SONG OF WAMPUMPEAGUE THE WARRIOR, SEPTEMBER 6, THE BRONX
(a dramatization based on known circumstances) : *The wampum crews were working hard to pile mounds of wampum beads that day. The greatest of the shell bead weavers, Kenoton, was supposed to come down from the north and sit before the loom and weave for us a special commemorative belt to honor our new peace accord with the brave Tenkitekes. There were piles of priceless shell beads everywhere, worth a fortune, so they say, but also sacred to our people, the People of the Wampum. Kwan no day kwan no day koy yo koy yo hey!*

A message comes from the Rechgewonks, our weaker cousins to the west, a member of the Wappingers Confederacy that we are foresworn to defend, mainly from a sea attack. He tells us that a strange canoe with five strong white skinned warriors within was seen paddling up the Kikeshika ["the Elder River" aka The Harlem River] not long before, and they were looking here and there for something, yes, or someone. Kwan no day kwan no day, koy yo koy yo hey!

One of the chief's advisors and some members of the tribal council say they've come to steal our wampum beads. The Cokoe, or the "owl" of our

nation, organizes teams to gather up the mounds of beads and place them in
five sacks, to wrap them all in bundle cloths, then bury them in the ground.
"This task takes too long," some others say. "We'll be wiped out by surprise!"
"Let us call Wampumpeague, hero of the Siwanoy! Let us call Wampeague,
the enforcer of the laws. He alone can save us!"

Wampumpeague, only thirty winters old, father of the newborn child
Wampage, but clearly blessed with special powers, one of the greatest
warriors of the age, and a deadeye shot with a bow and arrow, meets with
Chief Shomaroke and tells him he is ready to defend our western borders,
and our treasured shells, at any cost. The chief responds, "The economic
structure of this entire region is dependent on our wampum bead supply. You
must not fail!"

Wampumpeague rounds up twenty-eight, the finest of the Siwanoy,
but two of them are not so brave and go back home. It's not our way to
judge them bad. Everyone hears God's will differently. The steely twenty-
six however leap into two dugouts, each one large enough for battle on the
sea if they are driven out that far. A rainy fog comes down upon us, but
Wampumpeague's not discouraged. On one knee, he kneels down at the front
of the leading boat, pointing out the way.

Faintly in the distance and the fog we see their strange and cumbersome
canoe come pass right by us, but it is a diversion, and they turn around and
boldly come right at our Clasons Point wampum bead collection station.
The night comes on, the rain comes down so hard, it's hard to see. A deep
voice yells out strange words from the enemy boat which none of us, not one
of us can understand. The words sound neither Mohawk-like nor Munsee,
Wappingers nor Matouac. We shout out to them to turn back, to go home.
As they continue coming closer, our leader, Wampumpeague yells, "Turn
back and we will spare your miserable lives. Come one boat length closer,
we'll destroy you!"

Suddenly, the fog banks part for just a moment and we see five men
there, but dimly. The large man in front shouts something, but none of us can
understand him. With uncanny aim, our man Wampumpeague stands up
at the prow of the canoe and fires a shot at their imposing leader. Although
both boats are bobbing wildly up and down upon the tide, the arrow finds
its mark in "Loud Man's" throat and pierces him with the awesome power of
Wampumpeague's legendary bow. Kwan no kwan no day, koy yo koy yo hey.

Who within this bay, who within this world, would not have known
about and feared such keen ability? The leader of their gang collapses and
keels over, sinking below the gunwales of his craft. Our archers shower his

crew with arrows and two more men are badly injured, but they get away.
We could have killed the rest of them, but chose to spare their lives, as they
were eager so to go. Let them tell their people, we the Siwanoy are not to be
invaded, not to be disturbed by vandals, and that Wampumpeague, father of
the newborn child Wampage, is the Chief of all the Warriors of this world."
RED LEAF MOON, HALF MOON, (WAXING) NINTH DORSAL PLATELET OF THE
CALENDAR TURTLE.

JUET'S JOURNAL, MONDAY, SEPTEMBER 7 : *Was fair, and by ten o'clock they*
returned aboard the ship, and brought our dead man with them, whom we
carried on land and buried, and named the point after his name. Colman's
Point. Then we hoisted in our boat and raised her side with waste boards for
defense of our men. So we rode still all night, having good regard to our watch.

The men in the rowboat rowed or drifted about 21 statute miles from Hell
Gate back to Great Kills Harbor where the ship was anchored. We know that they
carried Colman onto a point of land. Edgar Bacon comments that Colman Point
is written on a Dutch map near Sandy Hook, but this is not correct. The cursive
script on the Blau map of 1635 actually says "Godyns Punt" at the end of Sandy
Hook, which refers to Dutch explorer Samuel Godyn (who helped start a Dutch
settlement in Delaware Bay) bears no relation to John Colman. There is only one
truly sharp point on Staten Island and that is Wards Point at Tottenville, a traditional place for Algonquin people to bury their dead. This burial region is on a
bluff near the Old Conference House, where Ben Franklin, John Adams, and other
rebels met with Lord Howe on September 11, 1776,[250] shortly after the battle of
Long Island. There are no known maps that mark Wards Point or Tottenville as
Colman Point, but there is another mysterious clue that warrants our most serious
consideration.

The earliest known name of the Arthur Kill, as mentioned before, is Rivierten
achter Kol. This appears on the Nova Belgica et Anglia Nova map of 1635, created
by master cartographer Willem Janszoon Blau (1571-1638). Note the unusual capi-
talization. The word achter, which means "after" has no initial capital, while the
word Kol does, indicating it is a person's name.

There is no word similar to "Kol" in Dutch that makes sense here. Therefore,
the Blau map indicates that this term is not the name of the river, but is written
as a comment, "...the river named after Mr. Kol." I propose that this was short for
Kolman, one of the spellings of John Colman's name in the historical records.[251]
Wards Point marks the eastern corner of the mouth of the river that still, in its
own weird way, bears his name, the Arthur Kill. There is no Arthur and there is

no *kill,* or stream, just a channel named after the unfortunate senior officer who unknowingly broke the taboo against eating the sacred fish, a river where there are few if any mantas, ironically.

While reading a dozen or more books on Hudson's journey, each with a different answer to one of the greatest mysteries of colonial history, ie, "where was John Colman buried?" I did not find a single source which suggested the possibility of Tottenville's Wards Point as "Colman Point," and yet it seems obvious, especially when you take Princes Bay as their hypothetical starting point. Wards Point is four miles west of Lemon Creek, the ideal landing spot where a deep channel lies "hard by the southern shore."

What makes this hypothesis even more compelling is that Willem Blau, perhaps Holland's greatest mapmaker, who was 38 in the year the Half Moon sailed, was a student of the cartographer Petrus Plancius, the very man that Henry Hudson reported to before his voyage of 1609, and the authority he was supposed to have reported to afterwards. Apparently afraid of retribution for not searching hard enough for a true northwest passage, Hudson remained in London and was thoroughly debriefed by Dutch consul, Emmanuel van Meteren, the same person who had brought Hudson to the VOC's attention in late 1608, and who wrote about the events Hudson spoke of.[252] He reported the circumstances surrounding Hudson's return directly to the VOC and presumably to Plancius. If Hudson had made a map, it would have shown Staten Island in greatest detail, including Wards Point and the Arthur Kill aka "Rivierten achter Kol," and van Meteren would have seen it.

Tottenville is one of the most famous Native American burial sites on the Eastern seaboard. The decision to bury Colman there may or may not have been a coincidence. On one hand, Hudson would not have discussed the burial with the local natives, as all on board were afraid they would ask questions and perhaps become hostile, as is clear from reading Juet's notes. On the other hand, Hudson may have already known the spot was a native cemetery, either by a chance comment or from observation. If Tottenville was in use as an Algonquin burial ground, it would have been dotted with characteristic wooden and stone markers. Tottenville seems to be an English twist on Todesfall, a Dutch or German word meaning "death or casualty."[253] It was supposedly named after the Totten family in 1869, but isn't it ironic that Henry Hudson's crew, a mixed bunch of Dutch and English speakers, wanted it to be named in honor of John Colman, and history, in its bumbling, accidental way, obliged?

Archaeologist George H. Pepper spent quite a while excavating this ancient burial ground, near the Old Conference House, built in 1668, a site of a great massacre many centuries before Colman's demise. Harrington and Skinner found thigh bones pierced right through with huge arrows, their shafts still in place. Bolton describes Tottenville as a Raritan village site at contact, and attributes to these Raritan people a Unami Delaware affiliation. This Raritan settlement may have stretched eastward to Great Kills Harbor, but this region itself was not highly populated. The Canarsee had an outpost called Arraochar village at the narrows to the east, to guard the bay from attack, but their territory stretched from Great Kills Harbor to Stapleton. There was also a Canarsee "Nyack" village at the narrows, but not necessarily members of the Canarsee Nyack Nation on the Brooklyn side, less than two miles away, as the term means "point of land." However, there were also Eghquaons Raritan Munsee along the Arthur Kill, perhaps at a different time.

Though not expressed clearly, it seems that the wayward men reboarded, then used the by-boat to bury Colman on land before returning to the main ship.

The small boat was hoisted up with the burial crew inside, with additional side boards (waistboards) to guard against further arrows. Most shallops and yachts at this time were equipped with outboard swiveling oval "lee boards" which could be nailed in an upright position to catch the wind from a sideways direction, in order to move the ship sideways in a narrow space. These waistboards were similar in concept, but cruder in design. The by-boat rode low in the water when full of sailors, and had short sides in any case, making the men an easy target for archers sitting in a higher position. They would simply have nailed wooden panels to the sides of the little boat and kept their heads down for their own protection.[254] Once hoisted onto the 85-foot long deck of the main ship, the boat's waistboards would have been removed. The main ship then stayed anchored in place during the night.

This is perhaps the most compelling clue of all as regards their location. In my mind, it settles the issue. According to Gerald de Weerdt, the only reason to nail waistboards onto a rowboat is if there are potentially archers or sharpshooters at a *higher elevation nearby*. Coney Island had no elevation to speak of, and neither did Sandy Hook. These wide-open beach areas offer no place for warriors to hide and no elevation whatsoever to offer a tactical advantage. However, Wards Point is flanked by a twenty foot cliff, atop which lies not only a prominent burial ground but a seasonal village of the Eghquaons Raritan branch of the Unami.

The scenario suddenly becomes crystal clear. Here's what happened, as if recorded in a secret diary kept by Henry's son[255] Johnny, and never found by European historians, but perhaps found in an empty row boat on the shores of Hudson's Bay in 1612 by a Mistassini Cree fishing party. (Like the Aquehong and Siwanoy diaries, this is a fictionalization of actual events. No part of this account conflicts with known fact.)

My Secret Diary, John Hudson, September 7 (a dramatization based on known circumstances) : *"Shortly after ten in the morning, all turn to my father and ask what we should do with the clammy corpse of John Colman. Of course, we can't embalm him so he has to be disposed of quickly in some way or another. "Should we have a burial at sea?" we ask, afraid to go on land and be outnumbered by either Siwanoy warriors or the locals, alerted by Siwanoy messengers. "No," father says, "John Colman is our oldest and dearest friend, and our senior mate. He deserves a burial on terra firma. Some day we'll return to his grave and build a memorial for him, and name the point after him. I will find a safe place for you all to bury him and will cover your backs with our cannons if needs be."*

Father skillfully navigates our Half Moon towards the Bay, [the Raritan] sounding the depths and praying he can find a place where the [Ambrose] Channel comes right up against the shore, and a flat place to bury the body amid the steep embankments so typical of this island.

He comes to the end of the island, [in fact the southernmost point in New York State], and sees a spate of land [what is now Wards Point] to his right. He heaves a sigh of relief as the ship pulls right up to it without hitting no shoals. Not only is it a distinct point of land, but the soil appears sandy enough for easy shoveling while solid enough to withstand seasonal shifting. What luck! I think to myself, "Thanks be to God we don't have to bury him in a strand, where he'll come up again after a storm like a bloody clam." This triangle of land is right at sea level, ideal for our purposes. There is one problem, the high bluff hard to the north. I am told there is a Raritan Unami village up there and an old sacred burial ground which they guard with their best warriors.

I volunteer to go ashore. Although it is dangerous, we are so incredibly short-handed that father agrees. The Half Moon comes right up to shore, and quickly drops a rowboat in the water, equipped with two waistboards, which are sitting on the bottom of the boat, beneath John's lifeless body. The men onboard leave cables attached to our rowboat to help us escape. Bearing the corpse, a few of us, whispering hoarsely to each other, reach the shore in minutes, beach the boat, drag the body a few feet inland, dig furiously to make a hole deep enough for the body, meanwhile looking over our shoulders for attackers from the hill. Then, I hear what sounds like the steady beat of a drum from the top of the bluff above us. I think I hear the murmur of low voices from that direction. It seems to me there are a number of people standing around on the top of the bluff, just beyond view. Is that a "war drum?" We scramble back to the rowboat, nail one waistboard into place, then a second, one along each side, then we duck down behind the boards, and allow the men onboard to haul the rowboat back to the ship, since it's the devil to row a boat with the boards in place. We are lifted by pulleys, the rowboat is placed on the deck, and the Half Moon sails away to safety.

I'm thinking meself very brave through out the whole thing, but then a single arrow comes flying at us from the top of the bluff and it pierces the mast right by my head, and I nearly faint. But this is an endeavor I'll not forget, a brave undertaking!

Leaving a wooden stake or marker would have been unwise, so we name the spot Colman's Point, and then name the river that reaches the [Raritan] Bay at this point "The River Named after Colman," or in Dutch, "Der Rivierten achter Kolman."

Papa has drawn a map of the spot and is about to enscribe it with Colman's name. As I am trying to learn Dutch from the men, I ask if I can pencil in a note on the map in Dutch about the river. He agrees. I write, "Der Rivierten achter Kolman," and I take time to write neatly. Just as I finish the first three letters, "Kol..." there is a knocking at the door. It is Robert Juet. He says the men are concerned about the savages, fretting they might be next to die. I put my pencil down and drop the map on the table, to be with my father as he calms the men outside. He promises them a quiet day for rest and reflection on the morrow. They need time to put this behind them. Methinks Juet is stirring up their anxieties for his own purposes.

We have a meeting with the crew, who are not only afraid for their hides, but mightily sad about Big John. Everyone assumes I'd been named in honor of him, though dad never says yes or no, so they look to me for signs of grief. I am still in shock.

One old sailor looks woefully at me and says, "The manta!" in a low voice. I wince in pain. I'd forgotten about the manta. We'd all of us supped upon its carcass the last two nights in a row. We were feasting on it the moment John Colman died. And he himself had eaten of it the night before, his last night on the earth! What will happen to father and I in the next year? Have we been cursed?"

Later, a hypothetical Dutch mapmaker, copying Hudson's map (now lost) records the words "Rivierten achter Kol," on an official map of the New World, which later sailors mispronounce as "Arthur Kill." Sadly, no map still in existence bears the inscription "Coleman's Point," but many now do say "Arthur Kill," even though there was never an Arthur and it was never a kill at all but a channel or straight. John Colman will have to live with that.

THE AQUEHONG PEOPLE'S DAILY JOURNAL, YOUNG BEAR REPORTING SEPTEMBER 7, THE BRONX (a dramatization based on known circumstances) : *This afternoon we organize a burial ceremony for old Two Shakes, up on Aquehong, the bluff overlooking the sea, but only a few show up. Our women are all tied up elsewhere with making jewelry out of the new colorful beads we traded away our furs for the day before. He was approaching his 89th winter. According to custom we are burying him within one day's passing. During his all night vigil, his wife washed and dressed him in his finest smoke-tanned buckskin, with many feathers. He is wearing a choker and necklace made of wampum shells, plus several leather pouches. He lies upon bark. The Meteu or Medicine Man burns some cedar, closes Two Shakes' eyes, and straightens out his limbs. The Meteu paints Two Shake's face with paint, mostly red ochre and black charcoal. The procession, singing a song, carries the body on their shoulders slowly to the gravesite on the bluff where they place it on the ground. The young men carefully dig a hole the depth of a man's arm, from neck to fingertip. They line the grave with bark and with the boughs of trees. They place chips of yellow jasper where the head will lay. They lower the body with the closed eyes looking to the west by northwest, turned slightly downward. His wife begins to sob in mourning, and blackens her face with ashes. Soon her sisters are crying with her.*

They place into the grave a paint pot made from a fox's lower jawbone, and also a tortoise shell bowl.[256] *The Meteu says that he will come back to life some day. Twelve times he says, "Manitou, help this man on his spirit journey," one time for each of Manitou's helpers on the twelve levels in the sky. The prayers are heard by the Manitou on the lowest level in the sky who passes it on to the one above him, who passes it on to the one above him, and so forth. These are passed to Kitchelamookong, "The One Who Dreams Us Into Being."*

Then he sings the Washaniki or Journey Songs, accompanied only by a drum. These songs are mournful, but very hypnotic as well. We all feel as if we are going on the journey with our beloved elder. We release tobacco into the grave and then the young men cover up the body with earth. A nephew places a distinctive wooden marker over the grave, and we all eat in honor of the grandfather[257] *whose spirit goes on to the southwest a few winters before our own. I hold up a strawberry and say, "Here's to Grandfather, a fine Lenni [man] who taught us much. We do not weep for him but for ourselves, as we are the ones who are left behind, while he will be 'tasting strawberries' to his delight, along the pathway to the spirit world in the hidden valley in the clouds. May he not be detained, but sing like a raven in the sky.*[258] *May he long be remembered!" As a memorial gesture, I shoot an arrow to the sun, to honor this man who never broke any of our taboos and always kept his word.* RED LEAF MOON, SECOND LUNAR QUARTER (WANING), TENTH DORSAL PLATELET OF THE CALENDAR TURTLE.

JUET'S JOURNAL, TUESDAY, SEPTEMBER 8 : *Was very fair weather, we rode still very quietly. The people came aboard us, and brought tobacco and Indian wheat, to exchange for knives and beads, and offered us no violence. So we fitting up our boat did mark them, to see if they would make any show of death of our man; which they did not.*

The men were fearful that the Siwanoy might have followed them through the night. The crew was no longer located within Staten Island's Canarsie territory; Tottenville was occupied by the Unami-speaking Eghquaons Raritans of Aquehong. It is hard for scholars today to understand the relationship between the Siwanoy and the Unami at that time, except that they were relatives with dissimilar languages. Plus, they were trading partners, at least in wampum. But we can be certain that neither the Unami nor Canarsie would have defended the crew of the Dutch ship against the Siwanoy.

It seems that the native people who boarded knew nothing about the fighting of the night before, as it was a different tribal group. "*We fitting up our boat did mark them, to see if they would make any show of death of our man...*" While fixing their sails they kept "marking," or making mental note of their behavior, to see if they made any signs of guilt, as murderers were believed to do during the Middle ages, but these people did not. Word never seemed to reach these people from the Siwanoy, confirming to some extent that these were Unami-speaking Raritans (as Skinner and Bolton have suggested) citizens of Tottenville and the southwestern portion of Staten Island (Aquehong), and not the Canarsee people the crew may have met at Great Kills harbor. Unami is so different than Siwanoy that it would have arguably been difficult for them to communicate.

THE AQUEHONG PEOPLE'S DAILY JOURNAL, SEPTEMBER 8, STATEN ISLAND (a dramatization based on known circumstances) : *It is excellent weather today. We bring corn and tobacco on board, eager to see what new and interesting objects these white men will offer us in return. They take both from our hands and give us knives and beads, but their knives are totally different than ours and are shiny. And their beads have unnatural colors to them that look like fruit dies. They offer us no violence, however they kept looking at us funny, as if suspicious we have done something to them or stolen something. This one they call Joo-wit is particularly intimidating.*

They continue to work as a team on their ship each day as we would build a wigwam, but never seem to be satisfied. They wash it over and over again as if by compulsion. We see a great deal of dried blood in the bottom of one of their canoes, but decide not to ask about it. It could have been a deer they shot and brought aboard. RED LEAF MOON, ELEVENTH DORSAL PLATELET.

JUET'S JOURNAL, WEDNESDAY, SEPTEMBER 9 : *Fair weather. In the morning, two great canoes came aboard full of men; the one with their bows and arrows, and the other in show of buying of knives to betray us; but we perceived their intent. We took two of them to have kept them and put red coats on them and would not suffer the other to come near us. So they went on land, and two others came aboard in a canoe; we took the one and let the other go; but he which we had taken, got up and leaped over-board. Then we weighed and went off into the channel of the river, and anchored there all night.*

Juet's words are jumbled and confused. Is he grieving for his fellow Englishman, John Colman, or fearful for his own life? Clearly, he and the others are afraid, but are trying not to show it. Apparently, the trading canoe was accompanied by an armed escort. Did Hudson's men take two captives, then let them go and take two more, only to lose one? Juet is not being clear and honest about it. Why did they dress them in red coats if not to Anglicize and possibly enslave them? Bacon believes it was to make fun of them.[259] We don't know why he let the first one go free, but the second escaped as well, both of them taking their red coats with them we presume. It is likely they would use these boys to try to learn the language, a long term investment in developing future trade in furs. It is possible that a few Algonquins had already been captured and sent to Europe, (we don't know the details, the famous ones were captured after Hudson's voyage) and word had apparently spread.

In April 1787, Heckewelder was astonished to hear one of the great Delaware orators, a chief Pachgantschilias by name, say of white men: 'They do what they please. They enslave those who are not of their color, although created by the same Great Spirit who created them. They would make slaves of us if they could; but as they cannot do it, they kill us. There is no faith to be placed in their words."[260]

In 1611, Adrian Block and Hendrick Christaensen (other spellings) came up the Hudson to trade in furs. They captured two Algonquin natives, whom they named "Orson" and "Valentine" after two characters in a popular English novel by that name. They took them back to Europe as translators.[261] Sullivan's *History of New York State* reports that these captains came in 1612 and that they "carried back to Holland two sons of Indian chiefs."[262] We don't know for sure but it seemed they were taken against their will, and were not always treated well. Everyone was shocked when the Algonquian captive (probably Orson,) killed Hendrick Christaensen on board the Swarte Beer while anchored in the Hudson River in 1619. Hudson was taking his life in his hands by capturing these very independent-minded people. Wassenaer states that Christiaensen was murdered "not long after" he completed Fort Nassau, or Fort Orange.[263] Fort Nassau was placed on Schodack Island in 1614 at its southern tip to displace the Mohican stronghold there. It was wiped out by a winter ice storm in 1617 and never replaced. Fort Orange rose up a few years later on the west bank between the mouths of the Hannacrois and Onesquethaw Creeks, facing the old fort ruins, about the time the Pilgrims landed at what is now Plymouth Rock.

"...Then we weighed and went off into the channel of the river, and anchored there all night..." If they did not go far from the newly Christened "Colman's Point," I would think that the channel is one in the river Christened "Rivierten achter Kol," or Arthur Kill as we call it.

AQUEHONG DAILY JOURNAL, AS REPORTED BY SHINING OTTER, SEPTEMBER 9, STATEN ISLAND (a dramatization based on known circumstances) : *More excellent weather, wallumdayoo, as we say. A Siwanoy messenger comes by canoe today and says there had been a skirmish a few days back, with warriors from some white skinned tribe trying to steal their wampum. Do we know of any? We send them back saying the white skins are all right, that they are very kind for the most part. But then we begin to worry. We send a large canoe out but are beginning to feel uncomfortable with the white men. So we send an escort along with it, as we would do when trading with an unfamiliar nation. The escort canoe bears some of our guardians. We have found the white man's knife to be rather useful due to its shape; no sharper than our own obsidian, but much easier to grasp. We trade generously for them, but are cautious. Out of that trading party, the white men invite two to come aboard and send the rest of us back to the land. As it turns out they force them to put on coats similar to their own leaders', and then proceed to mock them. There is an unpleasantness to the treatment, but neither man wants to talk about it afterwards. After a while, it seems that a lot of time had passed and two of our men row back to the Great Floating Bird to reclaim their relatives, but the whites want to keep them as their servants. Who do they think we are? We get one man back but they refuse to release the other. Our canoe goes back to shore unable to get custody of our own brother, and we are all amazed and upset. Where do these people come from? Are we not all equals? Later in the day, our captive brother seizes the opportunity; he struggles to freedom and runs through the ship to the deck railing, springs from the top of the railing and leaps through the air, landing into open water. He swims to shore and is free. Back on shore, he pulls off the bright red jacket, now sopping wet, and throws it to the ground, and then steps upon it, as a way of saying these people and their ways are not worthy of our people, but refuses to tell us what happened onboard the big canoe. He doesn't want to talk about it. He says, "These are not divine Manitouwak. They are crazy people!" That night, he has nightmares of being held captive and of being taken eastward to a place across the great waters with walls of stone, a place of manmade cliffs, where your eyes burn and your throat feels like its choking, and everyone looks upon one another with mistrust, a place where they fear the Creator, the One that dreamed them into being. We send the poor fellow to our meteu, or medicine man, for healing.* RED LEAF MOON, SECOND LUNAR QUARTER, TWELFTH DORSAL PLATELET.

JUET'S JOURNAL, THURSDAY, SEPTEMBER 10 : *Fair weather, we rode till twelve o'clock. Then we weighed and went over, and found it shoal all the middle of the river, for we could find but two fathoms and a half, and three fathoms for the space of a league; then we came to three fathoms, and anchored, and rode all night in soft oozy ground. The bank is sand.*

Notice the lack of rain at this time. They seem to be experiencing a cold, dry weather cycle. Also notice the absence of dolphins; it seems they have already gone out to sea for the winter, headed south. "*Then we weighed and went over, and found it shoal all the middle of the river, for we could find but two fathoms and a half, and three fathoms for the space of a league; then we came to three fathoms, and anchored, and rode all night in soft oozy ground. The bank is sand...*" If it was shallow in the middle of the river, they certainly were not at Verrazzano Narrows. Nautical maps made in 1778 show a deep, wide channel in the middle of the Narrows. Neither the Dutch nor the English had the technology to dig such deep channels before 1778, so Hudson is not at the Narrows. It is perfectly plausible, however, that they ventured yet further northward on the Arthur Kill, either to the shallow passage between Rossville and Port Reading, New Jersey now called "The Arthur Kill Ship Graveyard," a "spooky" place where several hundred ghost vessels lie rotting in the shallows; or to the mouth of the Rahway River, where they also would have found it shallow in the middle of the river.

Perhaps they turned eastward along the Kill Van Kull, only to find more shallows and narrows, and anchor for the night. On September 10, 1609, the moon bore a slim shadow on its left side, but was otherwise bright. They were heading past the Hackensack section of Staten Island.

It seems that Hudson wisely gives the men a second day to collect their thoughts and talk about what happened, reminiscing about John Colman and making their plans for the next leg of their trip. Do they go home? Or do they pull themselves together and go inland, where they will face many more dangers and hardships? Like the story The Lady and the Tiger, there are three doors to choose from.

There is the first river, a great estuary, a river of steep hills, which lies directly before them as they pass Bayonne. Then there is a second, rather muddy river that seems to be a channel in the harbor, and a third river that is also a channel, surrounded by sand. Rather than explore the "third river," Rockaway Inlet, which looks to be a small back bay, or the "second river," the East River that brought them so much tragedy, they decide to go up the "first river," the one that fits Verrazzano's descriptions and bears so much promise as the long-sought after western passage to Cathay. The men agreed with Hudson, that they would not give up and go home, but would help him look for Verrazzano's lost passage to China. This is the reason the Mohicannituck, "greatest of rivers, the one that ebbs and flows," now bears the name of that accidental tourist, Henry Hudson.[264]

THE AQUEHONG PEOPLE'S DAILY JOURNAL, AS REPORTED BY SHINING OTTER, SEPTEMBER 10, STATEN ISLAND (a dramatization based on known circumstances) : *We refuse to send out any more trading parties. What are we going to do with all this junk anyway? The Great Floating Woodpile leaves us finally. Our expectations had been too high. We were sure it was a divine being coming to visit us, as our Powwows and "Dreamers" had foreseen. They only saw part of the story. These travelers are powerful as manitous, but less than giants in matters of the heart, especially that man they call Juet. Now we are left in disillusionment and sadness. What a let-down. All we have are these material objects, and no promise of future alliances. Several of our people feel disrespected and abused and all of us feel their pain. One of our men follows them in his canoe up the western channel [Arthur Kill] until they disappear in the distance. He stands in the canoe and spreads both arms out to salute them, but no one salutes back, except the one they call Johnnyboy, who waves secretly where the men can't see.* RED LEAF MOON, THIRTEENTH DORSAL PLATELET OF THE CALENDAR TURTLE 392ND YEAR OF THE GREAT PROPHECY

Chapter Five

PEOPLE OF THE RIVER

One River Twice

*T*he river of history usually moves slowly, and at least in the Algonquin view, the river we step into today is not that different from the one that others stepped into before us. Hudson was seeing a river in 1609 that was largely the same as the one that was there in 1608. With that first glance, at least, he was seeing the last traces of an unchanged past even as it was merging into a drastically different future, swirling with eddies of ambiguous implications. But what Henry Hudson saw in 1609 was changing because he saw it, and to a degree that should have been instructional to quantum physicists such as Schroedinger and Heisinger, who say that we cannot separate ourselves from that which we observe, at least on the quantum level. The longer he stayed, the more it changed. A single gift could change the fortunes of a whole family. He could not, to extend the metaphor, have stepped into that same river twice.

If he had not disappeared two years later in what is now Hudson's Bay, and had come back as an old man to the harbor where the river meets the sea, he would not have recognized it—the river would have already borne his name. But the ship's log still preserves our cultural link, however rusty, to that unchanged past. Let us explore that log, and that link to the past and that month in time which both preserved (in writing) and destroyed (in fact) what was arguably one of the most ecologically sound societies on earth.

JUET'S JOURNAL, FRIDAY, SEPTEMBER 11 : *Was fair and very hot weather. At one o'clock in the afternoon, we weighed and went into the river, the wind at south-south-west, little wind. Our soundings were seven, six, five, six, seven, eight, nine, ten, twelve, thirteen and fourteen fathoms. Then it shoaled again, and came to five fathoms. Then we anchored and saw that it was a very good harbour for all winds, and rode all night. The people of the country came aboard of us, making show of love, and gave us tobacco and Indian wheat, and departed for that night; but we durst not trust them.*

"We went into the river..." It is clear that the ship entered the river now called the Hudson on September 11, as Juet plainly says so. By doing so, some would argue that it was on that day that European culture truly penetrated New York's native boundaries and defenses for the first time (although there were no "New York" boundaries then). This is significant, for reasons that will become clear later on. Although some would say September 11, 1609 was a day of invasion of Native people by whites, one could also say it was a day that a prophecy was fulfilled, perhaps even the day a new rainbow race was born. It all depends on how you look at it.

Although Hudson's first day on the river was peaceful, his voyage was to end in outbursts of violence. Readers must come to their own conclusions as to why these things happened as they did.

Although Juet is vague as to which direction they go after crossing the threshold, Michael Sullivan Smith believes that on September 11 of 1609, Henry Hudson's ship The Half Moon traversed the narrow Kill Van Kull, the only exit northward from the Arthur Kill, crossed New York Harbor, and landed somewhere near the Battery Park area of Manhattan. As there is no marking of distance in this entry, they could have easily made it to Battery Park either from Fort Wadsworth or from the Kill Van Kull. In any event, if we take Juet at his word, they must now know that the Mohicannituck is a "river" and not a "channel," and therefore not a passage to China.

In *A Century of Dishonor,* Jackson writes, in a somewhat dated fashion, "When Hendrik [sic] Hudson anchored his ship, the Half Moon, off New York Island [sic] in 1609, the Delaware [sic] stood in great numbers on the shore to receive him, exclaiming, in their innocence, 'Behold! The gods have come to visit us!' More than a hundred years later, the traditions of this event were still current in the tribe."[265]

The pointed end of the battery was nothing but a series of large rocks jutting out of the bay in those days, which the Canarsie called "point of rocks," or Kapsee. No sailing vessel would have wanted to pass within a hundred yards of such a dangerous spot, especially with prevailing winds so unfavorable. The only good landing spot in 1609 on the southwest side of Manhattan would have been at the future site of the World Trade Center, which was where many historians believe Adrian Block's ship the Tyger crashed trying to land four years after Hudson. There was apparently a valley here in Dutch times sloping from the ridge to sea level in a westward direction, which the Dutch later called "Murderer's Valley," after the murder of a Sunksquaw (female chief) eating a peach at that spot triggered the first of the Peach Wars, according to Washington Irving. There must have been a creek or rivulet at some time running down the center, but no mention is made of this before the British landfill project extended the shoreline out quite a

distance. It is due to this landfill extension that rescue workers after September 11 of 2001, found more pieces from the wreck of an old sailing ship underneath the World Trade Center so far from today's shoreline.[266]

Hudson's landing was at the great crossing place of the Tulpehoken Trail. The word "tulpehoken" has several meanings. There is a town by that name on the trail itself, but it has generally been translated as "turtle island," as it crosses a large part of North America. In Dankers and Sluyter's account of life in New Netherlands, an 80-year-old Ahakinsack (Hackinsack) man named Jasper came to their house on October 16, 1679. "Jasper" was old enough to have seen Henry Hudson just before his tenth birthday. His native name was Akinon. They asked him where he believed he came from. He said from his father and grandfather. They apparently were interested in finding out about Lenape migrations so they kept asking. Finally, he took a piece of coal from the fireplace and knelt down and drew a circle on the floor, then inside the circle he drew an oval, and then drew four little feet, a head and a tail. This was a terrapin surrounded by water. As it rose up, he said, the water ran off and it became dry. He then placed a piece of straw inside the oval and said, "The earth was now dry, and there grew a tree in the middle of the earth, and the root of this tree sent forth a sprout beside it, and there grew upon it a man, who was the first male. This man was there alone, and would have remained alone; but the tree bent over its top and touched the earth and there shot therein another root, from which came forth another sprout, and there grew upon it the woman, and from these two are all men produced."[267] This was Turtle Island. In this story, Turtle Island is the earth, but it also refers to North America, and in one Hackensack story (published in my book *Native American Stories of the Sacred*), it seems to be Staten Island.

The Tulpehoken Trail (Turtle Island Trail) is now roughly preserved as Route 22, from Montreal to Corn Island, Kentucky (now called Shippingsport Island, at the Falls of the Ohio River). It traveled due south from Montreal to a spot where it crossed the Harlem River (Kikeshika). It followed the course of Fifth Avenue then curved to the west around a Werpoes Village at Park Avenue South, then, following Fulton Street in Manhattan, it entered into a valley that ran east to west, the foot path following the course of a small rivulet. Then the Tulpehoken Trail came to the edge of the great river and made a crossing.

The landing here was a main ferry crossing for the Lenape, and the path continues on the western shore at Communipaw, which is a Double Dutch interpretation of Kamunipaw, from Kamn, or "across the river." Paw usually means waterfall, which doesn't seem to work here. Pough could be a grassy field. The entire word means "landing place on the other side." The Double Dutch version, Communipau, as lampooned by Washington Irving, suggests a place of communal living.

Henry Hudson seemed to have a penchant for anchoring at important trail crossings, which makes sense if you want to do trade with travelers. Plus one can invariably find good landings for canoes and rowboats on both sides. From this point on, Hudson will anchor almost exclusively at such crossings. It is important to understand where these trails led in either direction, as native people were running to see the Half Moon from great distances along well-made trails that now form the foundations of our highways.

The Tulpehoken Trail had different sub-names for each section. In Westchester it was called "The Common Path." In Manhattan it was called "The Path to the Wading Place." In Communipaw it was the Communipaw route. From Elizabeth, New Jersey to Reading, Pennsylvania it was called the Maxatawney Path. This section of trail was named after the populated and popular Delaware community of Maxatawaney, (Village of the Bear) now called Kutztown, which remained in "Delaware Indian" possession straight through its turbulent colonial history and into the United States history, until it was totally surrounded by white settlers for miles around. Then, whatever natives, and whatever bears, disappeared into the western woodlands unnoticed.[268] From Reading it followed the Tulpehocken

Creek Trail to the village of Tulpehocken (now Meyersville) and then it was called
the Allegheny Path to Harrisburgh, although Harrisburgh was called Paxton,[269]
which means "Flat Place," or, "Place of Still Water."

Manhattan's southwest corner was a highly populated spot, where even in the
cold winds of December, four years later, when their ship the Tyger accidentally
burned, Adrian Block's men would be quickly rescued by friendly Algonquins
living nearby. I have often walked from the site of the Kapsee Chief's house at the
foot of the Mohican Trail (now Broadway) to this spot, and it is a short walk of less
than a half hour, either following the Mohican Trail / Broadway or the shoreline
trail, now Greenwich Street. It was near this chief's wigwam that Peter Minuit supposedly made his first thwarted attempt at "buying" Manhattan, but some dispute
it ever happened.

Edward Hagaman Hall begins his account of Juet's locations starting with
September 11. He feels the ship traveled from the Verrazzano Narrows to Liberty
Island, or perhaps Governor's Island at this time. Linda Pulaw, retired Delaware
chief from Oklahoma, stated once that both Ellis Island and Liberty Island were
sacred meeting places for their ancestors, and places to pray. They are both located
at the crossing of the Tulpehocken Trail, or Route 22, so it does seem likely from
a geocultural point of view.

Governor's Island was a council fire island for the Canarsee, who called it
Pagganck, which means "hickory nut island," which was translated to "nut island"
by the Dutch. Hickories were good for making bow wood, but also good bee trees
for making honey.

THE MANNA-HATTAN PEOPLE'S DAILY JOURNAL, WHITE CLOUD REPORTING,
SEPTEMBER 11, MANHATTAN : *A hot day today. After night-fall we see what
appears to be a great floating bird in the middle of the harbor beyond the
Kapsee Rocks. It comes up the Mohicannituck and lands at the Tulpehoken
Trail crossing, across from Communipaw. Our people had heard good things
about this marvelous canoe, and we ride out in our canoes to greet it. They
take us on board and accept our corn and tobacco as an offering of peace and
a promise they will be good to us.*

*The Sapohannikans, our Unami-speaking tobacco-picking friends, came
running down the shoreline trail [Greenwich Street] to see the Great Floating
Bird, bringing with them some ears of corn hastily picked from the field
near the canoe harbor at the end of the verdant Sapohannikan Trail [now
Gansevoort Street/Greenwich Street] with its blossoming bushes and trees.
It ran slightly uphill into the cluster of garden-like bushes, passing the large
Sapohannikan Fort with its ten-foot tall cedar palisades just to the east. Corn*

and other trade goods were stacked high everywhere around the fort, but the men who were busy moving goods here and there suddenly abandoned their posts and were racing down to Kapsee Rocks with the others, grabbing whatever potential trade items they could.

They had chosen a good landing spot. The people of the Kapsee [at Bowling Green] the Ashibk Village [near the site of the later Quaker Meeting House], "The Safe Landing Place" [now Whitehall Slip], the Catiemuts village [near Broadway at Tribeca], the Ocitoc Village [at what is now Broadway and Canal], Shell Point Hill, [now Leonard Street], Indian Hill [at what is now Chatham Square], the Ishpatena Village [at what is now Varick Street], and the Aspetong Village [at what is now Broadway and Houston], all came running as fast as their legs could carry them. It was general pandemonium.

Our elders had very specific instructions to look for a sign this day concerning the outcome of the Seven Fires Prophecies. These teachings from the north coast [Partridge Island, St. John's, Nova Scotia] are very specific and describe the coming of white men from the east. If they come bearing gifts of friendship, the outcome of their arrival will be good, and a new rainbow race will emerge, and an era of peace will come at the end of the seven fires. Then the people of Turtle Island will come together to light the eighth fire. If the visitors come bearing weapons, there will be destruction at the end of the seven fires and we may not be able to light the eighth fire, without a great deal of purification.

It is to be understood that a "fire," according to the prophets that came long ago from the east, is the full span of a man's life as it was in the time of Creation, which is understood to be two cycles of the stars, each of which is 56 winters. [By "cycle of the stars"they actually meant the planets; 56 years is two complete Saturn cycles, a planet which returns every 28 years. The wheel is based on the seven year cycle associated elsewhere with Mercury and Uranus, but also with female reproduction (Joan Boresenko), financial markets, earth cycles, and the Sabbatical cycle in the Bible].[270] The prophets requested of our brothers to the north to tell all the people that the time of prophecy was to be seven of these fires, and no longer. Using the "fires"[112 year periods] as a reference, they told us precisely when there would be certain signs, including wars, visitations, and eclipses, that would let us know how the Turtle Island experiment was progressing. There would be crossroads and choices to be made every few winters. They predicted that choices would have to be made but said that we were free to make whatever choices we thought wise, and would suffer from our mistakes if we chose poorly. They instructed some of us to migrate westward "to the place where food grows on

the water," to preserve our culture. Others stayed in the east to guard over the
land, in honor of the ancient Landkeeper Covenant. These teachings would be
preserved by our Medicine Lodges who would meet four times a year for four
days each time.

Until this day, there were few signs of trouble along the northeast; the
Basque whalers left for us their wonderful copper kettles so that we could
make jewelry and copper pipes from them. But this autumn marks the time
long foretold after the half way point in the entire span of time known as the
seven fires. It has been one solar year since the midpoint of the Great Cycle, a
year of signs and omens. Our Medicine Chiefs and star watcher women have
counted the winters and kept careful count. Certainly we would be given a
great opportunity to meet the strangers from the east and welcome them, in
order to insure a peaceful future for the coming generations of Turtle Island
dwellers.

When we saw The Great Floating Bird swimming to shore, just before the
equinox when day and night are equal and the sun rises directly in the east,
we knew that we were about to come to a crossroads in the history of Turtle
Island. We are filled with joy and optimism. In the 784th year of the Great
Prophecy, or the year of omens to follow, we hope to look back on these days
with pride. If we and the strangers fail to grasp hands together in lasting
bonds of friendship, and if we the new people of Turtle Island continue to fail
in friendship and love, we will know that we all must willingly face a great
purification of spirit and of the earth at the end year of the seven fire cycle.
And if we do not face it willingly, by choosing the simple, humble way of life as
our ancestors lived, the purification will be thrust upon us unbidden and there
will be great suffering. We, the people of Manna-hatta, and of the Eastern
Door, do not want this to happen.

When the strangers arrive, we go onto their ship, and go out of our way
to show the greatest gestures of good will, oratory, stroking their hair, feeding
them, even punching them in the shoulder, which is our way to show masculine
brotherhood. We play the hand-bone game with them; we hide two colored
and two plain pieces of bone in the fists of two players and they guess where
the colored ones are hidden. Then one of the Dutch sailors kneels and draws
a sacred circle in the dust with his finger. We gasp with excitement, hoping
he will reveal to us their deepest spiritual teachings, but instead he brings out
some toys called marbles and shows us a game called "Knickerbocker," which
we learn eagerly even if it apparently is not a sacred game. Then we depart for
that night, filled with joy that our prophecies have been fulfilled. They come in

friendship after all, and just ten suns [days] short of the equinox of the central
year of our great eon, as it had been foretold at Partridge Island. RED LEAF
MOON, SECOND LUNAR QUARTER, FOURTEENTH DORSAL PLATELET.[271]

This is only one of several prophecies that predicted the arrival of Henry
Hudson. There were others. This is why the inhabitants of Manhattan rolled out
the red carpet for this motley crew and their captain. As they understood it, the
fate of a future world was at stake.

When the Munsee wrote to Zachary Taylor in 1849 and said, "Our forefathers
highly respected the arrival of their Great Father, and did instantly spread white
Beaver skins from the shore where the vessel landed to a certain tent where the
wise men and counselors were assembled together, for the Captain to walk on,"
they may have still been thinking of this prophecy, and worrying that things were
not going well between themselves, the Wisdom Keepers of Turtle Island, and
the strangers they had been told to expect. Although shared with few Europeans
until the late 1960s, the existence of the Seven Fires Prophecies has been a well
established fact for centuries, preserved by the Chippewa Medicine Society and by
a number of Midewiwin Lodges, as mentioned before. At least a few of the Munsee
who wrote the letter in 1849 would have already been instructed in the seven fires
prophecies.

The Fourth Fire of the Seven Fires Prophecies was a time period extending from
1552 to 1664. The year 1609 falls in the middle of this cycle. While Grandfather
William Commanda of Maniwaki, Quebec, Canada, holds the wampum belt of
this prophecy and has traveled extensively speaking about these ancient teachings, Eddie Benton Banaise, who is a full blooded Ojibway with a master's degree
in World Religion from the University of Toronto, is perhaps the foremost scholar
researching the significance of the Seven Fires Prophecies. He is also Medicine
Chief of the Three Fires Midewiwin Lodge and has inherited the complete oral tradition of the seven fires through his family. Recording the delivering of the fourth
fire, Banaise writes, in *The Mishomis Book:*

"The Fourth Fire was originally given to the people by two prophets. They
came as one. They told of the coming of the Light-skinned race. One of
the prophets said, "You will know the future of our people by what face
the Light-skinned Race wears. If they come wearing the face of nee-kon-
nis-i-win, (brotherhood) there will come a time of wonderful change for
generations to come. They will bring new knowledge and articles that can
be joined with the knowledge of this country. In this way, two nations will
join to make a mighty nation. This new nation will be joined by two more
[races] so that the four will form the mightiest nation of all. You will know

the face of brotherhood if the Light-skinned Race comes bearing no weapons, if they come bearing only their knowledge and a handshake."[272]

Upon reading this famous passage, one can immediately see why the Algonquins of Manhattan and elsewhere along the river were so careful with Henry Hudson. They had an abiding interest in forming a brotherhood with him. The incident at Clasons' Point was probably a case of mistaken identity and bad timing for John Colman. Whether the killing of the manta ray was the cause or not may never be resolved; it strikes at the heart of what is different between the two cultures. Hudson was wise to try to keep it a secret. Indeed, there was a lot of hand shaking and brotherhood on the way north, and as we see, Hudson shared his knowledge about the proper use of the metal tools he had brought. But there was much violence on the way south, and it is this about which we should be as concerned as those Native Americans on shore were then. Why did this have to happen? What caused it?

William Commanda, keeper of the seven fires wampum belt, once wrote, in reference to the fourth fire, that they "will live amongst our people and therefore mix the blood of our blood." This is a reference to the coming of the "rainbow race" predicted in the prophecy, a movement that New York City has been at the forefront of for years. The *New York Times* published a story on January 20, 2009, by Jodi Kantor, noting that newly inaugurated President Barack Obama had all four colors represented in his immediate family, black from the African continent, specifically Kenya; white from the European continent, specifically Irish, French and German; yellow from the Asian world, specifically Indonesia; and red from North America, specifically Cherokee, including the Gullah of the Carolinas. There is also a rabbi.[273] It was announced at that time on the news that he would be the first world leader in history to have all four "colors" in his immediate family. With this extraordinary "rainbow family" living in the White House, the Sachem Seat of Turtle Island's southern regions, one might be taken as a promising sign concerning the rainbow race prophecy and the advent of the eighth fire. Perhaps it is, but there is still much racial and cultural intolerance to be overcome, and we still have a long way to go before the spirit of the eighth fire can be lit.

The rainbow race cannot be created by assimilation. The colors of the rainbow do not lose their individual qualities, but only blend at the edges. According to William Commanda, keeper of the Seven Fires wampum belt, even if racial hatred is erased, and all people live in harmony, if we lose indigenous knowledge and the Native American way of life, which is centered on connecting with and listening to the mother earth, we will not be able to survive the purification that must still happen before the lighting of the eighth fire. To try to light it prematurely or from a purely European approach is to kill the eighth fire. William Commanda, the keeper of the seven fires belt, spent four years as a youth living in the northern wilderness, by his wits and his prayers, sometimes eating only beaver tails. He learned to make canoes from the birch trees, and snowshoes from the ash trees. His ordeal taught him strength and self-discipline and it was there he found his connection to spirit that prepared him to carry the seven fires wampum belt. He had been hiding from the agents from the residential schools. When he emerged from hiding at the age of 16, he was ready to defend his way of life; he knew he could survive without the white man's things. Today, the wilderness is weakening, the web of life is dissolving. It will be much harder for future children to do what he did then. According to Commanda, the Eighth Fire is not one you can light with matches and twigs, it is a spirit. It must be allowed to take birth at its own pace.

On September 11, 1609, matters looked well in hand, and it seemed as if the arranged marriage of at least two races, the red and the white, was going swimmingly, moving effortlessly toward the goal of racial harmony. But the fortunes of nations and of great men ebb and flow like the tides; Hudson had good fortune smiling upon him going upstream, but a bit of misfortune would follow him down. Even in the Eighth Fire, according to the teachings, we must remain vigilant, keeping an eye on those we entrust with power. Why Hudson kept entrusting Robert Juet with such power even to his last breath is a mystery, and it has affected his legacy.

Hudson's journey on the river into Wundjiyalkung was off to a great start, as was the second half of the Great Age of the Seven Fires. Hudson was a man who knew how to make a dramatic entry. The Algonquins of the Great River were in a celebratory mood. Clinton Weslager tells it this way: "This encounter supposedly occurred on Manhattan Island at a time before the Indians had seen a person with white skin or a sailing vessel. Some coastal Algonquins who were fishing in their canoes saw something on the horizon that appeared to be an uncommonly large fish or a huge canoe. They paddled to shore and reported what they had seen. Runners were sent to carry the news to their scattered chiefs, who came with their warriors to view the approach of the strange object. Meanwhile, as the vessel came closer it appeared to be a large house in which Kee-shay-lum-moo-kawng lived, and they thought he was coming to pay them a visit.

"Preperations were made to greet the Creator; the women prepared the best of foods, meat was brought for sacrifice, and arrangements were made for a dance and for entertainment."[274]

Edgar Bacon, writing in 1908, recounts a few of the many tales about the native view of Hudson's arrival on Manhattan, which seems to have been on September

11 of 1609. Whereas the previous Native American diary entries are dramatizations, the following are reportedly actual eye-witness accounts by the Delaware descendants of those who first greeted Hudson, handed down from generation to generation as part of the oral tradition. While my own "accounts" do not contradict Juet's writings in any way, (simply a matter of having read Samuel Purchas) it is impossible to match these actual accounts completely to Juet's journal. Again I warn the reader to keep Juet under close scrutiny and remember that he withholds quite a bit of information; exactly what or why we can't always guess. So we cannot say the native accounts are wrong just because they don't acknowledge or agree with his words. Bacon writes,

> *Some red men, so the tale runs, were quietly fishing, somewhere between Manhattan Island and the ocean, when one of them discovered upon the horizon an object that filled them with amazement. It suggested an enormous bird, and such they were at first inclined to think it....Gigantic birds were unheard of on that coast, and the appearance of one from the seaward side must portend some supernatural event.*
>
> *After a while, there arose a dispute, a difference of opinion between the occupants of the canoes. What had at first seemed to be a bird soon suggested some sort of a wigwam, of architectural style not hitherto known to the simple savage....The house idea rather gained ground. One of the fishermen suggested that it might be a wigwam in a canoe, but a canoe of such size and a house of such capacity as no man had ever seen before.*
>
> *Clearly this vast structure, that came towards the fascinated occupants of the canoe like a thing of life, riding the waves without the use of a paddle, and looming more and more as it approached, could be none other than the abode, or at least the vehicle, of the Manitou.*
>
> *...when the Half Moon came to an anchor, all the population of Manhattan was congregated on what is now the Battery to hail and bid it welcome.*
>
> *From the great canoe a smaller one was lowered into the water and into this descended the supreme Manitou, clad in a gorgeous coat of scarlet, with lacings of some substances brighter even than the copper of which the Indian's pipes and ornaments are made...*

This part agrees somewhat with the Munsee letter of 1849 quoted elsewhere.

HENRY HUDSON'S JOURNAL, SEPTEMBER 12 : *In latitude 40 ° 48'—It is as pleasant a land as one need tread upon; very abundant in all kinds of timber suitable for shipbuilding, and for making large casks or vats. The people had copper tobacco pipes, from which I inferred that copper might naturally exist there; and iron likewise according to the testimony of the natives, who, however, do not understand preparing it for use."*[275]

By mentioning the latitude, Hudson shows that they sailed up the west shore of Manhattan to the bay of a tributary, which was at what is now 96th Street. From old maps it looks like a great place for oysters, salt water mixed with fresh from the creek and to some extent, the river. In the month of September and at that time period, the salinity might have been 2/3 that of sea water, (20-22 ppt).[276]

"In latitude 40 ° 48'—It is as pleasant a land as one need tread upon;" In 1609, 96th Street Manhattan was indeed heavily forested, so perhaps the date is not wrong. Here they see more yellow copper, which must have been plentiful in those days, however little of it shows up in museums or in archaeological excavations today. Therefore we must conclude that most of it is in the possession of private collectors and pot hunters.[277] It is also possible the pipes were collected by the Iroquois (Hodenossuannee) at a later date as tribute. That would explain why so many metal pipes (not necessarily copper) show up in Seneca graves in New York's western regions.[278] The question still, as with the copper, is: who fashioned it into a pipe? Basque fishermen? Or the Algonquins themselves? Juet implies that these pipes really looked like native copper.

The Basque had been trading with the natives of the northeast for nearly a hundred years. "French explorers in the North Atlantic complained that coastal natives in Canada tried to address them in a kind of pidgeon Basque. One chronicle from the seventeenth century claims that Basques had taught the natives to respond to the greeting *nola zaude?* ("How are you?") with *Apaizak obeto!* ("The priests are better off!") "There is evidence that the whalers traded with natives, particularly for furs.[279]

As far as iron is concerned, it seems they pointed to something of Hudson's that was made of iron and gestured that they had some, or knew of it, but perhaps gestured that they did not know how to make it themselves. North American sign language was quite prevalent both in the northeast and in Central America and quite similar, so that a Taino or a Mi'kmaq could probably communicate with a Unami through sign language at this time, and perhaps without.[280]

Hudson's earlier journeys presumably exposed him to Indian Sign Language. He spent quite a while socializing with natives in the Maritimes a month earlier. The message "I cannot make this," can be communicated with four easily understood gestures. 1. Pointing to self, (I) 2. Hands forward and palms pressed together, with right hand an inch above the left, followed by a chopping motion; (make) 3. Pointing to the object of iron (this). And 4. Right hand turned over with palm up, (cannot) Similarly, In the grammar of NASL, "not" always comes at the end. "We've seen this before," could be expressed with four more stylized gestures.[281] It seems there was an iron mine on Canopus Island in the middle of Lake Mahopac, which was worked by natives in some way, probably for red paint. The Canopus were driven out by the British in 1671, and many departed for the Catskill Mountains, but the secret of the iron mine was not shared until sometime thereafter.[282]

As Hudson says that Manhattan "*is as pleasant a land as one need tread upon,*" we take it that he himself tread upon its rocky soil on this day, and possibly the day before, but does not say what he did there.

JUET'S JOURNAL, SEPTEMBER 12 : (Here he describes the same journey as Hudson did, so we cannot add the miles northward. It's a second opinion, as far as we're concerned.) *Very fair and hot. In the afternoon at two o'clock we weighed, the wind being variable, between the north and the north-west; so we turned into the river two leagues and anchored. This morning at our first rode in the river, there came eight and twenty canoes full of men, women and children to betray us; but we saw their intent, and suffered none of them to come aboard us. At twelve o'clock they departed. They brought with them oysters and beans, whereof we bought some. They have great tobacco pipes of yellow copper, and pots of earth to dress their meat in. It floweth south-east by south within.*

There is a rumor that the excerpts copied from Henry Hudson's journal were not dated, and that those dates were placed later, by guesswork, disconnected from the original sequence. This entry matches Juet's very closely, so we can be sure it is dated correctly.

Hudson and his crew were offered oysters on many occasions. Oysters are the food perhaps most associated with estuarine bays and rivers. New York City was one of the world's great depositories of oysters in 1609, and they were everywhere in large quantities. New York's oyster industry started to expand quickly around 1885, and hit a peak in 1900, when New Yorkers consumed over 500,000 bushels of local oysters per year. In the following years, concern about domestic pollution of oyster beds created worries about typhoid, caused by the organism *Salmonella typhosa*. In 1906, the U.S. Congress passed several "pure food" laws, and processing changed, but public opinion went against oysters. In 1924, many people, mainly in Chicago, had become ill or even died from eating oysters harvested in Raritan Bay, just south of New York City. During Prohibition, all bars, including many who provided oysters to clients, were closed, damaging the oyster industry further. New York remained a world capitol of oysters until about 1929, when stocks started to deplete, but the famed Oyster Bar in Grand Central has its legitimate origins in this major local Native American menu item.[283]

In the late 1950s, a disease called MSX caused by the *Haplosporidium nelsoni* parasite, began to kill millions of oysters in the Delaware and Chesapeake and later the James Bay estuaries. New York's remaining oyster beds would have also been affected. Another disease, *Perkinsus marinus,* added to the depletion of oysters along the Atlantic Coast.

It is interesting that Hudson did not describe pearls being worn as ornaments, but later Dutch traders found them being worn in abundance, culled not from oysters but from mussels.

Oysters harvested from particular estuaries had their own loyal followings. For oysters on the half-shell, many establishments served 10-15 varieties simultaneously. Some famous oyster names were Rockaways, Perth Amboys, and Raritan Bay oysters, harvested from those locations around New York. Gourmets claimed they could identify each one by its taste.[284] Many of the oldest shells in the middens such as at Croton Point, are about 7000 years old, however many are of more recent origin.[285]

"Very abundant in all kinds of timber suitable for shipbuilding, and for making large casks or vats." The "trees suitable for ship building" were probably Liriodendron, or "tulip trees," which are good for shipbuilding and for dugout canoes as well. They grew in abundance on Manhattan, along with oak and Scots' pine, which are excellent for ship masts. Marine wood must resist white ants, teredo, shipworm, and of course, marine rot.

Hudson would have seen "oaks, chestnut, hickory, walnut, beech, butternut, buttonwood, birch, elm, pine, maple, ash, cedar, spruce, hemlock, poplar, willow, and many other Native American trees..."[286] Elm was prized because it does not split.

"Pots of earth to dress their meats in.." seems odd to comment, but apparently they used clay pottery to "dress" meat. The beans were the kind called Turkish Beans by Dankers and Sluyter, and others, but were certainly native beans indigenous to the area. There were many kinds of pottery being used. This is also called grog or "tempering," and may be made of sand, crushed shell, crushed rock, fired clay or vegetable fibers. One Richmond style castled pot I saw had a kind of grout in the clay apparently made from ground-up black flint powder, perhaps from deboutage.[287]

M.S. Smith sees them traveling from Battery Park to 86 Street. Hudson believes he is at 40 degrees 48 minutes, which is 91st Street to be exact, but I would place him the same distance in the opposite direction, at 96th Street, for reasons mentioned earlier. According to Hall, they were on Liberty Island, or perhaps Governor's Island still. Allan Keller places them at Yonkers, but the latitude is wrong.

What might they have seen, sailing four or so miles northward along the west side of Manhattan? At least some rubbernecking was in order. Less than a mile up the shore was a little stream where the Dutch later built a water mill. That water mill is now the site of the entrance of the Holland Tunnel. One of the first areas they would have come upon was a small hook of sand stretching into the Hudson, creating a perfect harbor for canoes, and nearby, a verdant cornfield. Just to the south of it was the entrance to a beautiful trail, surrounded by blossoming bushes and trees. It ran slightly uphill into the cluster of garden-like bushes. Just up the pathway was a large palisaded fort, used as a trading post. This was the Sapohannikan Trail, and the palisaded fort made of ten foot high cedar logs was the Sapohannikan Fort.

Corn and other trade goods were stacked high everywhere around the fort, and men were busy moving goods here and there. This stretch of the trail is now Gansevoort Street, part of the grimy meat packing district with its sticky cobblestone streets. David De Vries bought a plantation near here some time in the 1630s, with thirty-one morgens of maize-land already cleared.[288]

The edge of the landing was where the first U.S. Customs house was built. The street was named after Peter Gansevoort, a friend of George Washington's who helped the American colonies win the Revolution and who was named the first Head of Customs. Among others, whaling ships would come into port to declare their valuables for sale. Peter Gansevoort's grandson Herman Melville also worked at that customs house, absorbed the stories he heard from the whalers and wrote *Moby Dick* in which the character Tashtego was an Algonkian whaling expert, the shamanic and spiritual guide of the ship.

Around the palisaded fort was a cleared area, and a star-like crisscrossing of trails brought traders to this fort from all directions. Today there is a large vacant plaza of cobblestones, the only one like in it New York City. The Dutch would build a tavern nearby within twenty-odd years, and the fort would remain under Native American control until 1666. There was a coastal trail along the edge of Manhattan next to the Hudson that we now call Greenwich Street. The Sapohannikan Trail continued across the island, southeast towards a good crossing place for Minetta Brook. (It is now Greenwich Avenue.) Beyond that, the trail heads north again, to the Kintecoying, the powwow dancing grounds at Cooper Union Square. Then it continues to Stuyvesant Place and St. Mark's Chapel, built by Peter Stuyvesant. Beyond that is the site of the old Shepmoes Village, along Shepmoes' Creek, now St. Mark's Place (aka. 8th Street).

The Half Moon continued northward, along the shore of Manhattan. There was a small island at the mouth of a winding stream at 42nd Street, which had plenty of elbow room to bend south and then north again to the corner of 45th

Street and 7th where it was fed by a babbling spring. That spring is now near the site of the old New York Times building, a national landmark.

As they continued north they would have seen a small inlet at 60th Street. At 67th Street there was a bay, or large inlet fed by two small streams, and at 79th Street was the V-shaped mouth of a small stream, that wound down the slope of Manhattan Island to the west. At 96th Street, there was yet another sizable bay, near where Michael Sullivan Smith thinks they anchored for the night. All of these waterways are now paved over.

O'Callaghan writes, "Throughout the whole country, vegetation was rapid and all the natural productions luxuriant, owing to the constant decomposition of vegetable matter—plants, wild grass, and the deciduous foliage—which, annually dying, furnished an ever-renewing supply of rich manure."[289]

There were two or three major trails that passed through the wilds of upper Manhattan. One was of course Broadway, which split into two post roads. One was called the Mohican Trail, and crossed into the Bronx past Marble Hill, at what we call Kingsbridge. The other, the Path to the Wading Place crossed at 5th and 90th Street. In colonial times there was a Harlem bridge at 3rd Avenue and 106th to 109th, which must have had native ancestry.

But there were many other trails just out of view. The Bowery was a trail that met with the Path to the Wading Place (5th Avenue) at the location of our 23rd Street. The Dutch called that 5th Avenue trail Euner Beinhauer Middle Road.

Some seem to think Hudson was located much further upstream, at Inwood Hill. There is a statue of Henry Hudson on top of the cliff above Spuyten Duyvel, at a place called Nipnischsen, "where two rivers meet." There was a Native American fort built there, and it appears to be true that Hudson's ship was attacked from that fort on the way back. The statue there of Hudson, erected in 1909, is by Karl Bitter.[290] Author Harry Hansen writes, "The island of Manhattan was separated from the mainland by a small erratic creek that the Dutch called Spuyten Duyvel. The English thought it meant Spitting Devil...it proceeded from a brook that flowed on the western base of the...hill in Riverdale...flowed through Marble Hill to West 230th Street."[291]

An armada of twenty-eight canoes came at once, each one bearing probably six to ten people. Although there were well over 200 people on the river coming to see them (8x28=224) they were women and children more than men, and so it is unlikely they were a war party. Juet is overreacting when he says, "... *men, women and children to betray us; but we saw their intent, and suffered none of them to come aboard us.*" Juet seemed to think these might be Siwanoy again, and was petrified by the thought of encountering the "savages" that killed John Colman, but it was hardly possible. There was no easy water passage between the East River and the Spuyten Duyvel in those days before the Harlem Channel was built in 1903. Marble Hill was in the way, literally a "marble hill" rich with deposits of Dravite crystals, which the Algonquins of the area considered sacred. According to Dutch records, some would make the crystals into ornaments for the body, however if they did, it apparently is not remembered as part of the Delaware oral tradition today. The Army Corps of Engineers blasted through hundreds of tons of marble and crystal in order to build the waterway in 1903, a project which turned the Harlem River, an estuary, into a strait, shortened Manhattan, and placed much of Tibbet's Brook, called Moshulou by the natives, "a field that has been cleared by burning," underground. It also left Manhattan's Marble Hill in the Bronx, and the island at Kingsbridge underground as well.

If it was the Siwanoy, and not his own men that started the fight on September 6, and if it was only Colman who died and no Siwanoy warriors, why would he think they'd be so far afield looking for them? Surely they would be satisfied with such a one-sided victory, if Juet is telling us the whole story. Perhaps there is more. Some suggest Colman did something awful to annoy the Siwanoy, and that is why they were constantly in pursuit of Hudson, and why Juet feared them. But Juet feared everything.

In any case, it couldn't have been the Siwanoy, who would have to wait three hundred more years for the Harlem Channel to be built. Where were these people coming from? The Weckweeskeck fort atop the cliff called Nipnichsen ("Two Rivers"?) Paparinemin, at Kingsbridge, a Weckweeskeck "island of fire" and the main crossing place to enter Manhattan from the north? We don't know.

Paparinemin means "diverting aside," as the waters of two streams, the Moshulou (later called Tibbet's Brook) and the Muskooten or Kikeshika (later Harlem River), collided there and diverted aside, one flowing into the sound and one flowing into the Mohicannituck (later the Hudson). It was a main defensive point for the entire island of Manhattan, which the British, after 1664, made a great effort to control, hence the name King's Bridge. It was situated on the west bank of Tibbet's Brook. The crossing of what is now Broadway was on the east side.

Bolton writes: "The present Kingsbridge, an island in ancient times and a favorite resort of the Reckgawawanc. Shell-pits and objects attest its use as a place of residence; a fine earthen vessel now in the Museum of the American Indian, Heye Foundation, was found at 231st Street by Calver and Bolton."[292]

Bolton writes, "[Chief]Reckgawac's sale of Harlem land...at Yorkville, at Harlem, on Washington Heights, and at Inwood, as well as on the *island of Kingsbridge...* seems quite definite." It seems that the sachem of the Weckweeskeck who supposedly sold Peter Minuit Manhattan in Novermber of 1626 was from Paperinemin.

According to lore, they planted a tulip tree at Shorakapkock (spellings differ) at what is now Inwood Hill Park. A rock with a commemorative plaque now stands at the site of the tulip tree. The inscription on the plaque reads:

> SHORAKKOPOCH [alternate spelling of Shorapapkock]
> ACCORDING TO LEGEND, ON THIS SITE OF THE PRINCIPAL
> MANHATTAN INDIAN VILLAGE, PETER MINUIT IN 1626, PURCHASED
> MANHATTAN ISLAND FOR TRINKETS AND BEADS THEN WORTH ABOUT
> 60 GUILDERS. THIS BOULDER ALSO MARKS THE SPOT WHERE A TULIP
> TREE (LIRIODENDROM TULIPIFERA) GREW TO A HEIGHT OF 165 FEET
> AND A GIRTH OF 20 FEET. IT WAS, UNTIL ITS DEATH IN 1938 AT THE
> AGE OF 280 YEARS, THE LAST LIVING LINK WITH THE RECKGAWANC
> INDIANS WHO LIVED HERE.
> DEDICATED AS PART OF NEW YORK CITY'S 300 ANNIVERSARY
> CELEBRATION BY THE PETER MINUIT POST 1247.

The crew did buy some oysters, and also beans. This is the first mention in Juet's diary of beans, the littlest of the Lenape's "three sisters." First came squashes, and gourds. (Whether they could have known watermelons or not in 1609 is a point greatly disputed.)The natives developed a taste for squash blossoms, a delicacy that is still appreciated by old timers. Then came the middle sister, corn, slowly developing between 200 and 1100 CE, becoming more cultivated with age. Finally the natives of the New York area were introduced to beans around 1300. [293] No one ever said the "three sisters," corn, beans and squash, were triplets!

Again yellow copper is mentioned. It was apparently quite common then, but there is none left today, and no new veins of it being found anywhere.

JUET'S JOURNAL, SUNDAY, SEPTEMBER 13 : *Fair weather; the wind northerly; at seven o'clock in the morning, as the flood came we weighed and turned four miles into the river; the tide being done we anchored. Then there came four canoes aboard, but we suffered none of them to come into our ship; they brought very great store of very good oysters aboard, which we bought for trifles. In the night I set the variation of the compass, and found it to be 13 degrees. In the afternoon we weighed and turned in with the flood two leagues and a half further and anchored all night, and had five fathoms soft oozy ground, and had a high point of land, which shewed out to us, bearing north by east five leagues of us.*

"Then there came four canoes aboard, but we suffered none of them to come into our ship; they brought very great store of very good oysters aboard, which we bought for trifles." The area of the five boroughs has always hidden great stores of oysters in its waters. *History of Westchester County* states that the ship is anchored on the opposite side of the river from the present town of Yonkers. "The dawn of the following day disclosed the residents of the village of Nappeckamak gathered upon the eastern shore, and viewing with wonder, but with a kindly interest, the strange revelation before them."[294] Nappeckamak is a planting field near a fish trapping place. That would be Untermeyer Park, and the fish trapping place is next to the large waterfall now underground, east of the train station, where Larkin Plaza and Warburton meet.[295]

"In the afternoon we weighed and turned in with the flood two leagues and a half further and anchored all night, and had five fathoms soft oozy ground, and had a high point of land, which shewed out to us, bearing north by east five leagues of us." It was the full moon that night, what the natives called "The Red Leaf Moon." A nice companion for the night owl Juet, who would have enough white light to add onto his precious dairy his meticulous scratchings just visible without a lamp. It was rising in the east, so if the high point of Spuyten Duyvel Hill were to their right, it would have shone brightly in the moonlight, or "shewed out to us." Five leagues is at least 11 miles. Juet's language is abstract like Haiku, but it seems they sailed towards the high point eleven miles until they reached the base of it at Inwood Park. This high point would have been Spuyten Duyvel Hill, and the fort would be the one called "Nipnischen, ("Two Rivers"). There was another fort in the area of Harlem, possibly facing Wards' Island at 105th St. It appears that they continued north, past Spuyten Duyvel Hill by the light of the moon, until they reached the shore opposite Yonkers, and dropped anchor.

Let us assume for a moment they were at Yonkers. It is commonly said that the word Yonkers is probably "from *jonker* meaning a "young squire" or from *jonkheer* meaning "young nobleman" or "gentleman," referring to the honorific applied to Adriaen van der Donck, who acquired his estate in 1645 where Yonkers is now situated." [296] However, given the probability of word play on the loose with such an odd place name, we need to look deeper.

The tribal group who lived at that spot were the Nepperan, who may have been called the Montawak in Algonquin times, relatives of the Matouac, the Renneiu-speaking people of Long Island. Like Matouac, Montawak implies "young men" ("those, including women, who frequent small islands" is implied) and Yonkers is the English interpretation of the Dutch translation *Jangers*, for young men. I presume that the reason the Matouac called themselves "young men" was because a large part of the population seems to have been descendanded from immigrants from what is now Puerto Rico, the "new kids on the block," even though those first Taino Indian immigrants had passed away 150 or so years earlier, of old age.

The Saw Mill River, or Nepperan, empties into the Hudson at Yonkers. This

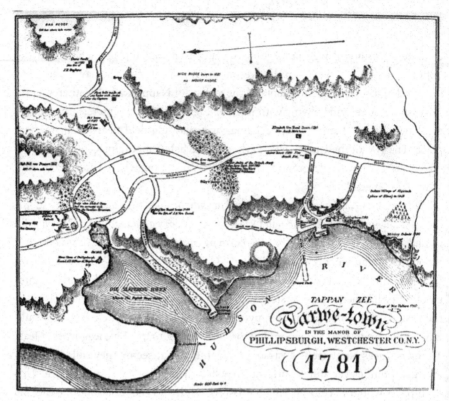

TAPPAN ZEE

𝕮𝖆𝖗𝖜𝖊-𝖙𝖔𝖜𝖓

IN THE MANOR OF

PHILLIPSBURGH, WESTCHESTER CO.N.Y.

((1781))

important river was made into a canal and now flows under the city, though there are plans to open it up again. The terminus (where fresh water begins) of this estuarial river was a "pawtucket" or waterfall, fresh water cascading over a ridge into salty. The ridge is still visible elsewhere, north of the enclosed outlet. The waterfall, in alignment with the eastern wall at Warburton Street to the north, at one time circled to the north before exiting into the Hudson.

Just to the east of the waterfall is an island and a crossing place, also now underground. This island was called Chicken Island by later settlers, and that trail, the old Mohican Trail, is now Route 9, Broadway, and it crosses the Saw Mill there, but deep under the ground. This was paved over and is now Getty Square. This small island was most likely a council fire or rendezvous spot in early times. According to *History of Westchester County,* Henry Hudson landed here on September 13, 1609 and captured two native men.

The *raan* in Neppe-raan is a Renneiu (probably Siwanoy) variant of *wan*, a fresh water stream running into salty. Nepperham is an English interpretation, and Nepperham Street generally runs along the shores of the covered-up creek, now called the Saw Mill. Harry Hansen writes that the original word for Yonkers was Nappechamack, which is translated as a "trap fishing place," but the ending indicates a field.[297] This trap fishing place was "where the Nepperhan flows into the Hudson."[298] Hansen notes alternative spellings for the river's name, including Neperan, (my choice) Neperhan, Neperhaein, and Nepperhan.[299] Its source is northeast of Tarrytown at a place the natives called Wiquaskeck, from Wiquajek, "head of the creek," and the name of their village there. This village is probably now under the Kensico Reservoir. The creek at that elevation is called "Saw Mill Run" today,[300] and as the term "run" is only used in North America, mainly in Eastern Algonquin territory, there is every reason to believe it is an English word "borrowed" from the Wappingers/Powhatan "run," or creek. There was another creek in Yonkers known to the Algonquins as *Amackassin*,[301] probably from "moccasin," or shoe.

The original Philipse Manor Hall still stands on the hill above Dock Street, used from 1682 to 1745. Philipse received his patent from Sir Edmund Andros, April 1, 1680 for much of Westchester and Putnam Counties.[302] This Manor Hall, plus the restored Philipse Castle and the Old Dutch Church are "the only structures that remain of the large Philipse estate."[303] In 1684, Kawanghis, a sunksquaw, participated in the deed for the "Neppiran" tract in Yonkers.[304]

Frederick Philipse, who came over to America from Holland in 1647 on the same ship as Peter Stuyvesant, was originally a carpenter, but he began to make his own wampum and trade it to the Indians for furs; he traded with everyone, but made his fortune through marriages to two wealthy widows Margaret Hardenbroeck, and after her death, Catharyna Van Cortlandt Dervall. He bought land from the Wappingers and amassed over 90,000 acres along the Hudson River. Cassidy writes, "Philipse took over a Dutch saw mill and built a manor house at Yonkers, where the Nepperhan [now the Saw Mill named after the one he bought] River runs into the Hudson. He put up a grist mill and a stone house, which he called his "castle," at Philipsburg, where the Pocantico River joins the Hudson. These places were known then as "Lower Mills" and "Upper Mills."

History of Westchester County describes Yonkers as the largest in Westchester of several villages of the "Manhattan" Indians, although this is stated unclearly. The term Manhattan Indian seems to be a generic term for those who live on Manhattan, regardless of tribal affiliation, and the Rechgawawank were the most prominent at the north end of Manhattan,[305] and on coastal inlets along Manhattan's shores. Their sachemdom seat was at Yonkers, hence the confusion. They were Renneiu-speaking people who occupied mostly sandy, coastal areas at the mouths of streams. This would reinforce the possibility that Yonkers is from "Matouac," as both were coastal peoples.

"At the southern end of the original township of Yonkers, overlooking the Hudson River...and Spuyten Duyvel Creek (Papirinimen) they had a fortress which they called Nipinichsen."[306] According to this source, "they" are the Manhattan Indians in their northern expression, an extension of the Nappeckamak.

Chapter Six

PEOPLE OF THE WATERFALLS

*T*he following entries from Juet's journal, September 14 to September 22 describe the Europeans' experiences along the middle part of the river as they are headed north. While the peoples towards the mouth of the Hudson experience the estuary as a marshy, wide open, salty bay, prone to winds and storms and home to great whales and porpoises, the people of the upper river are more apt to prize the protective canyons of the tributaries along the shores.

These canyons usually feature beautiful waterfalls created as the tributaries cascade and tumble down the slopes of mountains and hills towards the deep valley. If towering forests are indeed the "cathedrals" of the "woodland Indian," these narrow, protected hollows where waterfalls hypnotically gush forth are their chapels. One waterfall over to the west, in Munsee territory, is called, appropriately, Pataukunk, "the waterfall where we pray." It is the only one so named, but it speaks for all of them.

The native words for "at the side of a rocky hill or mountain," (kong) and "a waterfall pouring down the side of a mountain" (hong) sound very similar. Honk is clearly plural for waterfall, and konk is plural for mountain, meaning "near the mountains," as the suffix K is plural, however here the ear is fooled because honk (waterfalls) is preceded by the plural for prayer Patauk. Patau clearly means "to pray," as the word in Munsee for praying is Patau (or Pachtau), and so Patauk is "to make prayers." [307] I believe that the root Pach-ta for prayer was later "Double Dutched" to Pater, the Latin word for God, hence the two spellings. (The Munsee would drop the R) As the Munsee word for God is "that to which we pray," and prayer is that which we say to God, there is an appropriately reciprocal logic there, which is something to contemplate while watching the swirls and eddies below the falls.

The following is from "The Complete Official Program, Ottawa Centenary,

August 16-21, 1926: "They go through a peculiar ceremony accurately described by Champlain the founder of Quebec, who was here in June 1613. It is called the Tobacco Dance. All dances of the Indians were fraught with symbolism and cryptic (?) meaning and seems to have constituted an important adjunct [to] rather than basis of the social, military, religious, and other activities and were designed to avoid evil and secure welfare. Bits of tobacco gathered on a wooden platter were thrown into the seething waters of the Chaudiere [*Asticou* in Algonquin, "a cauldron", the name of the waterfall] as a propitiary offering to the Manitoo or spirit."[308]

There are a number of drawings from the early contact period showing the sacred pipe being smoked at the island at the base of Chaudiere Falls, and explorers such as Champlain described ceremony going on around the falls itself. Champlain reported that it was here that he accidentally fell in the water and found himself in a highly dangerous situation, which frightened him with the possibility of imminent death. According to William Commanda, Champlain in fact drowned. He was rescued by people of the Asinabka village, (possibly located on the island of Hull) and gladly did prayer ceremony with them celebrating his recovery. He found these ceremonies, which would have included tobacco being placed in the water, very helpful and from that point on was very open-minded about Algonquin spirituality. It seems appropriate to honor those "rescue workers" by honoring their island, and also to honor their spiritual traditions, as Samuel de Champlain did. A red ochre burial ground was found during the construction of the National Treasury which is located just to the east of the falls at the crest of the bank.

I knew Pataukunk well. There is a small, hand carved wooden sign on a pole even today marking the spot where the Samsonville road passes through Pataukunk. And it was certainly near some hills. But when I realized that the spot that gave Pataukunk its name was a waterfall less than two miles from that little sign, all the pieces of the puzzle fell together for me. Pataukunk doesn't just mean "where we should pray," it means "The waterfall pouring down the rocks where we should make prayers," It was the proof I was looking for, and a powerful statement about Algonkian spiritual values. The small letters on the topo map had a message for modern man, "waterfalls are for praying."

There is other evidence for this conclusion.

Former Sand Hill Band Chief, Dr. Sam Beeler, recently told Robin Hill-Chandler, "tribes from all over the eastern sea coast would meet at Paterson, N.J.['s Passaic Falls, derived from Pow-saic, deep valley of the waterfall] for 'peace' talks. They would meet even if they were on bad terms. If seems that at the falls there would be a lot of fish and feasting and good will would follow."[309]

This reverence for waterfalls is not exclusive to the Delaware by any means. A Cherokee medicine man living with the Sand Hill Band of New Jersey, recounted how in the old days waterfalls were considered sacred. Rivers were called "long people" and the falls on a river were considered to be a place of ceremony, the heart of the "long person."[310] Waterfalls are the river's heart and sacred places of meditation and ceremony for many aboriginal cultures around the world. Mary Pat Fisher writes, "In New Zealand, the traditional Maori people know of the re-vivifying power of running water, such as waterfalls (now understood by scientists as places of negative ionization, which do indeed have an energizing effect). The Maori elders have told the public of the curative power of a certain waterfall on North Island; the area is dedicated to anyone who needs healing.[311]

But the old Cherokee added something that many had forgotten. "The bottom of the falls was the place where cleansing happened, not just of the physical body, but old hurts, bad feelings, and ill health were cleansed away too. Even relationships were healed at the base of a waterfall. This process would lead to a new beginning for the people participating in the ceremony."[312]

Abenaki author and PhD scholar Joseph Bruchac, when asked if waterfalls were sacred and important to Algonquian culture, responded, "Absolutely! It just goes without saying! You can't always prove something like that about a particular waterfall, but everybody involved in traditional culture would know it! They are all sacred, every one of them."

For centuries, the Scatacooks, for example, lived at the falls at New Milford, Connecticut, until there were only about thirty of them. When their "teachers," the Moravian missionaries, left for Bethlehem, Pennsylvania, the Scatacooks scattered, some going to Stockbridge, Massachusetts, some to Bethlehem, some to Scatacook, some to Kent, some to the banks of the Hudson, some elsewhere. By 1774, there were no Scatacooks still living in New Milford, but they still held their rights to this fishing place. Even in 1849, John William de Forest (quoting John Warner Barber) observed "when a straggler presents himself, his claims are acknowledged, and he is allowed his turn." There are two cemeteries somewhat near the falls. "One is on the west side of the river opposite the village; another on the east side at no great distance from the ancient residence of the sachem. Many of the graves have great trees of considerable size growing out of them. The mounds are circular in shape, and, on opening them, the skeletons are found in a sitting posture. The grave of Weraumaug is still supposed to be known, and differs from the others only in being of large dimensions."[313]

Ojibway author and professor, Gabriel Horn, (White Deer of Autumn), when asked, stated that waterfalls were at the heart of Algonquian tradition, and commented that there were scientific as well as spiritual reasons for meditating at waterfalls, noting that the negative ions generated at waterfalls were very powerful healers. He also described the hypnotic and deep-relaxation-inducing qualities of the visual and sonic elements, different for each waterfall. As White Deer described it to me, each waterfall has a unique and different "song" from any other in the world. Each of these songs were medicine. They changed from season to season, and from one part of the cascade to another, but all were powerful healers in different ways." He also added that when he and some traditional friends founded the American Indian Movement (AIM) in Minnesota, they did ceremony together at the base of St. Joseph's Falls, one of the largest in North America, right on the Mississippi, and also at Hiawatha Falls, nearby. The decision as to location did not even have to be discussed. They all knew instinctively that waterfalls were the ideal places to conduct such high ceremony. The organization has undergone many changes since those idealistic days, but it is still very much intact almost forty years later.

There are no waterfalls in the main course of the Hudson River until Troy, New York, but there are dozens of beautiful waterfalls on each side, gracing with an extra splash of beauty almost every tributary that leads down to the Hudson. In honor of the quadricentennial, the Garrison Institute, whose mission statement is dedicated to the notion that rivers and spirituality are intimately linked, hopes to repair the trails to some of the waterfalls along the Hudson and provide audio self-guided tours to help hikers understand the connection between Native American spirituality and these still-vibrant chapels of the forest.

The people on the readily accessible east bank speak the same languages as those to the south; Renneiu (R dialect speakers, including Wappingers, Canarsie, etc.) on the east bank, and predominantly Munsee (with another R dialect, either Renneiu or Owasco remnant here and there) to the west. And they are part of an ancient estuarial culture as are those just to the south, but responding to a different part of the same watershed.

This remarkable stretch of river is the central realm of the Wappingers, the "Houghland Indians." In a real sense, they are the people of the waterfalls. Up to this point, Hudson has been meeting and greeting mainly members of the lowland Matouac culture, those connected to the cradle of Long Island. As the Matouac people moved north, they changed, marrying into families who call themselves "men of the east," or Wappanoes, later Wappingers.

The Wappingers

According to most accounts, the Wappingers Confederacy was a loosely organized chain of tribal nations most of them situated along the east bank of the Hudson, an area known for waterfalls. Among the nations that can be counted in this group are the Mana-hattans, (including the Rechwanis, Shepmoes, and Rechkawonks) Weckweeskecks (including Matouac, Wyskwaqua, Quorropus), Kitchewank, Sintsink, Patchem, Nochpeem, Matouac, and Wappingers (Indians of the Long Reach) proper. Further to the east are Siwanoy, Tenkitekes, Kent and Wicopee. Very little is known about a Connecticut group called Sequins.

The Wappingers are what anthropologists call Delawarian (but not "Lenape") peoples, whose territory was originally Mohican, who became distinct from the Mohican in the 1300s. A new group of people with probable Caribbean roots migrated up from Long Island, most notably of Canarsie stock, and intermarried with the northern Algonquian peoples of the region to create a new culture.

We know this for sure by the introduction of what is called Clasons Point material culture in the archaeological record, as clearly established by William Ritchie, the greatest of New York State archaeologists. The group that spread Clasons point material culture developed politically out of the Canarsie. The boundaries of the main area of Canarsie territory are more or less the boundaries of Brooklyn today, however the Canarsie also controlled lower Manhattan below Houston Street and east of the Bowery, to 14th Street. They also controlled all islands around Manhattan and were masters of the waterways. The "new" Wappingers inherited not only many words from their language but their ease with canoe travel. The Canarsie seem to have had many influences from the Quiskaian peoples of what is now the Dominican Republic, some of which may date back to 1300, while others may date back to the exodus of Tainos from Hispaniola during the conquest of the islands by Columbus.[314]

The term Wappingers was originally Wappings, (Wapani[315]) or "Eastern People." These were the people of lower eastern New York state and extreme western Connecticut and identified themselves with the Mohicans, (Muheakannuk) a people strongly identified with estuaries. The term Mohican derives from Mohicannituk, which I break down as *maugh* a superlative indicating the largest and greatest of all;[316] *hikan*, a river that ebbs and flows; although in several documented cases, and agreed upon by Electa Jones, Brinton and Trumbull, it means "sea" or "sea water"[317] as in an estuary; and *-ituk*, a stream, although in my research I have never found a *tuk* that is not tidal and salty at its base. Jones indicated that such a river would "flow both ways."

Mohicannituck refers to the Hudson, an estuary that is almost an inland sea. However, many of the people referred to as Mohicans in Dutch times were north of the Hudson River estuary's terminus at the steep rapids now the Troy dam in Troy, New York. The Wappings were located much more in the heart of the estuary region, and were the caretakers of most of the waterfalls mentioned above.

Some Wappingers today still refer to themselves as "Mohicans" out of respect for tradition, although the Wappingers language is the Taconic dialect of the Renneiu language (much like Quiripi of Connecticut and the Canarsie of Brooklyn). It is distinctly different from the Mohican written down in catechisms by Hendrick Apaumut, a Mohican chief, in the 1600s.

Cassidy states, "The Wappingers, sometimes known in English as the Wappanachki, meaning in the Indian language "Men of the East," lived along the east bank of the Hudson River from Manhattan to Dutchess County. They were Algonquins, members of a widely-dispersed group of North American tribes, linked by speech in a single linguistic family."[318]

Cassidy describes the Wappingers in less than glowing terms, propagating the usual stereotypes about laziness and sloth: "The Indians, at first, caused no trouble. They were tall men, lean in their leather loin clouts, leggings and moccasins, clean with their shaven heads and scalp locks. They were no good for work, unless to carry an occasional message, which they did with great willingness and speed, but they were cheerful, friendly neighbors."[319]

This image does not match the one we have of Daniel Nimham, confronting lawyers, magistrates and governors and challenging them on the loopholes in the terms of the land treaty known as the Rombout Patent. Daniel made his own way to London and back to seek audience with the King, but was refused. Perhaps the King was afraid of the legal mind of this Wappinger who was "no good for work."

As many Shawnee, Canarsie, and people from the Caribbean came into the lower Wapping area and intermarried with the Wappings, so they could no longer call themselves "Eastern People." These new people were from the south. However, if they changed their name to anything else, they would lose their longstanding identity as a nation. Today, we would not think of changing West Virginia's name just because people from eastern Virginia moved there, but Algonquin political systems are people-oriented, not state-oriented.

The Wappingers in particular were very progressive and sensitive to multicultural issues. They changed their name to Wappingus, which means possum in several different interpretations, either from "mu-wap-pink-us," (he has no fur on his tail) or "wap-ping-us," or "little white face." Some have said the name is similar to "Wapendragers" which is Dutch for "weaponbearers," probably another case of "Double Dutch."

The Algonquin languages in everyday use lend themselves nicely to puns, and wordplay was the rule, not the exception, even in serious matters, as we shall see. The possum is not a totem or power animal. The possum was an animal of scorn because it was said they robbed human graves as a source of food, and reverence for one's ancestors ranked higher than most other considerations, so we clearly have a "gang" type of naming phenomenon. The original "gang" (the Wappings) stayed north of the Wappingers Creek and north of the east-west line extending from Mawenawasik, where the two main branches converge.[320] These were the ones also known as "Indians of the Long Reach." They remained closely linked to the Mohicans, and retained the custom of having Mohican chiefs approve and sign land deeds. The split-off group became known as the Wappingus, now Wappingers and stayed south of the Wappingers Creek, covering a vast territory, now including not only shoreline parts of Manhattan, but the Bronx, Westchester, Putnam and Dutchess counties.

The extent of what can be called Wappingers territory has been disputed. Most Wappingers did not primarily call themselves that, but those in Dutchess county did. In an affidavit recorded in Albany by "King Nimham" in 1730, who would have been Daniel Nimham's grandfather, it is stated that the tribe of "river Indians," the Wappinoes" were "the ancient inhabitants of the eastern shore of Hudson's River from the City of New York to about the middle of Beekman's Patent."[321] This is in agreement with what Ruttenber wrote in his *Indians of Hudson's River*. Some Wappingers lived above the Beekman patent. For example, in 1956 at Cruger Island, Funk and Ritchie identified both Wappingers and Mohican artifacts in the late-pre-contact strata. Such cohabitation seems to have been common above the old boundary markers at Rhinebeck.

The presiding sachem in the 1683 Rombout Patent's name was spelled "Megriesken," however it can be assumed to be a variant of Amorgarikakan. The first signature actually says "Sakoraghkigh" but this means "high chief" in Wappingers, and Megriesken was the ruling family's name.[322] So in a sense, we don't know what the person's real name was who presided over the treaty that gave birth to Beacon, Fishkill, and Wappingers Falls.

Placenames in Wappingers' R dialect show up in Staten Island, in Ramapough territory on the New York/New Jersey border, and on the west side of the river. We will deal with these as they come up. The Wappingers' various holdings, and ultimately the northern Wappings, all became unified into a confederacy (not necessarily for the first time) under the rule of the family of Amorgarikakan (dozens of spellings). We see this name on the Rombout Patent in Beacon, NY, in Staten Island, Saugerties, and around Newburgh. This name is generally translated from Taino trade language as it has no Wappingers meaning. *Amor* (love, Spanish) *gwa* (love, Taino) *rika* (lord, Spanish) *khan* (lord, Taino). This family approved and signed deeds much as the Mohicans had done for their uncles to the north. The most famous was Kaelkop ("Old Bald Head" in Dutch) whose real name was possibly "Kaelkoptl" which has several Taino interpretations, similar to Quetzalquatl. (It is believed, in the oral tradition, that some of the Taino traders of 1000 BCE intermarried with the local Algonquins, but other than comparing similar "killed pottery," it is hard to trace in the historical record. It is also said that the Wappingers sachems or sagamores were descended from these Taino/Wappingers marriages, at least from 1300 onward.)[323]

The long line of the Nimham family of chiefs, outlined in the appendix of *Native New Yorkers,* were under the jurisdiction of the Amorgarikakan family, and probably not related, although it would not be surprising to find that they were. It is often observed that the name Amorgarikakan sounds Mayan or at least from the Caribbean. Many such names appear in Munsee and Wappingers territory. In 1677, the local natives deeded a plot of land near Springtown Road in present-day Rosendale which they referred to as "Tawaeri Taqui." Ta in Taino infers "sacred," and Tawaeri Taqui implies sacred land and sacred blood, perhaps a church site or a place where sacred offerings were made.

> JUET'S JOURNAL, MONDAY, SEPTEMBER 14 : *In the morning being very fair weather, the wind south-east, we sailed up the river twelve leagues, and had five fathoms and five fathoms and a quarter less, and came to a strait between two points, and had eight, nine and ten fathoms; and it trended north-east by north one league, and we had twelve, thirteen and fourteen fathoms; the river is a mile broad; there is very high land on both sides. Then we went up north-west, a league and a half deep water; then north-east by north five miles; then north-west by north two leagues and anchored. The land grew very high and mountainous; the river is full of fish.*

Michael Sullivan Smith pointed out to me that this entry is the key to deciphering the entire journal, as the river's crooked path is so distinctive at this point. Juet is clearly trying to estimate a 2.2 mile league, as Lossing supposed in his book of 1866 *The Hudson River,* but varies by a half mile over or under. If Smith's map is right about their locations on September 14, Juet is unable to maintain such a perfect standard league, and is using recognizable landmarks, estimating the distances between them. He was, I conclude, winging it.

"...*In the morning being very fair weather, the wind south-east, we sailed up the river twelve leagues and had five fathoms and five fathoms and a quarter less, and came to a strait between two points...*" If the wind pulls the sail into it, the wind was blowing towards the southeast, pulling them northwest. It is twelve miles due north from the center of the river at Hasting on Hudson to Croton Point, and six more miles headed northwest from Croton Point to the strait between two points, which is clearly the passage between Stony Point on the west and Indian Point on the east, a crossing place. This means that Juet's league was 1.5 statute miles at this entry, however as the river is very broad at this latitude, they might have tacked back

Croton Point Peninsula

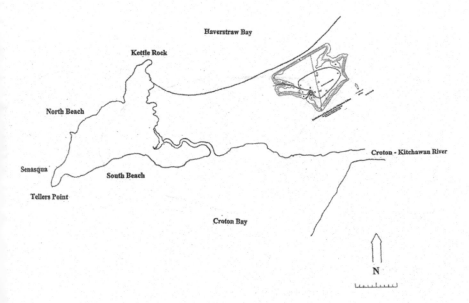

and forth. This leads me to believe Juet's leagues were based on time of travel as well as visual distance.

Although Juet does not comment, there was a fairly large population right on these shores, and even on these points. "The Sint Sinks had a village called Ossing-sing, where "The Kill" empties into the Hudson at Sing Sing. They had a smaller village at the mouth of the Kitchawan or Croton River."[324] There was also a village near the first waterfall of Ossining Creek, which is hidden in the bottom of a deep canyon. The bridge at Central Avenue crosses over it at such a height it cannot be seen from the road.

"The Kitchawancs had a large village upon Van Cortlandt's Neck, connecting Croton Point with the mainland. They had here the strongest fortress of any in the county. Like Nipinichsen, it was a heavily-palisaded stockade. They had another village upon Verplanck's Point [hence the name "Indian Point"] and a larger one called Sackhoes, where Peekskill now stands."[325]

"... had eight, nine and ten fathoms; and it trended north-east by north one league.." Above Indian Point, the Hudson veers sharply to the northeast for a distance of three miles to the Peekskill Inlet at the mouth of Annsville Creek. Here Juet's league is three miles, or perhaps a little less.

"...and we had twelve, thirteen and fourteen fathoms; the river is a mile broad; there is very high land on both sides." The river is one statute mile across from the mouth of Annsville Creek to Jones Point on the west bank. When you are at this point

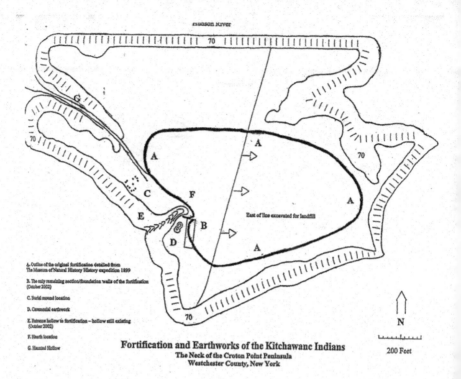

Fortification and Earthworks of the Kitchawanc Indians
The Neck of the Croton Point Peninsula
Westchester County, New York

A. Outline of the original fortification detailed from
The Museum of Natural History History expedition 1899

B. The only remaining section/foundation walls of the fortification
(October 2002)

C. Burial mound location

D. Ceremonial earthwork

E. Entrance hollow to fortification – hollow still existing
(October 2002)

F. Hearth location

G. Haunted Hollow

200 Feet

in the river, you see a southern view of Bear Mountain towering to the west at an altitude of 1284 feet and Manitou Mountain to the east with an altitude of 774 feet above the surface of the Hudson. Not only is it one of the most impressive sights on the eastern seaboard, both names may even honor their original Algonquian ones.

About sailing north along this same stretch less than thirty years later, David DeVries wrote, "Passed the Averstro [Haverstroo, or Haverstraw, which means Oat Straw] where a kill runs out, [Buttermilk Falls?] formed from a large waterfall, the noise of which can be heard in the river. The land is also very high. At noon, passed the highlands, which are prodigiously high stony mountains, and it is about a mile going through them. Here the river, at its narrowest, is about five or six hundred paces wide, [at Breakneck/Storm King Mountain] as well as I could guess."[326]

"...Then we went up north-west, a league and a half deep water;" At this point the Hudson River turns sharply to the northwest. It is then three more miles from Jones Point to the strait between the point at Bear Mountain and Anthony's Nose. Each of his leagues are exactly two miles long at this entry.

"...then north-east by north five miles;" The Hudson does indeed angle gently to the northeast at this point, but for six statute miles, from Bear Mountain to Cold Spring Harbor. Here his mile is a little lengthy, perhaps a thousand extra feet. This is why I feel that Juet's "league" is a ballpark figure, which would include the distance sailed side to side while tacking. It is here that the ship passes West Point, as Donald Johnson describes.

"*...then north-west by north two leagues and anchored.*" The Hudson angles to the northwest here. It is four statute miles from Cold Spring Harbor to the strip of beach just to the east of Plum Point and the mouth of the Moodna Creek, so his league is two miles long.

"*The land grew very high and mountainous...*" Alpine-steep, Storm King Mountain to the west was apparently called Pasquaskeck by the people of the village across the river, who have come to be named after her. The range suggests a woman lying on her back and Storm King mountain suggests the shape of her breast. Pasquaskeck means "the large, prominent female formation" in Munsee. To the east is Breakneck Ridge, also very high, and Mount Taurus just off the river. It is the only sea level passage through the Appalachian Mountain chain from Canada to Georgia.

"*...the river is full of fish.*" Some of the best fishing on the river is said to be at Cornwall Bay, and there are several spawning zones as well. Fishermen still flock to Cornwall bay at specific weeks of the year for hatchings, but as to the exact week, the fish wouldn't want me to give that away, nor would Cornwall's fishermen. When I asked former Newburgh mayor Donald Presuti just how good the fishing was at Cornwall Bay, he showed me a map of the spawning zones, and there seemed to be a number of colored zones between Beacon and Cornwall, although this can change over time. Then when I asked him for further proof, he gave me an article he had clipped from the local newspaper. The headline read, "Bass Caught in Hudson Breaks Record." A man named Ian Kiraly of Walton, New York, caught a 55 pound 6 ounce striped bass in the Ulster County section of the Hudson River, a few miles above Newburgh. The NY DEC measured and weighed it and found it to be the largest in history.[327]

The author of *Charting the Sea of Darkness,* Johnson, notates, "In the vicinity of West Point," but given Juet's last logging of "north*west* by two leagues," for the day, it hardly seems possible, as West Point can only be reached by sailing north*east* from the southerly direction.

Edward Hagaman Hall sees Juet at Rose Town (not Roseton, which is near Newburgh) and Indian Point to the east. He then has them at "The Race," (no anchorage), which may refer to the river between Indian Point and Peekskill, and then later the same day passing the Worragut. (*Gut* is a kind of gate or hole, or passage between two points of rock in Dutch, so it may refer to the gap where the Bear Mountain Bridge now stands, which is the gateway to the land of the Woeranecks.)

Using a longer league, Johnson then places them at a point in the river between Cronomer Hill near Newburgh, and Castle Point north of Beacon. Cronomer Hill was named after a Native American who came to be known as Cronomer who lived there in his old age. I believe this is a kind of English nautical timekeeper, or is a misspelling of Chronometer. His actual name is now forgotten.[328]

Castle Point is named after a Native American fort built at that point, probably not too long before Hudson arrived. It was probably built to keep a lookout for Hodenosuannee (Iroquois) coming down the river, but Etaoquah, a Mohican, adds that such forts were good for protection against wild animals. Usually these forts seem strategically placed to defend a council fire island or village. It's not clear why one was built at Castle Point. It is across the river from Roseton, which is near the Danskammer, or Kintecoy grounds, a flat rock jutting out into the river which is over a half acre in size. Lossing states that it was Henry Hudson's Dutch crew that named it "Den Duyvel's Dans Kamer,"[329] or "Devil's Dance Chamber," however there is no actual proof of their authorship other than it makes for a good story. It was already called thus thirty years later, when David DeVreis wrote in his diary of April 16, "At night, came by the Dance Chamber where there was a party of Indians, who were very riotous, seeking only mischief, so that we were on our guard."[330]

Waterfalls and Wisdom

Like a weekend tourist, Juet and crew had missed some of the most beautiful and most culturally rich areas of the Hudson Valley, perhaps the entire East Coast, while rushing to find their lost northwest passage. The Half Moon attains remarkable speed as it makes its run from Hastings (perhaps Yonkers) to Cornwall, but it is a shame Henry couldn't have stopped and smelled the roses here instead of on the nearly vacant coast of Staten Island. In a single day, Hudson passed most of Wappingers territory, and passed up a chance to visit some of the best waterfalls and Indian hospitality in New York.

Some of the sites of Native American interest he missed include Van Courtlandt Park and the Moshulou village there; Wickerscreek Falls and the Wysquaqua village, a great crossing place now called Dobbs Ferry, and a village occupied (on and off) since perhaps 7,000 BCE; Sunnyside, at the Besightsick Creek;[331] Tarrytown and the Alipconck village; Pocantico Falls, the haunted "dancing falls" of Sleepy Hollow. (There was a squarish bay at the manor of Phillipsburgh called Slapering Haven, or "Sleepy Hollow," which was the entrance to Pocantico, however the waterfall itself is in a shady "hollow."[332] Hudson missed Sintsink Falls deep in the canyon, and the three Ossining Villages; Kestaubatuck, Crawbuckie and the falls at Quakers Bridge; Croton, including the Kitchewan River, the Kitchewank Village, Little Croton Falls, Croton Point and the Senasqua Village, the Tanracken River, and Teller's Point; Indian Point at Meahagh; the Sackhoes Village at Peekskill; the Konighawach River, now called Annsville Creek; the little waterfall at Annsville, with Sprout Brook and Peekskill Hollow Creek beyond, and also Oscawana Creek.

The village site at Garrison (near the train station) and the rapids and falls of Philipes Brook; Indian Brook Falls up Indian Brook, one of the most sacred sites of the Hudson Valley; Foundry Cove in Cold Spring and Foundry Brook; Mattawan Creek, Mattawan Falls, also called Fishkill Falls, and Fairy or M'singwe Island, an "island of fire," were all passed by in a day.

Along the way, and out of sight, Hudson also missed many of the strange and puzzling rock formations, petroforms, perched boulders, solstice alignments, effigy stones, cairns, star maps, and rock sculptures that are hidden among the Hudson Highlands, some left behind by glaciers, some left behind by Native Americans, or so I believe. For example, (and this is according to *The History of Westchester County*) at Somers, which is just inland, east from Yorktown and Cortlandt, there is a "curious rock that has the appearance of an Indian's face. It is an immense mass of red granite, said to be the only specimen in the county, and is perched upon three lime-stone points, two feet or more above the surface of the ground, and four hundred feet above the Muscoot Valley."[333] It is sometimes called "The Cobbling Stone."[334] Five miles to the southeast is the "bear rock" petroglyph at Ward Pound Ridge, a rock drawing of a bear on a rock the shape of a bear's head.[335] Many miles due north of Tarrytown is a large cairn that resembles a turtle, with a sculpted head resembling the Mullenberg Mud Turtle. The tail is a stepstair allowing the ritual leader to climb atop the back of the turtle to face the east. The "shell" is inlaid with beautiful quartzite rocks laced with Shawangunk conglomerate, or a similar stone from the Berkshires to the northeast. Of course, Hudson rarely left his ship, and so missed all of these strange wonders. There was a "face" on Storm King Mountain, called "The Turk" by English seamen, but an excavation crew blasted it to pieces, so we'll never know if it was carved by native hands or by nature itself.[336]

On the west bank, they passed without comment the following meditation spots: Nyack Creek, (the Nyacks weren't there yet); Minisciongo Creek; Rumachinack Village (now Haverstraw); Buttermilk Falls, and Popolopen (or Poplopen) Creek. Popolopen Creek, also known by the name Senkapogh, was the southern boundary for the Waoraneck territory.[337]

JOURNAL OF THE WAORANECK PEOPLE, SKY WOMAN REPORTING, SEPTEMBER 14 (a dramatization, based on known facts) : *The people on the western landing* [Newburgh Marina] *see the Great Floating Bird arrive in the afternoon from behind the Menahtes* [one of its names, "small island'] *called Po-laup-pee-el* [Bannermans' Island], *catching the beautiful light from the west in its white wings. Runners spread the word. Soon our relatives are coming at us from all directions. We can see our eastern relatives gathering on the Mattawan shippa* [Fishkill Landing] *near Tioronda,* [Dennings Point] *and M'singwe Island* [Fairy Island, near Madame Brett's Park]. *Some canoes are coming forth from Matumpseck* ["A bad standing rock," the original name for Breakneck Ridge] *and Moschachtinne* [this is the original term for Storm King; As seen from the east it is called Pasquaskeck, large prominent woman. According to Zeisberger, *mosch* means clear and *moschachgayoo* means "it is ground that is cleared of trees." In Munsee, *tinne* would be a word for fire. Much of Storm King is barren of trees.] *Some come sailing out on canoes down Quassaic Creek,* [rapid, shallow creek in a deep canyon or valley] *some down Paquenocknok* [Idlewild] *Creek and some down Kowawese Creek* [a hill of young pines, now Murderer's Creek, or "The Moodna"] *to the point of land we call Kowawese Hill* ["a hill of young pines," now Plum Point][338]. *Some come down the Waoraneck Trail along the stream gulley* [Washington Street] *from the spring down to the landing while others trundle south along one of the two west shore routes, the ridge road* [9W] *and the shoreline road* [Balmville Road, named after a Balm of Gilead poplar that grew in the middle of the road, connecting with what is now Liberty Street to the south and the River Road to the north.[339] The road stopped in the south at Quassaic Creek, but the River Road section went directly to Dans Kammer Point, and then one jagged west and joined 9W. Barclay says it was "a path that had been trodden by Indians for ages."[340]] *There is a gathering going on at the Great Flat Rock* [Dans Kammer Point] *but some of them jump in canoes and row south along the shore to get a better look. Eventually, we start to see some of our relatives coming in on the Waywayanda Trail* [Route 94] *from the crossroads* [Vail's Gate] *area. We gather together in a great beautiful gathering, a Metchkentawoom, at the meadow just south of the gulley* [Washington's Headquarters behind Hasbroucke House]. *We have long heard the prophecies about the visitors from the east arriving in brotherhood and are greatly pleased. The crew of the great canoe does not come ashore at all, and we are mystified.*

Early the following morning, as a mist was clearing from the bay, two

young men are seen squeezing out of a hole in the side of this large canoe.
They leap awkwardly to the river below, screaming, and make a loud splash.
There are two of our watchmen there, and they row out to pick them up as
they swim frantically into shore. They pull them onto the boat and they are
fuming about something. They keep saying a word we are not familiar with,
"Joo-it, Joo-it." We ask what "Joo-it" is, but the one starts stuttering and
speaking words we never heard before and screaming in scorn at the Great
Floating Bird. The other man seems to be crying. We wrap him in blankets
and he shivers, but it is not just the cold that affects him.

Something has gone wrong with the prophecies! RED LEAF MOON,
SEVENTEENTH DORSAL PLATELET OF THE CALENDAR TURTLE, WANING MOON.

JUET'S JOURNAL: TUESDAY, SEPTEMBER 15 : *The morning was misty until the*
sun arose, then it cleared; so we weighed with the wind at south, and ran up
into the river twenty leagues, passing by high mountains We had a very good
depth, as six, seven, eight, nine, ten, twelve, and thirteen fathoms, and great
store of salmon in the river. This morning our two savages got out of a port
and swam away. After we were under sail they called to us in scorn. At night
we came to other mountains, which lie from the river's side; there we found
very loving people, and very old men, where we were well used.

"The morning was misty until the sun arose, then it cleared; so we weighed with the wind at south." Most writers agree that on the morning of September 15, 1609, Hudson and crew awoke to view Cornwall Bay, with Plum (or Waoraneck) Point behind them, looking east towards the red sphere of the sun rising over Fishkill Landing. The wind blowing to the south would have pulled their ship northward, which is where they were eager to explore, so they fixed up their rig and got ready for adventure. However, there is much history to this place. Let us disembark from this white man's narrative for a moment and explore the shorelines of the river from a native perspective.

A Native History of Cornwall Bay and Fishkill Landing

Cornwall Bay is the crossing place of the Waoraneck Trial, which is now Route 52. There were Waoraneck settlements on both sides of the crossing. This trail came up from the Atlantic via Connecticut's Route 7 and passed through Westchester and then Putnam, where it was called by some the Wiccopee Trail as it passed by the old Pachem Wappingers villages in Carmel, near Gleneida Lake[341] and then through Dutchess county along today's 52. Here it can be called the Mattawan Trail as is follows the Mattawan (or Fishkill Creek) westward as it crossed today's

Route 9 (the Mohican Trail), Glenham, and Mattawan village. The path followed today's Tioranda Road and came to Dennings Point, right near Matawan Falls (Fishkill or Suckerfish Falls today) and Fairy or M'singwe Island.

The Waoraneck Trail picks up again on the western bank of the Hudson at the marina, a bit north of Kowawese (now Plum) Point and Waoraneck (now Moodna, original name also Kowawese) Creek. It ascends the slope via Washington Street, which runs by the old Hasbrook House, George Washington State Historic site. Washington Street was originally a stream that started as a spring in what is now St. George's graveyard, with a Native American pathway to one side. The Hasbrouckes stoned it in some time during the 1600s. Nearby Spring Street at the top of the hill is named after it. A brewery was built there due to the quality of the spring water.

Washington Street winds north and crosses 17K and then is marked as 52 again. This road goes by Sam's Point (Ioskawasting) Preserve and out to the Delaware (Lenape Sipu and other names) River. Route 52 is sometimes called the Oswego Trail in its western reaches past the Delaware.

Fairy (or Fairie) Island, which lies at the foot of Fishkill Falls (also called Suckerfish Falls because of the predominance of the Suckerfish, a freshwater fish there) was believed to be the dwelling place of a powerful spirit or Manitou,[342] and of "the little people" which the Munsee called M'singwe and which the Wappingers called "Puckwadjee." It was an important "rendezvous," or "island of fire," where council fires were held. The trail that is now approximated by Route 52 stretched from the Atlantic to the Delaware, and passed through this important hub of activity via Tioronda Road. A prominent sub-chief of the Wappingers made his home nearby.[343] Fairy is a common translation of a native word for "little people," and the Celtic descriptions of fairies, "brownies," and the like, are quite similar to the M'singwe. The early settlers transformed this into Melzinger, a curious bit of word play. If they were Walloons, they might have meant Sweet (mel, from Old French for honey) Singer (from Dutch zinger). If Dutch, they might have meant simply mill-singer (moul or muhle=mill). Whoever lived there before Madame Brett then made up a story about an "Indian Princess" whose name was spelled "Melzingah," who jumped from the falls to her death, leaving us with a Melzingah Reservoir, and a road by the same name three miles south of the falls itself.

The Benton Institute found submerged stone walls at the Pollepel Island site. It would appear to be a fishing weir from 1000 BCE, with two parallel S-shaped walls. The water was much lower then. It was between Pollepel Island and the east bank. It is possibly the greatest spawning site for striped bass in the Hudson River, and very muddy. One canoer stated that the walls were at least four and half feet tall, but buried deep in sediment.[344]

Most crossings feature islands half way, though some do not. Here the island now known as Bannerman's is about a hundred yards too far south to be a convenient rest stop, but it was used that way nonetheless. It is interesting that Juet does not mention Pollepel, now Bannerman Island, at all.

Pollepel is a Dutch word for a ladle, or wooden spoon, but the island does not really resemble an "upturned ladle," nor was there a Dutch Miss named Polly Pell, as folklore suggests. According to more well-informed folklore there was a Munsee (or Wappingers) word for the island that meant "Divider of the Waters,"[345] and the rules of Double Dutch decreed that Pollepel would sound just like it. That word would presumably have been *pough-laup-pee-el*; *pough* (rock) *laup* (plow or divide[346]) *pee* (fresh waters[347]) *el* (suffix, meaning "their"[348]) giving us "the Rock that Ploughs Their Waters." It is perhaps one of the most poetic of all Algonkian place names, describing the island more vividly than any postcard home, and the Dutch word does sound remarkably similar. Here then is at least one instance where the Double Dutch process preserved a Native American place name where it had once been lost.

But that name Poughloopee-el may have another level of meaning in Algonquian. The Crawford family have continued to be caretakers of the island until recent times, and according to the family there are a number of "Indian" ghost stories about the place. It seems there was a long standing belief the island was haunted and some angry spirits lived there, and may still live there to this day. The bad spirits, *manetta* in Munsee, called "Der Heer of the Dunderbergs" (the Army of Thunder Mountains) by the Dutch, was said to rule the waters upstream to that point and no further. *Pough* is a great rock, while *loo* is a syllable that means "bad" or even "haunted" or "evil" (as in *loo-way-woo-dee*, "bad things in my heart.") The *pee-el* could refer to their water.

There are also stories of drunken Dutch sailors being lowered to the shores of Pollepel by a big bucket off the stern of the ship and the bucket was called a "soup ladle," or Pollepel. But Pollepel also shows off the classical education of the Dutch. Pelops was the son of Tantalus in Greek mythology. Tantalus served Pelops up to the Gods as food, but the Gods restored him. The large island called the Peloponnesus was named after him, and its shape is something like that of Pollepel Island. During the 1600s, the people of Holland were the best educated in Europe,[349] and the geographic double entendres were filled with references to Greek mythology, so this would be no surprise. Pelop-Hölle (Pelop's Hell) would be fitting. Today, we also call this spot Bannerman's Island, after Bannerman Castle, built around 1901.

Fishkill Creek, the mouth of which was directly east, was called Mettaewan, or Trout Stream, by the Wappingers. Vis Kill or Fishkill is a translation of the word into Dutch. The local Wappingers called themselves "Mattewan Indians" according to this same source. Just to the south, there was a larger group with a larger river called the Kitchewan, which means "Great River," and this group called itself Kitchewank, which means "People of the Great River." In the same self-denegrating humor seen in the name Wappingers, the people of the Mettawan changed the name to Mattawan, which means "humble little stream," and themselves Mattawan Indians, "the people of the humble little stream." It was a backhanded poke at the self-important Kitchewank Indians because Algonquins are expected to be humble, so humble in fact that in some places it is considered rude to use the word "I" or "my" (*nee* or *neen*) in decent company, and even today, you (k') generally comes before I (n') in a proper Algonkian sentence.[350]

Mount Beacon was also originally called Mattawan Mountain. A reference to this has been found in Madame Brett's Diary. Beacon was called Mattewan in the eastern uplands and Fishkill Landing by the shore. Fishkill Creek is the major creek in the region and empties into the Hudson just below Beacon at Denning's Point. On the map of the Rombout[351] patent by John Holwell, 1689, there is a teepee marked "wigwam" at a westward bend in the Mattawan River on a parallel with Wappingers Falls. This map is difficult to correlate with modern landmarks, but it would probably be Wiccopee Pass, called Fishkill Hook by the Dutch. The name (*wick-coo-pee*) means "dwelling place near the water, in the pines." There is such a spot, across from the Old Dutch Reformed Church in Hopewell Junction.

There was a Wappingers village right at the parking lot at Madam Brett park, at the old mill and factory, overlooking the island, and wigwams still stood at that spot until 1648. Paleo Indians were among the first to discover this as an ideal village spot, so occupation goes back quite far. Some remains and artifacts have been dated to about 5,000 BCE. Most Wappingers had left the area by 1760, and the last "full blood" died around 1800, according to Dutchess County, (1937). According to a lecture by Jim Heron, the Wappings who lived there had bronze- to golden-toned skin, recorded in the diaries of white men who came to visit.

The river is salt and tide up to the bridge. There have been sturgeon seven feet long and 45 pound striped bass, called operamack by the Wappingers and Long Island natives, caught here. There were also yellow fish. The Dutch were able to ship beaver pelts down the Fishkill Creek to this spot. In 1656, Wappingers helped load beaver pelts onto ships that would come up to Dennings point. Shiploads of over 80,000 pelts were not unusual.

In a pit on Dennings Point, not far from the bay, 300 skulls were found dating between 3000 and 5000 BCE. This spot was a focus for Algonquin life on and off from that point until at least 1656. The grandfathers of the many oaks that are there today may have been planted by ancient Algonquins, which was part of an early practice for harvesting acorns. (See *Native New Yorkers*.)

Just south of Newburgh is Moodna Creek, which is a very important estuarial tributary of the Hudson. The salt water enters into the creek at Plum Point and at one time reached inland as far as the waterfall at Salisbury Mills near Blooming Grove. Near this spot, the old Algonquin trail now called Route 94 crosses Moodna Creek. Thurston Cottage still stands there, associated with Vincente Matthews, who befriended the early Indians and may have lived with Awissawa, a chief of the Amorgarikakan family. There is no island, but as you might imagine, there was an Algonquin village there and a trading center. It was here the Dutch would go to meet with Nanawheron, (locally based songwriter Jay Unger still sings a folk song about Nanawheron) Awissawa, Winnesook, and Kaelkoptl (Kalkop). Salisbury Mills was the headquarters of the governing family of the Confederacy, the Amorgarikakan family, and after Awissawa,[352] Kaelkop was the chief for about seven years; he signed the Saugerties and Rombout Patents. He reportedly blew up the brewery at Kingston, and returned to Long Island. Moodna Creek today shoots over a large dam at this spot.

Wor or *wer* is the Wappingers equivalent of the Munsee *"woolay"* or "good, peaceful..." as it is an R dialect with no L phoneme. Nock means "a place near the water," and often describes a spit of land, also called a "sac" in Algonquin, or a "neck" in English. So therefore, *Weronock* is clearly "a good place by the water." But in Dutch/German the root *waren-* is a common prefix meaning "trade goods, dry goods," for example as in the German word *warenlager* (warehouse). Plus, the suffix *–ecke* means "corner," and Plum Point is also a "corner" of land jutting out into Cornwall Bay. So Warnock may have been Double Dutched into Waren-ecke, "the corner where goods are traded," and then the ending turned into "neck" by the English. Its history suggests that it was an international trading spot, dating back thousands of years, so this term would be quite fitting.

In 1963, an archaeological excavation of a large burial mound at Plum Point revealed much that spanked of Taino culture, from what is now Puerto Rico. Mel Johnson, who is still alive today, was one of those who examined those exotic and strangely foreign carved objects in that mound. Included was a statuette of a jaguar in the Taino style, dated to about 1000 BCE. Jaguars rarely travel north of the Rio Grande. Those findings further suggest that it had long been a trading point for merchants from thousands of miles around, "Sagamore Mike" D'Amico, a Mohican, has said that these Tainos would occasionally intermarry with the Mohican ancestors of the time, and that Sachems or Sagamores, were generally selected from their descendants.

"*...and ran up into the river twenty leagues, passing by high mountains...*" If we use Benson J. Lossing's standard, a league was 2.2 statue miles in Juet's time, twenty leagues would be forty-four miles. It is 44 miles from the southeast corner of Cornwall Bay to the mouth of the Esopus at Saugerties. Of course there is no indication here as to east or west bank, so Tivoli Bays, and North Bay in particular, across from the mouth of the Esopus, must be kept in mind as a possibility. Magdalene Island, an important fishing camp for Native Americans, and possibly an "island of fire" used for council meetings, lies close to the east bank. The south tip of South Cruger Island had been steadily occupied by Algonquian peoples from 2500 BCE to contact, so Tivoli Bay cannot be dismissed.[353] The modern town of Tivoli is directly across from the Esopus and its Broadway (turning into West Kerleys Corners Road to the east) may have been a Native American access road to the bluff overlooking the Esopus.[354] David DeVries came here thirty-some years after Juet and wrote, "The 27 [May?] we came to Esoopes, where a creek runs in, and there the Indians had some maize-land, but it was stony."[355]

The high mountains are the Catskills.[356] The so-called Wall of Manitou is a chain of mountains from Woodstock to Albany that are rather impressive from the Hudson River and form the front "wall" of the Catskills. Meads Mount, Overlook Mountain, Indian Head Mountain, the Plateau, Hightop and Blackdome, South Mountain, North Mountain and Windham High Peak form the southern portion of this wall,[357] the first three of which combine to form a beautiful backdrop for sailing before reaching the Esopus' mouth. They all have sacred connotations to those of the Catskill region today, who hike them, paint them, and take shoeboxes full of photos of them whenever possible.

Plattekill Clove in West Saugerties is a notch in the mountains that is very picturesque. But as it turns out, it is more than just a pretty rock face. It seems to have been a sighting for the summer solstice sunset various Native American nations observed along a 23 degree solstice line stretching from Montauk on Long Island to Fleishmann's New York, and beyond, perhaps even to the grave of Handsome Lake in Syracuse. We know through numerous eye witness accounts and stories that the Algonquins and other sub-cultures in North America honored the summer solstice above all other days, and the setting sun on that day had special significance in relationship to burial ceremonies. We can just begin to gage the reverence with which Eastern woodlands people viewed the setting sun by the extraordinary number of stone markers along this line.

According to Reider T. Sherwin, there was an Esopus Island at one time in the Esopus River, and this is the key to understanding why the next generation of Dutch turned "the little river," E-see-poo-us or Sheepush, into Esopus. (*See-poo* is "river," plus the diminutive *us* ending which means "small.") Any quick glance through the pages of Greek mythology will reveal that Asopus was a famous island, where the perfect utopian country of Arcadia was situated. If you look at a good map of the Mediterranean, near the modern country of Greece, and the Peloponnesus, you will find an island of Esopus, but Greek people will tell you, "That's not the real one! We have yet to find Utopia on this earth!" Perhaps the Esopus Indians living on the lost "Esopus Island" had found it, with their harmonious ways and closeness to the mother earth, but no one was paying attention, and now that island is no more, its happy people scattered.

"*We had a very good depth, as six, seven, eight, nine, ten, twelve, and thirteen fathoms, and great store of salmon in the river.*" There are regretfully no Atlantic salmon in the Hudson River today. Some say Juet was wrong, that there were never any salmon in the Hudson, but others say these fish became another casualty of industrialization, pollution, and over-fishing. Salmon tend to prosper in the waters of estuaries, and although many fish have returned to the river since the Clearwater Organization started in 1969, the salmon is not among them. Elsewhere, salmon are now being depleted by blooms or swarms of jelly fish, so a return to the Hudson River seems yet more unlikely.

"*This morning our two savages got out of a port and swam away. After we were under sail they called to us in scorn.*" As to his use of the word "savage," it is curious that this is the first time he uses this term, and in a situation in which the natives showed disrespect to the crew. On one hand, savage comes from the French "sauvage," or "in the woods." This seems appropriate, given the surroundings. But in the King's English, it may have already had other connotations. In fact, King James had used the term himself in casting aspersions on the indigenous peoples of the New World. Pearce writes, in his book, *The Savages of America*, "In Letters Patent issued in 1606 for the colonizing of Virginia, the King urged the furtherance of a work 'which may, by the Providence of Almighty God, hereafter tend to the Glory of His Divine Majesty, in propagating of Christian Religion to such people, as yet live in darkness, and miserable ignorance of the true knowledge and worship of God, and may in time bring the Infidels and Savages living in those parts, to human civility and to a settled and quiet Government....'" [358]

In 1828, Noah Webster, in his *American Dictionary of the English Language*, defined savage as follows: *savage; n. A human being in his native state of rudeness, one who is untaught, uncivilized or without cultivation of mind or manners. The savages of America, when uncorrupted by the vices of civilized men, are remarkable for their hospitality to strangers, and for their truth, fidelity and gratitude to their friends, but implacably cruel and revengeful toward their enemies...*" [359] It is not clear which connotation Juet intended us to read into the word savage. In that he seems either irritated or embarrassed about what has just occurred, I believe he wanted to discredit their escaped captives in his diary with this scornful word.

"*...This morning our two savages got out of a port and swam away.*" The port is a small window, square or round on the side of the ship, usually with a porthole cover attached. The Half Moon would have had several on each side, but I would guess seven to ten feet above the surface of the water. It seems they disembarked at Cornwall Bay or just to the north. If things were going well, why would the men not have simply asked for a ride to shore, or jumped from the deck? It seems likely that they were being held against their will.

With a long history of explorers capturing Algonquins for slaves all along the coast dating back at least to Gosnold and West, including famous ones like Tisquantum, (whom we now call Squanto, "the Wrath of the Creator") it would not be surprising to learn that Hudson was attempting to bring home exhibit A and B, at least to increase the commercial value of this otherwise failed mission to Cathay. Remember Cathay? Hudson's employers back in Holland were imagining him bowing and shaking hands with Chinese diplomats at about this time. A few strong and able-bodied slaves might ease their wrath at him upon his return.

Karen Sivertsen, in her master's thesis, plays with the idea that it was Hudson who captured the two Algonquins known in later years as Orson and Valentine after characters in a novel, and brought them back to Europe, but does not have a source for this theory. Charles Gehring concludes that Adraien Block picked up Orson and Valentine in 1614, perhaps at Cape Cod, and brought them back to Europe.[360]

Algonquins were among the first North American inhabitants to be captured for the slave trade, but the plan was abandoned when they proved to be talented escape artists, at least on their own turf. Failing that, the Dutch paid the Algonquins a small amount of money to help build Fort Amsterdam, but the amount was found insulting. Then they turned to slaves from Africa, which the English and Spanish were finding in great numbers.

The port holes were not very large, so for these native men to squeeze out of them, they must have wanted out very badly As we shall see on the return trip, Juet comes to believe that these two "savages" were quite angry about something, but exactly what, we'll never know. He fears their return, and indeed there is an incident on October 1, as the Half Moon is floating south, which he seems to attribute to these same individuals, although that would be at about Peekskill. In *History of Westchester County,* we read that Hudson picked up the native men at Yonkers two days earlier. "By Hudson's own statement, he himself first violated faith with them. He detained two of their number on the vessel, and, although they soon jumped overboard [apparently at Cornwall Bay], and swam to the shore, his act was nevertheless an outrage upon the universal rules of hospitality."[361] Would these disgruntled natives walk south 16 miles to what is now Indian Point just to get a better angle of attack? If they were originally from Yonkers as suggested, it was just another stop on their way home. Indian Point does jut out almost to the center of the river, increasing their chances of intercepting Hudson's ship. Perhaps that was the plan. The results however were tragic for the natives.

It is generally acknowledged that the Native American population has produced some fine swimmers, and it is a point of pride for Eastern Algonquins in particular, some of whom may tell you with a smile that they are "part fish." However I know of no studies proving they are better swimmers than their European counterparts, and have not even so much as come across a good Lenape word for "swimming." It's something you just do.

"At night we came to other mountains, which lie from the river's side ... there we found very loving people..." Every town along the Hudson River makes the claim that they are the place of "the very loving people," and in fact, there are very loving people in all of those towns today, which is the important thing, but in terms of Hudson's "loving people," they must have been from Saugerties. I believe that by "which lie *from* the river's side," he means to say that the mountains were not close to the river, but were *far from* the river's side. That would describe the lofty peaks of Mount Tremper, Meade Mountain, Overlook Mountain, Indian Head Mountain, Platt Clove, and the hills northward, which appear very dramatic from the river, but which lie at least six or seven miles inland. The strongest reason to choose Saugerties to the west over Tivoli to the east as their location is the mention of tall mountains far from the river. These are on the west side. There are either wetlands or cliffs on the east bank, immediately in from the water, hence no villages with access to the water. Also, there are no major mountains on the river between Newburgh and Esopus to the south, hence, *"we came to other mountains"* tells us they are not at Catskill where they would have passed ten miles of mountains already. Plus Catskill is too far from Cornwall Bay, their previous point of departure. Juet said they traveled 20 leagues, or about 44 miles. According to Mapquest it is 54.4 miles from Newburgh's exit 17 to Catskill's exit 21, but only 41.7 miles to Saugerties' exit 20, and the Half Moon was at least three miles further south. Following a parallel route upriver, the Half Moon could not have shortened this distance, and could not have made it in a single day to Catskill. On the journey homeward, the theory that Saugerties is the home of the "very loving people" becomes even more compelling, as we shall see.

"..and very old men, where we were well used..." Partly due to their vigorous lifestyle, Algonquins were known to live a long time in those days. Membertou was "well over a hundred," White Eyes was 79, today's William Commanda is 95 at this writing. Recent studies show that fresh air, clean water, exercise, sunlight, natural foods, and circadian sleep rhythms are the best thing for preventing cancer and insuring old age. Studies show that gratitude is equally effective and say-

ing "thank you" was the cornerstone of Algonquin spirituality.

"Our boat went to fish, and caught great store of very good fish." The estuarial portion of the Esopus below Cantine Dam is great for fishing. The Hudson is not salty at this point. I believe the rapids were sufficient in size to baffle most tides, however the waterfall at the bend would most likely be called the Sunkheague. That waterfall is now submerged in Esopus Lake, as people call it, which gathers behind Cantine Dam as it crosses the bridge at 9W, the old "west shore trade route," known as the King's Road during early English times. The original waterfall was at Saugerties' Stony Point, at the bend in the river a half mile further inland from there.

Michael Sullivan Smith agrees they traveled from Cornwall to Saugerties, and that the loving people were from Saugerties. If Juet's league was indeed 2.2 miles, the Saugerties solution does seem likely. Ruttenber speaks of a "Catskill Munsee" Indian tribe living along the river, but seems to place it north of Saugerties, perhaps in the modern city of Catskill, New York.[362]

The ship and crew had passed right by the following points of interest on the eastern shore. Pough-laap-pee-el Island, "the rock that plows their waters," called "Pollopel" by the Dutch, (various spellings) now called Bannerman's Island; Castle Point, a fort (east bank); Wappingers (Mahwenawasik) Creek, Wappingers Falls; "Trimuni;" Casper Kill; Rust Plats; Poughkeepsie, *uppuqui-ipis-ing*, reed covered lodge by the little water place; Valkill (or Winnakee) Falls, upper and lower, at Waryus Park; Maritje Kill (north of CIA); Crum Elbow (FDR); Indian Kill at Norrie Point; and Landsman Kill. This is the main stream in Rhinebeck. Not known as an estuary, it is very small today. However at one time "grist and saw mills stood so close together that the water from one mill pond occasionally backed up and interfered with[363] the operation of the water wheel of the mill above."

The ship and crew also passed these ports of call on the west bank. Moodna Creek, Idlewild Creek and Plum Point; Quassaic Creek; Danskammer Point; Rondout Landing, and Rondout Creek; and the Wallkill Creek and Sturgeon Pool, plus Towpath Island, Connelly Caves and Catskill Creek.

Chapter Seven

PEOPLE OF THE UPPER RIVER

JUET'S JOURNAL: WEDNESDAY, SEPTEMBER 16 : *The sixteenth, fair and very hot weather. In the morning our boat went again to fishing, but could catch but few, by reason their canoes had been there all night. This morning the people came aboard and brought us ears of Indian corn and pompions and tobacco, which we bought for trifles. We rode still all day, and filled fresh water; at night we weighed and went two leagues higher, and had shoal water so we anchored till day.*

"*The sixteenth, fair and very hot weather*" At the mouth of the Esopus, there are prongs of land that extend far into the Hudson River on each side, with a narrow slice of land in the middle, although the terrain has changed slightly since Hudson's visit. There was a Native American village site just to the south of this formation, and now the location of the largest mussel shell midden still to be found along the Hudson. The midden is one acre in size and 40 to 60 feet deep, and was discovered "under Glunt's lawn."[364] (A shell midden is located at the tip of the spit which extends into the middle of the river, property of Chester and Ruth Reynolds Glunt.[365]) Today the Saugerties Lighthouse sits firmly in the palm of the hand of the upper arm, as if the land were holding out a lantern or torch for the benefit of riverboat sailors. The spit of land is narrow and inundates at high tide, but lies on solid rock.

"... *In the morning our boat went again to fishing, but could catch but few, by reason their canoes had been there all night.*" By telling us they sent the rowboat "there" but the fish were gone, Juet seems to be referring to a small nook rather than the middle of "the greatest estuary." This must have been the popular fishing spot that is now below Cantine Dam. Algonquins of the northeast are famed for their night fishing, often using torches to attract the fish and then spearing them with three pronged spears, two wooden spring clamps on the outside and a nail-like spike in the center. Their night fishing techniques were reputed to be excellent and so it is not surprising they had fished out the Esopus creek below the rapids. However unfortunate for Henry Hudson, the supply would probably have recovered by the next day. There are still today a wide variety of fish living in the long, curving body of sea-level waters that make up the entrance-way of the Esopus. Here one finds both seagoing and freshwater fish, well protected from storms. One sees large fishing boats below the falls at all seasons of the year, but in 1609, shallow water and mud flats would have prevented the Half Moon from entering the Esopus.

The mouth of Sawyers Creek is north of the two arms of the Esopus and forms a small secondary estuary where it empties into the Hudson. The saw-mill which gave the creek and the town its name can still be found at Seamans' Park. According to Vernon Benjamin, the "little sawyer" was Randall Roswell Hoes, who owned the mill before 1660, but one hears various stories.[366] This was not good corn planting area and was deeded to the Dutch by Kaelkoptl. According to Funk there is a rock shelter archaeological site along the Esopus Creek, but Funk does not identify its location. There were caves at one time along Mudder Creek, a tributary of the Esopus, and an old route used by the Mohawk tribute gatherers from Scoharie Creek (according to Vernon Benjamin) but they are now inaccessible.

The main village was atop the bluff overlooking Lighthouse Cove, and corn and maize were definitely grown there. Mynderse Street was almost certainly an original pathway, and it is at this location that a number of artifacts have been found, including a projectile carved from crystal.[367] Some of the first Dutch settlers also lived on this bluff.[368] In 1998, Vernon Benjamin interviewed John Bubb for a documentary video in which Bubb, an "old timer," recalled stories from his youth about Native Americans (including Iroquois) coming down the Platt Clove Road on foot with pelts to trade, tramping down Mynders Street to a certain estate where they would trade fur for fish. Some of the fish was cooked over a fire at a rock shelter, the rest they took home. The (Mynders) trail followed the side of the ridge down to the cove.[369]

"This morning the people came aboard and brought us ears of Indian corn and pompions and tobacco, which we bought for trifles…" Perhaps the local sachem had heard that the young men had fished out the stream, leaving these powerful men carrying thunder-sticks with nothing for breakfast. Pompions are generally translated as "pumpkins," but it might instead have meant pignolia, pine nuts, a favorite delicacy among the Eastern Algonquins. From "ears of Indian corn" we can suppose that these were rather large "ears," and that the kernels were multi-colored as we know "Indian corn" kernels today, displayed in bundles on American doorways and walls in the autumn, much as the Eastern Woodlands people did four hundred years ago to offer thanks for an abundant harvest, or to ward off evil in some cases. This may have been the most advanced type of corn cultivated at the time.

Elsewhere, Juet refers to another stage of corn as "Turkish Wheat," which doesn't have "ears" as we think of them. Apparently, the natives cultivated many varieties of corn, in various stages of domestication. This is the only time in Juet's narrative where he uses the word "Indian" in any context, so we know this usage is already widespread among explorers as a word for Native Americans, but Juet doesn't use it carelessly.

There is a colorful teaching heard now and again, where the colors of the kernels of "Indian corn" represent the various races and colors. According to the oral tradition, we can study the pattern and learn much about how the Creator wants us to live. There are no two kernels alike, each tiny face a different hue and shade. They are not regimented in straight rows (like the pale sweet corn, preferred by whites) but each one finds its own space, without gaps, and without any one crowding upon the other. The natural processes of growth and change have moved each kernel to its rightful place, and the whirling patterns hold the ear together even more solidly than would straight rows.[370] This bit of philosophy explains why Native American villages were rarely designed along straight lines or perfect circles. People's wigwams found their own space according to the flow of the land and natural processes, just like the corn. Many descendants today do not like living in developments where every house is the same color and every street is in a straight line, parallel to the next one. That's a "sweet corn" solution, and not the "Indian" way of life.

"*We rode still all day, and filled fresh water . . .*" It seems that by "rode still" he means that they remained anchored, and gathered fresh water from the Sawyer's Creek, which remains at sea-level for about thirty feet, a secondary estuary, but then further inland affords a great deal of fresh water cascading down the mountainside.

"*. . . at night we weighed and went two leagues higher, and had shoal water so we anchored till day.*" This means they lifted the anchor out of the water on a chain and traveled 4.4 miles north (using Lossing's standard for a league) and then ran aground in shallow water, so dropped anchor again. Michael Sullivan Smith of Saugerties estimates they ran aground at Smith's Landing. There are a lot of islands there, between Green Point and Smith's Landing. There was a riverside town called Pes-squaw-nach-qua, or "woman's breast,"[371] now Dewitt Point. The name refers to an island of that appearance. There are water lilies stretching far out into the water, suggesting a shallow place.[372]

However, according to Shirley Dunn, "The Half Moon had probably reached the mud flats lying between the present City of Hudson and the village of Athens. These obstructions in the center of the river, covered with shallow water at high tide and exposed at low tide, later became notorious as the "middle ground" or the "Hudson flats." The extensive flats appeared on maps as early as 1630, hampered cross-river transportation between the developing communities of Hudson and Athens in the eighteenth century, and remain in the river today."[373]

Near Claverack is the town of Kinderhook, a town that claims to have been named by Hudson. One of the most famous stories about Henry Hudson is that he saw Native American children dancing at the point of land at the mouth of the Kinderhook and bestowed that name on the entire community. It is interesting that *kinte-hoking* could represent a "land of dancing" in a corrupted form of Munsee/Unami. We know from Dans Kammer Point and Indian Point (formerly Verplanck Point near Peekskill) that *kintecoy* spots (powwow dancing spots) are often "hooks," flat ground that juts out into the river. This is most likely true because the canoe was such a basic mode of transportation for long distance travelers. A fur trader could travel from one powwow to another with a sack of inventory for trade and never have to walk more than fifty feet. Kinderhook is a squarish "point" of land that juts rather far into the Hudson and was probably used for that purpose. Renaming the Kinte-hoking "Kinderhook" could be the first example of Double Dutch word play in history. We'll never know—Juet never mentions it.[374]

Surprisingly, Bacon agrees that "the explorer again set sail and tried the channel for fifteen or twenty miles farther."[375] There is nothing in the text to indicate this exact mileage, but I agree with Bacon, Hall, *et al*, that some miles are missing in Juet's account, and it seems to be at this entry. It is only three miles from Catskill to the mudflats, but twelve from Saugerties, and the mud flats are at Athens, so that is where the ship ends up.

They passed Catskill Creek, to the west, and were now in Mohican Territory.[376] Even up in the north, 130 miles or so from the ocean, the tides in the river rise four to five feet, and the tributaries are tidal as well, including the Catskill Creek, which rises three to four feet. There is no detectable salt here, but the incoming seawater 50 miles to the south pushes the fresh water back to Troy on the Hudson, and has the same tidal effect on the tributaries such as the Catskill.

There was a Mohican village at Catskill called Potick.[377] We can still see how the old trade route now 9W crosses the Catskill at a prominent island. A mile or two inland from here, after a turn in the stream, there are rapids and then a few natural stone steps (a waterfall in other words) with a rise of about two feet. (These steps have since been reinforced with block and concrete) When an unusually high tide comes in, the effect is apparently quite remarkable. The water from the Hudson climbs the cascade stairs gradually until it overwhelms the waterfall and breaks free over the top. As it rises above the top of the stairs, the estuarial fish are then more easily able to swim further upstream to the terminus, or head of the tide, which lies another mile or so upstream. (State Routes 47 and 30, Cauterskill Road. 30 is Cauterskill Avenue.) There is a small island just below that falls, and it looks as if a mill was here. Another mile or so in is where trade route now 23 B crosses the river and this was an important Mohican village. Just east of that crossing, on 23 B, is the site of Casteel Hoogte, (High) Indian fort. A marker shows that an Indian footpath ran along what is now Brook Street to Coxsackie, running through the Catskill Country Club.

Hop O Nose village lies along the river near Catskill Point, which is the mouth of the tributary. Just to the north in the Hudson, is Rogers Island where a trade route now called 23 crosses the Hudson and connects with Route 9, the Mohican Trail, on the east side.

The Stockbridge Munsee Band of Mohicans has acquired property at Leeds. They have been interested in sites about two miles west of Thruway Exit 21, near where skeletal remains of children believed to have been Mohicans were uncovered in the mid-1990s close to the Hudson River.

Edward Hagaman Hall positions the crew in Athens, New York, north of Catskill.[378] After reviewing compelling evidence compiled by state historian Paul Huey (see next section), I believe that, after traveling north six leagues, they were about to land at Schodack Island. It is not two leagues (4.4 miles) from Saugerties to Catskill, but more than four (8.8 miles). And it is not six leagues (13.2 miles) from there to Schodack Island, but at least seven (15.4 miles). Perhaps Juet misstated one of the distances. On the return trip, it is seven leagues back to the mud flats, the Hudson-Athens Middle Ground. In any case, Huey believes they somehow end up the next day at Schodack.

John W. Quinney, a Mohican chief, in 1854, said, "Two hundred and fifty winters ago...the Muh-he-con-new, for the first time, beheld the 'pale face...'." He explained that the experience "overwhelmed the senses" of his ancestors.[379]

Shirley Dunn writes, "At first they thought the ship with its sails was a sea creature. When they realized it was a ship containing men, they thought the men were ill because they were so pale. After the first moments, the Mohicans were not afraid, but intensely curious."[380]

Elsewhere Dunn writes, "When the Mohicans first viewed Hudson's decorated wooden ship with its billowing sails, they were mystified. A legendary account of this event was reported by one of their tribal orators, Hendrick Aupaumut, almost 150 years later at an Indian conference in 1754. Aupaumut recalled, "Our forefathers had a castle on this river. As one of them walked out he saw something on the river, but was at a loss to know what it was. He took it at first for a great fish."

Dunn goes on to report an account dated from 1649 which noted "those natives of the country who are so old as to recollect when the Dutch ships first came here, declare that when they saw them, they did not know what to make of them... some among them, when the first one arrived, even imagined it to be a fish, or some monster of the sea, and accordingly a strange report of it spread over the whole land."[381]

JUET'S JOURNAL: THURSDAY, SEPTEMBER 17 : *The seventeenth fair sun-shining weather, and very hot. In the morning as soon as the sun was up, we set sail and ran up six leagues higher, and found shoals in the middle of the channel, and small islands, but seven fathoms water on both sides. Towards night we borrowed so near the shore that we grounded: so we laid out our small anchor, and heaved off again. Then we borrowed on the bank in the channel and came aground again; while the flood ran we heaved off again and anchored all night.*

Here again seems to be a solid point of reference in the strangely ambiguous journal of Robert Juet. As we shall see, solid points of reference present answers that sometimes raise a hundred other questions. This diary entry truly seems to be describing Schodack Island, a unique spot of great importance to the native people. *"...The seventeenth fair sun-shining weather, and very hot. In the morning as soon as the sun was up, we set sail and ran up six leagues higher, and found shoals in the middle of the channel, and small islands, but seven fathoms water on both sides..."*

Throughout this book we have been using a "two mile, give or take," system of determining a league; 2.2 miles per league based on Lossing. Juet's journal entry of September 14 shows us this is a fair estimate, however, here the leagues are longer; 2.5 miles each if they started at the mud flats, heading for Schodack. If they traveled 15 miles north (2.5 x 6) they might just reach the lower point of Upper Schodack, a shallow place between the islands as described.

Paul Huey is a New York State historian, with a special focus on Native American history. He has greater access to New York's historical records concerning native settlements than perhaps anyone else. He writes, in his landmark booklet, *Historical and Archeological Resources of Castleton Island State Park* published by the State of New York in May 1997, that "Henry Hudson arrived at Schodack Island on September 17, 1609." Without overwhelming evidence to the contrary, it seems unwise to argue with such a learned man, one who is so certain about his conclusions.

Another possibility is that they arrived at Hotaling Island, which has a similar disposition in the river to Schodack. M.S. Smith suggests that the "loving people" were at Saugerties, the mud flats were at Smith's Landing north of Saugerties, and

that the place of the two channels was not at Schodack but at Athens. But the entry
for September 18 seems to disprove this theory.

*"Towards night we borrowed so near the shore that we grounded: so we laid out our
small anchor, and heaved off again. Then we borrowed on the bank in the channel and
came aground again; while the flood ran we heaved off again and anchored all night..."*

The tides of the Hudson rise four feet above sea level twice a day, six-minus
hours rising, six-minus falling. Not all sections of the river rise at the same time.
The moon pulls on the overall surface from New York City to Albany in waves and
bulges, low tide in some places, high in others. They were stranded by a severely
low tide, but by waiting six hours, the "flood ran," the tide came in, and the ship
buoyed up on the water and broke loose of the sand. If "towards night" he meant
about 1900 hours (7 PM this time of year) the boat would have risen at least three
feet by midnight, five hours later.

HENRY HUDSON'S JOURNAL; FRIDAY, SEPTEMBER 18 : *"In latitude 42° 18'—
I sailed to the shore in one of their canoes, with an old man, who was the
chief of a tribe consisting of 40 men and 17 women; these I saw there in a
house well constructed of oak bark, and circular in shape, so that it had
the appearance of being well built, with an arched roof. It contained a great
quantity of maize or Indian corn, and beans of the last year's growth, and
there lay near the house for the purpose of drying, enough to load three
ships, besides what was growing in the fields. On our coming into the house,
two mats were spread out to sit upon, and immediately some food was served
in well made red wooden bowls; two men were also dispatched at once
with bows and arrows in quest of game, who soon after brought in a pair of
pigeons which they had shot. They likewise killed a fat dog, and skinned it
in great haste with shells which they had got out of the water. They supposed
that I would remain with them for the night, but I returned after a short time
on board the ship. The land is the finest for cultivation that I have ever in
my life set foot upon, and it also abounds in trees of every description. The
native are a very good people, for when they saw that I would not remain,
they supposed that I was afraid of their bows, and taking the arrows, they
broke them in pieces, and threw them into the fire."*[382]

Paul Huey has positioned the crew at Schodack Island from the previous
day's landing. However, the latitude mentioned is that of Kinderhook Inlet and
Kinderhook Creek, or possibly Stockport (where remains of an Indian Village have
been found) or Stuyvesant instead of Schodack. There are mudflats at Claverack,
near Kinderhook, but Huey believes that Hudson's latitudes are off. *"In latitude 42°
18'—I sailed to the shore in one of their canoes, with an old man, who was the chief of a*

tribe consisting of 40 men and 17 women;" Huey places this event either at Papscanee Island (Jameson 1967: 21-22, 49) or at present Castleton.

Hudson probably mentions the numbers of men and women because it is unusual that there are so many more men than women, and no children. Shirley Dunn (Columbia County Historical Society, Vol. 8, no. 1, p. 36) suggests that some of the women were in hiding with the children, which makes sense. With so much food for so few people, it seems certain that this was a regional distribution center for food, but does that mean the old man was a Grand Chief or Sachem? Yes, or perhaps a retired chief. But where would there be such incredible farmland? For one thing, this disproves the idea they are at Athens; there is no great field of grain near the shoreline. Where is this fantastic site, this breadbasket of the Hudson Valley? We'll get there.

Hudson is usually more gregarious, and also more descriptive in his diary than Juet, so it is quite surprising we don't learn of this old man's name, as he is obviously someone of great importance. Again, great age was not uncommon. Many believed that the course of a person's life was not to exceed "two turns of the wheel," each wheel being 56 years long. This wheel refers to the teaching wheel or medicine hoop made of willow, which the elders hold in their hands to explain to children what they can expect to experience as they go through life. Few today expect to live to 112, but it was apparently more common then. Each direction was marked with a color and divided into two seven-year portions. For example, east represented birth, southeast represented 7 years of age, and south represented 14 years.

"...these I saw there in a house well constructed of oak bark, and circular in shape, so that it had the appearance of being well built, with an arched roof...." Some less permanent houses were thatched with reeds and rushes. This sounds like descriptions (in Ruttenber) of the houses of high-ranking sachems. There was a gerontocracy in traditional times among Algonquins, so I suspect this old man is considered a wise elder and perhaps a grand chief. A grand chief as a rule would live near a council fire spot, and these were usually on islands. If so, it supports Huey's idea that Hudson was anchored at Schodack, one of the most well established council fire islands in the Algonquian-speaking world, one which Frank Speck wrote about to some extent.

Schodack is not only at a major river crossing, it is just below the "head of the tide," and "the head of navigation," and somewhat further below the confluence of the Mohawk and Hudson Rivers. All of these geographical factors add to the importance of one particular island over another. The "head of the tide" was called *sunkheag* (or spelled sunkheague) in Munsee language, a term which means "she is at the head of the estuary (sea-river)." *Sunk* is short for *sunkskwa*, (also spelled

sunksquaw) or "head woman," used for female chiefs in some cases. *Heague* is generally an estuary, a "river-sea." It implies that both the river and the waterfall itself are feminine, as rivers are called "the blood of our mother earth" among most Algonquin people. Mi'kmaq elder Joe Mike Augustine said about Red Bank, New Brunswick, "I can remember this was where the Indians always made their villages, head of a tide. That's where the fish come up, low tide or high tide. There's a head of a tide here, see?"[383] He called that place in the river *"geezegikshuk."*

"It contained a great quantity of maize or Indian corn, and beans of the last year's growth, and there lay near the house for the purpose of drying, enough to load three ships, besides what was growing in the fields." This is a well-known passage, and folk lore has it that this hill of beans was located at Red Hook, Rhinebeck, or Hudson, but 42 degrees 18 minutes is quite far north, and there could never be so excellent grain production as this near the shore at any of these locations due to the terrain. These stories are therefore not worth, as they say, a hill of beans.

This passage is one of several indications that the "savages" of the river were living comfortable lives, with little fear of starvation. It also shows that while Eastern Algonquins have a clear sense of "living in the now," (with a great deal of spontaneity and trust as even Juet's sparse diary suggests) and though the practice of "acting on behalf of seven generations to come" is a cornerstone of Native American philosophy, there is also a time for thinking ahead to the immediate future, in a practical sense. In *No Word For Time*, I recalled how a Mi'kmaq elder explained to me that there are times of the year when the people will gather

certain plants to dry them for teas and medicines for next year. There is also a time for harvesting and smoking oysters and for catching and salting fish to be eaten through the winter, not to mention piling firewood for months to come late in the fall. Samuel de Champlain wrote that the residents of the St. Lawrence River valley "continue until they have enough for three or four years' provisions, for fear lest some bad year, barren and unfruitful, should come upon them."[384] Henry's hosts seem to have had three years' store of grains as well.

In addition to their turtle shell calendars, marking 28 edge platelets around the outer rim of the shell to mark days, and the 13 large platelets in the center to mark moons (28x13=364, plus a "day of the dead" once a solar year),[385] indigenous people have certain signs they look for "in the bush" to know when to harvest. For example the Lenape knew that "...when the leaf of the white oak was the size of a mouse's ear," it was time to plant the corn.[386] The Aboriginal Australians today have preserved much of this type of knowledge as it pertains to their "bush." Some of these activities can be managed by a family or clan, but here we can see a sachem, perhaps the Grand Sachem of the Mohicans operating a food management system worthy of a great and generous people, insuring that no one would go hungry with winter frost only one or two moons in their future. To quote *History of Westchester County*, "Next in importance to maize was the sieva bean. It was extensively raised and boiled alone or with the green corn. The latter dish was called "succotash." The boiling was accomplished in bowls of steatite, or in vessels of rude pottery. In addition to these, pumpkins were grown. These were readily baked before the fire. Wild fruits and nuts, in their seasons, also contributed to his support and enjoyment.... With their requirements for food thus met, the Indians here were not destitute of the means of comfortable clothing."[387]

Succotash comes from the native word *m'sickquatash*, "maize not crushed or ground."[388] The traditional "Indian" succotash included not only beans and squash, but the cob and the cut kernels of corn, stirred into the mix separately.[389] The traditional people of New England, descendants of colonists and Algonquins, continue to serve succotash on December 21, winter solstice, each year, probably in concordance with some Native American ritual, calling it "Forefathers' Day," not specifying which set of forefathers they meant.[390] In Algonquin tradition, winter solstice is celebrated each year by honoring the ancestors and telling stories about relatives who have passed on; winter solstice is thought of as "the night of the year," and it is said that the veil between this world and the spirit world is thin at that time, so communication with the dead is easier. Our modern "spiritualist church" movement with its séances, was the brainchild of Andrew Jackson Davis, the Euro-Lenape "seer of Poughkeepsie," who probably saw such practices as a child around Winter Solstice. Mrs. Davis must have also served succotash, cobs included.

The spirit of the "giveaway" ceremony (similar to "potlatch") has always been a vital part of Algonquin culture, and a grand chief, if he was to retain his position, would be expected to give away more than anyone else. It is the reverse of status seeking in the white world, but it is still status seeking nonetheless. Food in Algonquin culture is a symbol of life, and more than a symbol, it can bestow life to those who are hungry. There was power in being able to give it generously, and this man had that power. If Henry was at Kinderhook, or perhaps Stuyvesant, we are just west of the home and historic site of Martin Van Buren, another prosperous old gentleman.

"...On our coming into the house, two mats were spread out to sit upon..." The mats, along with birchbark implements, quillworking, and basketry, were traditionally made by women.[391] Around the world, women are often the prominent weavers in a given culture, due to the finer motor skills the majority of females develop before reaching adolescence. When beadworking arrived to the Hudson Valley some years after Hudson, again it was the women who excelled in this craft, although most men were expected to be proficient as well. Studies (as quoted in *Women in Ancient America* by Bruhns and Stothert) show that this was true in South America but that when it came to commercial or "royal" ventures, men replaced the women because men were free of child-rearing responsibilities and could work long hours.[392] In other words, women were superior weavers in a communal setting where children were swapped off among various "mothers" and other relatives during the day, but in a "deadline" situation, men were more available as they were not already burdened with such an important duty as childrearing.

The mats weren't necessarily made from reeds; they could have been made from tree bark, or again, the dogbane. The Eastern coastal Algonquins were famous for their beautiful, intricately woven mats. The Natives who greeted Father Andrew White and the passengers of the Ark and the Dove at St. Andrews' Island, Maryland, had created such mats, and White describes them at length, as his people ended up living in the richly matted homes of the Algonquins there. This artistry with reeds was probably a regional adaptation; we don't hear much about such mats further north, where other methods were used to keep out the cold. Danckaerts wrote that villagers of Nyack used reed mats and sheets of chestnut bark (in combination) to cover the frames of their wigwams.[393] This seems to indicate a northern adaptation to a southern-based building tradition, or perhaps a summer-to-winter adaptation.

"...and immediately some food was served in well made red wooden bowls." The red wooden bowl may have been made from the Eastern Yew bush, from the heart, which is the reddest and oldest part of the tree. It could also have been from what is called "heart cedar," for the same reason, as it is quite red. Alder is often red also. Osage wood is more of an orange color, and is not soft.

Cedar is one of the four sacred plants; the others are sweet grass, sage, and tobacco. Another possibility is that it was made from a burl, a bowl-like outgrowth of a large tree. It could have been of pine, basswood, or other soft white wood, stained red with red ochre, a sacred mineral that has immune-boosting properties. The ochre is made from limonite, (also called Goethite[394]) which is rich in iron. When mixed with water it forms iron oxide, which supports the red blood cells in the skin when rubbed on and thereby in the blood stream, giving a feeling of greater strength. Once in a while the limonite is found naturally in an "Indian Paint Pot," which holds rainwater in its cup as if waiting for a native to place a brush inside and go to work. To this day, Algonquin medicine people use red ochre (and the color red as a modern adaptation) ceremonially because "it makes the thing it touches stronger."[395]

Hudson does not mention wooden spoons, but this is a popular product of woodcarvers and whittlers all over the world. In *History of Westchester County* we read, "They had wooden bowls for holding their food and wooden spoons for handling it."[396] Peggy Turco writes, "Dried mountain laurel wood, hard, and fine-grained, can be carved into unparalleled forks, ladles, and spoons, which led to its other name, spoonwood."[397] This tree or shrub is now considered endangered in some areas, however it is not a "protected plant" in New York State. According to a New York Times article of June 3, 2007, by Nancy Polk, "Despite persistent rumors, the Mountain Laurel receives no more protection under state law than other plants."[398] As with the yew, it is difficult to pass legislation to protect plants or shrubs.

"...*two men were also dispatched at once with bows and arrows in quest of game, who soon after brought in a pair of pigeons which they had shot....*" They were trying to impress the sailors with their hunting skills. Dropping a pigeon in flight with a bow and arrow is not that easy, because they are fleet of flight and as they are overhead targets, the pull of gravity must be taken into consideration. These birds were most definitely *Columbidae, ectopistes migratorius*, in other words, passenger pigeons. Due to their great plentitude, they were probably not the most expensive item on the menu, but a welcome meal nonetheless for the weary travelers. A Sand Hill band member and elder interviewed for this book said that passenger pigeons "were killed usually using a blowgun. There was a certain time of year when the pigeons were plentiful and could be killed easily."[399] There did not seem to be a sense among the people that passenger pigeons were especially sacred or spiritual, but were great game birds. These particular birds were probably not killed with blowguns, as their hunters carried bows and arrows with them.

"John James Audubon described migrating flocks [of passenger pigeons] that stretched for miles in the sky and took three days to pass over, and which he estimated to contain over a billion birds."[400] The Munsee also have preserved in their old stories and oral traditions of a time in Wundjiyahkun, their "old homeland back east," when the sky would become so blackened with the flocks of passenger pigeons that it would seem as if night had descended on the Munsee people in broad daylight.[401]

It is ironically noted that this indigenous form of the species, fetched for Hudson's men by the Algonquins that day, was completely replaced by the gray-suited European form within a few hundred years, helping to drive this once-predominant eastern woodlands bird into extinction. How the descendants of these same Algonquin peoples have avoided extinction over these last centuries is a remarkable tale of courage and persistence, perhaps best told elsewhere.

Few alive today have ever seen a passenger pigeon, which has been extinct since 1914 —but natives of 1609 would have known them well. The bird we think of as a "pigeon" which now crowds New York City, is a very different bird, the Blue Rock Pigeon. The male passenger pigeon had a reddish or tawny-colored breast and blue-gray head, and a long, wedge-shaped tail. The female had a brownish-gray breast, more like our mourning doves in appearance. These tasty birds were logically a main source of food for Algonquin hunters of the 1600s. In line with the Algonquin cultural rule of never harvesting the last of any group of plants or animals, the river peoples must have felt that the passenger was a gift from Father Sky, very sure that these plentiful creatures could never be wiped out, at least not in their lifetime. Alsop estimates that in Hudson's era, passenger pigeons may have made up an astounding one quarter of the North American bird population. According to Alsop, "they nested in large groups…from Virginia and Kentucky, northward into southern Canada." As the deciduous forests were cut down and replaced by farms, the "gregarious" passenger pigeon had nowhere to hide. Alsop comments that their demise coincided with the disappearance of their thickly forested eastern woodland habitat. In addition to this was the introduction of the feral rock pigeons, their competitors who thrived in cities and towns. After thousands of years of prolific expansion, the passenger pigeons were doomed by forces beyond their control. It would not be appropriate to quote novelist James Fennimore Cooper here as regards the Mohican people, whose descendants still exist, such as Etaoquah, a consultant to this project whose name means "River Keeper" and whose language is preserved in the writings of Schmeck and Carl Masthay, but the Last of the passenger pigeons was named "Martha," and she died of old age at 29 in the Cincinnati Zoo in 1914.[402] A good thing the Mohican people never came to such an end, as Cooper insinuated back in 1826.

Native Americans not only hunted the passenger pigeon, they also ate their eggs, as did numerous Americans of various stripes before 1898.[403] A monogamous pair of passenger pigeons will create two to three white eggs in a season, (much less prolific than chickens) feeding their featherless young after hatching with "pigeon milk," a liquid secreted from their crops.[404] These eggs, too, gradually became too easy to find, a very short-lived blessing for the less perspicacious hunters of the 1800s.

Passenger pigeon songs were not very uplifting or musical; one was a loud, grating sound, another a croaking or chattering, but they were capable of short clucking notes as well.[405] Although passenger pigeons are North American birds exclusively, Hudson would have recognized them as similar to the English racing pigeon (various species, related to the Blue Rock). All pigeons around the world, including postal carrier or homing pigeons used in Baghdad in 1150 CE, are descendants of the Blue Rock Pigeon of ancient times, presumably the kind used by the Pharaohs of Egypt in 3000 BCE. Racing pigeons were particularly popular in Belgium, whose fame would have overflowed into Holland with great ease.[406] Although Hudson was English, at least 11 of the 15 remaining sailors were Dutch or Flemish.

"…They likewise killed a fat dog, and skinned it in great haste with shells which they

had got out of the water..." I presume this was an unusual decision made in order
to provide food for unexpected visitors held in great esteem. Most dogs, especially
terriers, would have been domesticated for hunting, some with names. A good
hunting dog would dine on his catch with the hunters. Algonquins had special
burials for such dogs, and covered their graves with a circle of crushed oyster
shells. Two dog burials dating from about 1400 were found at 209 Street and 9th
Avenue. The graves are found with bodies intact. A dog would not have expected
to be hunted or to make such a sacrifice and would not defend himself. Their skill
in preparing the meat quickly is more remarkable because they did not have shells
that were already sharpened as scrapers, but had to fish them out of the water.
Should we suppose that they were oyster shells? If so, doesn't that mean the water
was brackish, not fresh? Some have suggested that the natives near Croton Point
found a way to open oyster shells without breaking them, and without exposing
them to fire.[407] Clearly, Hudson stood there and witnessed how the young men
managed to open and then sharpen the shells without fire, but he fails to share
that information. Today, they would have cut the hinge muscle at the corner with
a standard-issue oyster knife and pried it open.

Algonquins were not ritual dog eaters like the Lakota. It would be a mistake
to read anything of "Black Elk" into this narrative. Black Elk, the Oglala man of
knowledge of the Sioux, received many visions (in 1932) and his elders told him
that twenty days later he should do the "dog vision" cleansing ceremony, but with
heyokas, who are divine tricksters, or "coyotes" in that tradition. "...he and his
heyoke helpers had to kill a dog and put it to boil in a big kettle. Every person in
camp was called to join in the ceremony around the area where the stew was cooking." Lame Deer added in explanation in 1972, "Well, the heyokas dance around
that steaming kettle, sing and act contrary. If the dreamer says, 'A good day tomorrow,' well, it will be a hell of a day next day..."[408] Hudson's dog meat dinner was not
a cleansing ceremony, and there were no heyokas dancing around the pot. It was
an ad-hoc version of the feasting ceremony, which would honor the four elements.
This feast should normally have meat to honor fire, herb tea to honor water, greens
to honor the earth, and birds to honor the air, although there are many other com-
binations to feast the four directions. Bread could honor fire, potatoes could honor
earth, for example.[409]

"...*The land is the finest for cultivation that I have ever in my life set foot upon, and it
also abounds in trees of every description.*" Such grain production so close to the river
is rare and our best clue as to Hudson's whereabouts. On the east bank of the river,
the best soil and terrain for farming (in either Dutchess or Columbia Counties)
is at Stuyvesant, New York,[410] formerly called Kinderhook. The village sign says,
"Stuyvesant, site of the landing of Henry Hudson's Half Moon in 1609." The lower

border of this township is precisely at 42 degrees, 18 minutes, at the mouth of Kinderhook Creek, but the sign marking the landing spot is a half mile north of the intersection of trade routes 9 and 26A, a few minutes north by astrolabe. The marker reads, "Henry Hudson landed here September 19, 1609, and was entertained by Indians who encamped here called Kinderhook." (State Ed. Dept. 1932) I believe they meant "...landed here September 18, departing on the 19..." but its position does match the unique terrain described by Henry Hudson, as well as the latitude. So here are three reasons to believe in all the hoopla about Stuyvesant. But wait a minute.

If true, it means the Half Moon either drifted a few miles backward from Huey's Schodack location for September 17, or that Huey is wrong and they were at Stuyvesant already, suggesting that the small islands were at Athens. Another possibility is that they never landed at Stuyvesant but did in fact land at Schodack, finding a place of rich soil near the island, meaning Hudson was wrong about the latitude. But where would Hudson find rich farming soil way up there when the best farming on the east bank of the Hudson is at Stuyvesant?

On the west bank. David De Vries described fertile farming soil at the foot of the mountain on the west bank at Schodack Island. David De Vries writes; "The 28th, [April] arrived at Beeren (Bears') Island, where were many Indians fishing. Here the land begins to be low along the margin of the river, and at the foot of the mountains it was good for cultivation."[411]

In fact, some of the most excellent farming land was right on Upper Schodack Island itself. Huey writes, "The alluvial islands that form Castelton Island State Park consisted of rich, fertile soil ideal for farming. One or more of these islands must have been cleared and used by prehistoric Indians as well as the historic period Mahicans who lived nearby if not on the islands. Geologically, the area is distinctive also because of fossil clam remains that have been found at Schodack Landing. In 1973, tests on a fossilized clam found on the river bank there indicated that it was about 570 million years old, making it the oldest-known fossil clam in existence. (Blanchard 1973)

"As early as 1844 Henry R. Schoolcraft had identified Schodack as the Mahicans' "seat of their council fire" (Huey 1992–1993: 111). It is possible the 17th-century Mahican village was in present Castleton and was moved to Schodack Island in the early 18th century. Arthur C. Parker in 1922 reported a Mahican village site in Castleton on a hill owned by Jacob Seaman. The site contained Iroquoian late Woodland pottery but was unfortunately excavated for sand."[412]

Parker in 1922 also noted "traces of occupation" just south of Castleton on the mainland near the north end of present Castleton Island (Parker 1922: pl. 209). Van Rensselaer's map of 1632 shows extensive corn fields north and south of Fort

Orange, and on the islands as well.[413]

Huey writes, "...it appears that Hudson may have anchored *in the Half Moon* between the Papscanee Island area and the north end of Upper Schodack Island opposite present Castleton, where his mate probably went ashore to visit with the Mahican chief who lived there. If there was a settlement or village of Mahicans on the hill in Castelton, those Indians most likley grew crops conveniently nearby on Upper Schodack Island."[414] I believe that if Hudson was correct about the six leagues, the Half Moon was anchored not near Papscanee Island but below Upper Schodack, and that Hudson traveled by Indian canoe, as he himself states, to all the areas Huey describes. This also suggests he was riding in a swift birchbark canoe, not a slow-moving dugout.

"Known to the Mahican Indians as Cachtanaquick, Lower Schodack Island was called Moesmans Island by the Dutch in the 17th Century.... Lower Schodack Island was apparently not yet cleared of timber and was perhaps to be the source of Moesman's lumber. As late as 1978 wood was still to be cut on Lower Schodack, or Moesman's Island." (Huey 1992–1993: 101)

"A crude map made in 1730 attached to the deed from the Indians of Lower Schodack Island conveying land to Maes Hendricksen van Buren shows the location of the Mahican Indian village on the northwest corner of this island. The village is identified as including "Ampaments house" (Huey 1992-1993: 104). Ampamet was living as early as 1703 and was chief of the Mahicans living on Lower Schodack Island by 1722. They were still there as late as 1755 (Dunn 1994: 219-223; Huey 1992-1993: 105)."[415]

"It was possibly in this area, somewhere north of Upper Schodack Island, that Henry Hudson anchored the Half Moon and on September 18, 1609, sent his mate on shore to meet with the 'old Savage,' presumably a chief, 'Who carried him to his house.' On September 4, 1648, Wanemenhett and three other Mahican chiefs, who must have been among the children greeting Hudson in 1609, sold the Muitzeskill with land north and south of it to Jacob Jansen Gardenier. The Mahican name for the Muitzeskill was 'Paponicuck,' described as a 'river with bordering thickets.' A short distance inland is a substantial water fall, and here Gardenier soon built a mill."[416]

Huey continues, "Since the Schodack islands evidently served as the traditional central council fire place of the Mohican nation, Mahican descendants today are very concerned about park development and preservation of the island, the village site and Indian burials."[417]

I have identified well over a hundred "council fire islands" (or "rendezvous islands" as they were called in New England) around the United States and Canada, and they seem to play a significant role in the history of the political development of those two nations. Situated near the head of tide and a major trail crossing where creeks enter from the side, it is not surprising that "Schodack Island" became the seat of power of such a large Algonquin nation, and not surprising that the "white man's" Fort Orange stood in watch over it, as that was the general pattern. Also typical is the way the state capitol grew out of that interface over time. There are dozens of similar examples elsewhere, but few as significant.

But much of what Hudson describes is not right at the lower end of Upper Schodack, which is the furthest point the Half Moon could have possibly reached on September 17, as far as I can determine, traveling six leagues north from the Mud Flats. It's probably seven. The answer is simple. As Juet describes, Hudson and his men have ditched the Half Moon and are exploring the area by a much more suitable means of transport, a birchbark canoe. These light, buoyant canoes are much faster than dugouts and do well in shallow water. In a few hours, he could visit the Castleton site on the east bank, the main fort on Schodack Island, and the rich planting fields on the island and on the west bank as well.

Edward Hagaman Hall positions the Half Moon anchored off the shore at New Baltimore, going up to the mouth of the Hannacroix (formerly Hannacrois) Creek, which is just south of Schodack Island, also near Houghtaling. This is close to the lower end of Upper Schodack.

Hannacrois is a rare French example of a Double Dutch word game. The *crois* ending is clearly intended to convey the French word *croiser*, the verb "to cross,"[418] as in the phrase *J'ai croisé la chemin*, "I have crossed the road."[419] Hannah is a probably French woman's first name, so it suggests "Hannah's Crossing." It is presumably derived from the Mohican *hanna-qua*. *Hanna* is the equivalent of the Munsee *wanna-* the Wappinger *ranna-* and the occasional *tanna-*, all referring to a fresh water stream that runs into salty or brackish estuarial water, plus the connecting vowel A which adds no meaning. The *qua* ending means shallow water, as we see at Sinasqua, Nissequa, Massapequa, Renaqua, and countless others.

The Algonquian *qua* does not sound the same as the French *crois*, so it is clearly a play on words. However, the English or Dutch would probably not pronounce the French *R* correctly, and would substitute it with the *W* phoneme, which is more like the Algonquian *qua*, which sounds like *KWA*, returning it to its correct pronunciation once again.

Hannah's Crossing makes a lot of sense because Hannacrois Creek crosses a probable native trade route, now 143, at Coeymans Hollow and also near the Star Road, and crosses trade route 9W a mile north of the modern-day town of Hannacrois and two miles south of Ravena, New York. Its mouth is right next to that of Onesquethaw Creek, which implies a place where one looks down from a high ridge.[420] That high ridge and landing below faces Schodack Island, the original Island of Fire of the Mohican nation. Across the island on the opposite shore is Schodack Landing.

According to a map created by Jo(h?)an Vinckeboon in the early 1600s, Fort Orange was built right between the mouth of these two creeks on the west shore of the Hudson facing an island just north of "Castals Eylandt."[421] Could it be that the creek that the early Dutch had to cross to get to Fort Orange from the southerly direction was "Hannah's Crossing?" It was only recently that signs were erected spelling the creek's name as Hannacroix, referring to a crossroads or Christian crucifix.

The name Castle's Island refers to the Mohican palisaded fort located on the island, which also gave rise to the naming of nearby Castleton on Hudson. Fort Nassau was placed on the island in 1614 at its southern tip to displace the Mohican stronghold. It was wiped out by a winter ice storm in 1617 and never replaced. Fort Orange rose up a few years later on the west bank facing the old fort ruins, between Hannacrois and Onesquethaw as mentioned, replacing a fort built so early in American history that it disappeared three years before the pilgrims first placed their feet on Plymouth Rock.

Fort Orange, (built in 1630 after the establishment of Rensselaerwyck that year) was nicknamed "The Fuyck." It gave rise to Beverwyck in 1652, which became Albany in 1664 when the English took control, and City Hall was erected at the site of Fort Orange in 1668, within sight of the original Native American council fire. It was called Willemstadt in 1673 (for one year, under the Hollandistas during the short-lived Revolution of New Amsterdam) and then Albany again in 1674. So it is not a stretch to say that the Mohican "castle" and its council fire was the seed from which New York State's capitol grew.

This then is the answer as to the question "Where's Henry?" The Half Moon was anchored to the south, possibly even at Houghtaling Island. The hill of beans was on Upper Schodack, and the fort was there to protect it and the Grand Council fire as well. The Grand Sachems were there to wisely distribute the food in case of hard times. And Henry Hudson was there to bring the Dutch to that spot, using his diplomatic skills, such as they were, to introduce the Dutch Master's Mate and others of his Dutch crew to this jewel of Algonquin civilization, to its best farmland and its most generous leaders, so that they could get a foothold in the so-called New World and give the English a run for their money. It all makes sense. Except that he was himself an Englishman and that his latitudes were ten miles off.

"The native are a very good people, for when they saw that I would not remain, they supposed that I was afraid of their bows, and taking the arrows, they broke them in pieces, and threw them into the fire." The word *ah-kink* in Munsee means "it is not worthy,"

and the Indian hand sign for "bad" is to pantomime throwing something down to the ground with the right hand.[422] Even if there was no fire, the throwing of the arrows on the ground would have been a nonverbal way of saying "arrows between friends are bad." This was clearly a nonverbal form of demonstration—there were other less dramatic ways to communicate this message in sign language. The sign for "friend" for example uses the index and middle fingers of the right hand held together, pointing up, with thumb crossed over the remaining fingers, facing out. It represents two men who join forces. This sign became a logo for Boy Scouts of America in the 1950s. The intertribal sign for peace and getting along is with the right hand palm up grasped by the left hand palm down.[423]

> JUET'S JOURNAL, FRIDAY, SEPTEMBER 18 : *The eighteenth in the morning was fair weather, and we rode still. In the afternoon our master's mate went on land with an old savage, a governor of the country, who carried him to his house and made him good cheer.*

We wonder, is this the same "old man?" I believe it is a different one. We see no sign of them moving from this place, and small wonder. They are being treated very well. A governor of the country would be a grand sachem. This suggests that the other elder was a retired grand sachem. The people of this location would be part of the Mohican Nation. Huey believes the chief may have lived on Papscanee Island (Jameson 1967: 21-22, 49), or "present Castleton."[424] Who is Juet referring to as "our master's mate?" It is not Juet himself because, at least according to *God's Mercies* by Douglas Hunter, he is of the "Dutch majority" on the ship. Elsewhere Juet refers to the master's mate and others as "they."

> JUET'S JOURNAL, SATURDAY, SEPTEMBER 19 : *The nineteenth was fair and hot weather. At the flood, being near eleven o'clock, we weighed and ran higher up two leagues above the shoals, and had no less water than five fathoms we anchored and rode in eight fathoms. The people of the country came flocking aboard, and brought us grapes and pompions, which we bought for trifles; and many brought us beavers' skins, and otters' skins, which we bought for beads, knives and hatchets. So we rode there all night.*

They traveled about two more leagues north, which Huey says would bring them to the Port of Albany.

"...*many brought us beavers' skins, and otters' skins, which we bought for beads, knives and hatchets. So we rode there all night...*" In November of 1624, no less than 675 otter skins were shipped back to Holland.[425] "In Wassenares' 'History of the New Netherlands,' it is narrated: 'The tribes are in the habit of clothing themselves with otter skins, the fur inside, the smooth side without; which however, they paint so beautifully that at a distance it resembles lace. When they bring their commodities to the traders, and find they are desirous to buy them, they make so little matter of it that they rip up the skins they are clothed with and sell them also, returning naked to their homes.[426] Wassenares also mentions that they use the beaver skins mostly for sleeves, and otter for the rest of their clothing.

Beaver skins were plentiful still, but were being hunted out in order to do business with traders and trappers. They would be wiped out within twenty years. Otter on the other hand, were not as plentiful, and their skins were symbols of initiation, at least to the Midewiwin, a sacred teaching lodge to the north, mostly under the auspices of the Ojibway, whose name implies that they wrote down ancient stories and histories on birchbark. The place the Dutch later called Otter Hook lay only three miles up the river. Can we assume this was where these furs came from? Again, the word "pompions" is unclear but most scholars agree it refers to a pumpkin.

If the "flood" or high tide was 11 AM then the high tide mentioned from the entry of the 17th was 11:40 PM, 36 hours earlier, minus forty minutes.

Hall locates Juet at Schermerhorn Island, and Selkirk. He indicates the ship stays anchored there from the 19th to the 22nd "while the small boat explores up-river to Pleasantdale."

JUET'S JOURNAL, SUNDAY, SEPTEMBER 20 : *The twentieth in the morning was fair weather. Our master's mate with four men more went up with our boat to sound the river, and found two leagues above us but two fathoms water, and the channel very narrow, and above that place seven or eight fathoms. Toward night they returned: and we rode still all night.*

Juet was the ship's mate, not the master's mate. There is a difference, obviously, as here Juet refers to "they" as including the master's mate and not himself. If a league is 2.2 miles, they traveled 4.4 northward by row-boat and found rather shallow water, but deeper water beyond.

Schodack is one of the most important council fire islands in the east, and served as a meeting place not only for the Mohicans, but for the Wabanaki Confederacy grand council, even though the Mohicans are not part of the Wabanaki.

Schodack means "place of fire." I have also found a word in the Innu language of the Naskapi, *akaam-iSKUTA-ahch*, holding a similar meaning, "across the fire." William Mameanskumw, a fluent speaker of the Naskapi dialect of Innu, recognized the word Schodack as one relating to "fire" in his own Algonquian language.[427] Then there is the Cree word *iskotew*, (pronounced is-ko-**tay**-oo) which means fire. Schodack is the same word with the "I" dropped and the T softened to a D, plus a locative ending, meaning "place of."

There has been extensive research into its history as a council fire place. The Mohawks were referring to the Mohican council fire there, not their own, and the Mohican word for fire is *staau*, but few remember that today. It was the Mohican capitol at contact, as it probably had been an Algonquin capitol since the days of Allumettes Island. Route 890, the Berkshire Section, an extension between 90 and 87, crosses the island today. There is a new state park on the island, and discussions are being held concerning a Native American cultural center.

The town on the shore nearby is called Castleton, after the Mohican fort or "castle" which was there. There were considerable rapids to the west of the island, which served as an excellent defense in case some Mohawks decided to attack from the west. Even early 19th Century maps show difficult waters to the west. The river was reconfigured in the 1820s to allow easier boat passage to Albany.[428] On the eastern side is a modest slip of water called Schodack Creek, easily crossed from the eastern banks, which is where the Mohican village settlements were, including their capitol city, although some did live on the island itself. Civil engineers have used the island for dumping the spoil from dredging operations, which has changed the landscape entirely. What was once several islands clustered together is now one long island called Schodack.

> JUET'S JOURNAL, MONDAY, SEPTEMBER 21 : *The twenty-first was fair weather, and the wind all southerly: we determined yet once more to go farther up into the river, to try what depth and breadth it did bear, but much people resorted aboard, so we went not this day. Our carpenter went on land and made a fore-yard, and our master and his mate determined to try some of the chief men of the country, whether they had any treachery in them. So they took them down into the cabin and gave them so much wine and aquavita, that they were all merry, and one of them had his wife with him, who sat as modestly, as any of Our countrywomen would do in a strange place. In the end one of them was drunk, who had been aboard of our ship all the time that we had been there; and that was strange to them for they could not tell how to take it: the canoes and folks went all on shore, but some of them came again and brought stropes of beads; some had six seven, eight, nine, ten, and gave him. So he slept all night quietly.*

With the wind "all southerly" they were moved further upstream, which was where they were bound. *"Our carpenter went on land and made a fore-yard..."* A foreyard is the lowest yard on a foremast. A yard is short for yardarm, which is the entire crosspiece that intersects the mast, supporting a square sail, and also possibly signal lights. A foremast is the mast nearest the bow (or front) of the ship.[429] In some cases it would be a yard long; the Dutch called it a "ra"[430] (perhaps because its length is similar to a cubit.) This indicates that one of the two 3-foot long spars that make up the lowest arm on the first mast (to use everyday terminology) had broken off and needed to be replaced.

"...and our master and his mate determined to try some of the chief men of the country, whether they had any treachery in them. So they took them down into the cabin and gave them so much wine and aqua-vita, that they were all merry, and one of them had his wife with him, who sat as modestly, as any of Our countrywomen would do in a strange place. In the end one of them was drunk, who had been aboard of our ship all the time that we had been there; and that was strange to them for they could not tell how to take it." None of our experts comment on location, but it is interesting that one of the Natives had "been aboard the ship all the time we'd been there." This shows a growing familiarity between the two parties, however it sounds as if most of that buddy-buddy stuff was a trick to get the natives drunk. It is true that anyone who is planning a crime or murder is likely to talk about it when drunk, and Hudson was far from the sea and needed to know what he was dealing with.

Hudson and crew had had an unusual number of mishaps and hostilities, much of which can be traced back to his taking captives, a custom the Algonquins had been wary of by 1609. On the other hand, it does seem highly unethical by our modern standards for Henry to introduce alcohol to unsuspecting Native Americans who had no way of knowing what they were imbibing, and perhaps becoming addicted to. According to Samuel W. Eager, "this was the first instance of intoxication among the Indians in this part of the continent."[431] Budke writes, "In their aboriginal state they had no intoxicants, their only drink having been cold water, but alcohol once tasted, they willingly gave up any, or all, of their possessions for the joy of getting drunk. Rum and beer was part of the consideration in most of the land purchases, and about the only consideration in some of them."[432]

Aqua Vita is a word for ethanol, a grainy drink that has a high alcohol content. Even if these Native Americans did not have a low tolerance for alcohol due to a blood-type-related deficiency in ALDH (Aldehyde Dehydrogenase) and other factors, not all of which are conclusively proven,[433] ethanol would have a dizzying effect on almost anybody. However, there is another interesting possibility. Aqua Vita is also the English slang term for French Cognac, which is highly distilled ethanol. The Shannessee brewery in Ireland distills thousands of gallons of Cognac from ethanol every year, keeping the tradition alive. It is possible that Hudson saved his best aged Cognac, "Aqua Vita," for this special occasion, to spare no expense to entertain his Native American guests, but this is terribly unlikely.

By bringing the intoxicated man a strope of wampum, his friends were demonstrating a belief that he was possessed by a bad spirit. Many traditional Native Americans today still hold to the belief that alcohol is in fact a "spirit," perhaps a "plant spirit," one derived from the energy of the original plant, or perhaps a human one which becomes attached to the drinker.

The well-known painter and historian John Trumbull, at the age of ten, met Zachary Johnson, a "full-blooded Mohegan," and considered after Uncas' death the regent of the tribe, who visited his parents for dinner. Zach had foresworn liquor, but young John tried to tempt him with a mug of home brewed beer. He said, "Zachary, this beer is excellent: won't you taste it?" The knife and fork dropped from the Indian's hand: he leaned forward with a stern intensity of expression: his dark eyes, sparkling with indignation, were fixed on the young tempter. "John," said he, "you don't know what you are doing. You are serving The Devil, boy. Don't you know that I am an Indian? I tell you that I am; and if I should taste your beer I could never stop until I got to rum, and became again the drunken contemptible wretch your father once knew me. John, while you live never again tempt any man to break a good resolution."[434] Even if he overstates his case, Zachary made an indelible impression in the eyes of the young John Trumbull about alcohol in general.

Alcohol causes problems not only among Native Americans, but around the world wherever it appears. However there are cultural aspects to the problem as well. Each of the "seven deadly sins" are fairly harmless and natural when taken in small quantities and experienced in a sacred context, but highly dangerous when taken to excess. When a people have no experience with a "habit," they have no traditions or customs by which to modify their expression, and the results are generally disastrous. One could argue that alcohol was disastrous for the Native Americans in part because they had no experience with it as a culture (at least across most of North America). Europeans had the Christian ritual of communion as a sacred space within which wine was made harmless, or possibly beneficial, but the Europeans had trouble with tobacco, as they had no spiritual context in which it was made harmless.[435] By the end of World War II, a vast number of Europeans were addicted to tobacco, but in a way that was almost in defiance of the sacred, just as a vast number of Native Americans were drinking themselves to death in defiance of the very society that introduced Aqua Vita to them.

"...the canoes and folks went all on shore, but some of them came again and brought stropes of beads; some had six seven, eight, nine, ten, and gave him. So he slept all night quietly..." The stropes of beads must have been fathom-long strands, or wampum belts, (from wappa-bee-el, strung together) usually one yard long and varying in width. Before the introduction of Dutch muxes, which are steel drills to speed up the process, it would take a man days to create one belt of wampum beads a yard long. I believe Juet is saying that some of them were carrying between six and ten belts. They were concerned about the man who was acting strangely, not having seen alcohol before. It is possible that they thought he was possessed by a demon and offered some sacred belts to him, whose purple and white patterns may have represented or spelled out some powerful blessing or prayer. The idea would have been to let him hold it to drive the bad spirit out of him. Sometimes tobacco would be presented, wrapped in strings of wampum or a belt, both in diplomatic and in healing circumstances.[436] Unless Juet is mistaken, this is not the case here. Apparently, it worked, and he slept quietly.

Some think of wampum as a form of "money," but this use was a later development. Originally it was a sacramental object for ceremony, then a form of medicine, then a form of writing, then a political tool, and only now and then was it used for trade. In the book *Three Strands in the Braid*, author Paula Underwood writes, "When given to another, the giver transferred energy to the receiver." Although she is Mohawk, I feel this also expresses Algonquin views about the use of both tobacco and wampum, and explains how a wampum belt can be used as medicine. She attributes to Tehanetorens (Ray Fadden, also Mohawk) the following insight, which also applies to Algonquin culture; "Wampum also served as a concrete representation of agreements and promises. This was especially important during treaty ceremonies. No treaty was recognized as valid unless wampum was exchanged. This wampum was Iroquois documentation."[437]

These were not trinkets they threw together and gave away, these were most likely heirlooms that had been passed down for generations for just such emergencies. He would have had to give them back soon enough. Juet may not have seem wampum before: it does not age or yellow with time and always looks like it was "made yesterday." Ironically, these beads were probably made at the same Siwanoy "wampum factory" where John Colman was killed, at the Snackapins village near the mouth of the Bronx River.

Juet mentions the word "canoes" here, but does not specify birchbark or dugout. Again, it would have been instructional to us today if he had. The current understanding is that dugout canoes were used in salty or brackish water, usually hollowed from tulip trees that thrive in salt water, while birchbark was used in clear water, in that birchbark tends to dissolve in salt water. Other accounts say birch were used north of Albany as it was not tidal. On September 4, Henry Hudson described their "canoes, which are made of a single hollow tree" but my guess is that Juet would have said "dugout" if the boat was a hollowed-out tree, but would have used the term canoe as we would, to refer to the birchbark type with the gunwales and ribs stretched with bark and sealed with pitch. Since the next day's journey brought them to waters that were too shallow for the Half Moon to navigate in, the canoe would have been necessary in that it barely displaces any water as it is being paddled.

As to the behavior of the women, Juet didn't say the woman in question had anything to drink. They might have seen the folly in that right away, and steered her clear of it, meanwhile intoxicating her husband with red wine and "hootch." Nonetheless, it is highly significant that she maintained such aplomb. There was a waning half moon in the sky this night, and just as the ship the Half Moon was reaching its halfway point in terms of miles up and down the Hudson, the shadow that had been charting its course across the rounded face of the moon had also reached the halfway point.

JUET'S JOURNAL, TUESDAY, SEPTEMBER 22 : *The two and twentieth was fair weather: in the morning our master's mate and four more of the company went up without boat to sound the river higher up. The people of the country came not aboard till noon, but when they came and saw the savages well they were glad. So at three o'clock in the afternoon they came aboard and brought tobacco and more beads and gave them to our master, and made all oration, and shewed him all the country round about.*

Then they sent one of their company on land, who presently returned and brought a great platter full of venison, dressed by themselves and they caused him to eat with them: then they made him reverence and departed all save the old man that lay aboard. This night at ten o'clock, our boat returned in a shower of rain from sounding of the river, and found it to be at an end for shipping to go in. For they had been up eight or nine leagues, and found but seven foot water, and unconstant soundings.

"The two and twentieth was fair weather: in the morning our master's mate and four more of the company went up without boat to sound the river higher up." We don't know who the master's mate was—it was not Juet; but on the morning of September 22, the master's mate went on foot a short distance with a few of the men to sound the depths of the waters around the islands, and came back shortly.

"The people of the country came not aboard till noon, but when they came and saw the savages well they were glad." As the few who were on board came down with the mysterious illness we call "drunkenness," their relatives were concerned, but were amazed and relieved to see that all traces of this strange "sickness " had disappeared by noon that day. "So at three o'clock in the afternoon they came aboard and brought tobacco and more beads and gave them to our master, and made all oration, and shewed him all the country round about." Those first scouts went back on land and three hours later, returned with more wampum beads, valuable gifts often given out on special occasions,[438] and of course tobacco, the gift to spirit. Their oration would have been in Mohican. It is interesting to think how Hudson would have responded. Perhaps he was learning the language already.

There are disagreements as to the correct form and pronunciation of Mohican. To illustrate this, I will show a comparison between the short Mohican word list from *History of the Indians of Connecticut*, and the highly regarded word list from Jonathan Edwards' "Observations" on the Mohegan Language from 1789. This may help readers experience for themselves the difficulties Hudson would have to face trying to understand the oratory made in his honor.

> Man: neemanaoo (JE: that man=uwoh)
>
> Woman: p'ghainoom
>
> Ear: towahgue (JE: towohque)
>
> Eye: ukeesquan (JE: hkeesque)
>
> Teeth: wpeeton (JE: His teeth=wepeeton)
>
> House: wekuwuhm (JE: weekumuhm)
>
> Shoes: mkissin (JE: mkissin)
>
> Sun: keesogh (JE: keesogh)
>
> Fire: staauw (JE: stauw)
>
> Water: nbey (JE: nbey)
>
> Bear: mquch (JE: mquoh)
>
> River: sepoo (JE: sepoo)

The following Mohican words in parenthesis are from more recent sources, as quoted in my *Introductory Guide to Lenape Indian Words and Phrases*)

> One: ngwittoh (nu-kut)
>
> Two: neesoh (neesh)
>
> Three: noghkoh (naukhh)
>
> Four: noghkoh (na-wuh)
>
> Five: nunon (nau-non-nu)
>
> Six: ngwittus (n'quit-taus)
>
> Seven: tupouwus (taup-ow-waus)
>
> Eight: ghusooh (khau-soow)
>
> Nine: nauneeweh (nau-ne-weh)
>
> Ten: mtannit (don-n)
>
> *Some additional words*
>
> Moon: neepauhauck
>
> Day: waukaumanw

Night: t'pochk

Rain: thocknaun

Snow: msauneeh

Tree: machtok

Dog: n'dijau (?)

Nose: okeewon

Mouth: otoun

John de Forest, the author of this source spent some time among the Mohegan of Eastern Connecticut, an offshoot of the Mohicans, and states that as of 1849, "English is the language of most of the community; but a few old people still cling to their ancient Mohegan, and have only a broken knowledge of the tongue of the white men." Such was the case with many Algonquian languages just before the Civil War, and yet most of them survived well into the Twentieth Century.

Then they sent one of their company on land, who presently returned and brought a great platter full of venison, dressed by themselves and they caused him to eat with them: then they made him reverence and departed all save the old man that lay aboard."[439] There was yet another feast, a symbolic blessing for the hungry travelers, as food is the gift of life. In contrast, the people of Dartmouth England were to scorn the starving crew (who had run out of all provisions probably three quarters of the way home) upon their return, refusing to let them land or to offer them food or any other basic necessity. Finally one Englishman offered to buy their anchor from them for a small sum of money, only enough to buy a few days' provisions. They were forced by weakness and dizziness to succumb to his cruel offer, and then continued to wait for permission to dock anywhere in England that would allow them,[440] docking would be difficult without an anchor.

"This night at ten o'clock, our boat returned in a shower of rain from sounding of the river, and found it to be at an end for shipping to go in. For they had been up eight or nine leagues, and found but seven foot water, and unconstant soundings." Juet forgot to mention that at some point early in the day, a number of men had gone north in the tender (row boat) in search of an unlikely northwest passage to China in this long stretch of shallow water. Using 2.2 miles for a league, some members of the crew traveled a total of 19.2 miles northward above Schodack Island. That is the distance from the northern tip of Upper Schodack Island (just south of today's Castleton-on-Hudson) and the mouth of the Mohawk River. So it would not be unreasonable to assume the mother ship was located at Upper Schodack during their expedition.

On the way, they would have ascended some steep rapids as they passed the town of Troy, an ancient village site spanning many eons of Native American "time." Here they might notice the great trade route now called Route 7, the Hoosic Trail. That trail crosses the Hudson at Green Island, which I believe to have been an inhabited site in ancient times, and possibly an "island of fire" for a while at least. River Street, aka Route 4, is another old trail site that runs along the eastern bank of the river. Route 32 from Newburgh/New Paltz runs along the west bank. South of these islands is the modern capitol of New York State, Albany. High atop of the State Capitol building is a bust of Henry Hudson, next to a bust of Chief Joseph Brandt. They are looking out across the city towards Schodack Island to the southeast, but it doesn't look like they are saying much to one another. Brandt was a Mohawk who lived 150 or so years later.

The state capitol building is at the T intersection of Route 32, aka the New Paltz Road, and the terminus of the Mohawk Trail, and borders the Mohican Trail aka Route 9 on the other side. Route 9 crosses the Hudson for the first time (heading north) at the narrow crossing from Rensselear a few yards south of the capitol. Clinton Avenue completes the square of that historic block. There is a long peninsula or sand bar in the river there, but only Route 90 crosses it today; the Route 9 crossing is just a mile or two too far south.

They must have navigated around Peebles Island, which was called Nach-te-nack, or "council fire," in reference to Moenimins Castle situated there.[441] This route would have taken them to Cohoes Falls, well past the mouth of the Mohawk River, a large body of water with slow current flowing in from the west. One would think that Hudson might have thought it the northwest passage, or at least a way to the Great Lakes. In the Velasco map that was issued soon after Hudson's return, this river appears, and a connection to the Great Lakes is shown, though a fanciful one.

The Mohawk River does lead to a northwest passage, but Hudson would not have found his way without Mohawk assistance; There is a two mile portage called Oneida Carry, which Henry would have had to cross, traveling from the Mohawk River to Wood Creek. Fort Stanwix is still there. Then he would have passaged west to West Oneida River, to Three Rivers, to Oswego River, Oswego Falls and then to Oswego.[442] From Oswego, Hudson could have launched a different ship onto Lake Ontario, portaged around Niagara Falls, ran through the straights at Detroit, run the rapids at "Soo" Ste. Marie and found himself in Lake Superior. If he had found the Brule River, he could have gotten onto the St. Croix and headed south to the Mississippi. If he had then turned right at St. Louis, he could have taken the Missouri all the way upstream to the Rocky Mountains. He could have then gotten on the Milk River, and made it all the way to Glacier National Park. From there he would have had to walk many days to get to the headwaters of the

Snake River, which would lead to the Columbia, which would rapidly descend to the Pacific. From there China was only a few weeks away by shallop, which he would have had to build on shore out of green timber.

It is remarkable, due more to luck than skill, that Hudson's little by-boat, did, as far as we know, find the Mohawk River, and an admittedly difficult passage to China, on its final day heading north. It is reasonable to think that somewhere along the line, either Verrazzano, John Smith, Samuel de Champlain, or Henry Hudson himself, had been told by a Native American about this interior route westward, and shared this information with Henry. It seems more likely than the alternative, which is blind luck.

And yet Juet does not mention it. Clearly they were unable to explore it further because they could not get the Half Moon past the shallow waters at Albany nor could they have gotten the big ship past the rapids at Troy (where the dam is now) and could not go too long without supplies. It also surprises me that they do not mention the large rapids at Troy.

It seems that Henry did not go with them, and may have been skeptical of their claims when they got back. Hudson told Van Meteren when he got back to London that the *ship* (The Half Moon) had only reached as far as 42° 40' which is hardly past Albany. Juet wrote in his account that the crew had reached to nearly 43° latitude before turning back. Obviously he meant the men of the *row boat* or tender they had been using every day, or another boat of larger dimensions stored somewhere on the ship in easy-to-assemble pieces. Even so, for them to row this distance seems almost impossible. 43° is half way to Saratoga Springs from Albany. The Mohawk River reaches that latitude at Fort Johnson, but that is too many miles west. "Half Moon Point" (one spot where folk custom has them turning around) is right between these two estimates, at 42°47', and this is also the general area that Sweet suggests.[443]

It is also probable that a Mohawk met with the exploratory crew and somehow explained to them that they could travel far into the interior via the Mohawk River and get to the Great Lakes via that route. We know this because the Velasco map issued in 1610 includes a schematic water link between the Hudson River and the Great Lakes at this latitude.

Therefore the crew of the Half Moon had to keep the remarkable discovery a secret, so that other nations would not learn of this passage. They clearly planned to come back the following year, to explore this duty-free passage to China (Spain demanded a tax on all ships traveling around the Cape of Good Hope).

One wonders if they got to see Cohoes Falls. The Algonquin are not the only people who loved and cared for their waterfalls. The Mohawk revere Cohoes Falls just as much. It was here that the Cohoes Mastodon, on display at the New York

State museum, was found in a large pothole. The falls also play a role in the original "Hiawatha" story.

At Cohoes, NY, the Mohawk River and Hudson meet, and there is a great waterfall, most of it dry, but very tall. This is Cohoes Falls, and there are the twin islands of Peebles Island, and Van Schaick Island at the meeting of the two waters. That a spot on the north shore was an important meeting place was brought down to us through Mohawk oral tradition. The stories of Hiawatha (Iatwenta) and the Peacemaker tell of walking along what is now Route 5, west to east, bringing four of the five nations together. The Peacemaker had a double row of teeth (which I believe to be a genetic trait that still runs among descendants of the Wyandot, including some Munsee) so it was difficult to speak clearly and Iatwenta (Hiawatha) went along as a translator. The Peacemaker stopped at a place a few yards northeast of Cohoes Falls to meet with the chief of the Mohawk, the largest of the five nations. According to one story, the Mohawk Chief tested the Peacemaker relentlessly. He told him that, if he was the messenger of the Creator (and the Mohawk today say he was of virgin birth), they could tie him to a tree at the top of that falls of solid rock, then cut the tree down, and he would survive. If this Peacemaker could do that, they'd adopt his League of Nations. According to the story they tied him up, cut the tree down and then left him for dead. The next day they saw his campfire smoke rising up the falls, and went down and found him cooking some fish for breakfast. He was without a scratch.[444]

It was at this moment that the Mohawk realized his medicine was strong, and began to adopt his Great Law. When the three men shook hands it was a turning point in world history. The Peacemaker and Iatwenta returned to what is now Rochester with the Mohawk guarantee of solidarity in place, along Route 5, and to make a long story short, convinced the Tonadaho of the Onondaga to join them as the fifth nation, to become the leader of the other nations in the League of Peace. The bicameral government they formed became a model for the United States via Ben Franklin, who attended the Council of Albany and observed the "Iroquois League" in action. The Delaware were present as well. So to say the island next to Cohoes Falls has all the earmarks of an "island of fire" and an important meeting spot is underplaying the possibilities quite a lot. Route 4 (River Street) crosses the Hudson less than a quarter mile north of Peebles Island, and today's Route 470 crosses Van Shaick. The configuration there is almost exactly like that of Victoria Island, except the waterfall is about a mile further downstream, and in the other river. It also has a north-south orientation rather than east-west.

Just north of the Mohawk River but to the west, was the mouth to the Hoosic River to the East, the later site of the Sghagticoke settlement, where natives from all over the New York area went in refuge after King Philip's War. One can read about this in *A Clash of Cultures on the Warpath of Nations, the Colonial Wars in the Hudson-Champlain Valley.*[445] The small boat crew turned around, having unknowingly found the closest thing to a "northwest passage" that existed on the continent at that time. They somehow came down the rapids and made it back to the ship, the Half Moon, without incident.

Chapter Eight

THE RETURN TRIP

*H*owever peaceful and pleasant Hudson's one-week sojourn in the far north was, in the sachem's seat of the Mohicans, so the week of his return was quite the opposite. Whereas his time with the Mohicans at Schodack was remarkably happy, even blissful, Juet's accounts of the trip south become filled with fear and apprehension, exploding into violence and bloodshed. What is it about the Half Moon that attracted these extremes, when to our knowledge today, there did not seem to be such a pronounced difference of temperament between the Mohicans and the Wappingers, who as far as the oral traditions were concerned, were themselves Mohicans, or at least their descendants and protégés? The Munsees on the west bank were not prone to unprovoked violence either. Why was there so much violence in this final Shakespearian scene? Thirteen to fourteen Native Americans dead, a spate of bloodshed that has marked New York's colonial history for four hundred years. Why did this happen?

Edgar Bacon suggests that even though Hudson was temperamental, he was much more diplomatic than his hot-headed crew, and fingers Robert Juet himself as a perpetrator of some of the conflict. He points out the fact that Hudson showed nothing but admiration for Native Americans when discussing his travels on his return to London,[446] while Juet's journal is full of expressions such as "savages," and "we durst not trust them."

Juet is a contemporary of fellow Englishman King James, so it follows that his language would be at times reminiscent of this most famous Bible. There are two passages, which were being translated circa 1609, that contain the expression "durst not..." which is the past tense of "darest not..." One is in Job 32.v 6, the other in Matthew 22 v 46.

Juet is the hero of his own diary. He presents himself as his master's (humble) assistant. He is never at fault, he is always there to be of help. He is the archetypal butler. Except for the three or so glowing pages translated from English to Dutch and back to English from Hudson's writing, all we know about what occurs on the ship is through Juet, his squirrely eyes, his tightly gripped and secretive pen, stingy not only with praise, but with words of any kind. Not once does he even acknowledge the beauty of the landscape. He is hiding his feelings throughout, constantly defending his own actions. A frustrated riverboat poet with the heart of an assassin, he is a cross between Mark Twain and Marcus Brutus.[447]

Suddenly we think back to the several Native American passengers, apparently willing at first to ride with the men, each of them becoming terribly offended by what happens on board, leaping out of port holes to get away. Juet never explains why these natives might have been so angered and upset, but the reason for his reticence is obvious if his own ill deeds were causing all the enmity.

Note that Juet's possessions were the ones that were "stolen" and thrown in the water on October 1 of 1609. This is generally thought to be coincidence, but a number of natives had explored the inside of the ship and could have seen the disagreeable old Juet go into that cabin and close the door. It may be this selective attack was revenge against Juet for hostile actions, which the cagey Mr. Juet would certainly have left out of his own report. After all, it is Juet who says, on October 2 of that year, "*we* discharged six muskets." Perhaps two of them were in his two clenched fists, knuckles white with rage. It's Mr. Juet with the cook in the row-boat, gathering his relatively worthless possessions, when the cook cut the Native American's hand off. It's Juet who fired the falcons, the cast iron cannons, on two different occasions, killing many men, some at close range. As Hudson said, "It's Juet that's done all this."

The incidents of this week provide a case history in the annals of the Algonquin "Way of the Heron," the peacemaking tradition that was shared with Henry David Thoreau in the 1830s by Joseph Polis and Joseph Attien, two Penobscot trail guides. Thoreau then wrote about one small portion of the "Way of the Heron" in his work "On Civil Disobedience," which was later published at Cambridge while Mohandas Gandhi was a student there. Gandhi later credited Thoreau with the coining of the phrase 'civil disobedience," which he often borrowed, never realizing its Native American origins. Juet's writings are about to show us examples of Algonquin-style civil disobedience, but the Englishman fails to hear the message.

They show us the anatomy of a failed encounter, the calculus of catastrophe if you will. In this account we see how one rash act can lead to another and another, until, step by step, all lives are at risk. The guilt is bipartisan. It is a "teaching tale" in the traditions of the native people themselves, such as when (in the Washo story) Weasel, Coyote's little brother, kills a powerful Waterbaby to acquire her scalp and brings calamity upon himself and his big brother. The charming

Coyote is something of a rapscallion himself, but becomes almost fatherly in his efforts to curb the enthusiasm of little Weasel for big trouble.[448] This would be Hudson and Juet. In this chapter, we will reconstruct the fateful events referred to in Juet's journal between Wednesday, September 23 and October 5, 1609, as they flee southward toward the sea.

> JUET'S JOURNAL, WEDNESDAY, SEPTEMBER 23 : *The three and twentieth,*
> *fair weather. At twelve o'clock we weighed and went down two leagues to a*
> *shoal that had two channels one on the one side, and another on the other,*
> *and had little wind, whereby the tide laid us upon it. So there we sat on the*
> *ground the space of an hour till the flood came. Then we had a little gale of*
> *wind in the west; so we got our ship into deep water, and rode all night very*
> *well.*

The chain of islands we call Schodack are 4.4 miles long, "two leagues" according to Lossing. That means they started out at the uppermost point, near where New York State Throughway's Birkshire Extension begins, and traveled to the bottom of Lower Schodack, as Huey suggests. Here we find "*a shoal that had two channels one on the one side, and another on the other.*" The single channel is the eastern one next to Schodack Landing, the water not a hundred feet across from shore to shore (William F. Link's map of 1878). The double channel is the one to the west, split by Mull Island and then Beeren Island. (This means Bears' Island, but the English renamed it Barren Island.) There is hardly 300 feet clearance between Mull and Lower Schodack and about the same between Barren and Mull. According to William F. Link's 1878 map, the main shipping channel passes through the narrow space between Mull and Barren Island at what is now the meeting place of four counties. Fort Nassau was located here at the southern tip of Lower Schodack, and Fort Orange was located on the western shore facing Beeren Island.

Hagaman Hall has the ship going south 4.8 miles back to New Baltimore, near Houghtaling Island. Johnson writes, tersely, "Return down river." But Juet has the final say; "*...so we got our ship into deep water, and rode all night very well.*" The deep water, 130 feet, was west of the southern tip of Houghtaling Island, according to Link's map, which would be one more league south.[449]

> JUET'S JOURNAL, THURSDAY, SEPTEMBER 24 : *The four and twentieth was fair*
> *weather; the wind at the north-west, we weighed and went down the river*
> *seven or eight leagues; and at half ebb we came on ground on a bank of ooze*
> *in the middle of the river, and sat there till the flood; then we went on land*
> *and gathered good store of chestnuts. At ten o'clock we came off into deep*
> *water, and anchored.*

"...the wind at the north-west, we weighed and went down the river..." As the wind was blowing from the northwest, it herded them downstream. Here, after an hour's time they would have passed Coxsackie on the right. Coxsackie was a flint quarry for millennia. It is interesting that the natives traded for Dutch knives and hatchets. The best Munsee knives and hatchets were made from Coxsackie flint, which was mined just miles away, some of the finest in the world. I guess these knife specialists were interested in studying the competition. Famous as the home of the polio-like Coxsackie Virus, this town was once an incredibly important rhyolite mine, producing green chert or flint thousands of years ago, and the Munsee went well out of their way to maintain control over that mine. You don't hear much about green chert mining these days, and hence the town is now rather small. Johannes Bronck, the founding father of the Bronx, was murdered by accident in an Indian raid, possibly the second homicide in the illustrious history of that fine borough after John Colman, and young son Pieter was sent to Fort Orange (now Albany) to grow up in a safe place. When he came to manhood, he purchased the territory of Coxsackie and spent his life there, so the Dutch had an early introduction into the area, and one can still swim in Pieter Bronck's Lake today, just to the west of town.

The suffix *hakee* means "territory," or "land of," in Munsee. The prefix *kahak* should already be familiar as "wild geese." The problem then is the stray letter S in the middle. From a Munsee point of view, the original word may have been Kahakus, the –us ending meaning "small," as in "small geese," with the U dropping out over time. But why would anyone want to know that, and why would one area feature only small geese, when small ones generally come from large ones and their eggs? If it was a nesting area, that would make sense. It is also possible it was once Kahak-sac-hakee, "a point of land into the water which is the territory for wild geese." It is not off the table as a solution, but there is no record of this name being used in colonial times. There is a "sac" or spit of land into the Hudson at the northern tip of the township, but most of Coxsackie is built along straight coastline and was used as a whaling and steam ship port in the 1800s. Instead we should again look to the English settlers, who took one look at Kahak-hakee, and decided to celebrate English crew championships, Cox-sackee, although the sack would be filled with rhyolite (flint) and not gold. People today still forget to insert the S when writing letters to their friends in Coxsackie.

"...wind at the northwest...seven or eight leagues." This was a favorable wind, so they made good time and traveled about 15 miles south. It is about 17 miles from New Baltimore to Catskill. This would bring them to Rogers Island just above the town of Catskill, at a Native American crossing place for a trail now marked more or less by Route 23, sometimes called "The Catskill Turnpike." This is the

site of today's Rip Van Winkle Bridge, and heading east, the trail forks and joins with Route 9, roughly speaking the Mohican Trail, in short order. The town of Hudson, whose namesake at this point is floundering, stuck in the mud, is just beyond that. Heading west, the turnpike takes us through Leeds, Cairo, Stamford, and Harpersfield; it crosses the East Branch of the Susquehanna at Oneonta and continues.

Just north of this crossing is a mud flat in the center of the river, which is still there today. I would assume that Rogers Island and the mud flat were used as resting places while swimming and wading the wide river. This was the same mud flat Hudson became stuck in on the way inland. Edward Hagaman Hall agrees, imagining the ship traveling 18 land miles south to a place between Mt. Merino and Olana. (By Lossing's measure, eight leagues is 17.6 miles, almost 18) and again suggests the Mud Flats just north of Catskill, near Claverack.[450] He doesn't say on which side of the river they found chestnuts. If it is the same mud flats, it does suggest that the journey of six leagues of September 17 was really seven leagues.

JUET'S JOURNAL, FRIDAY, SEPTEMBER 25 : *The five and twentieth was fair weather, and the wind at south a stiff gale. We rode still, and went on land to walk on the west side of the river, and found good ground for corn, and other garden herbs, with great store of goodly oaks, and walnut trees, and chestnut trees, yew trees, and trees of sweet wood in great abundance, and great store of slate for houses, and other good stones.*

With the wind blowing from the south as they were heading home, they had no choice but to slow down and smell the flowers, and in this case, hug a few old-growth trees. They went for a stroll on the western shore, but where? Where is there good corn and excellent slate so near a huge mud flat in the center of the Hudson River?

Chief Kaelkoptl once supposedly commented that Saugerties was not a good place to grow corn, suggesting they might be at Catskill, which is much better suited, and which also has some slate deposits. On the other hand, Saugerties is extraordinarily good for slate mining. Saugerties is the home of the best bluestone quarries in the Hudson Valley, and Blue Mountain is a famous local landmark. Much of the bluestone found in Greenwich village sidewalks today was cut from Saugerties blue stone, which breaks off at straight angles, almost as if God had intended men to build New York City by providing them with such accommodating paving material. According to New York State geologist William Kelly, Saugerties slate is far superior to that of Catskill, New York,[451] in terms of both quality and quantity. But there are no mud flats right at Saugerties and little corn.

"*...and found good ground for corn...*" Juet doesn't say he saw corn, just good ground for it, but how would he know from the ship unless he saw the harvested September corn stalks? The Mohicans mostly grew corn on intervale land, (flat land along a river) and such plots were recorded by colonists at Catskill Creek, on the Kinderhook, and on Roelof Jansen Kills [452] (The Jansen Kill is near Linlithgo, the corn is along the ridgetop to the north of the creek). Kinderhook is on the east bank and the Jansen Kill is too far north, so Henry Hudson is at Catskill. The tide at Catskill Creek rises and falls four or five feet and it must have been at the outer edge of this intertidal zone that the Mohicans were planting the corn Hudson saw. David DeVries writes, "Found the river up to this point, stony and mountainous, unfit for habitations. But there was some lowland here and the Indians sowed maize along the Cats-kill."[453]

So, without waiting another four hundred years for better information, we have to assume that they were located at Catskill, specifically the village of Potic, not Saugerties, even though Saugerties has better slate. This in turn affects our views on where they were on the trip upstream as well.

It is a shame Juet did not list the "garden herbs," as most he saw would have been wild crafted for their medicinal properties. Chestnut trees were once plentiful in the east, but were nearly wiped out by a blight in the early twentieth century. Their wood has always been highly valued for its texture, and the Algonquins used its bark to cover their domiciles, sometimes stripping living trees for that reason.[454] The wood was used by whites to make a good many barns over the centuries. A few healthy chestnuts, like the ones examined by Juet, still exist, and are priceless today. Native people see them as a symbol of the ancient ones, the ancestors, because they survived off of "ground nuts," the nuts that fall to the ground, including chestnuts, acorns, walnuts, and hickories. Now the chestnut is the rarest of these by far, preserved to some extent by Native American efforts, the Nissequogue for example, at Smithtown.[455]

A new kind of chestnut, a hybrid more resistant to disease, has replaced the old type. These new kinds of chestnuts are still roasted on pushcarts all over midtown Manhattan, filling the island with a distinctive burning odor, an acquired taste that most of today's "native New Yorkers" actually have cultivated, as opposed to non-native New Yorkers, who rarely make the cultural transition. It is safe to say that the smell of roasting chestnuts was well known on the Island of Manhattan long before Henry Hudson's little business trip took shape.

However, the tree Juet examines here that is soon to have the most monetary value is the Eastern Yew. This is the ground hemlock, *Taxus canadensis,* that grows through the northeast woodlands of North America and well into northern Canada. It is found mostly under a cover of forest canopy of mixed trees in a low-spreading bush form, but tends to grow taller in the open. It flowers in May and

June, and actually produces a fruit that is highly prized by certain animals. It was used in Juet's time to make excellent archery bows, axe handles, and canoe paddles, with a rugged lifespan of 25 years or more as the handle of a favorite tool.[456] When the famous 5,500 year old Tyrolean Ice Man was found in Europe under a melting glacier, his axe handle was of yew wood, still in good condition.[457]

While its European relative, *Taxus baccata,* is the basis for English topiary (or shrubbery sculptures), popular among Henry Hudson's patrons, its close relative, the Pacific yew tree, *Taxus brevifolia,* has been found to have astounding cancer fighting properties, and has been used by native women for centuries, such as the Saanich tribal women of the great northwest. The yew, a form of hemlock, is a slow-growing shrub. Not only does the Pacific Yew, called "chief of the forest" by some western nations, grow to a maximum of 60 feet tall, 56 inches around, Yew, in all its forms is the only known source of taxol, which has been called "the gold standard of cancer treatments." Taxol has been proven in laboratory tests since 1960 to be effective against twenty forms of cancer, most notably ovarian cancer. It cannot be produced synthetically.[458] If the yews become extinct, which is not impossible at this point, as bushes cannot usually be classified as endangered, it would set the National Cancer Institute back forty years at least.

It is interesting that female deer eat the needles of these conifers, as they are poisonous to humans, yet also contain the highest concentrations of taxins, which fight uterine cancer. Algonquins, who use a large range of tree barks in medicinal teas, also associate yew bark with boosting the immune system and the prevention of colds, viral and bacterial infections, fungal growth, flu, sciatica, kidney and lung problems, and much more; however it is not recommended for amateur harvesters, due to its extremely high level of alkalids, especially in the eastern variety. One can, for a much lower price, simply buy Vital Yew tea made from the Pacific Yew needles off the Internet for about $11.50 a bottle.[459] Although the eastern yew has not yet been marketed in this way, recent studies have shown it, too, to be a good potential source for taxol, though not in industrial quantities. The yews Juet saw may well have been grown, tended and harvested by Algonquian women of the region, not in neat rows in the open sun, but in optimal conditions, scattered throughout the shady forest floor, their "farmers" remembering the location of each bush through the subtlest of markers along the way. If so, they must have known the secret of detoxifying it, one which still eludes top scientists.

The Abenaki use the same name for the Canadian yew and the spruce. It is known that the leaves of *Taxus canadensis marshall* are used as a tea, good to heal rheumatism. In Caughnawaga, the Mohawk make a beer or ale with the fruits and leaves; the fermentation takes one week, using maple water.

Taxine, from which Taxol is made, is found in the bark, the needles, and the seeds, but not in the fruit, which is called arille. Not found in dry areas, this indigenous bush grows abundantly in deciduous forests and in conifer forests, as far north as Lake Mistassini. Called the dwarf yew, it is also known as ground hemlock. The pacific coast cousin is called Chief of the Forest, used by native women as a tea, and is the type used to extract for taxol for curing cancer of the uterus. The eastern yew's branches are used for fever and colic, however the taxine is an alkalid which is toxic and provokes vomiting, colic and vertigo, and is potentially fatal. [460]

Juet also mentions walnuts, which are rarely found today between Saugerties and Catskill. But apparently, they were well tended by the Algonquians, who honored all ground nuts as symbols of the ancestors.

> JUET'S JOURNAL, SATURDAY, SEPTEMBER 26 : *The six and twentieth was fair weather, and the wind at south a stiff gale; we rode still. In the morning our carpenter went on land with our master's mate and four more of our company to cut wood. This morning two canoes came up the river from the place where we first found loving people, and in one of them was the old man that had lain aboard of us at the other place. He brought another old man with him who brought more strips of beads and gave them to our master, and showed him all the country there about, as though it were at his command. So he made the two old men dine with him, and the old man's wife; for they brought two old women and two young maidens of the age of sixteen or seventeen years with them, who behaved themselves very modestly. Our master gave one of the old men a knife, and they gave him and us tobacco; and at one o'clock they departed down the river, making signs that we should come down to them, for we were within two leagues of the place where they dwelt.*

The wind was blowing from the south, but they needed a headwind to proceed, so they stood still. Juet writes, *"In the morning our carpenter went on land with our master's mate and four more of our company to cut wood...."* If the place of "the loving people" were at Saugerties, then they were presently at or just above Catskill.[461] It seems as if the man *"who had lain aboard"* was from the place of the loving people, and the other old man may have been his sachem. *"He brought another old man with him who brought more strips of beads and gave them to our master, and showed him all the country there about, as though it were at his command."* If the man was a grand sachem, it is likely that he would not be Mohican, but Munsee, as they had just left the Mohican Grand Sachem. This suggests that the home of "the loving people" was Saugerties, at the mouth of the Esopus, which was Esopus Munsee territory. If he was the grand sachem of the Esopus, he was an important personage indeed.

It is one of the largest of the Munsee political units. It is frustrating to historians that Hudson never tells Juet these people's names, and perhaps can't remember. Or perhaps Juet is hiding something.

"So he made the two old men dine with him, and the old man's wife; for they brought two old women and two young maidens of the age of sixteen or seventeen years with them, who behaved themselves very modestly." Hudson insisted the two elders and their wives dine with him, a sort of state dinner. The two girls may be daughters or granddaughters of these elders. They were at an age where young Algonquin women were expected to marry, and marriages between nations, specifically between the families of their leaders, was considered an important part of diplomatic protocol. Therefore one must ask if the young ladies were being presented as potential wives for Henry Hudson, who was perceived as the chief of the ship, and was in fact its "master." Marriage would probably have involved relocation for the explorer, and a messy divorce back in London, as well, to be sure. Hudson wisely chose to decline, if the offer was ever made.

"Our master gave one of the old men a knife, and they gave him and us tobacco..." It appears that the diplomatic party gave each member of the crew some tobacco. Clearly they expected that some major diplomatic breakthrough could be achieved, but it would depend somewhat on his formal visit to their territory the following day. Perhaps they were concerned that Hudson had spent entirely too much time with their allies to the north, the Mohicans, and needed him to feel equally beholden to them to maintain an old balance of power. As it turns out, Hudson caught a good wind the following afternoon and breezed right by the diplomatic greeting party that the Munsee of the Esopus had prepared for him upon the shore.

Even today, age brings with it considerable honor and prestige amongst Algonquian-speaking people, assuming honor is otherwise merited. The old man, representing a large body of people, brought "strips of beads," in other words, several wampum belts, indicating that he was on a diplomatic mission. Again, the gift of wampum suggests that messages were being conveyed, histories were being told, and promises might be made. Did Hudson "promise" to stop by the next day on his way to the sea as he accepted the wampum? If so, he was about to break a sacred oath for the sake of a good breeze.

Incidentally, September 26 was the only day during Hudson's time on the river that the moon in the sky resembled the carved moon on the back of the ship.[462] It was interesting that the natives spent that day on board the Half Moon.

JOURNAL OF THE LOVING PEOPLE: SEPTEMBER 26, 2009, PRAYMAKER

REPORTING : (a dramatization) *It is good weather. The grand chief and I* paddled upstream in the canoe, bringing our wives and my two teenage daughters. We took wampum with us and some tobacco because we were hoping to engage this powerful war chief in a diplomatic foray. He had been spending too much time with our formidable allies, the Mohicans, and we are afraid it will upset the balance of power, as happened with Samuel Champlain. We went quite a ways north and met with ship. It was very interesting to be on board again to look around. Everyone had a marvelous time. Hudson served us all a wonderful meal. When the clock rang one time it was time to go, so we came back down the river.

I thought that by accepting our wampum Hudson had sworn to us by oath that he would be on time for dinner. I thought we had exchanged clear hand signals that we wanted him to come back to "the place of the loving people" the next noon, but he did not. What is going on in his mind?
RED LEAF MOON, 29TH DORSAL PLATELET OF THE CALENDAR TURTLE.

JUET'S JOURNAL, SUNDAY, SEPTEMBER 27 : *The seven and twentieth, in the morning, was fair weather, but much wind at the north we weighed and set our fore-topsail, and our ship would not float, but ran on the oozy bank at half ebb. We laid out anchor to heave her off, but could not; so we sat from half flood, then we set our foresail and main-topsail, and got down six leagues. The old man came aboard, and would have had us anchor and go on land to eat with him, but the wind being fair we would not yield to his request, so he left us, being very sorrowful for our departure. At five o'clock in the afternoon, the wind came to the south south-west; so we made a boord or two, and anchor, in fourteen fathoms water. Then our boat went on shore to fish right against the ship. Our master's mate and boatswain and three more of the company went on land to fish, but could not find a good place. They took four or five and twenty mullets, breams, basses and barbils, and returned in an hour. We rode still all night.*

The ship's progress was stalled by unfavorable winds, then from being pushed into a sand bank, and being a proper Englishman, Henry was becoming concerned about the time. "*We laid out anchor to heave her off, but could not; so we sat from half flood, then we set our foresail and main-topsail, and got down six leagues.*" They lifted the anchor, anxious to leave, but the ship was stuck even though it was mid-tide. "*The old man came aboard, and would have had us anchor and go on land to eat with him, but the wind being fair we would not yield to his request, so he left us, being very sorrowful for our departure.*" When a favorable wind finally blew up, Henry was itching to go. So what if they had a dinner appointment with a great chief in

Saugerties? They hadn't found a passage to the west and had to report back to their superiors. When they passed by Saugerties, and the leader came up alongside the ship to come aboard, and to guide them personally to shore, Henry had an important decision to make. He knew from experience that no state visit could possibly be short. Eastern Algonquins have no word for time even today, and many do not respect "short visits," unless the reasons are made clear in advance and by mutual agreement. Leaving after an hour or two would be interpreted as a sign of anger or hostility, just as the English would interpret it if the King walked out on a concert being held in his honor. If Hudson stopped in, he would probably have to stay until evening and thus lose the perfect wind he had been looking for these many days. He decided to bring the distinguished VIP on board and show good will towards him, but then planned to try to explain that they had to be going.

The native people of the Hudson River did have rude sails they attached to their canoes from time to time, so they understood about favorable sailing winds, but Hudson's decision must have seemed cold and unfriendly to them. The Esopus chief had probably told a hundred people to prepare to entertain a great Sachem from far away, and was probably quite embarrassed by the rejection, especially after he'd heard rumors about how eagerly Hudson had received hospitality from the neighboring Mohicans. But why would he want to avoid "the loving people"?

Hudson then went four more leagues southward, in other words 8.8 miles from Saugerties, which would bring them to Kingston, New York. Rhinecliff is across the river.

"*At five o'clock in the afternoon, the wind came to the south south-west; so we made a boord or two, and anchor, in fourteen fathoms water.*" According to *Where Hudson's Voyage Ended, an Inquiry* by Harry Montford Sweet, the disingenuous Robert Juet is pulling our leg here. He suggests that these lines may be from a sea chanty. He writes that when Tri-centennial historians read these lines, "we began to feel suspicious; for the phraseology and the rhythm were so like a fragment of one of Dibdin's sea songs that it began to dawn upon us that we were being fed salt-water literature to the exclusion of historical facts relating to the furthest point north on the Hudson where at least five of the crew of the Half Moon, if not all, were privileged to land."[463]

They are trying to head south, but again the wind blocks their progress. A traverse board, or "boord" represents a four-hour watch. "..a boord or two" refers to four-to-eight hours of watch duty. The traverse board had a series of holes in it like a cribbage board. The watchman would run a sand clock (an hour glass) that marked a half hour's time. Each time it emptied there would be a bell, marking the half hour. At that time he would place another peg in a hole on the traverse board. Eight bells was the end of a four-hour watch, and by that time he would have filled a single "boord" with pegs. Two boards was a poetic way of saying that eight hours of watch duty had been measured and passed. They were anchored in deep water over 60 feet in depth, the length of a shot cable.

"Then our boat went on shore to fish right against the ship. Our master's mate and boatswain and three more of the company, went on land to fish, but could not find a good place. They took four or five and twenty mullets, breams, basses and barbils, and returned in an hour..." Basses would include "stripers" or "striped bass," (*Morone saxatilis*) still common today in the Hudson, and Large Mouth Bass (*Micropteros salmoides*). By "barbils" he means "barbels," (*Barbus vulgaris*) which is a European member of the Cyprinid family. They grow to 50 pounds, and have four "barbels" hanging from the corners of the mouth, something like Fu Man Chu whiskers. Barbels comes from the Latin root for beard, *barb*, which is also where barber comes from. There are no indigenous barbils so he is mistaken. It seems that he was probably looking at rather large specimens of the Channel Catfish, which are common in the Hudson.[464] The other fish he mentions, the bream, is also a European non-indigenous fish, (at least the *Albramis brama*) so again he is mistaken. The Silver Bream (*Blicca bjoerkna*) is also European, as is the carp. The bream is a laterally flattened fish with a small inferior mouth. He doesn't mention its size, so they may have caught some "Sunnies," or Sunfish, (Machgalingus in Northern Unami), thinking them baby breams. Many fishermen call them "white breams" today. They are both types of perches. Mullets are a leaping fish that grow to a maximum of 47.2 inches and are found around the world, largely in estuaries. These may have been red mullets (*Parupeneus heptaconthus*) or white mullets (*Mugil curema*) but were probably striped mullets (*Mugil cephalus*). For more information about which of the 231 species of fish in the Hudson River today were caught by Native Americans for their breakfasts, go to Appendix I.

Juet does not say whether the fishing boat landed on the east or the west. If on the west, it had possibly rowed a few hundred yards up Rondout Creek to Kingston Landing.[465] Kingston Landing is the terminus of the Minisink Trail, as described in my book *Native New Yorkers*. It was an important spot for making contact with native peoples in 1609. Back in about 2000, I boarded the replica of the Half Moon at that spot and took a tour of the ship. It is the site of the Maritime Museum which hosts events through the warm months. But the depths there are not 14 fathoms, so the main ship was in the Hudson. There was a creekside trail from the foot of the Minisink Trail to Kingston Beach, called Ponkhakee, ("place of biting bugs" in Munsee) and then turning east and following along a narrow spit of land out to the center of the river. On the other side of this crossing was Rhinecliff and the Sepasco Trail, now roughly followed by Route 308.[466] Note that they were able to catch so many fish (24 to 25 mullets, plus all the others) in a single hour.

There is a local legend about a "lost fisherman," Jacobus Van Horen, captured by wild Indians, apparently Wappingers, from the crew of the Half Moon, a tale that still floats from camp fire to camp fire up and down the Hudson River Valley. This entry is the only one that remotely matches the details of the story, as there is in fact a fishing party, and yet Juet does not mention a lost passenger. Perhaps it was a crew member that Juet didn't like, or one that he may have had an argument with. An encounter with the Wappingers would have occurred near Rhinecliff, perhaps at Tivoli Bays or Cruger Island, which are good fishing spots. This story may or may not have any truth to it, but it should not be left out of the narrative, as it has become so well known to those who collect folklore about Hudson Valley's Native Americans. This version is quoted directly from Peggy Turco's classic, *Walks and Rambles in Dutchess and Putnam Counties*.

"On Hudson's trip downriver, he anchored at Newburgh Bay for two foggy days. An unarmed party of sailors went ashore near Glenham. They were attacked by Indians, an undocumented but persistent local tale says, and Jacobus Van Horen was wounded and captured while the rest fled back to the Half Moon.

"Van Horen[467] was taken into the hills around Matteawan, today's Beacon range, and we cringe to think what his captors contemplated. Princess Manteo, daughter of the chief, saw the captive, fell in love with him, and pleaded for the white man's life. He was given to her, their marriage planned for a year hence. An excellent fisherman, Jacobus was allowed to roam freely in the Indian Brook area, each day bringing in a supply of trout.

"But one day, when they were swimming in the pool below Indian Brook Falls (a spot still popular with young lovers), Henry Hudson's man spotted a European ship on the river. Jacobus abandoned Manteo and bolted for the shore. He was seen and picked up. Manteo's body was found in the pool. Some say Jacobus murdered her to escape. Others say that after her lover fled, Manteo walked broken-hearted and weeping up Indian Brook, a white flower springing up where each tear fell to earth. At the falls, she hurled herself from the clifftop to her death in the pool."

Peggy adds, "Now you know why it's called Indian Brook."[468]

Did Juet fail to mention the loss of a crew member in his diary? Certainly they would have noticed the loss of an angler with such ability that he impressed the Wappingers with his skill. There were no two days of fog at any time on their voyage up the Hudson River. Juet mentions some "mist" near Glenham the morning of September 15, but it is short-lived, and the Half Moon does not linger long enough for a fishing expedition. Manteo is also a man's name, specifically that of a leader of the Lost Colony just to the south. Could this story possibly be fictitious? Perhaps it was told by Jacobus' descendants as a tall tale to be shared at campfires. As Peggy Turco comments, "This tale, while totally European in origin, does give insight into the numerous misunderstandings and intermarriages typical of the early contact between Europeans and Natives."[469]

Although some Wappingers lived at Tivoli Bays and Cruger Island, this was mostly Mohican territory. Why would Mohicans allow such an unfriendly gesture? It doesn't make sense.

"We rode still all night." This night and the following one was at the dark of the moon,[470] and this might explain why they rode still, as visibility was poor to nonexistent.

MUNSEE VILLAGE JOURNAL: CHIEF PRAYMAKER OF THE "LOVING PEOPLE" OF THE ESOPUS; SEPTEMBER 27 : (a dramatization) *I don't understand what happened. I thought I had his word that he would visit our people. I tried to explain to him that we were not Mohicans, but we're Munsee, and that we wanted to be sure he spent as much time with us as he'd spent with our friendly rivals. I got my helpers to create a great banquet area, and arranged for musicians to entertain. I gathered together twenty family members to offer gifts and make speeches, and eighty others besides. I thought of everything. There was a great feast prepared. I felt very excited when his ship rolled by down the river. I had my canoer row me out to the ship and I boarded. I asked him four times to come to the feast, but he just laughed it off. I showed that I was very sad. The Chief of the ship said the wind was finally right after three days, and he had to keep going. He showed me great on-board hospitality below deck, but would offer me nothing to help me save face among my people. I got back into my canoe, feeling very embarrassed. I had asked a hundred people to go out of their way to be there at this ceremony, and they had all been waiting four hours already. I had to dismiss them! There was much grumbling.*

My cousin from Atharhakton had prepared roasted corn on the cob, using a big pit. Then my uncle Lone Bird from Waughkonk had some turkey meat he cooked and his wife brought some leftover acorn soup. There were selected herb teas, and various corn breads and sapsis breads. There was venison stew and then beaver tail for desert. As the sachem of the Esopus Indians it was up to me to pay for all this, and I did. Everyone was very understanding, but I felt humiliated. I had told people how he hung on my every word and now they can see that he doesn't think much of me. I may be voted out of office over this. Hudson is a great chief, but obviously cares more for the Mohicans than he does for us. RED LEAF MOON, 30TH DORSAL PLATELET OF THE CALENDAR TURTLE.

JUET'S JOURNAL, MONDAY, SEPTEMBER **28** : *The eight and twentieth being fair weather, as soon as the day was light we weighed at half ebb, and turned down two leagues below water, for the stream doth run the last quarter ebb, then we anchored till high water. At three o'clock in the afternoon we weighed and turned down three leagues until it was dark, then we anchored.*

Edward Hagaman Hall sees them starting out in the river between East Kingston to the west and Mount Rutsen to the east. They leave there and come to a place between Cave Point[471] and Staatsburg to the east. This is a distance of ten miles. This seems to be the case.

"...*we weighed at half ebb*..." To weigh at half ebb means to pull up anchor as the receding tide reaches the halfway mark. In the Hudson River below Albany, this is at about two feet above low tide. "...*and turned down two leagues below water*..." To "turn down" means they would come upstream to where the anchor lay by hauling to it, passing the anchor, then turning around to go back downstream from whence they came in order to continue their journey untethered four miles further.[472]

"...*For the stream doth run the last quarter ebb*..." This sentence is as clear as a drink of spring water to a salty sailor of an estuary, but to most landlubbers, it is mud incarnate. I asked Courtney Anderson, the man who designed, created, and strung the rigging for the scale replica of the Half Moon—perhaps the closest one can come to meeting Henry Hudson in the flesh today—what this sentence meant. He told me that the Hudson River's tide is a separate issue from its current. Water can fall and rise at the same time. As I understand him, as the tide finishes the last quarter, there can be a tidal bulge coming upstream even as the swift current is going downstream.[473]

"...*then we anchored till high water.*" They lowered the anchor and stood still until high tide, as they were unsure of the depths ahead. "*At three o'clock in the afternoon we weighed and turned down three leagues until it was dark, then we anchored.*" They caught up with their anchor, pulled it aboard, then headed south at least 6.6 miles, (possibly ten, as Juet seems to go more by time than by distance and they were riding on a strong ebb current). This would bring the ship to Poughkeepsie.

On the way they would have passed, just north of Poughkeepsie, "Shagabak," now erroneously called "Shagbark" by locals, which is a form of hickory (*Carya covata*). There is a cove and peninsula on the riverbank where some artifacts have been dug up, some of which is now submerged with a rise in water levels.[474]

There was an important crossing in the river at Poughkeepsie, and a Native American ferry service that continued well into colonial times. This route was then continued by a more modern type of ferryboat in the 1700s. The eastern landing was at the foot of Main Street, where Waryus Park is today; the western one was about a half mile upriver at Highland Landing, the closest spot that afforded a manageable walkway to the top of the bluff to the west, and to the trail that became "The King's Highway" after 1664, now 9W.

One translation of Poughkeepsie not usually heard is that it is derived from Powk-eap-sinck, "place of waterfalls near the bank of a river"[475] which would be the cascades of the Vallkill, or Fallkill, a series of dramatic waterfalls, the last of which crashes into sea water just a few feet inland from the Hudson. In pan-Algonquin terminology, the lowest tier of Valkill Falls would be a *pawtucket,* fresh water falling into brackish or tidal waters.

The Fallkill is a secondary estuary for less than hundred feet. There is a significant waterfall near the first road crossing, at Water Street, at the old Arnold Cotton Mill, and then a rather spectacular one (hence the name Fallkill) a quarter of a mile inland near the Post Road, formerly Mohican Trail. On a map of 1798,[476] the village at the conjunction of the Hudson and the Fallkill was called Pondakrien. This was the site of the Dutchess Avenue Dock and the Poughkeepsie Whaling Company in the 1830s. This company was renamed the Dutchess Whaling company and had seven whaling ships, one of them the "New England," which was mentioned in *Two Years Before the Mast* by Dana. This once-prosperous inland port was shut down in 1844. This is interesting because the harpoonists on such ships were so often of Algonquin stock. Also called "The Upper Landing," it was one of the busiest on the waterfront. It was a ferry dock from 1798 until 1879, continuing the tradition started eons before by the "Indians of the Long Reach."

A mill was built in early times at the terminus of the waterfall. The once-beautiful waterfall behind that one is now awkwardly positioned behind parked trains at the Metro North Train station. When trains are parked there, the largest waterfall and most potent tourist attraction in Dutchess County is invisible even to those determined to glimpse it. If the station were two hundred feet further north, at least paying passengers could enjoy the view while waiting for the train to board. Pow is the best-known Algonquian word for waterfall, so it is not surprising that the term Poughkeepsie has also been translated "where the water falls over," referring to the falls at Fallkill, and also was said to refer to the little cove at the mouth of the Fallkill. This is probably incorrect. In 1683, a Wappingers named Massany, deeded property to Pieter Lansing and Jan Smeedes, possibly for the riverfront near the Fallkill (or possibly Casper Kill).

Lossing writes, "Between two rocky bluffs was a sheltered bay (now filled with wharves) into the upper part of which leaped, in rapids and cascades, the Winnakee, called Fall Kill by the Dutch. The northerly bluff was called by the

Dutch Slange Klippe, or Snake or Adder Cliff, because of the venomous serpents which were abundant there in the olden time. The southern bluff bears the name of Call Rock, it having been a place from which the settlers called to the captains of sloops..."[477] Pronounced Wennakee, it would be a Mohican word for "good land," in reference to Poughkeepsie, and might have been the name for Valkill Creek, which zigs and zags its way across that good land, which is now the city of Poughkeepsie.

Although it was once a small bay, that landing, Waryus, is approximately in the center of the long straight shoreline that Juet calls "the long reach." Many sailors have called it that since. The Algonqun word for such a reach, coincidentally, is "Shippa." Beacon is at the end of that long stretch of straight shoreline. The Wappingers of this area north of the Wappinger Creek (Mahwenawasigh) were called Indians of the Long Reach,[478] whereas those just below were known as Mattawan Indians.[479]

That crossing trail, Route 44, extended all the way from Plymouth Rock aka Pawtuxett ("small waterfall at the estuary"), or "First Encounter Beach" to Kerhonksen, New York, where it meets the Minisink Trail, Route 209. The whites took over the ferry service in 1740.[480] Just a few hundred yards to the north is Fox's Point, (now part of Marist College, marked by a gazebo of recent excavation), from which two ships were launched in 1775, before the Revolutionary War. That point, and Forbus Hill were used as lookouts over the river, where the Long Reach Wappingers could keep an eye on all water traffic in both directions. There was a Wappingers burial spot there as well. It is claimed by Marist that the name of their famous sports teams, "the Red Foxes," has nothing to do with local Native American history, but one has to wonder.

"...*until it was dark, then we anchored.*" September 28 was still at the dark of the moon, so they could not see very well after nightfall.

JUET'S JOURNAL, TUESDAY, SEPTEMBER 29 : *The nine and twentieth was dry close weather, the wind at south and south by west we weighed early in the morning, and turned down three leagues by a low water, and anchored at the lower end of the long reach for it is six leagues long. Then there came certain Indians in a canoe to us, but would not come aboard. After dinner there came the canoe with other men, whereof three came aboard us; they brought Indian wheat which we bought for trifles. At three o'clock in the afternoon we weighed, as soon as the ebb came, and turned down to the edge of the mountains, or the northernmost of the mountains, and anchored, because the high land hath many points and a narrow channel, and hath many eddy winds; so we rode quietly all night in seven fathoms water.*

Michael Sullivan Smith identifies this leg of the journey as taking the crew from Poughkeepsie to the place in the river between Cornwall, New York, to the west and Beacon, New York, to the east.

Edward Hagaman Hall has the ship traveling 7.2 miles south to a point between Maritje Kill to the west and Crum Elbow Point to the east. Then he supposes they travel 18 more miles south to a point in Newburgh Bay, across from Beacon, New York, in agreement with Smith. Johnson merely writes, "Below Poughkeepsie."

Just after shoving off, they pass the Rust Plaets Kill, a small stream that enters the Hudson from Poughkeepsie. This is the same water that originates at the "safe sheltered spring," now next to Route 9, which is the official namesake of Poughkeepsie, New York. Poughkeepsie, one of the more famous of Native American place names in New York, most likely derives from *uppuqui-ipis-ing*, "reed covered lodge by the little water place." This spot, a natural spring at Teahan and Constantino's office, has just been designated an historic site. This marshy spot, opposite the Locust Grove Poughkeepsie Rural Cemetery, creates a stream that runs through a culvert and under Route 9 (Mohican Trail), then into the Hudson.

Poughkeepsie became the county seat in 1717 as the courthouse became ready by 1720. This courthouse was situated near the grounds which are now the headquarters of the *Poughkeepsie Journal,* a few hundred feet from Fallkill Creek, (formerly Winnakee) one block east on Mill and one block north on Conklin Street. A church and a cluster of houses went up about this time near the intersection of Mill and Main, after the post road was authorized in 1703. The courthouse was burned at the advent of the revolution, so the Van Kleek House became the center of politics.[481] Poughkeepsie was the capitol of New York state between 1778 and 1783, and in 1788 the Van Kleek House became the site of the famous debates on the Bill of Rights between Malancthon Smith and Alexander Hamilton. The Dutchess delegates remained firm in their demand that the proposed U.S. constitution be amended to include the New York Bill of Rights as a condition.[482] They had to remove the word "condition," but ended up getting their wish anyway.

Sixty years later, a descendant of the Munsee Indians (in fact, I believe both parents to have been at least "half" Munsee), Andrew Jackson Davis, lived and worked in a cobbler's shop near the Poughkeepsie Courthouse. It was here that the teenage boy took part in a demonstration on hypnotism, and unexpectedly became "the Seer of Poughkeepsie." The father of American Spiritualism, his prodigious and inspired writings have a distinctively Algonquian slant to them, though he never uses the word. His vision of oneness and of a great harmony that encompasses all, plus his use of the term "summer land," to refer to a level of heaven, are all classic pan-Algonquin concepts.[483]

JUET'S JOURNAL, WEDNESDAY, SEPTEMBER 30 : *The thirtieth was fair weather, and the wind at south-east a stiff gale between the mountains. We rode still the afternoon. The people of the country came aboard us, and brought some small skins with them, which we bought for knives and trifles. This is a very pleasant place to build a town on. The road is very near, and view good for all winds, save an east north-east wind. The mountains look as if some metal or mineral were in them; for the trees that grew on them were all blasted, and some of them barren with few or no trees on them. The people brought a stone aboard like to emery, [a stone used by glaziers to cut glass,] it would cut iron or steel; yet being bruised small, and water put to it, it made a colour like black lead glistening; it is also good for painters' colours. At three o'clock they departed, and we rode still all night.*

"*The thirtieth was fair weather, and the wind at south-east a stiff gale between the mountains.*" This suggests that they were at or just above the pass between Storm King and Breakneck Ridge, where two weather systems collide, hence the European name Storm King.

"*The people of the country came aboard us, and brought some small skins with them, which we bought for knives and trifles.*" De Laet wrote: "From Stony Point to Dans-Kammer were the *Waoranecks*, 'the people of the country' who sold the 'small skins' to Hudson on the 30th of September [1609], and who were subsequently known as 'the Murderer's Creek Indians.' Their castle was on the north spur of Schunemunk mountain, and their place of worship the Dans-Kammer. Above them were the *Warranawonkongs*, subsequently known as 'the Esopus Indians,' whose hunting grounds extended through the valley of the Wallkill. West of the *Warranawonkongs*, and occupying the country drained by the Delaware and its tributaries, were the *Minsis* or *Minnisinks*."[484] This confirms that the crew were at Cornwall Bay.

To some people, "*the road is very near,*" may seem to refer to a place where a large trade route came near the shore, and such is the case on the Beacon side of Cornwall Bay. But every nautical type and old salt I interviewed said that "road," or a "roadstead" to a sailor means basically "a good place to anchor." To anchor well, the water under the keel must be "good," or of sufficient depth. It must be protected from the wind, and the river bottom must be able to hold the anchor.[485] As to what "near" means here, it probably does mean, "near the shore," but this is less certain. Michael Sullivan Smith sees them at Cornwall. Johnson, to my surprise, interprets the "*...pleasant place to build a town,*" as a spot in the vicinity of Peekskill, NY. There is also a narrow place between two mountains where the wind can be strong, what the Dutch called Warragut.

"...and view good for all winds, save an east north-east wind." My nautical experience is limited, but expert seafarer Courtney Anderson explained that when a boat is anchored, it can blow about in all four directions of the compass depending on the wind. One must be sure then that one of the "winds" won't blow your ship into a cliff or onto a sand bar. Also important is that your ship's "watch" can see for some distance in any direction regardless of which way the wind blows.[486]

"The mountains look as if some metal or mineral were in them; for the trees that grew on them were all blasted, and some of them barren with few or no trees on them." Yellow copper leaches out of rocks as a yellow stain, and various minerals show a similar stain, spreading downward on rock cliffs. The natives showed the Dutch settlers a few decades later where these places were "in the Highlands." It is difficult today to tell where these spots were. "That the trees that grew on them were all "blasted" may have possibly indicated maple trees, that neither Juet nor Hudson were familiar with. The entry of October 2 seems to confirm this, and I have commented on it further there. The black metal he mentions is not identifiable, although lignite, andacite and asphaltum have been suggested.

Many writers have praised Indian Brook Falls; William Livingston, writing in the 1800s, penned "The Legend of Indian Brook Falls," a not-so-tragic poem about a young maiden who loved a young warrior, Eagle Wing. He wrote, "Each young lover who stops beside the fall at eve, will feel the spell and his companion will be his bride, ere the new year's blossoms perfume the dell." In the Ballad of Breakneck, from the same period, the maiden's name was Nekima. In other stories, Captain Kidd the pirate buried some of his treasure near the falls. Many have searched for it; caves were found somewhere to the east, perhaps in what is now Fahnstock State Preserve, but no treasure has been discovered as yet.[487]

Benton J. Lossing sings the praises of this brook and the magnificent falls from which it flows. "We crossed Indian Brook on a rustic bridge, just below the Indian Falls, whose murmur fell upon the ear before we came in sight of the stream. These falls have formed subjects for painting and poetry, and are the delight of the neighbourhood in summer." He is not alone in his admiration. Many great writers, naturalists, and thinkers have come to this spot for inspiration. It brings out the poet in Lossing, as he writes, "We were on the Indian Brook on a bright October day, when the foliage was in its greatest autumnal splendor, and the leaves were falling in gentle showers among the trees, the rocks, and in the sparkling water, appearing like fragments of rainbows cast, with lavish hand, into the lap of earth. At every turn of the brook, from its springs to its union with the Hudson, a pleasant subject for the painter's pencil is presented."[488]

Just north of Indian Brook Falls is Cold Spring, the place of the Pasquawskeck, "the place of the prominent woman," which is Storm King as seen across the

Muhicanituck from Breakneck. North of Breakneck is the mouth of Matteawan Creek, where there is a waterfall land, an island, and a crossing place.

Tioronda Road has been translated different ways, all of which are impossible. It is most likely from Ti-a-ran-tuck, in Wappingers, the council fire place between the river and the estuary. This leads to the Howland Cultural Center, just to the right is Mary Ann's Bridge, which spans the Fishkill. Beyond it is the Hiker's Trail, which was a pioneer trail in the 1700s sometimes called the Danbury Road. It crossed the mountains directly, entering a deep ravine north of Mount Beacon and skirting the slopes of Bald Hill. Here one finds the abandoned Greer Farm. It went to the Clove at Fishkill and on to Danbury and New England.

Much of Beacon was a popular residence for the Algonquins, including both "Waoranecks" and Mattewan Indians. The Waoraneks were associated with Kowawese Point, now Plum Point in Cornwall, NY, and the Mattewan were associated with Mattewan Creek, now Fishkill Creek. Ruttenber refers to these Waranecks as Munsee people, and the Mattewan as Wappingers, which is probably accurate, although Waraneck is not a Munsee term, as they have no R phoneme. Both were living in Beacon. The Waoranecks referred to mount Beacon and the Highland as the "Matteawan Mountains."

The first white family to live at the mouth of Fishkill Creek was the Nicholas Emigh family in 1682. It is suggested in the book "Dutchess County, written in 1937, that they lived in cave-like dugouts to keep warm. An important trail ran along the entire length of Fishkill Creek on the north bank. Some call it the Madam Brett Trail. This is now Tioronda Road (which passes within a block of Madam Brett's homestead today), East Main, to Fishkill Avenue, to Old Glenham Road, then back to Route 52 past Route 9 becoming the Hopewell Road, to Hopewell Junction and onward, turning east towards Carmel (Mt. Nimham) and Lake Mahopac.

If you crossed Mary Ann's Bridge, (now downhill from the Howland Center) near Madam Brett's, you would find yourself on the Mountain Road that was a trail that led to Route 9 (the Mohican Trail). However there was another trail you could take by turning left onto what is now Washington Avenue, Beacon, which heads into Glenham and meets up with 52.[489] It is said that "All roads lead to Madam Brett's Mill."[490]

A native ferry service left from the mouth of Fishkill Creek and landed at the foot of Washington Street at the marina in Newburgh. Franklin Delano Roosevelt crossed many times here (landing not at Dennings Point but Fishkill Landing) and George Washington took the ferry and landed at Dennings Point, resting afterwards beneath a row of oak trees on the shore which became the "Washington Oaks," one of which was replanted at Walcott Avenue. Alexander Hamilton passed through here as well.

The Mohican Trail, now Route 9, ran through the Wiccopee Pass near what is now the location of the Van Wyck Homestead and the Dutchess Mall. It was named for the Wiccopee Indians, a branch of the Waranoaks (not my spelling)[491] Wickopee means "homes near the water." They were a large subgroup of the Matawan Indians. Originally there were many Wiccopee passes, but during the Revolution it mainly referred to the one mentioned above. There is a town of Wiccopee to the east of Fishkill, on Route 52 next to East Fishkill. It borders on Fishkill Creek and appears on the map of the Rombout patent.

Cassidy states, "Madam Brett's Indian neighbors, the Wappingers, kept their council fire at Wiccopee, about ten miles up Fishkill Creek from her homestead." This was certainly true in later times, but the name Tioranda and other records indicate that what is now called Fairie Island was the most likely site of council fires in the area in ancient times. He continues, "It was a place of fertile clearings, lush foliage and rare fragrances, sheltered in what the Dutch called "The Hook," the corner formed by the creek and the Highlands." He states, "In the Algonquin language Wiccopee meant 'nut trees.' The nuts grew on hickory trees and black walnuts."[492] Actually, *pagank* means hickory or nut trees in Wappingers (*sagabun* in older Algonquin) and *wiccopee* means dwelling-place near the water, in the pines, and may have also been named "a place of nut trees." Cassidy states that they also planted apple orchards and pear trees. "All the other food they needed came from the forest and the fields and the creek. The Wappingers were a happy, loving people, and that was their undoing," he writes, in 1992.

Cassidy writes, "There had never been a war between them and their Algonquin brothers, the Manhattans to the south and the Mohicans to the north. They were at peace with their new friends, the white people, and particularly with Mistress Brett, who permitted them to live untroubled, as they always had, on the land that her father had brought from their ancestors." Cassidy goes on at length to describe how remarkably peaceful the Wappingers were. In regard to the Wappingers' ambush of a barge in 1644, from which hundreds of beaver skins were stolen, he quotes a Dutch record as such, "a nation with whom we had never had the least trouble before."[493] This hostility in fact was a non-violent protest against the actions of Governor Kieft.

"There lived a vast many Indians in this place when we first came here," Catharyna Brett wrote years later."[494] Cassidy states that "The entire Wappinger population has been estimated at its peak, at no more than 1,000," however he does not state the source of this figure.

Although generally described as "seasonal," a village used for summer farming only, Mawenawasigh must have been a very important village, as it was the main boundary reference for the Rombout Patent. In 1683, on August 8, the Rombout patent was signed. The new governor Thomas Dongan assigned to Kipp, Rombout and Van Courtlandt, the following territory:[495]

"...all that tract or parcel of land situated lying and being on the east side of Hudsons river at the north side of the highlands, beginning from the south side of a creek called the fish kill and by the Indians Matteawan, and from thence northward along said Hudsons river five hundred rods beyond the great Wappins Kill called by the Indians Mawenawasigh, being the northerly boundary and from thence into the woods four hours going that is to say sixteen English miles always keeping five hundred rods distant from the north side of said great Wappingers Creek however it runs, as also from the said Fishkill or creek called Matteawan..." The deed describes the southern boundary as following the Fishkill 16 miles inland and then joining the two with a north-south line to the east.

According to Armbruster, this creek was part of an ancient boundary between the old "Mohican" Wappings and the "southern" Wappingers. If you follow Wappingers Creek 18 miles, you arrive at the Salt Point, also known as Mahwenawasik. Eighteen miles is a long ways to walk in four hours, however it is possible. If you walked a line due east from this point, you would be tracing what I believe to be the old traditional boundary line between north and south peoples. It takes you to Kent, which is still a reservation today, of Schagticooks. It stands to reason that the family of Amorgarikakan could not have deeded lands they did not own, and could not have deeded lands past the Wappingers Creek or past Mahwenawasik. That land was under the jurisdiction of the Mohican. Just to the south of the joining point of the rivers is Nooteeming Lake, formerly a Boy Scout Camp.

Far inland, past the headwaters of the creek system was the Moravian mission at Shekomeko, to which many Wappingers were removed, as well as Mohicans. That mission operated from 1740 to 1744. In 1744 they were ordered to leave the country.[496] They migrated to Pennsylvania, Delaware, Maryland, and Ohio.[497] Some that held on up to the Revolution were sent to Stockbridge, Massachusetts.

It seems that Hudson's crew never got to explore Cornwall Bay and the remarkable Native American villages to the west of the bay. Quassaic, Moodna Creek, and Idlewild Creeks were left unexplored. The most remarkable secondary estuary in Orange County is what is now called Moodna Creek. There are two or three others. As mentioned earlier, Moodna was called Kowawese before it was Murderer's Kill. It enters the Hudson at Kowawese or Waoraneck Point, now called Plum Point. This was a headquarters for Munsee and Wappingers and became the site of one of the first trading posts along the Hudson. It was the Scotsman MacGregorie who built the trading post and was apparently able to communicate with Awissawa, who lived nearby. We assume then that Awissawa spoke Walloon (which he would have learned from the "Dutch" settlers, most of whom were not really Dutch). Walloon is related to Gaelic, but just close enough to afford some communication with the Scotsman.

Ruttenber categorizes the Waoranecks as Munsee, but the term itself is Wappingers and has several murky translations including "good camping place." The Moodna is fully tidal and brackish along its course between the old trail now Route 9W and the Hudson. At 9W crossing, we see the trail crossed Moodna at an island now inhabited by ducks and other estuarial animals and birds.

The Moodna travels westward through a deep canyon along Old Forge Hill Road. At one point Old Forge Hill Road, an old native trail route, crosses the canyon right at the head of tide, which is also the salt point, so I have been told by local historians and fishermen. Right above the bridge, the creek is joined by Silver Spring Creek, and the native trail that runs along its steep slope is still intact. There is a mill upstream and up the steep trail, and the home of Henry Knox, who served as an advisor to George Washington on matters of Indians. He had learned what he knew from the bookstores in Boston, but soon learned out west what the real Native Americans were like. The house has been completely restored and sits on the crossroads between Route 94, the Waywayanda Trail and the Old Forge Hill Road trailsite. Silver Stream runs nearby and under Route 94.

James Edmonston, from Tyrone, Ireland, came to Vail's Gate in 1727, and many years later his neice told Samuel W. Eager that she recalled seeing Indians. He wrote, "At this time, Indian huts were numerous along the brook west of Edmonston's. Their burial ground was on the hill west of the brook, and covered several acres. My informant, a niece of James Edmonston's, ...says she recollects seeing 100 of them, and that they looked like little haystacks, that the chiefs were buried at Schunemunk Mountain...."[498]

There is an island at the confluence of the two rivers, (Silver Spring and Moodna) at the bottom of the canyon, and it is conceivable that at certain full moon tides that the salt water from the Hudson would have reached the island. It was here that LaFayette tried to cross the Moodna one winter, on his way to a birthday party in his honor, being held at the Knox home. Afraid of getting his nice suit of clothes wet, he paid an Irishman to carry him across on his back. The Irishman slipped and fell on the slippery rocks, and LaFayette fell flat into the water with a big splash. LaFayette ran home shivering and never showed up for the party. This story may indicate that there was a trail on the east bank of the Moodna there, and a crossing at the island, but it is not evident today. It would have connected the island to the trail to the Knox residence, which climbs the west bank.

A few miles upstream is the terminus of Moodna Creek, a substantial waterfall (now reinforced by concrete and block) at Owings Mills. The mill building is still there, and Route 32, which was called the Fish Creek Trail, crosses just below the falls. A probable village site, a large flat landing, stands just to the south of the falls. There is considerable sign of tidal debris just below the falls and none whatsoever above. This place of both fresh and estuarial water fish is frequent home to large herons, which can be seen at all hours in May and June.

Just to the north of the river is the Owings Mills Road, which runs along the creek and leads us to another even larger waterfall, not part of the estuarial system as far as we can see today, but which was the home and political headquarters for some later members of the Amorgarikakan family who were leaders for the Wappingers. This spot is called Salisbury Mills today, and a large reinforced waterfall can still be seen near the power plant, more clearly in winter because of the loss of foliage. It is possible that certain "climbers" (waterfall climbing fish) could have ascended the falls down at Owings Mills (it is about three feet high) and would then reach this falls, which would then become a terminus for estuarial fish. The western source of Moodna Creek is the Otterkill, which was the home of Awessewa and Vincent Matthews for a time.

The spit, or "neck" of land at the mouth of the lovely "Murderer's Creek," now called Plum Point, was once Waroneck Point, and was an island-like "place of fire" or council fire seat, for the Waroneck, or Waweroneck Indians. Who the Weroneck, or Waweroneck were is quite the mystery. Ruttenber, who believed they were Munsee, was generally accurate, but here, and at other spots along the western bank of the Hudson, we have to taste these suppositions with a grain of salt, because Unami and Munsee dialects have no R phoneme, and have never had one, as a look at Zeisberger's word lists from 1776 (and O'Meara's Dictionary) will show.

It was here that Patrick Magregorie, a Scotsman and one of the most interesting of all the settlers of the Hudson Valley, once placed his home. According to Stickney, "Lord Bellomont, Governor of New York in 1701, says, in a letter to the lords of trade, that the country west of the Highlands, at that time, was a dense wilderness, there being but one house in all that section—on Captain Evan's grant, which was along the Hudson. This was the first house built within the present limits of the eastern part of Orange County. It was built some years before Bellomont's notice of it by Col. Patrick MacGregorie, a Scotchman, who came to America with a band of followers in 1684. They landed in Maryland, but, like the majority of the early emigrants, were continually roving around in quest of a better location. Magregorie was next located at Perth Amboy, New Jersey; but this was no better suited to his taste, and in 1685, he petitioned for leave to take up land within the bounds of Billop's Point on Staten Island, the place where John Colman had been buried only 76 years before.

"At the insistance, it is said, of Governor Dongan, he was persuaded to relinquish that design and remove to the Highlands. While here he devoted himself to the Indian trade and became master of the Indian language. The following year, 1686, he was appointed Muster Master General of the Militia of the Province of New York, and was next sent in command of a party to trade at Michilmakinac, [modern-day Michigan] but was intercepted on the way by a party in the French interest, and carried a prisoner to Montreal."[499]

MacGregorie was freed and later killed in battle in New York City, but his many children inherited some land in Cornwall, which is where Plum Point stands. Magregorie made friends with a certain young chief named Awissawa and wrote about him in his journal. According to one report, Awissawa later lived at Otter Creek and then Salisbury Mills. According to some, Awissawa was also known as Maringoman, brother to Nanawoeron, related to Kaelkoptl. In spite of extensive research on the lives of this family, it is still difficult to be sure who is who.

JUET'S JOURNAL, THURSDAY, OCTOBER 1 : *The first of October, fair weather, the wind variable between west and the north. In the morning we weighed at seven o'clock with the ebb, and got down below the mountains, which was seven leagues; then it fell calm and the flood was come, and we anchored at twelve o'clock. The people of the mountains came aboard us, wondering at our ship and weapons. We bought some small skins of them for trifles. This afternoon one canoe kept hanging under our stern with one man in it, which we could not keep from thence, who got up by our rudder to the cabin window, and stole out my pillow, and two shirts, and two bandeleeres. Our master's mate shot at him, and struck him on the breast, and killed him. Whereupon all the rest fled away, some in their canoes, and so leaped out of them into the water. We manned our boat and got our things again. Then one of them that swam got hold of our boat, thinking to overthrow it but our cook took a sword and cut off one of his hands, and he was drowned. By this time the ebb was come, and we weighed and got down two leagues — by that time it was dark; so we anchored in four fathoms water, and rode well.*

Juet writes, "In the morning we weighed at seven o'clock with the ebb, and got down below the mountains, which was seven leagues; then it fell calm and the flood was come, and we anchored at twelve o'clock." They pulled up anchor at 7 AM to float downstream as the tide was going out and traveled about 15 miles before noon. This would bring them to Indian Point. This point, extending into the middle of the river, got its name from regular powwows that were held there every year, up to about 1923. It has had many names, Meanagh Point, (*New York Times*, March 8, 1896) Montrose Point, (Funk, Johnson) Verplanck Point (Adams) and now Indian

Point, and yet for the most part it is not exactly a point, but a headland at a bend in the river. There is a shell midden there which covers at least a half acre along the river bank. There were oyster shell middens on the east side of Haverstraw Bay as well. The most intensive native occupation was between about 2200 to 1000 BCE,[500] but some middens predate this era.

Meanagh Point was purchased from Native Americans on August 24, 1683, along with the adjoining land called Appamagliopogh, (or Appamapough) to Stephanus Van Cortlandt. The sellers included Stecheam, Pewimme, Oskewaus, Turhum, Querawighint, Highgres, and Prackytt. *The Hudson River Guide Book*[501] confirms that the Half Moon stopped here on September 14 and October 1. This was called King's Ferry, a ferry crossing to Stony Point on the western bank. Stony Point became a fort to defend the ferry, as critical supplies and munitions were being transported across the river. Given its reputation and archaeology, it would have been a Native American ferrying point as well, for the Sagamore Trail, a continental trade route now called Route 6 which extends from Cape Cod to California, and also a trail that is now today's Route 202, from Bangor, Maine (near Indian Island) to Wilmington, Delaware, as well as local route 17A. Good river crossings were rare, so many trails would converge at such passage points. We have to assume that early large faunae, (mainly mastodons) followed by deer and other hooved animals, instinctively located these crossings, then animals maintained these trails and crossings with the help of Native Americans over the millennia. Although these roadways still pass through Peekskill as if to approach the old ferrying place, they are now redirected north to a bridge astride high cliffs of rock at Bear Mountain pass, with very deep water below. Travelers jumping off the Indian ferry would have headed back north along what is now 9W/202, however Route 17A to the west may also cover an alternate route of the Sagamore Trail from Stoney Point to Warwick then Goshen, where it again heads west as our Route 6.

When purchased in 1683, the water would have been brackish at this crossing, but boiling would have made it potable and healthy to drink. Today, according to a recent study, the water at old Verplanck Point crossing shows ten times the levels of Alpha and Beta radiation as at Albany. No amount of boiling will improve that figure, a poignant measure of the metrics of mechanization and the long transition from water power to nuclear power which began October 1, 1609. [502]

I have been told that in the 1920s, Mohawks from the Mohawk River would paddle south in canoes, bringing craft items to trade on weekends, then paddle back home on Sunday evening. The land was then sold to the firm that became Central Hudson, which developed the nuclear power plant. The Hudson River Day Line bought the point as a tourist attraction in 1923, calling it Day Line Point, and when they sold it in 1956 they claimed that "this place had been a meeting place for Indians."[503] From photographs I've seen, I'd estimate that these meetings had continued to 1923.

"The people of the mountains came aboard us, wondering at our ship and weapons. We bought some small skins of them for trifles..." Who were the people of the mountains if they'd already passed them?

"This afternoon one canoe kept hanging under our stern with one man in it, which we could not keep from thence, who got up by our rudder to the cabin window, and stole out my pillow, and two shirts, and two bandeleeres. Our master's mate shot at him, and struck him on the breast, and killed him..." This is a turning point in the narrative of the story, and perhaps in history. Until this time, the men have managed to keep cool about the sometimes frustrating intercultural exchanges they are attempting to make. On the other side of the equation, some Algonquins were understandably fearful of the Europeans while others felt the need to defend their land from these sometimes overbearing strangers, uninvited guests in their homeland. By this time the various Algonquin peoples had had time to discuss the people of "the great floating bird" and were perhaps now sure that there was nothing particularly divine and sacred about these men. Their disillusionment led to anger among some. Perhaps they felt that in their eagerness to acquire what was different and new they had been out-traded and over-charged for their furs. It seems from the description that the Dutch East India Company had at least one disgruntled customer, and unable to communicate clearly with Hudson, or perhaps feeling that their complaints (which Juet would be unlikely to pass on to officials in England and Holland via his ship's log) were falling on deaf ears.[504]

In the world of the River Indians, non-violent, symbolic action would be the first recourse when communication between parties broke down into a dispute. Here we see what appears to be a second or third recourse, similar to that which the Algonquins of 30 years later were to attempt with the tyrannical Governor Kieft: when other avenues of statesmanship had failed, the Algonquins resorted to the destruction of relatively insignificant property as a warning. Whatever symbolic action the Wappingers had taken back in mid-September must have been lost on Juet. The native in the canoe may have been being playful, but the paranoid Juet and his friend the cook were picking up on no small degree of hostility.

It may have been by accident that the canoer picked up the bandolier, filled with European ammunition, (unless it was the type with a musket holster attached, which is not likely) not knowing what it was. In any case, logic tells us that is why the encounter turned violent. For all they knew, one of them had stolen a pistol two weeks earlier and figured out how to use it. In spite of the aspersions that Edgar Bacon casts on Robert Juet's character, and I think rightly so, would he have started a war over his pillow and his two shirts, meager though his wardrobe might have been? I believe that after the death of his friend John Colman, his fear, mistrust and anger towards Native Americans was building up inside him like a volcano. The sight of his enemy, imagined or real, swimming off with his ammunition belt made him lose his tightly wound composure and "see red," in every sense of the word.

Another factor is the cultural difference between the two parties concerning material objects. To the Algonquins of this time, objects were either valued for their symbolism or for their practical value. If they had practical value they were to be shared by all, or traded for other practical things. If they were not so practical, they were to be used symbolically, to express feelings, thoughts, and intentions. In addition, a large number of practical Native American objects found by archaeologists are decorated. Their ability to embody powers and principles of the universe is much more important than their practical value, and if they could be used in both capacities, so much the better. Hudson had already seen the Mohicans use the universal *ah-kink* throwing-to-the-ground gesture with the arrows, to show that arrows were "unworthy" between friends, that they were displeased with having kept them in hand when Hudson arrived. Here we cannot escape the implications that this native man was saying that Juet was unworthy, that they were displeased with him. We find the same gesture described in Verrazzano's letter to King Charles, when he offers a potential captive some food, and she throws it dramatically to the ground. Though slightly different circumstances, in both cases, objects are not being coveted as property, they are being used to express something very important. It seems clear that an unethical deed had been done to the natives, and it seems to have involved Juet.

In stark contrast to the Algonquin view that this "robbery" was a pantomime to help redress grievances, the English view is that robbery is a felony and felonies, if great enough, are punishable by death. Here is an excerpt from William Blackstone's (1723-1780) *Commentary on the Laws of England*, Book IV, Chapter XVII, concerning laws in force and effect during Juet's lifetime.

"OUR antient Saxon laws nominally punished theft with death, if above the value of twelvepence: but the criminal was permitted to redeem his life by a pecuniary ransom; as, among their ancestors the Germans, by a stated numer of cattle°. But in the ninth year of Henry the first, this power of redemption was taken away, and all persons guilty of larciny above the value of twelvepence were directed to be hanged; which law continues in force to this day^p. For though the inferior species of theft, or petit larciny, is only punished by whipping at common law^q. or by statute 4 Geo. I. c. 11. may be extended to transportation for seven years, yet the punishment of grand larciny, or the stealing above the value of twelvepence, (which sum was the standard in the time of king Athelstan, eight hundred years ago) is at common law regularly death. Which, considering the great intermediate alteration in the price or denomination of money, is undoubtedly a very rigorous constitution...."

Astoudingly, the master's mate was only meting out English common law, but to a Draconian extreme. Blackstone reports that guests at an inn who walk away with property are committing a felony and those who rob an inn of an object of value greater than twelve pence can be put to death. No symbolic action, no communally owned commodities, no mercy for pity's sake, just crime and punishment. This contrast in values concerning the cultural use of objects is one of the best illustrations of the differences of understanding between the two parties. A bandolier full of ammunition was worth twelvepence, so they shot him, even though he most certainly was trying to make a political statement, bringing to their attention the need for better communication. If the objects were selected for symbolic value, readers must ask themselves what the symbolic portent of Robert Juet's pillow might be, and why the man would risk his life to show he felt it "unworthy," and "distasteful." Again, Robert Juet has a monopoly on communication with us via his logbook, and he isn't going to tell.

This passage also clearly indicates there was a window at the stern of the Half Moon, and a rudder that reached up fairly close to it. I have rarely seen a model of the Half Moon that includes this feature, but the fullscale replica is accurate in this regard. It seems that the natives associated Juet (and maybe Hudson) with this cabin, and with this window. The following day, they fired arrows at the window, another impractical and therefore symbolic gesture.

"Our master's mate shot at him, and struck him on the breast, and killed him. Whereupon all the rest fled away, some in their canoes, and so leaped out of them into the water." The master's mate is an important man throughout the journal, but he is never named. Again, it is clear it's not Juet, because Juet also uses I. Plus, Juet was the ship's mate, not Master's mate, and though it is intriguing to think of him describing his violent acts in the third person to deflect the blame, it didn't happen. Perhaps John Colman had been the Master's Mate, and this crewman filling in for him saw his first opportunity to wreak revenge, and took it, setting the wheels of prophecy in motion. Looking back in hindsight, we have to ask if it was really necessary to kill the man.

Judging from the rest of the entry, there were many canoes, and many ablebodied Algonquins, presumably Wappingers, at the scene, so the man was not acting alone. However, they were apparently unarmed. Their jumping from their canoes into the water indicates as much. They were not likely to leave their weapons in the boats and less likely to swim with them under water, but an argument could be made to the contrary. The crew of the Half Moon may have been outnumbered. If they simply knocked the man unconscious, they might have ended up having to shoot several others in self-defense. To the best of our knowledge, none of these people had ever seen a gun (or a matchlock rifle in this case, we presume) and though somewhat courageous and confident with their own fists, are caught off guard by this new weapon. By killing one by mysterious means, they scared away the others, thus, at least for the moment, sparing their lives.

"*We manned our boat and got our things again. Then one of them that swam got hold of our boat, thinking to overthrow it but our cook took a sword and cut off one of his hands, and he was drowned...*" By "boat" Juet means "row boat," which would have been lowered from the deck in this case. By "we" Juet probably meant the cook and Juet himself, as they were *his* things. They rowed over to where the soggy pillow stood adrift, to where the ruined bandolier and the two shirts lay floating, and gathered them up. Juet and the cook brought a sword with them just in case, a fact the swimmer may not have noticed, or cared about. The man may have been a good friend of the one that was killed so violently, and may have been beyond concern in his grief. We don't know. The cook whipped out the sword[505] and cut the swimmer's hand off. It seems to us that the cook over-reacted to this playful act, but if the man was filled with thoughts of revenge, the boat tipping may have been a way to get the two men in the water to do hand-to-hand combat to the death if necessary. If Juet was the cause and target of this incident, he probably would have died as well, and it is uncertain as to whether his diary would have survived, or at least come to our knowledge.

From the point of view of conflict resolution theory, there must have been some way to communicate with the Native American man climbing the rudder, asking him to hand over the bandolier at least, if not the other items. If the issue was "fair trade," they should have offered the young man something of considerable practical value for the bandolier, and then perhaps tried to put together some sort of conference, to sit down and "talk," to communicate at least in the language of loving symbols of reassurance, even if words were for the most part useless. Without strong guidance from Hudson, and perhaps because there were deep-seated moral issues underneath the surface, Juet chose instead to use violence to silence his critics, and it snowballed out of their control the following day.

"*By this time the ebb was come, and we weighed and got down two leagues — by that time it was dark; so we anchored in four fathoms water, and rode well...*" It appears they removed themselves from Indian Point, and traveled south to Croton Point, spending the night anchored in Croton Bay, where 12 feet of water can be found, a bay which tends to offer shelter from the winds, causing them to "ride well" during the night.[506]

Edward Hagaman Hall has the ship traveling 16.8 miles to Peekskill, New York, then 4.8 more miles to a point between Garnersville to the west and Furnace Brook to the east. There was a large Wappingers fort at Croton Point, and several different village sites over time, plus one of the oldest oyster middens in the Hudson Valley. The fort seems to have been unoccupied or abandoned at this time.

If the capture of Van Horen at Glenham north of Beacon were in retaliation for the skirmish over the bandolier, it must have happened at Croton Point.

JUET'S JOURNAL, FRIDAY, OCTOBER 2 : *The second, fair weather. At break of day we weighed, the wind being at north-west, and got down seven leagues then the flood was come strong, so we anchored. Then came one of the savages that swam away from us at our going up the river, with many others, thinking to betray us. But we perceived their intent, and suffered none of them to enter our ship. Whereupon two canoes full of men, with their bows and arrows, shot at us after our stern, in recompense whereof we discharged six muskets, and killed two or three of them. Then above a hundred of them came to a point of land to shoot at us. There I shot a falkon at them, and killed two of them, whereupon the rest fled into the woods. Yet they manned off another canoe with nine or ten men, which came to meet us; so I shot at it also a falcon, and shot it through, and killed one of them. Then our men with their muskets killed three or four more of them. So they went their way. Within a while after, we got down two leagues beyond that place and anchored in a bay clear from all danger of them on the other side of the river, where we saw a very good piece of ground; and hard by it there was a cliff that looked of the colour of white green, as though it were either a copper or silver mine; and I think it to be one of them by the trees that grow upon it; for they be all burned, and the other places are green as grass; it is on that side of the river that is called Manna-hata. There we saw no people to trouble us, and rode quietly all night, but had much wind and rain.*

The second day of October, 1609, was a sad day. Both sides would choose to take the path of war. It was the fifth day of the Falling Leaf Moon. "*At break of day we weighed, the wind being at north-west, and got down seven leagues then the flood was come strong, so we anchored...*" With a wind from the southeast to draw them forward, they leave peaceful Croton Bay, and with a wind at their back make excellent time heading south. They come to a place that is between Spuytil Duyvel on the East Bank and the Palisades on the West.

"*Then came one of the savages that swam away from us at our going up the river, with many others, thinking to betray us. But we perceived their intent, and suffered none of them to enter our ship....*" Juet seems increasingly paranoid (using a word employed by several respected writers including Bacon) and Henry seems to be in hiding. Juet uses the same word, "savage," to refer to the same individual who escaped capture before, but again, we have an issue with location. *History of Westchester County* suggests he was captured here near Yonkers, and then carried against his will as a prospective slave to Cornwall Bay where he escaped through a porthole. It seems as if he found his way home with a story to tell. "Guess what? These people are not divine! They are human like us!"

The editors of *History of Westchester County*, Edgar Bacon and others all suggest in a variety of ways that some kind of cruelty was being perpetrated, either in the manner the men were captured or in their treatment on board. In any case, it would seem that at least certain native men did not ask to be brought aboard, but were taken against their will. It would help to explain the seemingly unprovoked retaliations upon Hudson's return south, but not completely, We have to consider the possibility that Juet may have had a sadistic side to him, and may have felt a sense of power over these people he now called "primitive savages."

"*Whereupon two canoes full of men, with their bows and arrows, shot at us after our stern, in recompense whereof we discharged six muskets, and killed two or three of them.*" What provoked the volley of arrows at the stern? Does he mean "from the direction of the stern?" Why wouldn't the natives wait until they had a better shot? There are no cannons at the stern. What's there is the cabin window, and that seems associated now with Juet, because of the pillow. If this futile shower of arrows was merely a symbolic gesture of protest for the attempted captures (or some other horrible incident Juet fails to mention, perhaps something that happened in that cabin) were they justified in killing two or three of them as described? If the volley of arrows was a "warning shot" wouldn't a warning shot in return be enough?

"*Then above a hundred of them came to a point of land to shoot at us. There I shot a falkon at them, and killed two of them, whereupon the rest fled into the woods. Yet they manned off another canoe with nine or ten men, which came to meet us; so I shot at it also a falcon, and shot it through, and killed one of them. Then our men with their muskets killed three or four more of them. So they went their way....*" A falcon is a breach loading cannon in which cannon balls are inserted from the top. Some said they were "more dangerous to the attacker than the attacked," but this was probably an example of "navy humor." The falcons were positioned inside the ship, pointing out of the portholes. They were not large or highly accurate cannons, but in the narrative they seem to be highly destructive. Who was firing them with such determination to kill? Juet says "I" fired the cannons. Hudson, a veteran, we assume, of a number of broadsides and cannon volleys during his duty in the sea battle against the Spanish Armada as a lad of 18, seems to be absent. Based on Juet's skill with a falcon, perhaps we should assume that the older man also joined in the fight against King Philip of Spain, and ended up behind a breech loader.

It could be argued that this was the first "Wounded Knee" in United States history. On December 29, 1890, (at the beginning of the seventh fire) a deaf Minneconjou named Black Coyote, a follower of the "Ghost Dance" movement, was slow to put his newly acquired rifle down on the pile of confiscated weapons at the Wounded Knee camp, because he could not hear the protests of the soldiers. The rifle went off and shot into the air by accident, and the soldiers opened fire on the Ghost Dancers with not only rifles but then Hotchkiss guns, a more modern descendant of the falcon. When the smoke had cleared, three hundred Minneconjous were dead. Although the massacre at Spuyten Duyvel Hill was on a smaller scale than Wounded Knee, and although the natives at Spuyten Duyvel were not totally unarmed, as they were in 1890, there are some basic parallels. In both circumstances, small incidents escalated into greater ones, leading to the use of overwhelming force. In both cases, guns and cannons were used in combination, and at close range, on Native Americans who had neither guns nor cannons.[507]

Those who had survived retold the story to their children. Those children told their children, many of whom traveled west into territories of native people who had never seen a white man before, or a gun. In spite of all that Henry Hudson did to try to make a favorable impression on his new clients in the peltry business on behalf of the Dutch East India Company, the one Robert Juet left was probably the more long-lasting. When asked, "Did the strangers from the east come in brotherhood or with weapons of war?" those natives who saw only the bloodshed and thundering cannons at Spuyten Duyvel would have to answer, "the latter."

Where's Manna-hatta?

Most readers tend to think that *"the side of the river that is called Manna-hata"* would be the east side, where the island of Manhattan is. This would mean the attack was from the west side, possibly from Indian Rock above the Palisades. Edgar Bacon agrees with this notion, and presumes that the "one hundred" attackers were Mohawks, or at least Iroquoian people.

It is true that the Mohawks had a more organized military presence and frequently traveled down from the region of the Mohawk River in large bands of warriors on foot, along trails such as what is now called 9 W, or what is now Route 32, both of which are on the west side. However the ship was attacked first by "two canoes full of men," and approached by what Juet believed was a local man they had had an encounter with when they were in the area three weeks earlier, on or about September 13. It seems plausible that the disgruntled man and a few of his friends would approach the ship together, with two canoes of men from his clan or nation backing him up just in case. These too would then be local men. But what is not plausible is that one hundred Mohawks from a village a hundred miles north would show up on the bluff (not easily accessible from sea level) at exactly the same moment. This would imply a highly organized, brilliantly planned military effort, jointly launched by both Algonquin and Iroquoian (Hodenosuannee) people. At this time, these two groups had different military protocol, mutually unintelligible languages, and a history of conflict between them. Even fifty years later, when King Philip asked for Mohawk assistance (from war chiefs he was personally familiar with) in a fight that presumably would be to their mutual advantage to win, the details could not be worked out. There is no way the one hundred were Mohawk.

Who, then? The Mohicannuk had no argument with Hudson's men, and had established peaceful trade relations with the Half Moon, after considerable effort. Such an attack would have required sanction by the very chiefs that were so friendly to Henry Hudson.

There was no habitation at the foot of the Palisades to the west. The only major tribe to the west at that latitude was the Tappaans, and they were inland. It is somewhat questionable as to whether the Tappaans were a large enough group to muster one hundred men. Their subtribes included the Quaspeck (just below Haverstraw, from *poquashpeck,* "clear open water"[508]) the Nayack, (or whatever group was at our present day town of Nyack at that time, "point of land"), the Tappaan proper (possibly from *thuphanne,* "cold stream"[509]), the Kessa Waky, the Gessawakin (both far inland,[510]), the Uteneyik ("villages"[511]), the Achkinkeshaky (forerunner of the Hackensacks, this Sanhikan-affiliated tribe were located at a bend in that river;[512] *achkink* means "unworthy," *–es* means "small," but is generally translated as "stony ground" in reference to Teaneck Ridge), the Awapough ("bushy place"[513]), the Espating ("raccoon hill"[514]) and the Wiehaekse[515] at the far south of the Tappaan region. All of these small tribal groups were east of the Hackensack River, but west of the Hudson River.[516] They were relatives of the war-like Sanhikan, and possibly could muster one hundred warriors, but in my estimation it is not likely. These were only tiny, widespread villages. That leaves the Sanhikans, "the fire bow drill" people.[517] Explorers generally describe them as "warlike." They were Unami speaking people with a large population, living in a shifting border territory north of the Raritan, shared or disputed (that isn't always clear) between Unami and Munsee "cousins."

The ship's contacts on the way north were on the east bank at this latitude. Therefore it is more likely that the attack was from the east as well. This side of the river has high points such as Nipnichsen (Spuyten Duyvel) and settlements at sea level, with trails between them. However, according to Kevin Wright's map entitled "Indigenous Place Names in Northeastern New Jersey,[518] the west bank of the Hudson, south from Hoboken, was called Manatthans, as was the island we call Manhattan. The syllable "man" or "men" generally means island, (derived from menach'hen, an island[519]). And this group at Bergen Neck, which is not an island, was apparently a spillover group of Manhattan Island natives. If by this time Juet or Hudson had become more conversant in the language and therefore with the people, they might have learned that these people called themselves "those of the Manatthan," but mistakenly thought they lived on "the side of the river called Manahatta."[520]

This strangely named territory east of the Hackensack River included several subtribes of "commuters" to Manhattan; The Hobokan, at the foot of a trail from the inland, whose name means "smoking-pipe place," probably from a serpentine outcropping of stone used to make pipe bowls;[521] the Hackiing, the Aressechhonk, "the place at the far side of the river." This is now Communipaw,[522] derived from a native name that means "at the other side" of the crossing; the Ahasimus,[523] the Pembrepough,[524] the Minckaque[525], and the Nyacksick.[526] Further inland was the Penepack[527], and the Sikakes.[528]

If Bergen Neck is his Manahatta, that means the attack of the "one hundred" really did come from Nipnischsen, about eight miles north on the opposite side, where there was a large fort on top of a point of land overlooking Spuyten Duyvel. This is in fact where Henry Hudson's statue stands, and where most people believe he was attacked. It is also on the same side of the river, the east side, where most of their interactions had happened on September 13, and where some historians believe two native men from Yonkers were captured.

All told, Henry Hudson and the men of the Half Moon, killed 13 or 14 Native Americans on their trip to Albany and back, and as far as we know, all of those killings happened in the last few days of the trip. As regards the Siwanoy near Clasons Point, we don't know for sure if any were killed in that skirmish, as the exploration crew's match went out and visibility was very poor. Were these killings justified? Compared to other explorers and traders, the crew of the Half Moon was not the worst, certainly not like DeSoto's men, but certainly not the most peaceful either. Hudson fell far short of his hero Verrazzano in terms of diplomacy, if only for his inability to control Juet and others in his command.

THE MUNSEE PEOPLE'S JOURNAL, BLUE HERON REPORTING, OCTOBER 2 : (a dramatization) *The ship that carries the good and the treacherous brothers, the two "Manitous," Robert and Henry, is firing upon our people. We tried* symbolic action to warn them about the untrustworthy one, Juet, but it has backfired terribly. I feel the need to flee the carnage. It is no use trying to teach them anything. These weapons they have are very powerful and we are not yet prepared to deal with them. I need time to think things over. At least thirteen of our people, some of them my brothers and cousins, lie dead, due to a cascade of violence that has twice run out of control in these last two days.

My brother Arrowroot and cousin Medicine Tree were captured at Neppakamack [Yonkers] 15 suns [days] ago. My brother Tuckahoe and I were spared. They carried both of them to the bay near the island we call "The Rock That Plows Their Waters," Pough-laup-pee-el [Bannerman Island]. That man Juet had abused them so both jumped out a porthole to escape. They swam to the mouth of the Matteawan Creek, to the island of the Little Spirit People whom the Munsee call M'swingwe, but which we call Puckwahdjeedjk. They walked back to Neppeckamack and met with me and Tuckahoe. We couldn't find Medicine Tree. He brings me and my brother to Meanagh Point at the crossing of the Sagamore Trail where the old oyster middens are. The passage is somewhat narrow there, and for the most part, shallow, so we thought it a good place to intercept their ship. Arrowroot's plan was to create some kind of non-violent demonstration to illustrate to them how unhappy many of us are, and how he was mistreated. He said he'd been in the Captain's Cabin and knew where Juet's things were. At one point he had been locked in that cabin without a means of escape, so he looked out the window in the back and seeing the rudder, devised a plan. His plan was to cause a harmless disturbance that would bring attention to the other crew members that Juet was not behaving civilly. He thought a long time and decided that if he threw Juet's belongings down from the window, in the "ah-kink" gesture, which means "not worthy," "not good," they would eventually figure out the message, as they know our sign language. We agreed, they must already realize that he is mixed up in his mind, and would realize that we are angry with him and not them. We hope to give them cause to demote him in ranking. We are aware of the prophecy and know how important it is to make peace with them, but what good is peace when our people's voices cannot be heard? It is we who are supposed to lead them and show them the ways of our land. If the Salty Smelling Ones take over, it will be disastrous for not just human beings, but all beings on the earth.

My brother Arrowroot is always goofing around, and quite the athlete too; getting up that rudder and into the window is no small feat. I recall the many times he'd hide up in a tree and jump down on top of me to surprise me. He laughs as he throws down the pillow. It seems to have some significance to him. He is saying something but I cannot make it out. Suddenly there is this loud crack like lightning hitting a tree. It is a musket firing, something we have never seen or heard before, and the next thing I know, my brother is dead. He falls like a stone into the water. My other brother, Tuckahoe, is right there on shore, watching. When that man Juet comes out in a row boat with the cook to collect his soggy pillow and his flimsy shirts, I got a bad feeling. I saw Tuckahoe on the shoreline and his face was a knotted ball of anger. He grieved so for his brother Arrowroot that he was beyond all personal concern. Arrowroot was like his right hand, after so many moons hunting together as a team. I yelled to him not to avenge our brother's death against such musket power, but he yelled back, "I want merely to capture this Juet so he knows how it feels!" He lept into the water to swim over to Juet's boat. Tuckahoe, like the rest of us, was unarmed. He thought he could flip over Juet's row boat the way you flip a canoe, and hold Juet underwater, hold his arms behind him, drag him to shore and tie him up somewhere in the name of justice. But flipping that boat proved much more difficult. My brother Tuckahoe was strong, but he couldn't seem to push it over. I saw Juet hand the sword to the cook and the cook took a big chop at Tuckhoe's wrist and his hand flew off. All our native men heaved a sigh of wonder, for they had never seen anything so cruel. My brother's eyes glazed over. Without his older brother, and now without his hand, he did not want to live. He looked at me, mouth silently open, and sadly, shook his head at me, I'm not sure why, and then threw himself into the current where he was pulled under. I guess he was saying, "Don't try to save me! I am lost!"

And yet I have a younger brother named Black Hawk back in Neppeckamack who was also captured and placed on the ship, and he too escaped. Brother Black Hawk is not forgiving. He seeks justice for his people, but does not have the patience required to negotiate a just peace. There is loo-way-woo-dee in his heart, a darkness that eats at him. He is an angry man. I must run back to tell him not to try to protest the strangers' actions, but to let them go out to sea and hopefully never come back. I must tell him to hide all the people. I cross back to the east bank, and run down the trail to the Nepperan River. I run to the shoreline where I see the Great Floating Bird approaching, and there is my brother Black Hawk on the shoreline, shouting commands to a muster of his fellow warriors. Black Hawk is a renegade and does not do these acts by the will of the people. I grab him by the shoulders and tell him of my fears. He has organized a whole battalion of his young

friends, and they are good warriors. I say, "Don't try to fight them! They
have thundersticks of death. You must stop your men from attacking!"

He tells me that his warriors will never agree to such a thing as they
are proud, like the Siwanoy, and not afraid of the white man. I implore
him to tell them that it would be better to stage a non-violent protest, firing
a hundred arrows at the back of the ship where Juet's window is located.
No one would be hurt. A symbolic gesture. Perhaps this one will be more
clear than throwing down the pillow that our late brother attempted. We
could signal for a parley with the one called Hudson. He has an ear for our
concerns. The ship comes closer. He looks at me with frustration, and says,
"Okay. We will try the Way of the Heron one more time, but any show of
disrespect will block the path to the parley and we go to all-out war!"

Black Hawk and his warriors jump into their canoes and row out into the
river to engage the Half Moon. On his cue, they carefully fire one hundred
arrows towards the closed back window of the ship. Some points stick in the
stern of the ship, but no one is in danger. It is an eloquent warning shot. In
the art of nonverbal community expression, which is at the heart of the Way
of the Heron, the political system that has kept Algonquin society at peace
for thousands of years, it is a masterpiece. Some stand and admire their
work. Maybe now their voices will be heard. Maybe they will be granted a
parley.

Suddenly, not one, but six muskets billowing smoke open fire on us, and
many fall dead. I see Juet on the deck laughing as he fires at will, a musket
in each hand. He is running around on the deck, and then disappears.
The warriors back off briefly, upset by what seems to them a horribly
inappropriate response. Some of the young warriors become outraged and
overwhelmed by anger. They break ranks and start attacking the ship, in
earnest this time, trying to climb aboard; thoughts of killing and hatred
fill their minds. Bravely, they continue, but they are shot down by the
musketmen.

Brother Black Hawk blows the eagle bone whistle. Now the call has gone
up, there is no turning back. Our protest has failed, and our allies up at
Fort Nipnischsen come to the top of the ridge, one hundred strong, armed
to attack. Then I see Juet's face through a cannon porthole, and his face is
something to see. He is lighting and loading all these iron weapons they call
falcons and fires balls of iron right through our warriors' canoes on the water
and many are dying. My brother Black Hawk blows the eagle bone whistle
one last long note, and then a cannon ball destroys his boat and his muscular

body is torn to pieces. He floats face down in the bloody river and drifts downstream. Again I am overwhelmed with grief.

Then Juet begins to fire the giant smoking pipes on the east side of the ship, fires these thunderous falcons at the hoard on the top of the ridge atop Spuyten Duyvel Hill, and some are falling. Finally all retreat. Many of my friends and relatives are dead or badly injured. We have no medicine for cannon ball injuries. The big canoe the Half Moon floats away.

The first thing at least some of us want to know is, "How does this affect the prophecies?" Many of us retreat back to our shamanic healers and village prophets looking for answers. The answers are quick in coming, "It's a very bad sign for our people," we are told.

I go to my spiritual elder, an old man named Firefly. I offer him a bundle of tobacco and a piece of yellow jasper as a gift, and he accepts. I say to the seer, "Yes, it is a bad sign. But I thought the prophet of the fourth fire said that the strangers would come in brotherhood, that we would be at peace and all would learn from one other!"

The seer answers, "Yes, that was the first prophet. But don't forget about the second prophet. There were two. Only the fourth fire was presented by two messengers from Manitou. The second one foretold of another possibility.

The old man pulls out a large purple and white wampum belt from his sack, three feet long, three inches wide, and of magnificent workmanship. He hands it to Tuckahoe so he can feel its weight in his hands.

"As you see, there are three white diamonds on the left and three on the right. In the center is what is called "The Double Diamond.""

"I have heard of the double diamond, but I knew not what it meant. What does it mean?"

"Each single diamond represents 112 winters of our history, a length of time we call a "fire." I was born at the end of the third diamond. We are at the center of the fourth cycle, the middle of the seven fires. This time period alone is divided into two diamond figures, one overlapping the other. The events of this time period alone were predicted for us by two messengers of Manitou instead of one. We've known for 393 winters that something important would happen this autumn. But we didn't know what."

"What did the second messenger have to say?" Tuckahoe asked.

"The other prophet said, 'Beware if the Light-skinned Race comes wearing the face of ni-boo-win (death). You must be careful because the face of brotherhood and the face of death look very much alike. If they come carrying a weapon...beware. If they come in suffering...they could fool you. Their hearts may be filled with greed for the riches of this land. If they are

indeed your brothers, let them prove it. Do not accept them in total trust.
You shall know that the face they wear is the one of death if the rivers run
with poison and fish become unfit to eat. You shall know them by these many
things.'[529]

These are the exact words that he spoke, as handed down to him by his
medicine lodge chief.

I ask, "How will it turn out? Which side will win? What do the
prophecies say?"

He answered, "Some men shoot straight and true, and are full of virtue.
Some men's arrows miss the mark again and again. Some men's minds are
clear, and some minds are cloudy. Some are healers while others spread
disease and death. It has always been this way. Confirm what is good
and avoid or heal that which is destructive. As to who is winning at any
given time, it all depends on how you look at it. Some think the darkness
is devouring the earth, while others think everything is perfect, just as it
should be. They are both right, and both wrong. Throughout the stories
of the Manitou-wanini there runs a thread of tales about twin brothers, a
good brother who is the tool of the creator, and a brother who is a trickster
and destroyer. The good brother is known by many names, Glooskap,
Glooskabee, Nadabozo, Nanabush, or Waynaboozhoo. Glooskap's dark
twin, for example, is called Malsum, which means "He is related to you."
Waynaboozhoo in Ojibway has a dark twin as well. It seems that you, too,
had a brother who followed the path of selfish ambition."

[The following material is quoted from *The Mishomis Book* © 1976 by
permission of Eddie Benton Bernaise]

"In the stories they tell in the Midewiwin Lodges, the woodland spirit
Bug-way-ji-nini, not unlike the Maysingway spirit of the forest you heard
when a child, speaks to the good twin Waynaboozhoo of light and shadow.
Bug-way-ji-nini says, 'When your shadow is cast on the ground you are
able to see it. But even though you do not see it at times, you know that
your shadow is still there. Your shadow represents your relationship to
Grandfather Sun and the Four Directions, and thus to the Universe. It is
time for you to continue on your journey. I will be with you little brother,
wherever your steps may take you. There is one last thing I wish to leave you
and then we shall never talk again.'

Bug-way-ji-nini says, 'You have a twin brother whom you have wondered
about and whom you would seek. This I tell you: he is your other side in
all things and in all ways. He is with you…do not seek him. Do not wish to
know him, but understand him.

'You will walk the path of peace...he would not
'You are kind....he is not.
'You are humble...he is not
'You are generous...he is not
'You seek the good in things...he does not.
'You shall respect others....he does not.
'You will seek the goodness in others...he will not.
'You are the light....he is the darkness.
'Know that he is with you, understand him,
'But do not seek him!'
"With that, Bug-way-ji-nini left Waynaboozhoo and vanished like a
shadow into the woods."[530] That is one of the ancient stories, one I have
wanted to tell you for a long time.

"This is good teaching for you. You have lost three brothers; that is sad.
I am sorry for you. In the old stories, the good and the not-so-good happen
at once, and it's up to us to sort them out and to choose for ourselves how
we look at it and what we will do. But do not use it as an excuse to follow
the path of revenge, or as an excuse to destroy yourself. In our story of
Nanabush, the Hero, he is forever wrestling with the awful serpent Minetta.
He casts it into the Muscouten [East River], but it comes back to terrorize
the people. He casts it into the Muhikanituck [Hudson River] but it jumps
out and attacks him. He drives it underground, but it shakes the earth as
it passes. He turns it into a snaking stream that snakes across Manhattan,
and its waters bubble up like poison out of the ground. He may vanquish
it for a hundred years but it will some day return, because its not really a
snake or serpent, it is the fear, the hurt and anger in every person's heart.
The story asks you to face the greatest enemy, yourself, and to emerge
victorious...every day! That battle must be won each day through courage
and determination. The prophecies describe both the best in human behavior
and the worst, and say both are possible. It seems that every 56 years or so,
we who believe come to a new crossroads and must choose to change our
route. And it seems that at every crossroads half the people go down the path
of light and half go into shadow, they go the wrong way and make all the
wrong choices. It's a seesaw battle. Light wins the day if you choose to see it,
and Darkness wins the night, if you think it does.

"This island is a vortex for a creative power in the universe; we don't
know why, but the brighter that light gets the more the darkness will try to
destroy it. And the more dark and dangerous it gets, the greater and more
miraculous will be the deeds of those who would be heroes. You ask what will

happen at the end of the seven fires? I will tell you. It will get very interesting!

"The light from this island will light the world, and its darkness will engulf the world. In the last days, the greatest villains will come here and take everything with their trickery, and then the greatest of heroes will appear and take it all back in the name of the people. There will be great wealth and equal poverty. There will be brilliant leaders and unbelievably stupid ones as well. Towers will crumble and new ones will take their place.

"What the prophecies say is absolutely true, that if enough people choose to walk in balance, and tend good fires at night, awaken to the power of Manitou within them, and live and die for love and brotherhood, then we will all walk in the light and we will all ignite the glow of the eighth fire which will last 784 years. But they are also correct in saying if enough people lose hope and plunge themselves into destruction and the sleeping state of awareness, it will be as if they had cut down all the trees across the entire earth, and then the whole planet shall suffer for it, and no one will be able to light the eighth fire in the winds that will blow then.

"Many of our elders said the visitors would come only in friendship. Others said the visitors would come only in hatred and killing. But there was a third possibility few considered; that like the two brothers at the beginning of time, Tujiskeha and Tawiskarong, (as the Huron call them)the sweethearted one and the hard-headed one, one visitor would be kind and another would be cruel. One visitor would seek power while another vistor would seek love."

"Is that what happened yesterday and today?"

"Yes, I think we can safely say that."

"What will happen at the end?"

"Half shall wallow in insanity and dark thoughts, disrupting all around them, while the other half will have to fight every day to keep their balance, but they will do so, and become incredibly strong."

"And who on this island of Manhattan shall become more powerful?"

"The one you let get to you!"

I leave the wigwam of the visionary, our "powwow," and set out immediately on a journey to the top of the Highlands, to fast and sort out my angry thoughts. I find an abandoned rock shelter such as was used by our ancestors in ancient times, and set up camp. At night I ask Kitchelamookong to show me what will happen at the end of the seven fires cycle. I fall asleep and have a dream. I find myself back at the spot where the colorful floating bird first landed on Mana-hattan, three weeks ago, just above the Kapsee Rocks, at the Great Crossing. I was among those greeting the ship. In my

dream I am back at that place, but it is very different. There are tall cliffs
of slate, and frozen waterfalls like lakes on their side, reflecting the sun,
yet the heat does not melt them. There are holes in the cliff, like little caves
and people are sticking their heads out. Suddenly the cliffs catch on fire and
smoke billows out, the cliffs are collapsing. The people above us are jumping
off the cliff. There are great throngs of people on the ground and they are
running in every direction and screaming, as the cliffs begin to fall upon
them. Dust is everywhere. It clouds my vision, and gets in my eyes, until I
am blinded by it. Gradually, I also see a band of great heroes emerging from
the smoke. They are fearless and strong. They carry the injured and weak to
safety. They calm the bereaved. They ask for nothing but the chance to serve
others.

I dream I am grabbed by one of these heroes and taken to a quiet place of
rest. I wake up in a cold sweat, shaking. BLUE HERON, FALLING LEAF MOON,
5TH DORSAL PLATELET OF THE CALENDAR TURTLE.

Commentary on Juet's Journal, October 2, 1609, continued.

Juet's journal continues coolly as if nothing out of the ordinary has happened,
and yet he is the one who fired the cannons. *"Within a while after, we got down two*
leagues beyond that place and anchored in a bay clear from all danger of them on the
other side of the river, where we saw a very good piece of ground; and hard by it there
was a cliff that looked of the colour of white green, as though it were either a copper or
silver mine…" This spot is now Hoboken, New Jersey. It is often said that a form
of pipestone was mined at that place. It was written in 1902, as follows: "Of the
settlements made upon the New Jersey shore of the Hudson River and intimately
associated with the early history of the Dutch in New York was the locality known
as Hobocan-hackingh, where the Indians and fur traders crossed to trade gewgaws
for peltries. Here in 1609, upon the voyage of the "Half Moon," Henry Hudson
and Juet, his mate and historiographer, saw the "cliff that looked of the color of
white green" — now the Castle Point estate of the Stevens family, and which the
Dutch navigators supposed to be formed of copper or silver ore."[531] This is fairly
near Bergen Neck, which apparently was also called "Manna-hatta" by its natives
as revealed to Juet, explaining the source of the confusion.

"…and I think it to be one of them by the trees that grow upon it; for they be all
burned, and the other places are green as grass;" This has been interpreted as a reference to the red maple, whose leaves turn red and then brown, and then wither as
if scorched by fire. Neither Juet nor Hudson would not have seen such coloration
in Europe, nor in the far north or even in the Caribbean, for only the maple dis-
tinguishes itself so in the fall, and maples are mainly found in the northeastern

United States and across Canada. Due to the thick canopy cover of old growth trees at the time, the maple, which enjoys sunlight, would have been less numerous,[532] but it is interesting that no notice is taken of these "the chief of trees" (as called by Mi'kmaq) until October 2, at the height of the leafing season. It is ironic that it looked "burned" to Juet, as the maple is fire-intolerant.[533]

Each February and March the Lenape Trailside Museum in Cross River, New York, conducts workshops on Native American maple sugaring techniques. The Munsee Delaware consider the uncooked maple sap "water" to be a form of medicine, and still drink it today, as did their ancestors in 1609.[534] However similar it may look to water, it is not H_2O, and can make one dangerously thirsty while on a hike. In this form, it is only faintly sweet, but contains elements such as iron, potassium, and calcium that help boost the immune system.[535] Chief Seattle once said, "The sap that courses through the trees carries the memories of the Red Man."[536] The tree that carries the sweetness of that memory must then be the "tree of friendship," the maple.

THE MUNSEE PEOPLE'S JOURNAL: AS REPORTED BY BLUE HERON OCTOBER 3 : (a dramatization) *As dawn comes, I stumble back to my shaman, and tell him my dream, still flashing over and over again before me. I ask, "Are these the ghosts of things to come? Or can they be erased, and made not to happen?"*

The shaman answers, "Yes, these pictures in the sand can still be erased, but it will take a lot of time. Everyone must work together. We must treat each other as equals and try to communicate. We must find new pathways of peace, and constantly adapt to change as it happens. It will be hard. Such heroism as you saw in your dream should not be necessary. If we all do the right thing, no one will have to sacrifice anything. Everyone will be the hero. In the old days, heroes were not needed.

"And what if we can't stop the bad dream and the violence just continues until the end of the Age of Seven Fires? What then?"

"Even then it will not be the end, even though at times it will appear to be so. No, at about that time, all the people of Turtle Island will come to a crossroads, and will have to make a decision. If they decide to follow the ways of wisdom, and honor the earth and each other in all they do, there will be a time of purification, there will be hardship for a few years, but if we face that purification willingly, we will light the eighth fire together and usher in a new era of peace and prosperity. It will still not be too late."

I thank the shaman for his help and begin walking south along the ridge above the river, trying to collect my thoughts. I collect some tobacco and return to the place where the Great Floating Bird first landed on Mana-

hattan, and where my terrible dream took place. I kneel and offer a handful of tobacco to the earth on the shores of the Mohicannituck, with a prayer for peace.

I think of those two white men, Henry Hudson, who came as our brother, filled with curiosity, and Robert Juet who came with weapons in his hands, and a face full of anger, and hatred and a heart full of confusion and mistrust. We were only trying to find a way to warn Henry and the others about Juet, and in response they killed a dozen or more of us. Our lives will never be the same. We have lost our innocence. I pray that the Robert Juets of the world will awaken to Gitchi Manitou Great Spirit before it is too late. I pray that Mana-hattan will never see such terrible destruction, that we never need such heroes, and if it does, I pray that the heroes will come, and it will be healed. I pray that our people survive long enough to see the lighting of the eighth fire and hail it in our own language. I pray for a great awakening for all the people of the earth. BLUE HERON, FALLLING LEAF MOON, 6TH DORSAL PLATELET OF THE CALENDAR TURTLE.

JUET'S JOURNAL, SATURDAY, OCTOBER 3 : *The third was very stormy, the wind at east north- east. In the morning, in a gust of wind and rain, our anchor came home, and we drove on ground, but it was oozy. Then as we were about to heave out an anchor, the wind came to the north north- west, and drove us off again. Then we shot an anchor, and let it fall in four fathoms water, and weighed the other. We had much wind and rain with thick weather, so we rode still all night.*

If the wind was from the east, they would have run aground on the west bank with sails down, which was where their anchor was. They pulled that one up but this did not release them from the sand bank. So they tried to drop another anchor in the channel but were blown into the channel by a wind from the west and north before it hit bottom. So they dropped yet another anchor on a sixty-foot cable called a "shot," and managed to get a footing in twenty feet of water,[537] and pulled up the other anchor. They decided to stay right where they were until the storm blew over. It was just one of those days, but it showed that Hudson had considerable problem-solving skill in navigating shallow water.

But where were they? In the Native American accounts, it seems that Hudson comes onto Manhattan Island alone during his last day in the New World and shares his rum with the men. The stories imply that they have never seen him before and that he bids them a fond ado and heads back for Europe. Since we know he went to Schodack Island and back, we also know this is not possible. It seems very possible there were two visits to Manhattan, which have become one over time in the minds of the people.

That would mean Henry went ashore on this day, full of sorrow for what Juet and the others had done, wanting to do something remarkable, Manitou-like, to impress the Natives. Being a lifelong sailor, he thought of rum. Juet's lack of information about this last day in the river is actually a clue that "Hudson's Farewell" is true. Being by this time a confirmed Indian Fighter, Hudson would not want him anywhere near this last diplomatic gesture, and Juet in turn would not have admired Hudson for his last show of friendship, nor would he want to report it to the King and all his subjects. He can't say anything nice so he says nothing at all.

HENRY HUDSON'S LOST SECRET DIARY, OCTOBER 3 : (for dramatization purposes only) *I cannot bear being around these men much longer! I hold Juet accountable for the disastrous events of these last few days; he is a madman! When I get back to England....if I get back to England … they will probably hang me for establishing Newe Netherlands for the Dutch, then the Dutch will hang me for deigning to follow orders. I wish to jump ship, cast away my officer's uniform, don buckskin made by my own hand and join the Natives! Their life is so simple, so uncomplicated. I do admire them so. They are open with each other as are children and share every possession like saints on Christmas Day. They hold the earth so dear they call her "mother." I am so saddened about the violence that left so many of them in the throes of death ignoble. How will we deal with them now? Will we be welcome back next year when we come again to trade for furs? I so miss being their magic Manitou Man!*

In the tongue of symbolic action, which they seem to use so freely, I wish to show them that I admire and love them, that I am their greatest friend and elder brother. I wish to show them that I still have magic powers, other than the voice of death that proceedeth like thunder from our port holes— which they surely shall hear of by the end of the day. I shall impress these people of Manna-hattan with the pleasures of Portuguese rum, a sailor's greatest comfort. If their reaction is liken to that of the Mohicans up north, they shall never cease speaking in wonderment about my visit. They shall desire to see our arrival each year, to accept eagerly our rum for their furs. But my men are such beasts, I dare not trust them to come ashore, lest they blow off the peoples' heads with their blunderbusts. I shall row myself ashore and face them alone. If they know what happened yesterday, they shall kill me and I should not blame them. But if they welcome me, I will share with them my finest possession, the Captain's special rum, and they will be happy,

at least for a day, and shall be too blinded by bliss to afford a clear shot with
their arrows. I shall bring with me my quaich shell cup, and honor them with
a toast of the highest order, which they shall describe in their stories and pass
down for centuries to come. It will be my greatest gift, and they shall know
t'was not myself who fired the canons and muskets, but that damn fool we
call Juet.

The above diary entry is fictional, and should not be quoted out of context. It is meant to provide insights about Henry Hudson's psychological state at the end of the journey, and a logical transition to the following Native American account, a well known part of the oral tradition of the Algonquins of the region, and may in fact be a synthesis of two visits by Hudson to Manhattan.

The following is a continuation of the tale as told by Edgar Bacon, in *Henry Hudson His Life and Voyages*, based on Heckewelder, an early missionary who enjoyed close ties with the natives of New York and New Jersey.

"...he caused to be lifted from the canoe a vessel the like of which no one had ever seen before, and out of it he poured into a smaller but equally curious receptacle some liquid that had a strange but no unpleasant odour. Taking this in his hand and inkling his head to the company, he drank a little of the contents and handed it to the nearest chief, who carefully smelled of it and passed it, untasted, to his nearest neighbor. He in turn, lifted the cup to his nose and offered it, without drinking of its contents, to the chief next to him. So around the circle went the first flowing bowl ever offered by way of a convivial treat on Manhattan Island. The custom has since been somewhat abused."[538]

"Indian after Indian, teetotalers till that day, sniffed and declined, till the last man, who should have passed the liquor again to their entertainer, wavered and made a speech. With the glass of rum in his hand he harangued the assembled braves and sachems, and there was a curious mixture of Tammany acumen and Roman heroism in his words. The substance of his speech, translated into English, was somewhat as follows:

"If this singular thing, which is neither a shell nor yet a grape leaf, [the Quaich Cup] but which is capitally contrived to hold a liquor which hath a most admirable and seductive odour, is handed back to the great and powerful Manitou who hath poured it out for us and who hath himself partaken of it, no doubt he will be offended and may visit upon us some terrible calamity. It will be far better for one man to risk death than for all the tribe to be wiped out. I will drink this unknown concoction and if I die you may put upon my monument, 'he died for his country.'"

"He raised the cup to his lips and drank every drop, though the fiery stuff burned his throat and the tears came to his eyes. He was willing to perish for his tribe, surely he could endure choking for them.

"With awestruck faces the Indians gathered closer to watch their companion and champion. For a few moments they saw no change in him; then suddenly it was noticed that his eyes gazed unsteadily upon them; he swayed from side to side; presently he sank to the ground and lay as one dead.

"Now if the man in the red coat had not been regarded as a Manitou, it is probable that the whole history of Henry Hudson would have ended at this point and would ere this have been forgotten. Believing him to be superhuman, his red hosts waited and after a time their compassion revived. He declared in accents of unmistakable conviction, but in language that unfortunately has not been preserved, that he never had such a good time in his life. He wanted some more of the same seductive liquor."

When the other natives saw the man's pleasure in drinking the rum, they too wanted some, and soon everyone was drinking and there was a remarkable party. According to Heckewelder, only Henry Hudson had left the ship; Juet and all the other crew members had stayed on board. He suggests Hudson communicated in sign language. After everyone was drunk, Henry Hudson departed on the rowboat and went back to the ship, saying that they were going back home now but would be back in a year's time.

This is the most famous of all the stories about Henry Hudson's visit to the New World, and yet there is no mention in either Juet's or Hudson's journals of such a drinking party on Manhattan, nor did they return the following year. However, the natives to this day call Manhattan by its nickname, Manahachtanienks, "the place of general inebriation."

As Henry Hudson leaves, perhaps he notices a pile of tobacco perched on a rock, tobacco left there by Blue Heron just moments ago. Perhaps he picks some up, holds it to his heart, and says, "Some day, I would like to have the pleasure of living with such gentle children of mother earth." As he steps onto the canoe, he would release the tobacco into the river and say, "Amen!"

JUET'S JOURNAL, SUNDAY, OCTOBER 4 : *The fourth was fair weather, and the wind at north north-west we weighed and came out of the river, into which we had run so far. Within a while after, we came out also of the great mouth of the great river, that runneth up to the north-west, borrowing upon the more northern side of the same, thinking to have deep water, for we had sounded a great way with our boat at our first going in, and found seven, six, and five fathoms. So we came out that way, but we were deceived, for we had but eight feet and a half water; and so to three, five, three, and two fathoms and a half; and then three, four, five, six, seven, eight, nine and ten fathoms; and by twelve o'cock we were clear of all the inlet.* Then we took in our boat, *and set our mainsail and spritsail, and our topails, and steered away east south-east, and south-east by east, off into the main sea; and the land on the southern side of the bay or inlet did bear at noon west and by south four leagues from us.*

"The fourth was fair weather, and the wind at north north-west we weighed and came out of the river, into which we had run so far." They finally experienced nice weather and a strong wind behind them to fill their sails and give them speed. They soon "came out of the river," clearly the Hudson River, and found themselves in open water below Manhattan. They had navigated over 160 miles inland on this river, an unusual feat for a seagoing vessel. He implies they were lucky to get out alive.

"Within a while after, we came out also of the great mouth of the great river, that runneth up to the north-west, borrowing upon the more northern side of the same, thinking to have deep water, for we had sounded a great way with our boat at our first going in, and found seven, six, and five fathoms." This is an important passage. On one hand, the only body of water in the area that runs to the north-west is the Verrazzano Narrows, but it only runs that way just before high tide. It runs to the southeast at ebb tide. It is not a river at all, hardly even a channel or strait, but all other rivers slant to the northeast/southwest. Since the current in the center of the narrows is so strong, it is necessary to stay to one side, and it seems they stayed to the northern, or Brooklyn side, if that's where they were. But where would there be eight and a half feet water? On September 10, Juet had written, *"we weighed and went over, and found it shoal all the middle of the river...."* The narrows is not shallow in the middle, only on the edge. There is something fishy about this story.

But what if he got his directions reversed and said northwest but meant northeast? Then the entire passage makes a great deal of sense. South of Manhattan, the only river that runs at an angle (actually to the northeast) and has a great mouth is the Arthur Kill, or Rivierent achter Kol.[539] This river or channel is very deep in its southwest end, but very shallow in the northeast end. And the Kill Van Kull between Bayonne and Staten Island is very shallow as well. Either before or after burying John Colman at the edge of its mouth, it would then be clear that they had gone in and measured the depths of the lower Arthur Kill and found 35, 30, and 25 feet as they headed north. It is still this deep today. Clearly, they turned around, satisfied that the rest of it that lay to the north would be equally deep, but were wrong. Unsure of who had just attacked them, they attempted to avoid sailing by Arrochar, which was so populated with Canarsie, whose language is close to Siwanoy, where scouts would have reported they had camped. Perhaps they went around the back way and found it shallow and difficult, not to mention narrow. In fact it was so shallow that at one point they sounded a depth of just over a single fathom! On the trip up, they found shallows in the middle of the river. That's not the narrows either.

"*So we came out that way, but we were deceived, for we had but eight feet and a half water; and so to three, five, three, and two fathoms and a half; and then three, four, five, six, seven, eight, nine and ten fathoms;*" Somewhere in the Kill Van Kull they found themselves in water that was hardly eight feet deep. Elsewhere, probably in the upper Arthur Kill, they found 13, 15, and 25 feet, greater or lesser depending on where they dropped the plumb line. There was no channel, and no margin for error. A single encounter with a sand bar with a large rock involved could have ruined their trip. Finally they proceeded back to where they had sounded a month earlier, the lower part of the Arthur Kill where the channel gradually deepens to a chasm of fifty or more feet while still narrow and rocky.

"*.. and by twelve o'clock we were clear of all the inlet.*" The Arthur Kill is more of an inlet than a "kill" or stream. According to Wesbster's Dictionary, one definition of an inlet is "a narrow strip of water between islands." This correctly describes the Arthur Kill. Raritan Bay is also a large inlet, but is more correctly called a bay.

The Verrazzano Narrows is too short to be called a true inlet and certainly not a "great river" separate from the Hudson River. However it does angle slightly to the northwest, and at least in Verrazzano's day featured a spot that was very shallow. In 1524, Verrazzano wrote, "*...deep at its mouth, flowed out into the sea; and with the help of the tide, which rises eight feet, any laden ship could have passed from the sea into the river estuary.*"[540] If a laden ship could not pass unless the tide rose eight more feet, that is quite a shallow channel. However, Juet writes of being "deceived." There is nothing deceptive about the Verrazzano Narrows. They had been there before and sounded the depths. He can't be describing that most obvious route as "the other way."

Michael Sullivan Smith launches the final leg of their river journey from Hastings on Hudson, steers them through New York Harbor and out to sea. Edward Hagaman Hall writes, "Hudson leaves the river and the bay and enters the Atlantic Ocean." Johnson: writes, "The great mouth of the great river." However, Juet makes it clear that he *also* exited another great river, and "came out *that* way." I believe that river was the Arthur Kill, but also that he was hiding something. Sure enough, as Douglas Hunter writes in *God's Mercies*, "On October 4, 1609, when the Half Moon returned to sea where New York City now sprawls, the crew was on the edge of revolt. According to Emmanuel van Meteren, the Dutch consul in London, who relied on Hudson for his account, the Dutch mate said they should overwinter in Newfoundland and search for the Northwest passage the next season. But Hudson was opposed: 'He was afraid of his mutinous crew, who had sometimes savagely threatened him, and he feared that during the cold season they would entirely consume their provisions, and would then be obliged to return. Many of the crew also were ill and sickly.' Hudson's suspicions were raised when, as they discussed their options, nobody in the crew suggested returning to Holland. If he agreed to the overwintering scheme, the Dutch crew, bent on full-time piracy, more than likely would wrest the ship from him and his handful of English companions— now down to two, as a native American arrow had cut down John Colman soon after their initial arrival at the mouth of the great river."[541]

Did they travel once again through the Arthur Kill, past what they had called "Colman's Point" where their friend lay buried, to place a garland and a marker on his hastily-constructed tomb? Dead men tell no tales.

After Hudson left the area, the natives of Staten Island met various fortunes at the hands of the Dutch, some of which was described by David De Vries. Under English rule, however, they were quick to vacate the island. In 1675, according to Alanson Skinner, Governor Lovelace "bought the island for the last time from the Indians, and the exchange was made on May 1, 1676."[542]

Skinner continues, "After this sale, most of the Staten Island Indians withdrew to the mainland, and encamped, according to local tradition, about South River, a branch of the Raritan." They always pitched their lodges on the other side of the river from the Raritans proper. "As the years passed, they with their neighbors, withdrew to the Kittatinny Mountains, after joining the Stockbridges in New York. Thence they removed to Green Bay, Wisconsin, where perhaps some survivors may still be found among the Oenida and Stockbridge."

He adds, "A few Indians lived on the Island for many years after the departure of the main body. The best known of these people were an old couple called Sam and Hannah; and their daughter Nance. They lived on the Seaman farm at Fresh Kill Road, and gained a precarious existence by basket-making." He also mentioned one, Story, living near Rossville in 1909, and another named Homer Harris.[543] But there must have been many more, "in the woodwork," and their descendants are still among us, some of whom may still remember stories of the day the "Great Floating Bird" first appeared.

JUET'S JOURNAL, MONDAY, OCTOBER 5 : *The fifth was fair weather, and the wind variable between the north and the east. We held on our course southeast by east. At noon I observed and found our height to be 39 degrees 30 minutes. Our compass varied six degrees to the west.*

*We continued our course toward England without seeing any land by
the way, all the rest of this month of October; and on the seventh day of
November, stilo novo, being Saturday, by the grace of God, we safely arrived
in the range of Dartmouth in Devonshire, in the year 1609.*

It is symbolically fitting that there was a "half moon" in the sky the night the
ship left New York's waters, the completion of the October moon's first quarter.
Juet's account is so casual as to be humorous. Apparently, they knew they were
headed for trouble no matter where they landed, but Dartmouth had them on their
no-fly list. "Hudson persuaded the crew to sail home. Or, at least, in its general
direction. Initially they agreed to make landfall in Ireland. For some reason, the
Half Moon steered instead from the Hudson River directly to Dartmouth, neither
seeing nor touching land along the way during a month of sailing."[544]

Landing in Dartmouth was infinitely preferable to a return to Amsterdam,
where Hudson would face the anger of "powerful, wealthy, and litigious merchants."[545] Dartmouth's mayor was Thomas Holland, who detained Hudson and
immediately sent a message to Sir Robert Cecil, Earl of Salisbury and Secretary of
State of the Realm. According to Hunter, Holland considered Hudson's "imminent
departure from Dartmouth a matter of national security."[546]

Hudson spoke with Holland, who later wrote, "it seems to me, by conferring
with him, that he has discovered some especial matters of greater consequence
which he would not impart."[547] As Hudson was heading back to Holland with the
Half Moon in January of 1610, he and the other Englishman "were commanded
by the government there not to leave England but to serve their own country."[548]
The Half Moon eventually did float into the port of Amsterdam, with Robert Juet
in charge,[549] but Hudson was never to set foot in Holland again. His ship's papers,
maps, Juet's log and Hudson's journal, were all carefully inspected and scrutinized
by powerful merchants and map makers in London before being returned eventually to Amsterdam. Hudson must have had mixed feelings about not having to
appear before the governing board of directors of the VOC, or Dutch East India
Company, the largest multi-national corporation in the world at that point,[550] and
explain why he did not try to find a passage to China through Northern Canada as
he had promised in writing, and for which he had been paid handsomely.

Instead, he accepted a prestigious promotion from the folks at the Muskovy
Company. He was hired to "pick up in the northwest where George Waymouth
had left off in 1602, using Waymouth's old ship, the *Discovery*."[551] It was a double
victory for Henry. He was not only bailed out of what might have become one of
the biggest international lawsuits in years, he got the "moon shot" opportunity to
sail in one of England's legendary ships and complete the tragically interrupted

explorations of one of England's bravest explorers. Hudson, now soon to be legendary himself, had "arrived."

He knew that he had to at least *attempt* to find a passage across the arctic in a sea-going vessel or there would be trouble upon his return. He also knew there was probably no safe passage and that the harder he tried, the more likely it was that he would follow in Waymouth's footsteps to the grave. It was, for him, a golden death certificate. Having nowhere else to turn, he signed it.

The Escape of the Century

Hudson did indeed escape capture by the Dutch authorities by a whisker, but his ship the Discovery, got stuck near the Arctic circle in the endless sea of ice now known as Hudson's Bay, Canada. The ship was running low on food, and the men were becoming angry, but Hudson was determined to find a passage west. Hudson, upon realizing he had gotten them lost, was deeply apologetic, and tried to persuade the men that he knew how to get them out of dangerous waters and back to a certain island filled with the sounds of waterfowl they had seen earlier. Juet was not convinced and argued openly with Hudson on more than one occasion, threatening harm to him and some of the others.

Hudson removed Juet from duty because of insubordination, but in fact, Juet's internal stew was starting to boil over. Juet demanded Hudson call a meeting to denounce the rumors that were spreading about the reasons for Juet's demotion. The men responded with tale after tale, some under oath, some to Juet's face, that the demented scribe had been plotting armed mutiny all along, concealing loaded weapons in hiding places around the ship. Hudson, saying he understood their unhappiness, forgave them, and Juet as well, and all went back to their bunks to have a good night's sleep. But some months later, after several more attempts to head further west (or, as Ian Chadwick suspects, more time to check out Canada's natural resources) Hudson was bound in ropes by those he had forgiven and then was lowered to the small open boat tethered below to face a terrible death by freezing, starvation, exposure, and exhaustion simultaneously. Also bound and placed in the boat were his son John, and several others. The carpenter, a remarkably courageous man, shouted that he'd rather die with Hudson than stay on ship with such scoundrels, then leaped down to the shallop and untied his faithful captain and the others, but found himself in the same boat, quite literally as themselves.[552]

Bacon writes, "At this Henry called out, 'Juet has done this! He will overthrow ye all!'"

"'No!' called the scribe, (we have his word for it that he spoke not softly). 'It is that villain Greene!'"[553] Nothing could have been further from the truth, and no greater disrespect paid by this Judas to his lifelong discipleship with Hudson than this.

Someone threw the carpenter down his toolbox in scorn, then Juet hoisted all sails and made off in the opposite direction at full speed, but the old man began to self-destruct a few days later. Ironically, he died of sickness and hunger just as they came within sight of the British Isles (Ireland), so we must take the words of his shipmates under oath in place of his own. Although the year of Henry's birth is unknown, everywhere you will see the date of his death listed as June 21, 1611.

After all, how could he have survived the winter in such a climate? Remember the carpenter? Without his toolbox he was just another doomed passenger on a boat to nowhere, but with a hammer and saw in his hands, he might have become a force to reckon with. He might have helped them find an island with trees growing on it, and built an encampment. We can only imagine.

Or perhaps their captors helped them survive the winter. We don't know. But like the immortal twins, legends about Hudson and Juet don't die easily. According to the Ontario Provincial Historical Society of Canada, there is a rock that was found west of Hudson's Bay, in West Main Cree territory, and upon this rock is the inscription, "HH 1612, Captive."

Who else could have carved that stone and left it there in Canada's vast interior? Another intrepid explorer? A hoaxter? Or the indomitable Henry Hudson himself?

Who knows who would have "captured" him and for what reason—possibly a roving band of hunters? I like to imagine that there is truth to the numerous local legends still passing from lodge to lodge among the East Main Cree, that Hudson was rescued by the local Mistassini Cree population.

The following three accounts are from Ian Chadwick's website; www.ianchadwick.com/hudson:

Hello from Canada. I was recently in Inukjuak on the eastern shore of Hudson Bay, on vacation. On one of the Hopewell Islands (Harrison Island) I was told that there were stone houses of Dorset culture people there (they were early Inuit people). These same people also told me that there were graves of some of the Hudson crew. This might be a myth. I don t know, but the stone houses of the Dorset people are there. For me, I always liked the story of Capt James. It is sad that he is so neglected today. I have visited James Bay in the past. I hope that you find this interesting. — from Robert Prontack, 2004

There is a local legend here, I live in James Bay on the Quebec side, in a little Cree community called Wemindji. The story goes that it is quite possible that Henry Hudson is buried near here. There is a trapline nearby that is call "Wamstuksheesh" which means little white man in Cree. Apparently it was named after him because it is believed that he had lived peacefully among the Cree People until he was an old man. If this is true I would assume that he would have taken a Cree woman as his wife and they most likely had some offspring. Our history has been passed down from generation to generation orally, and I'm sure some history has been forgotten. Had it just been written!! I found that story so interesting that my main goal when I attended post-secondary school in Montreal was I was going to be an archaeologist and solve this mystery (I'm an early childhood education professional). But an archaeologist (can't recall his name) was here maybe about eight years ago or so and a few friends of mine and myself asked him if he believed that Henry Hudson was buried here.... he told us that the soil around this area was very acidic and that remains usually are non-existent when buried for a long time. The only evidence would be if he wore buttons, rings, etc....and even if they found such things it would be hard to prove it was Henry Hudson! So that's my little story on our local legend of Henry Hudson. . . . — from Lee Ann Gilpin, 2004

I used to live in the James Bay area, where Hudson, was reportedly last seen, and actually, there's this place near a reserve called Wemindji, where some of the locals told my father that there was a certain mound of large rocks assembled just 8 km south of Wemindji. The mound, apparently, was not made by any of the locals. What I find somewhat odd is that no team of archeologists has bothered looking in this area for any evidence. I never been there but my father has, since he wasn't any pro on archeology, he could not verify anything. We even had a non-fiction writer, Lawrence Millman (*Evening among Headhunters*) come to the place, and other suspected areas where Hudson could've been. Many of the locals also told my father and the writer, that "many" years, that their ancestors had seen several men, one in particular, was called "red beard." They could've been referring to the carpenter who was with Hudson. They were spotted at a cove, next to a small rocky island. I've been there. I couldn't find anything. There was another island just 7 km south of Wemindji, which was called "monkey island." The reason being, that the locals spotted two "ape men" on a boat going to that island. I know for a fact, back then, the Crees, who inhabited the area, were known for never having facial [hair] which strongly concludes, based off probability that those so-called "ape-men" were bearded Europeans, possibly Hudson's crew but so far, no one in the local area, has been able to verify if that is true." — from Tommy McGee, 2004.

The Henry Hudson Stone ended up in the Village of Chalk River, in Tenna-Brise Park, where it can be viewed today. It would be fitting if the Cree fulfilled his wish of two years before and took him in as one of their own, and that he lived the rest of his life fishing with the tribe, the blood of his descendants being mixed in with that of the Cree, so that his blood now runs in the veins of a hundred Cree Indian hockey players, the heroes of modern Canada, and a new race of people.

Ever since Henry Hudson brought white European culture to Manhattan in 1609, it has been a place of great racial and cultural interchange, largely in peace and harmony. In 1992, inspired by the visions of the Hopi prophecy of the "House of Mica by the Great Water," and by visionaries and wisdom keepers from many Native American nations, the United Nations held a special assembly on Manhattan Island called "The Cry of the Earth." William Commanda brought the Seven Fires Wampum belt to the United Nations and, holding it up, spoke before the special assembly. He spoke of seven prayers, seven dimensions, seven eras of history. He warned against what we now refer to as global warming and the pollution of our water and our air. These were his closing words:

"This is the history of the teachings from the first nation people and their prophecies. This as we all know today is the reality of the outcome that we experience that we cannot deny or refuse to believe. If we do not take action, according to these sacred messages and prophecies, there will be continuous harm that will come not only to man and creation but to our Mother Earth as well." Thus concluded William Commanda's historic talk in Manhattan at the United Nations on the Seven Fires.

And as for Henry Hudson, it is intriguing to think of him hunting and fishing, living the life of a traditional Cree for the remainder of his days, perhaps with a Cree wife, happy to be away from the likes of Robert Juet.[554] His eight peaceful days among the Mohicans may have turned out to be rather important. They spoke an N-dialect Algonquian language surprisingly similar to the East Main Cree, so that his contact with the Mohicans in 1609 would have been good preparation for his early retirement. Unlike Juet, he had listened well and was rewarded. To him I say, "Mau-mu en-do-dem-ik!" a Cree expression which means, "Let us all come together in peace, all my relations!"

Acknowledgements

First I would like to thank my Dutch collaborators, and those associated with the Onrust Project; Dirk Tang and his wife for assistance with Dutch terms and for encouragement; Gerald de Weerdt for his remarkable expertise in building ancient Dutch ships and knowledge of nautical terms; Courtney Anderson for generously sharing his remarkable nautical knowledge; Hendrick "Henk" DeBoer for his knowledge of sail-making, and Will Van Dorp for his knowledge of depth charts; Christina Sun; Eric Baard, and Ravensong as well.

Also I wish to express my appreciation for those closer to home; for historian and cartographer Michael Sullivan Smith's assistance in understanding Juet's journal and for his map of 2008. In sharing his approach to the September 14 entry, he opened my eyes to the possibilities before us, that someone may someday actually know what was going on in Juet's mind in 1609. Again I thank Richard Frisbee, a true champion of the Hudson's history who has gone out of his way to make this book possible; Shoshana Rothaizer for ongoing assistance with *Native New Yorkers,* and paving the way for this "prequel"; Vernon Benjamin on Edward Hagaman Hall's nautically-astute analysis of Juet's journal of 1609, and for providing material from his long-awaited work-in-progress, entitled *The Hudson River Valley: From Wilderness to Woodstock,* which is forthcoming from Overlook Press.

I would also like to thank those in Albany and New York City; Charles Goering, director of the New Netherlands Project, for navigating me in a good direction and answering many questions. I thank him especially for guiding me towards Donald Johnson's book *Charting the Sea of Darkness*; Donna Matyas at the Staten Island Museum for creative brainstorming; Ed Johnson for a great stream of reliable information about Staten Island; Ira Chadwick, who was generous enough to create a website celebrating and analyzing Hudson's voyages, from which I have quoted at times; Carl Schuster, whom I met on a stairway in mid-town Manhattan, a meeting which inspired me to rewrite some of my book; Marian Lupulescu, the curator of geology at the New York State Museum, for educating me on the difference between red, yellow, black, green, and copper-colored copper, not to mention red ochre. His contribution has been invaluable in understanding the Juet diary. I would also like to thank Dan Atchinson and Trao Ietaka, Beth Herr, and John Gambino of the Westchester Parks, Pete Seeger for his activism and positive involvement with Native American people, Stephen Mercier for his sunny outlook; I am indebted to the many Native Americans who helped with this project, too many to mention. I thank James Flowers, a native botanist (Meherrin/Nottaway) for his timely expertise on the flora of the New York City area, and plant identification; former Chief Mark Peters and those close to him for access to Munsee tribal knowledge; Raymundo Rodriguez, Nissequogue marine biologist, for his help in understanding the behavior of manta rays and "mulletfish"; I would like to thank Mike D'Amico and Maureen Kelley/Etaoqua for many insights and corrections along the way and support for the Center for Algonquin Culture; Roberto Borrero for providing a forum for a full presentation in the limelight of modern-day New York City; Brian Wilkes for Cherokee braininess, Monique Renaud for patience; Robin Hill Chandler for networking skills; Joanne Menchini for tireless service to the Native American community; Robin Kimmerer for writings that all should study carefully; Lynn Pritchard for drum songs and copies of the old maps; David Pritchard for brainstorms on the western horizon; David Bunn Martine for art and inspiration; William Commanda for constant guidance from the teachings of the Seven Fires; Ramola Trebilcock for taking care of us all; Eddie Benton Banaise for preserving the indigenous knowledge of the eons; Joe Bruchac for cheering on the light during the darkest part of the year; Barbara Three Crow for wisdom and perspective; Peggy Turco /Ani Yeshe Palmo/SheWhoGathersSumac, for permission to use her classic text on the Hudson Valley, *Walks and Rambles;* and the Putnam County Historical Society.

I would like to thank fellow scholars, including the historians at Ocean County, New Jersey, (and my helper D.D.), student research assistant Stephanie Lyons for helping out with background research for this project, specifically on oysters in New York City. On matters Paleolithic, I would like to thank Peggy Jodri of the Smithsonian for her time and an informative and candid interview. I would also like to thank Ron Kessler for his unique understanding of Pleistocene mammoths and their care and feeding. I would like to thank Dennis Stanford for ideas and insights; William Meyers and Leslie Kriesel at Columbia University Press for long-shot optimism in the face of opposition; Melvin Johnson for his straightforward answers where angels fear to tread; Larry Mumia for enthusiasm for this book and what I do for a living; and Rick Jarow and Banta for spiritual guidance through the academic maze. You were all right on target. This book is dedicated to the memory of Patrick L. Pritchard and Mike D'Amico, Madeleine L'Engle and John "Talking Leaves" Powell, each of whom left an indelible signature upon the soul of this book. May they enjoy the taste of strawberries along the pathways of the spirit world and not forget their destination.

A Short List of Estuarine Fish, Animal and Plant Species Available to the "River Indians" in 1609.

There are 213 species of fish currently in the Hudson River. Here are some of those that lived in the Hudson in 1609.

Salt Water Fish/Seafood

Eastern Oysters; *Crassostrea virginica* (various species)

Common or Forbes' sea star; *Asterias Forbesi*

Atlantic Shad; *Alosa sapidissima*

Brook Trout; *Salvelinus fontinalis*

Blue Craw Crab; *Callinectes sapidus*

Horseshoe Crab; *Limulus polyphemus* (natives used in chowders)

Black Bullhead Catfish; *Ictalurus melas*, or *Ameiurus melas*

Yellow Bullhead Catfish; *Ameiurus natalis*

Northeast Blue Channel Catfish; *Ictalurus punctatus*

Bluegill; *Lepomis macrochirus* (live in inlets and backwaters
    and bays, not in the main channel)

Black Crappie; *Pomoxis nigromaculatus* (aka sunfish,
    sun perch sunnies, "breams" "brims")

White Crappie; *Pomoxis annularis* (aka white perch)

River Herring; *Alosa pseudoharengus*

Blueback Herring; *Alosa aestivalis* ("Alewifes")

Common Mummichog; *fundulus heteroclitus* (aka Mollies)

Striped Mummichog; *fundulus majalis* (rainbow killifish)

Diamondback terrapin; *Malaclemys terrapin* (probably thrived
    in Tappan Zee)

Tom Cod; *Microgadus tomcod* (was common in Hudson,
    but no longer; aka Frost Fish)

Lake Sturgeon; *Acipenser fulvescens*

Atlantic Sturgeon; *Acipenser oxyrhynchus*

Shortnose Sturgeon; *Acipenser brevirostrum*

American Eel ; *Anguilla rostrata* (more green, red around gills)

Atlantic Salmon; *salmo salar* (wild ones are endangered, now
    farmed)

Freshwater Drum (Sheepshead); *Aplodinotus grunniens*
(aka "Porgies")

Sheepshead; *Archosargus probatocephalus*

Striper (Striped bass); *Morone saxatilis* (aka Rockfish)

Bluefish; *Pomatomus saltatrix* (as far inland as the Tappan Zee
according to DEC, fresh is 3 feet deep, but ocean water goes
50 feet below; they live there.)

Manatee; *Trichechus manatus* (sirens at the mouth of the river)

Manta ray; *Manta birostris*

Mullets; *Mugilidae*

Striped Mullet; *Mugil cephalus*

White Mullet; *Mugil curema*

Lobster; *Homarus americanus*

Bluefish; *Temnodon saltator*

Porgy/Porgy; *Pogrus argyropos*

Blackfish; *Tautoga americana*

Shad; *Alosa prstabilis*

Herring; *Engrau-lus- meletta*

Yellow flounder; *Pleuronectes ferruginea*

Winter flounder; *Pleuronectues americanus*

Summer flounder; (fluke) *Paralichthys dentatus*

Butterfish; *Gunnellus mucronatus*

Monkfish; *Iophius americanus*

Mackerel; *Scomber vernalis*

Spanish Makerel; *Scomber co lias*

Suckerfish/chub; *Catostomis communis*

More Seafood: Rare Visitors to the Hudson Valley

These species have appeared in the Hudson River at times, for various reasons.
Later generations of Native Americans have fished for them and dined well.

Sea trout (brown) *Salmo trutta lacustris* (mostly European,
but seen today in Hudson River)

rainbow trout; *Oncorhynchus mykiss* (mostly Pacific Coast US,
but seen today in Hudson River)

Steelhead (or sea-run rainbow trout) *Oncorhynchus myleiss*
(mostly found in California)

Brown Bullhead Catfish; *Ameriurus nebulosus* (native to Florida)
Central Blue Channel Catfish *Ictalurus furcatus* (Native to Mississippi River)
Mosquitofish; *Gambusia affinis* (native to Caribbean)
North American Guppy; *Poecilia reticulata* (Caribbean)
Rock shrimp; *Atyopsis* various species (see some at Breakneck Train Stop, not originally from New York)
Skate; *Dipturus laevis* (Barndoor Skate)

Fresh Water Fish/Animals

White Perch; *Morone americana* (not a true perch)
Green Frog; *Rana clamitans*
Crayfish; *Crustacean decapoda*
Spotted Turtle; *Clemmys guttata*
Wood Turtle; *Clemmys insculpta*
Snapping Turtle; *Chelydra serpentina serpentine*
Painted Turtle; *Chrysemys picta* (edible?)
Red-eared Slider *Trachemys elegans*
Freshwater Salamander, Tiger Salamander; *Ambystoma tigrinum*
Muhlenberg Mud Turtle; (edible?) *Geoclemys hamiltonii*
Newt (Red Spotted); *Notophthalmus viridescens*
Beaver; *Castor canadensis*
Tadpoles (various species)

Estuary-Dwelling Edible Plants (salty)

Cattail; *Typha latifolia*
Phragmites; *Phragmites australis* (upper edge of estuaries)
Sea Lavender; *Limonium vlugare*
Ulva Sea Lettuce; *Ulva lactuca*
Turtle Grass; *Thalassia testudium*
Dwarf Pitch Pines (boil baby cones); *Pinus rigida*
Starwort; *Stellaria Holostea*
Spirolina; *Spirulina*

Estuary-Dwelling Plants, Rare Visitors

Sea Cucumber; *Holothuroidea*

Freshwater Edible Plants

Spirogyra; *Spirogyra*

Lily Bulbs; *lilium* (bulbs on rhizomes)

Pond Lily; *Nuphar lutea*

Freshwater Cattail; *Typha latifolia*

Willow; *Salix* (tree bark), see NASS

Duckweed; *Lemnaoideae*

Water sprite (or Indian fern, water fern); *Ceratopteris thalictroides*

Arrowroot; *Maranta arundinacea*

Plantain; *Musa x paradisiaca*

Sassafrass; *Sassafrass albidum*

Estuaries are also home to birds such as herons, cormorants, coots, and skeets.

Glossary of Algonquin Estuarine/Geographic Terms

The pre-contact Algonquins were great anglers, and knew the characteristics of each feature of the estuary's landscape intimately, and had a special name for it. Many of the descendants of the Algonquin civilization today are great fishing people as well, and some still remember and understand these terms. Most of the following are ancient central Algonkian terms or roots, and are found everywhere throughout the Atlantic region. I have arranged them here by alphabetical order for the convenience of the English reader. They convey a sense of how intimately coastal Algonquin people knew and understood these waterways.

abachtuck ocean

akee territory or land of

ashokan a hard, forceful rapids, or extended waterfall

asiskung muddy place in Unami

cush a steep incline

cushnock a steep, lengthy rapids

cutt salt water, or sea water

-hakee, or -akee territory or land, whereas **-haking** or **-hoking** means dwellingplace

-hanna a river

heague or **hikan** a large body of salty or brackish water; Both the Hudson and the Connecticut Rivers are "heague" or "hikan." Hituck may mean a river that is both salty and tidal.

-ing or **ink** endings mean place, as do the endings **-ett** and **-ic** further north

keck, usually an ending

keek-hee-tuck a river (part tidal and salty) in Unami. **Heek** can mean "big." (Talking Leaves)

kin-ne-ke-la-bi "as far as the eye can see," often used to refer to the stretch of river between one turn and another

kitchewan great stream

kock, -quague, or **-cook** endings indicate a place near the water

kweeneepayoo the water is deep.

laach (or **rech** in Renneiu dialects) sandy

lakawana sandy creek or river in Unami

mas-peth "bad water"

mattawan shallow or literally humble stream, in contrast to kitchewan
   which means great powerful stream

maug fishing place

mawen to gather, as when two rivers meet

m'bee-sis lake or pond in Unami

meech-han-nek Great River in Unami

mell- or **meli** (**meri** in Renneiu) hundreds of-

metch or **mitch** food, a meal

metta-koo-honts a trout stream with pine bows offering shade

mettawan means freshwater trout stream; In New York, waan was translated
   into the Dutch word "kill." In English areas, stream.

mon-, man-, mono-, manna-, mannas-, min-, minis-, all indicate an island.

muscouten a river with a wetlands area on the shore, usually estuarine

muskeg an estuarial wetlands, related to the above. It is generally an
   intertidal biome.

na-keeh downriver in Unami

namos or naymetch fish; Namoskeg Falls in Manchester, NH became
   shortened to Amoskeg, retaining its message, "lots of fish." **Na-maes** in
   Munsee.

neck possibly a point of land like **nyack** (**narrag** or **narriok** in Renneiu). In
   all cases I know of, the point of land extends into salty or brackish waters.
   It is not to be confused with the English word neck which can refer to
   a cape, but more often an isthmus or natural causeway, connecting two
   areas of land.

neepee can refer to a river, and neep-ni-schen means "two rivers" meeting.

niskepek dirty water in Unami.

pak (or **pax** with a guttural x) flats or flat; it can be used to refer to intertidal
   mud flats.

paal-peh-oo it overflows (Munsee)

paw or **pow** a waterfall

pawtuckett a waterfall that empties into a tidal estuary. Fall River is a
   translation; Valkill (Poughkeepsie) is a Dutch translation of Pawtuckett,
   but is not as specific.

peck usually a small body of water such as a slip or inlet, however **Copeck** is
   a pond, and **Mahopac** may mean "Bear Lake."

pee water, but in a place name means lake or pond

peek "waters," or a bay

pocantico pow is waterfall, cantico is dance, is said to refer to a waterfall in a "hollow" or a canyon, literally "between two hills." The **ti-co** ending probably also means "council fire place."

podunk a freshwater marsh, or muddy place; **po**=field or meadow, dunk=where your foot sinks down

Pomopeehleoo stream in Munsee

powhattan a waterfall that is particularly rocky and therefore large

-qua as a suffix means shallow water, not usually drinking water.

quan short for samquan and implies drinking water

ran river (Renneiu); **tan**, **han**, and **wan** are variants

rch or **raach** sandy (Renneiu)

sac or **saco** a long strip of land

nyack, (or **narrag-** in Renneiu) a point of land

seepu means river.

seepus small river; also **shee-po-shish** or **w-shee-poo-shus** in Munsee

schauwunuppeque a shore of a lake in Unami

shin or **sinn** usually rocky or full of rocks

shippa a long straight stretch or "reach" of shoreline along a river or bay

sook-pay-hel-laak big waterfall in a river in Unami. **Sookpay** means "to fall down," **hellak** might mean "like rain," but further research is needed.

Shewan-haking at the [land of the] salty place in Unami

Sunckheague top or head of the — arm-of-sea

tan a variant on wan and ran

ti (usually in the middle of a word) often means a place of a council fire, ie. a seat of a sachemdom (usually near water)

tan-ghan-ayoo is a little creek in Unami.

tow-pat refers to a boiling spring or swirling water.

tshy-ta edge of the water in Munsee

tuck is a tidal river, one that "flows both ways," an estuary. A **tuck** is usually primary, a **ran** or **wan** is usually a tributary and can be a secondary estuary for part of its length. Algonquins loved to live on them, calling the lesser ones *wanis*, or a small stream.

wan (or **raan** in Renneiu dialects, **tan** in others) is a freshwater stream, usually large

wanis a small stream, possibly ending in a tertiary estuary

whil- head

winni- in some areas means muddy water

The Seven Fires

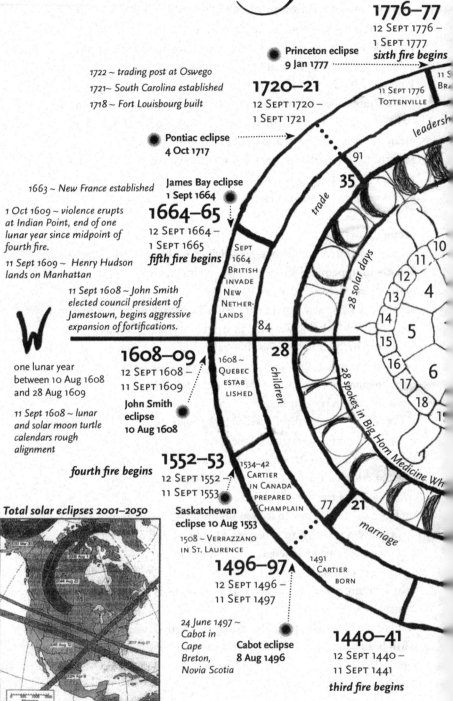

1776–77
12 SEPT 1776 –
1 SEPT 1777
sixth fire begins

Princeton eclipse
9 Jan 1777

1722 ~ trading post at Oswego
1721 ~ South Carolina established
1718 ~ Fort Louisbourg built

1720–21
12 SEPT 1720 –
1 SEPT 1721

11 SEPT 1776
TOTTENVILLE

11 S
BR

leadersh

Pontiac eclipse
4 Oct 1717

91

trade

35

1663 ~ New France established

James Bay eclipse
1 Sept 1664

1664–65
12 SEPT 1664 –
1 SEPT 1665
fifth fire begins

1 Oct 1609 ~ violence erupts
at Indian Point, end of one
lunar year since midpoint of
fourth fire.

11 Sept 1609 ~ Henry Hudson
lands on Manhattan

SEPT
1664
BRITISH
INVADE
NEW
NETHER-
LANDS

28 solar days

10

11

12

13

14

15

16

17

18

4

5

6

1

11 Sept 1608 ~ John Smith
elected council president of
Jamestown, begins aggressive
expansion of fortifications.

W

84

one lunar year
between 10 Aug 1608
and 28 Aug 1609

1608–09
12 SEPT 1608 –
11 SEPT 1609

**John Smith
eclipse
10 Aug 1608**

1608 ~
QUEBEC
ESTAB
LISHED

28

children

28 spokes in Big Horn Medicine Wh

11 Sept 1608 ~ lunar
and solar moon turtle
calendars rough
alignment

fourth fire begins

1552–53
12 SEPT 1552 –
11 SEPT 1553

**Saskatchewan
eclipse 10 Aug 1553**

1508 ~ VERRAZZANO
IN ST. LAURENCE

1534–42
CARTIER
IN CANADA
PREPARED
CHAMPLAIN

77

21

marriage

Total solar eclipses 2001–2050

1496–97
12 SEPT 1496 –
11 SEPT 1497

24 June 1497 ~
Cabot in
Cape
Breton,
Novia Scotia

**Cabot eclipse
8 Aug 1496**

1491
CARTIER
BORN

1440–41
12 SEPT 1440 –
11 SEPT 1441
third fire begins

Medicine Wheel

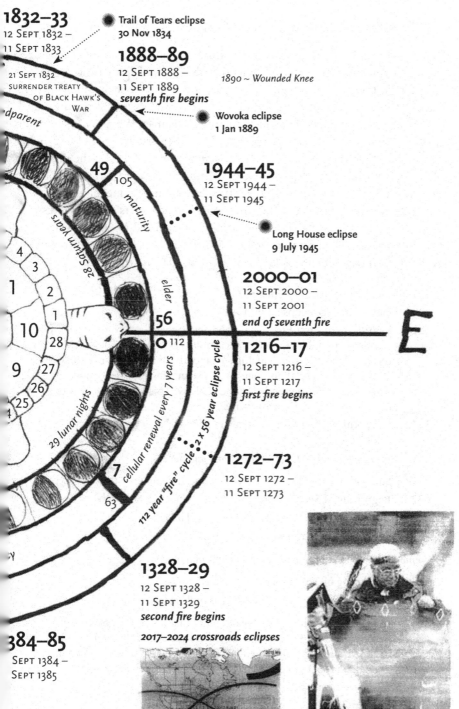

1832–33
12 SEPT 1832 –
11 SEPT 1833

21 SEPT 1832
SURRENDER TREATY
OF BLACK HAWK'S
WAR

...dparent

Trail of Tears eclipse
30 Nov 1834

1888–89
12 SEPT 1888 –
11 SEPT 1889
seventh fire begins

1890 ~ Wounded Knee

Wovoka eclipse
1 Jan 1889

1944–45
12 SEPT 1944 –
11 SEPT 1945

Long House eclipse
9 July 1945

2000–01
12 SEPT 2000 –
11 SEPT 2001
end of seventh fire

1216–17
12 SEPT 1216 –
11 SEPT 1217
first fire begins

1272–73
12 SEPT 1272 –
11 SEPT 1273

1328–29
12 SEPT 1328 –
11 SEPT 1329
second fire begins

2017–2024 crossroads eclipses

...384–85
SEPT 1384 –
SEPT 1385

49   105   maturity

56   elder

O 112

cellular renewal every 7 years

2 x 56 year eclipse cycle

112 year "fire" cycle

28 Saturn years

29 lunar nights

7

63

4   3
1   2
1
10   28
9   27
26
25

E

Timeline of the Seven Fires: Moon Turtles, Eclipses and Signs

There is no word for time in Algonquin culture, and no birthdays were recognized in traditional times. However it seems that those who followed the prophecies kept careful track of the days, months and years. There are many numbers here, but the turtle calendar is not a clock nor a mechanical system. It requires much moon-gazing and periodic adjustment to keep it on target. While some Algonquin people say the year begins in Spring, and others when the rivers first freeze in late fall, it seems that this particular calendar system may have begun the new moon of September 12, 1216, showing possible Taino influence, or perhaps a common influence not of this realm. Although the new moon at winter solstice of 1215 might seem to be a more logical starting point, its "new years" do not correspond nearly as well with eclipses and historical events related to Native Americans. So while the actual starting date of the prophecies remains secret, we will use Hudson's birthday, September 12, as the reference date for this book.

1205   Cahokia Eclipse, September 14

1209   East Main Cree eclipse, July 13

1216   **Beginning of First Fire**, new moon September 12, according to author's reconstruction. Lunar and solar calendars are set into motion, using "moon turtles" (*see chart*) as calculators. 13-month lunar calendar is approximately 18.655 days longer than solar, so first solar year ends September 11, 1217; while first lunar year ends October 1, 1217. This is the First Year of signs and omens (*keegaynolaywoagun*).

1272   **Midpoint of First Fire**, September. 56th year of Seven Fires Cycle completed.

September 1272–September 1273: Year of signs and omens.

1314   Sun and moon calendars end closely together, about 2 days apart.

1328   **Beginning of Second Fire**; 112 years completed, September.

September 1328–September 1329: Year of signs and omens.

1384   **Midpoint of Second Fire**, September

September 1384–September 1385: Year of signs and omens.

1440   **Beginning of Third Fire**, September

September 1440–September 1441: Year of signs and omens.

1451   Cornplanter's Eclipse (Cornplanter told that his predecessor Chief Sagonyuthna made peace among the Iroquois after the eclipse of January 28, 1451. Joseph White Norwood (p. 77) suggests this was also when Tamanend II of the Lenape [Unami] became grand peace chief.)

1491   Jacques Cartier born.

1492   Columbus' first voyage.

1496   John Cabot's eclipse (Atlanta, Ga.) August 8

1496   Midpoint of Third Fire, September 11

September 1496 to September 1497: Year of signs and omens

1497   John Cabot arrives at Cape Breton, Nova Scotia, June 24, 1497 (10 moons, 25 scute after eclipse). August 10 (one solar year after eclipse) Cabot reports to Henry VII about New World.

Third voyage of Columbus.

1534-1542   Cartier in Canada, prepares Samuel de Champlain.

1543   Copernicus publishes work, begins scientific revolution in Europe.

1552   Beginning of Fourth Fire, September.

September 1552–September 1553: Year of signs and omens.

1553   Saskatchewan eclipse, July 10

1569   Henry Hudson born, September 12

1608   John Smith's eclipse, Sargasso Sea, August 10

Close alignment of sun and moon calendars, September 8–11.

Completion of 392nd year, September 11.

First half of Seven Fires cycle complete.

1608   John Smith elected Council President of Jamestown, begins expanding English fort, September 10.

Samuel de Champlain in Quebec

September 12, 1608–September 11, 1609: Year of signs and omens; first solar year of second half of Seven Fires cycle.

1609   Hudson lands at Manhattan, September 11.

Hudson celebrates 40th birthday near location of today's Times Square, September 12.

Half Moon attacks protesters at Indian Point, October 1.

Hudson's farewell to Manhattan, October 3.

1663   Final Esopus Wars

1664   Beginning of Fifth Fire, September

September 1664–September 1665: Year of signs and omens.

James Bay Eclipse, September 1

British invade New Netherlands, negate all Native American treaties, New Amsterdam becomes New York, September.

1717   Pontiac's eclipse, October 4

1720   Midpoint of Fifth Fire, September.

Pontiac born in Long House at Fort Detroit

September 1720–September 1721: Year of signs and omens.

1769   Pontiac killed in Cahokia, by a Peoria/Kaskaskian along the Maumee River, April 2

Circa 1770   Tecumseh born.

1776   Thomas Paine's *Common Sense* published, January 9

Declaration of Independence, July 3- 4

Adams, Franklin, refute Howe's terms of surrender at Tottenville, (near John Colman's/Rarian's burial site) commit to Revolution on **last day of Fifth Fire**, September 11.

Beginning of Sixth Fire, September 12

George Washington crosses the Kitchi Sipi (Delaware River) at Sunqheague (Falls of the Delaware) December 25.

September 1776-September 1777: Solar year of signs and omens.

1777   Battle of Princeton, January 3·

Princeton eclipse, January 9

First year of Sixth Fire solar year of signs and omens completed September 11.

Battle of Saratoga, first major victory for US, one lunar year + one week after the beginning of the Sixth Fire.

US Articles of Confederation adopted, November 15, with input from Charles Thompson, honorary Delaware.

1778   Battle of Brandywine, many "Brandywine" Unami Delaware are killed or displaced, American flag flown in battle for the first time, Washington defeated on Sept.11, 1778, must move nation's capital from Philadelphia (Shackamaxon) to Lancaster (Okehocking).

Chief George White Eyes of Delaware assassinated, November.

1832   Midpoint of Sixth Fire, September

September 1832-September 1833: Solar year of signs and omens.

Peace/surrender treaty of Sac and Fox (relatives of Mohican) to end Black Hawk's Wars was signed September 21, nine days after midpoint of Sixth Fire.

1834   "Trail of Tears" Eclipse (Chattanooga/Memphis) November 30

Running River Treaty near Chattanooga, Nov. 27–30

1835   One lunar year after eclipse, (one day early) NY Stock Exchange burns, "The Great Fire." December 16.

One lunar year (plus 12 days) after eclipse, Trail of Tears Treaty signed at New Echota, December 29, 1835.

1888   Beginning of Seventh Fire, September 12

September 1888-September 1889: Solar year of signs and omens.

1889   Wovoka's Eclipse, Pyramid Lake, Nevada, January 1

1890   Wounded Knee massacre of the Mineconjou, one solar year after eclipse, December 29

1906   Mahatma Gandhi coins term "Satyagraha" to refer to Civil Disobedience techniques Thoreau learned from Penobscots, September 11.

1944   Midpoint of Seventh Fire, September.

September 12, 1944–September 11, 1945: Year of signs and omens.

1945   Last Long House "to prevent end of the world," ceremony, spring

Hitler dies April 30.

Long House Eclipse, July 9

Hiroshima destroyed, August 6.

Japanese prison camps on Borneo liberated, September 11, last day of solar year of signs and omens after midpoint.

1991   Fifth Sun begins for Maya, July 11 "UFO" Eclipse over Mexico City

1998   Al Gore unveils White House Global Warming Initiative, August 10.

1999   Solar and lunar calendars coincide September 11/September 12, within a day of each other, for first time since 1315. **783rd year completed**.

2000   End of Seventh fire. End of 784th year of Seven Fires Prophecy cycle, September 11-12. (New Moon) **Rough alignment of sun and moon calendars.**

September 2000–September 2001: Year of signs and omens.

Lunz memo on how to dismiss global warming in campaign. "*A Report of The Project for the New American Century, dated September 2000.*"

Disputed US presidential election, November 8

2001   World Trade Center falls, marking end of the first solar year of signs and omens after the Seven Fires cycle, September 11, 2001. Sixteen years until eclipse of 2017; 23 until eclipse of 2024. "Will we light the eighth fire?"

Appendix IV

The Best Kept Secret

Although the reader may not believe it possible for anyone to foretell the future, nonetheless, prophecies play a large part in human history, especially Native American history. Native American prophecies tend to be interactive rather than fatalistic, an attempt to guide the decisions of the people along more productive lines. The Seven Fires prophecies were handed down from generation to generation in secrecy by the Medicine Chiefs of the Midewiwin Societies and by the leaders of other related lineages. For this reason, there was almost nothing published about them until recently.

The Munsee letter to Zachary Taylor, which states that the Munsees knew when Hudson was coming, was written in 1849 and sent to the White House, but not published until 2002 when I included it in my book *Native New Yorkers*. Joseph White Norwood referred indirectly to the Seven Fires prophecies in his book *The Tammany Legend,* published in 1938. In the late 1960s, knowledge of these prophecies started to spread by word of mouth. Key words were "rainbow race," "earth changes," and "purification." When I recently asked a Canadian audience of adult aged Metis or mixed-blood Native Americans if they had heard about the Seven Fires prophecies while growing up, every person without exception decisively raised his or her hand. This surprised even me, since so little has been written about them.

William Commanda, already First Nations Chief of Canada, received the Seven Fires wampum belt in the 1960s and began to talk openly about the prophecies, but the mass media was not very interested. He taught that the reckless cutting of trees was going to lead to a global disaster of monumental proportions. People scoffed. In 1973, an up-and-coming Francophone journalist, Michel Merleau, now remembered for his groundbreaking pieces in *Le Droit,* interviewed William Commanda for a local publication in Quebec. It was one of the first publications of any kind to report on the Seven Fires prophecies wampum belt or to mention what we now know of as "global warming." It is surprisingly similar in language to scientist James Lovelock's book *Revenge of Gaia,* which was considered shocking in 2006, thirty-three years later. Here is an excerpt from Merleau's article:

> Chief Commanda is the oldest member of the lodge of the wampum belt. This belt has been a legacy from generation to generation, and Chief Commanda has learned to listen to the wampum belt, which is the medium between him and his ancestors.
>
> "While we're in the process of doing those ceremonies, the belt is giving warnings of our ancestors and of nature," says Chief Commanda, for whom nature is the mother of everyone, adding that we shall not try to dominate her or abuse her but that we shall live in harmony with her.
>
> "It is nature herself who leads the world. She is feeding her children and providing for them from her breast and is also giving reprimands to her children when they are abusing her."

The moon is also of great importance in the eyes of William Commanda. "The moon is our grandmother and even if some people refuse to recognize the influence she has on the earth, she has, for example, sway over the plants, the fish, and the fertility cycle of the human being."

The wampum had also given messages to William, "When the white people will have destroyed everything, and when the Indians will not be able to find signs of Nature like the bark of the birch, the skin of the deer or the moose to display in their houses, sixty percent of the Indian race will have been destroyed and it will be the same for a greater part of the white people."

The epidemics which the inhabitants of the globe are already acquainted with, may be in a great part the reprisal of Mother Nature who is fighting against the abuse of her children. The chief gave the example of a tree blight which may be a way for the mother to tell her children to stop the irrational cutting of trees.

(Excerpted from a published interview, "Pourquoi aurais-je besoin d'un permis?" ["Why Do I Need a Permit?"] by Michel Merleau, well-known Quebec-based journalist, 1973.)

Three years later, in 1976, Eddie Benton Banaise published his landmark *Mishomis Book,* describing the predictions concerning each of the seven fires, but giving no details about the exact lengths of the time cycles involved. In fact, although he agrees that the length of a fire might be "somewhere around 112 years" he reminds us that it is not an exact number. I have since come to understand that the sun and moon cycles dance together to an irregular rhythm as judged by European calendars. The truth is much more interesting. That book is still in print, considered a classic text by Native Americans of all tribal affiliations.

When mixed-blood Chippewa Vernon LaDuke ("Sun Bear") self-published his book *Black Dawn, Bright Day,* in 1990, he decided not to mention the Seven Fires prophecies by name, but it is certain that he knew of them and was referring to them in part when he wrote of the bizarre and chaotic irregularities in weather patterns that were beginning to appear all over the globe. The book was a grim warning, but even after it was picked up by Simon and Schuster in 1992, few listened. Al Gore's book, *Earth In the Balance, Ecology and the Human Spirit,* published that same year, brought news of these climate changes to the attention of the mainstream. The Cry of the Earth conference at the United Nations, where many predictions about climate change were shared for the first time, occurred later that year. Nonetheless, global warming has been slow to be accepted in the United States. This important aspect of the Seven Fires prophecies has finally been revealed. Perhaps there is still time.

Introduction
Great Floating Bird

1. The number 84 is partly symbolic as regards the number of Algonquian-speaking nations, but in fact there are more.

2 Also MAHKWA Miami/ Illinois; MAKWA Algonquin; MOSQ Massachusetts; MASKE Narragansett.

3. as found on Ian Chadwick's website; *Legends and Oral Histories*; www. ianchadwick.com/ hudson/hudson 05.htm

4. Samuel Purchas, *Henry Hudson's Voyage,* from *Purchas' Pilgrimes,* a facsimile, (New York, NY: Google Books, no date)

5. In *Native New Yorkers*, I quoted in full from the Munsee letter of 1849, in which they described the first European ship to land on Munsee shores as "a great water fowl, floating…" Other accounts, such as that published by Heckewelder, describe the ship as a "great floating house…" I have combined these poetic descriptions into one, with, I hope, a minimum of poetic license.

6. Donald Johnson, Vernon Benjamin (based on Edward Hagaman Hall), Michael Sullivan Smith (based on Lossing) Edgar Bacon, and Ian Chadwick all are seasoned historians who have tried to answer the question, "Where was Henry?" All arrived at different answers.

7. Edgar Mayhew Bacon, *Henry Hudson His Times and His Voyages* (New York, NY: G.P. Putnam and Sons, Knickerbocker Press, 1907; reprinted Kessinger Publishers, London, UK,), p. 144.

Chapter One
The Saga of the Half Moon, a Synopsis

8. Medicine wheels marked out with stones and dating back to ancient times exist across North America and testify to the importance of 28 day and year cycles in Native American reckoning. See, for instance, http://solar-center.stanford. The 28 spokes align with the 28 small platelets around the perimeter of the shell of the calendar turtle. These turtles, which have 13 large (month) and 28 small (day) platelets on their shells, can be used quite effectively to measure the 364 (28x13) +1 day solar year, or the 56 year life walk wheel, accomplished by dividing each platelet in two. By dividing only one platelet in two (or using the turtle's neck as a space) Algonquin people also measured 29 days/ nights of the lunar month, of which there were also 13, a 377 night "lunar year," adding seven nights at the end (to make 384). These two calendars, run simultaneously, would only coincide every 98 years, and would also be subject to periodic adjustments. Did Algonquin people make these adjustments? The seven fires cycle of 784 years, as proposed here, indicates that they did, and that they, or the prophets, had intimate knowledge of solar and lunar calculations on a par with any other culture on earth. In fact the actual synodic (lunar) cycle is 29.53058 nights, making the 13 month lunar year 383.89765 nights long, whereas the actual solar year is 365.24219 days. This means the lunar year is 18.65546 days longer than the solar year. If you noted the exact position of the sun and moon on the day you were born, they would come close to realignment (at the end of their respective years) on your 98th birthday. The solar calendar would have completed five more turns than the 13-month lunar calendar by that time. They would not come into similar alignment until your 783rd birthday, (you should live so long!) one lunar year before the end of the seven fires prophecy cycle. In fact, the middle of the fourth fire (the moment of Hudson's arrival) and the end of the seventh fire are the only moments when the 98 and 56 year cycles would come into similar alignment. This cannot be a coincidence. Using the turtle shells as abacus-like computers, the calculations could have been made in a matter of hours or days. What is more remarkable is that from the middle of the third "fire" to the middle of the seventh, the approximate beginning of each 56 year cycle, as reckoned here from AD 1217, is marked by a solar eclipse visible from New Brunswick, the site of the arrival of the seven fires prophets. As solar eclipses are rare, and

appear almost anywhere on earth, this author has yet to discover their method of predicting this highly unusual chain of variable eclipses. It suggests that these prophets had been part of a society that charted out the sun and moon for thousands of years.

9. Mentioned in Lee Francis' book *Native Time: An Historical Timeline of Native America* (New York, St. Martin's Press, 1996).

10. At least according to Ian Chadwick. Douglas Hunter doesn't express it that way.

Chapter Two
Their Destinies Linked by Water

11. Donald Johnson, *Charting the Sea of Darkness* (Camden, Maine, International Marine, 1993). p. x.

12. Washington Irving, *Knickerbocker's History of New York*, (New York, NY: Capricorn Books, 1965), p. 93.

13. From a display in the New York State Museum, 2008.

14. Donald Johnson, *Charting the Sea of Darkness*. (Camden, Maine, International Marine, 1993). see page 87 and footnote that states there were either "16, 18, or 20 crewmembers, but 16 is mostly likely correct." This number is almost always mentioned.

15. Douglas Hunter, *God's Mercies, Rivalry, Betrayal and the Dream of Discovery*; (no city: Doubleday Canada, a division of Random House of Canada, Ltd. 2007), p. 17.

16. New Netherlands project coordinator Charles Goering, June 4, 2008, Albany, NY State Library

17. Edgar Bacon, *Henry Hudson His Times and His Voyages*, p. 186.

18. Edgar Bacon often refers to Juet as "the ancient man," but Hudson was only 39 (I believe he turned 40 on September 12, 1609, while visiting Manhattan) so it is unlikely they were literally school chums at Limehouse. If part of the same fraternity, Juet would have literally been an "older brother" to Hudson.

19. Douglas Hunter, *God's Mercies, Rivalry, Betrayal and the Dream of Discovery*; (no city, Doubleday Canada, 2007) p. 19

20. Ibid p. 19

21. Edgar Mayhew Bacon, *Henry Hudson His Times and His Voyages* (New

York, NY. G.P. Putnam and Sons, Knickerbocker Press 1907; reprinted Kessinger Publishers, London, UK) p. 5.

22. Ian Chadwick website *Legends and Oral Histories*; www.ianchadwick. com/hudson/hudson 05.htm

23. Quoting from various sources, starting with Bacon and Hunter.

24. This spelling appears in John Bierhorst's *Mythology of the Lenape*, (Tucson, AZ, University of Arizona Press, 1995) p. 122. The translation is from former Chief Mark Peters.

25. That is if you accept the popular belief that he died on June 21, 1611. Carl Schuster for one does not, as we shall see.

26. If Tamanend III (The Affable) were fifty when he welcomed William Penn ("Miquon") to Shackamaxon, he would have been born in 1632. If his father, Tamanend II was twenty-three at the time, a likely age for a father of a first-born son in Algonquin society, he was therefore born in 1609, the first-born son of Tamanend I. This is an educated guess.

27. Reginald Pelham Bolton, *New York City in Indian Possession*, (New York, NY: Heye Foundation; Indian Notes and Monographs, Vol. 2 no. 7, 1920, reprinted 1975), p.126. Tackamack signed major treaties in 1639, 1646 and 1684, so we can estimate his birth to have been about 1599, as sachems signing major treaties were rarely younger than 40, and few live past 100. According to Scenic Hudson's brochure on Clauslands Mountain, he was also known as Jan Claus. This Jan Claus has been incorrectly linked to Ee-towac-chams (probably Ee-towac-chans, which means the Elder Brother of the Towacos) who appears to be about 30 in his portrait made in 1710, and was therefore born about 1680, eight decades too late to be *that* Jan Claus.

28. George H. Budke, ed. *Indian Deeds 1630 to 1748*, BCE – 88 of the Budke Collection, reprinted New York Public Library, Manuscripts and Archives Division, Fifth Avenue and 42 Street, NY, NY, 10018; (reprinted by Library Association of Rockland County, 1975), p.144.

29. Reginald Pelham Bolton, *New York City in Indian Possession*, (New York, NY: Heye Foundation; Indian Notes and Monographs, Vol. 2 no. 7, 1920, reprinted 1975), p. 117.

30. Will L. Clark, edited by Alvah P. French, *History of Westchester County, Volume One* (New York, NY, Chicago, Illinois: Lewis Historical Publishing Company, Inc. 1925), p. 29.

31. Conversation with Gerald deWeerdt, December 2008.

32. Conversation with Gerald deWeerdt, December 2008.

33. Edgar Bacon, *Henry Hudson His Times and His Voyages* (New York, NY: G.P. Putnam and Sons, Knickerbocker Press, 1907, reprinted London, UK: Kessinger Publishers), p. 92.

34. Edgar Bacon, *Henry Hudson His Times and his Voyages*, p. 3.

35. Henry C. Murphy, *Henry Hudson in Holland* (New York, NY: Burt Franklin,1972), p. 45.

36. Henry C. Murphy, *Henry Hudson in Holland* (New York, NY, Burt Franklin,1972), p. 45.

37. Smith sent his "True Relation" back to England via Lord Nelson June 2, 1608, which was entered for publication at the Stationer's Hall on August 13, 1608, and which is quoted at length on page 238, American Scenic and Historic Preservation Society's Fifteenth Annual Report, J.B. Lyon Company, 1910, Submitted to the Legislature of New York, April 19, 1910. Smith's letter to Hudson, written shortly thereafter, may have gone into yet more detail because *True Relation* does not mention a passage to the western sea.

38. Henry C. Murphy, *Henry Hudson in Holland* (New York, N.Y., Burt Franklin,1972), p. 45-46. Murphy adds, "….though his main dependence was upon a more northerly point, and in fact at or near the straits which he afterwards discovered and which bear his name."

39. Also along the 40 parallel were Native American villages that became Eureka Ca. (39), Pyramid Lake (40), Denver (40), Indianapolis (39° 50'),Cincinnati (40), Columbus (40), Harrisburg (40), The Mason-Dixon Line (39° 50'), and Camden (40).

40. John Fiske, *The Dutch and the Quaker Colonies in America*, Vol. 1, (New York,NY: Houghton Mifflin Co. 1899, 1927, renewed by Ethel F. Fisk), p. 60.

41. Desmarquets, *Memoires pour server a l'histoire de Dieppe*, Paris, 1785, i 100, as noted in Fiske, *The Dutch and the Quaker Colonies in America,* (New York, NY: Houghton Mifflin Co.,1899, 1927), p. 59.

42. *Eusebii chronicon*, Paris 1512, folio 172, quoted on page 59 of Fiske, *The Dutch and the Quaker Colonies in America.*

43. Donald Johnson, *Charting the Sea of Darkness*, p. 144.

44. From lecture on Dutch mapmaking, Huguenot Historical Society, New Paltz, Erik Roth, Director. February 17, 2008

45. Henry C. Murphy, *Henry Hudson in Holland* (New York, NY: Burt Franklin,1972), p. 47.

46. Henry C. Murphy, *Henry Hudson in Holland* (New York, NY: Burt Franklin,1972), p. 45.

47. Edgar Bacon, page 86, quoting a famous epithet of the time.

48. Verrazzano never traveled far enough up the Hudson to determine whether or not it was the passage to China he believed might lie through the middle of the continent.

49. The Union Jack was created in 1606, combining the Cross of St. George and that of St. Andrew. This was about the time Captain Smith began exploring the Americas.

50. Robert C. Ritchie, *The Duke's Province* (Chapel Hill, NC: University of North Carolina Press, 1977), This book documents an endless variety of Dutch rebellions and British Imperial edicts against them over a one hundred year period, from 1620 to 1720. Open to any page.

According to Ritchie, the Long Island towns of Easthampton, Southampton and Southold never ceded to the Dutch, but instead ceded to Connecticut, a British colony, during Peter Stuyvesant's time, better to do battle with him. On April 23, 1662, King Charles II granted that Connecticut colony rights to all land west to the Delaware River, and beyond, ignoring the burgeoning Dutch colony that stood in that gap. Peter had heard rumors of impending British invasion from the start; in fact a Britisher named John Scott had already solidified British claims to much of Long Island by1663, and sent a message to the English colonies in New England in the autumn of 1663 that the Duke of York already considered himself unofficially to be the proprietor of what he planned to call "New York," after his royal self. Considering New Jersey was in English control as well, little New Netherlands had been perilously surrounded, or perhaps only then realized that it was. Blame Hudson for this mess as well.

51. New York State's only true coastline today, not including Long, Staten, or Manhattan Islands, runs from Port Chester to Willis Avenue in the Bronx, a distance of twenty miles, as defined October 28, 1664, (*History of Westchester County*, p. 4). Then add to that the north bank of the estuarine Harlem River, another eight miles, and you have the entire tidal coastline of mainland New York, not including the Hudson River, 28 miles. Rye and Port Chester were disputed with Connecticut before the British attack, reducing it at times to about 15 miles. Although Holland claimed other territories in New Jersey and Connecticut from time to time, this was the circumstance of New Netherlands in the mid-1600s, surrounded by almost 3,000 miles of British coastline to the north and south. The Dutch were tenacious! It should be noted that the Greenland Company may have made an attempt to set up colonial trading posts from Maryland to New York in 1598 to further the commercial interests of Holland calling it 'New Netherlands." Evidence is scarce. Based on Bacon, *Henry Hudson His Times and His Voyages*; page 27-28.

52. Robert C. Ritchie, *The Duke's Province*, p. 149.

53. Robert C. Ritchie, p. 148.

54. Martha Bockée Flint, *Early Long Island, A Colonial Study;* (New York, NY., G.P. Putnam's Sons, 1896) p 406-407.

55. Herbert Kraft, *The Lenape: Archaeology, History, and Ethnography* (Newark, NJ: New Jersey Historical Society, 1986), p. xvii. According to this book, the term Munsee did not appear until 1727 among Minisink descendants living at the forks of the Susquehanna River, while the term Unami did not appear until 1754, originally at the upper branches of the Susquehanna. However, Ives Goddard (1978, p. 236) wrote that Kraft erroneously considered Munsee a "corruption" of Minisink. Word lists such as those by

DeLaet of the Sanhikan made in 1633 have been labelled "Unami" retroactively, though this is incorrect. It is Renneiu.

56. Peggy Turco, *Walks and Rambles in Dutchess and Putnam Counties, A Guide to Ecology and History in Eastern Hudson Valley Parks* (Woodstock, Vt.: Backcountry Publications, 1990), introduction.

57. Chief Mark Peters, former Munsee Chief at Munseetown, Ontario.

58. According to certain oral traditions, which are, unfortunately, poorly documented, the Amorgarikakan descended from Caciamarex, (who was born in Culebra or Spanish Virgin Islands) the father of "Towaco," the first Amorgarikakan. The name derived from a seastream mixture of Spanish and Taino, Amor (love, Spanish) / gwa (love, Taino) rica (rich; feminine ending, Spanish) /Kahn (great or wealthy lord or serpent Taino). The term most likely means "Beloved Lord," but there are various shades of meaning, for example, the name may carry with it missionary influence from the time of Christopher Columbus.

Towaco (or Ta-ho-a-co) should logically be a shortened Unami translation of Amorgarikakan, or "Beloved Lord." For example, it could be a shortened form for "Place of Love," K'tahoah=Love (Zeisberger) + *co*=place of; or a shortened form of the Delaware word for an "act of loving," *au-ho-le-to-wok-con*. But this is speculation. It most closely resembles an Algic root for "ear." The name Towaco remains present over such a long period of time, it is assumed there were three or four generations of Towacos, although spellings differ.

There is reason to believe that Towaco III's oldest son would have been Ee-towach-cham (or E Tow O Koam, "King of the River Indians, or Mohigans" as captioned in a portrait of 1710) (Ruttenber p. 188), who went to England to sip tea with Queen Ann. On May 1, 1710, he and the other three "kings" were entertained at Punch's Theater in London.(Wilson, University of Toronto Press Journals, VOl. 16 No 3/1935 pp. 266-275) His royal title as king over the river Indians or Mohicans, does not make him a Mohican, although his mother's lineage is unknown. His family was clearly from the south, but Queen Ann was quick to recognize that authority in order to treaty with him for a greater chunk of land further inland. This acknowledgement does give credence to the idea that there had indeed been a dynasty of sorts brewing amongst the River Indians. If it was spelled Ee-towac-chans, it means "I am the Oldest Brother of the Towacos," in Unami Delaware.(Zeisberger p. 5) Assuming they were following the patriarchal traditions of the Taino and Cebone, this makes a great deal of sense, as the eldest would be heir to such a distinguished title.

 * I believe that Ee-towac-chans (various spellings) was the elder brother to Ee-Towac-chak, (or Ee-towach-chac) (*chac* or *chanc* means "small") the *ee-* prefix usually means "His," but it seems more likely, "I am," similar to the Spanish prefix *Io-*). In Unami or Munsee it would mean, "I am Towaco the Small." (O'Meara) Ee-towac-chack seems to have been the most prominent member of the trio for a while after his elder brother. Ee-towac-chack had in turn a younger brother Awissawa, who was also short in height, the one who befriended MacGregorie at Newburgh and who became a co-chief with Maringoman under the sachem Werepekes by 1685. (Ruttenber p. 94 also Lewis Beach "Cornwall." 1873) Ultimately, the somewhat delicate Awissewa, whose eyes were "like pools of ink," became the reluctant heir to this casually administered "throne" after Ee-towac-chams' death or retirement and after his brother Ee-towac-chack. Awessewa's dynamic ambassador Kaelcoptl, who signed the treaty for Saugerties, was one of the most prominent "River Indians" of his time. He signed many treaties in the name of the Amorgarikakan family, but he must have mumbled, because it is spelled differently in each case.

The Amorgarikakan family may have been mentioned in the Rombout Patent of 1683 when Sackeragkigh ("a high chief" possibly Kaelkoptl himself) signed "for himself and in the name of Megriesken," (Ruttenber, p. 84) (presumably Amorgarikakan) along with Wappingers Chief One Shake (father of Chief Daniel Nimham). The name Maringoman, for example, whose "castle" is said to have stood near today's Blooming Grove, New York, (possibly at the foot of Schunnemunk Mountain) may be yet

another version of "Amorgarikakan." (Mel Johnson, June 2008) Dr. Johnson suggests it may be a word play or "conflation" of words meaning "dark of skin," from Marrano/ Morisco (a Spanish ethnic group).

59. John William De Forest, *History of the Indians of Connecticut, From the Earliest Known Period to 1850.* Published with the sanction of the Connecticut Historical Society (Hartford, CT: W.J. Hammersley, 1853)

60. Clinton A. Weslager, *The Delaware Indians, A History* (New Brunswick, NJ: Rutgers University Press, 1972), p. 104.

61. See John P. Hart, Hetty Jo Brumbach, Robert Lusteck, 2007.

62. See Jack Weatherford, *Indian Givers:How the Indians of the Americas Transformed the World* (New York, NY: Crown Publishers, 1988). He provides not only a list, but provides their original names in native tongues. Evidence to the fact that most if not all of the planting, hybridizing and experimentation was being done by women can be found in recent articles by Alice Mann and elucidated in my upcoming book *Sacred Knowledge*.

63. William A. Ritchie identifies early Munsee pottery as "Owasco," and dates it to about AD 1000 throughout his book *Archaeology of New York State* (Fleischmanns, NY: Purple Mountain Press, 1994). However, Michael P. Hart's recent articles such as "The Death of Owasco" challenge Ritchie's definition, suggesting that this pottery followed a different strain of Algonquian culture. Not surprisingly, Dean R. Snow, President of the Society for American Archaeology, defends Ritchie's position, challenging a number of Hart's points in his new book *Archaeology of Native North America* (Saddle River, NJ. Prentice Hall, 2010 release).

64. Like the Florentines, the Algonquins had to contend with a powerful neighbor whose military might and sea-power was increasing year by year, the Hodenosuannee. They were as much a threat to the Algonquins as were the Venetians who had kept the Medici up at night a hundred years earlier. The Algonquins rose to the occasion, building palisaded forts along the Mohicanituck (Hudson) which further centralized their populations, increasing the possibilities for cultural exchange and innovation.

65. The Dutch, rivals of the British, had created an English bible in 1535, but this translation did not apparently please King James.

66. The "Shakespeare Code," in the 46th Psalm, has been taken seriously by John Updike, Rudyard Kipling, and Anthony Burgess, and many other serious readers of Shakespeare. It appears that the Bard played an important role in creating more sublimely inspired translations of the Psalms. The word "shake" appears 46 words in and the word "spear" appears 46 words from the end, and these terms have since been recognized by other translators as interpolations. The clever Welshman was 46 years old in the year 1610, the year he presumably "ghosted" for Solomon much like Valentine had ghosted for Sylvia in "Two Gentlemen of Verona," written in 1592.

67. *Virginia.; Sir Thomas Gates, Governor.; His services and death.*

Sir Thomas Gates, we gather from a speech of Sir Ralph Winwood, our Ambassador at the Hague, in February 1611, had long been in the service of the United Provinces. He told the States General how some English Lords and gentlemen of quality, at their own expense, had undertaken to plant a colony in Virginia, and among those who had laboured for the success of this design, there was not one who had done more to advance it than "one of your captains named Sir Thomas Gates, who the past year was there, where the providence of God led him, after having run the risk of shipwreck, being cast in a tempest upon the Bermudas, where he dwelt with all his followers more than forty weeks. From: *'Preface', Calendar of State Papers Colonial, America and West Indies: 1675-1676* and *Addenda 1574-1674, volume 9* (1893), pp. V-LVIII. URL: *http://www. british-history.ac.uk/report.aspx?compid=70022.* Date accessed: 14 June 2008.

68. Based on comparing the short list of Powhatan words that survive to this day with the short list of Wappingers words.

69. Many sources describe him as an administrator on the Mayflower, some do not.

70. There seems to be some dispute about this, it may have been a less illustrious positon.

71. The abductee, Tisquantum, now a slave, was taken against his will to Spain, England, and Newfoundland. Five years later, he returned to his home at Patuxet (now Plymouth Rock) as a free man and navigator for Thomas Dermer. Like his friend Epanow, he wanted to become a great sachem and a peacemaker between the two races. (Incidentally, Main Street Poughkeepsie is part of a Native American trail that goes from Plymouth Rock to Kerhonksen, New York) A forgiving man, he helped the Pilgrims and taught them how to work the new land, In return, the Pilgrims dug up and ate all the Wampanoag winter corn provisions. The year was 1620. Edward Harlow came to Martha's Vineyard in 1611, capturing six or more natives and killing at least six more. Epanow, a rather tall Wampanoag, was one of those captured. He was taken back to England where he was forced to entertain on the streets of London as "a wonder of the world." He quickly learned English, told his captors that there was a large gold mine near his home on Cape Cod and that only he knew where it was. Eagerly they took him back, and as they sailed by his home, he urged them to come closer to shore to avoid rocks… no, closer! To their surprise, he leaped into the sea and swam safely to the beach. He ran into the woods and successfully avoided recapture. He later became a sachem and friend to Squanto. Oddly enough, the gold mine was never located.

72. Charles C. Mann, *1491: New Revelations of the Americas Before Columbus* (New York, NY: Vintage Books, 2006), p?xxx

73. http://www.inventionofthetelescope. eu/400y_telescope/content/view/53/1/ lang,en/ accessed June 11, 2008.

74. from http://crystalinks. com/galileo.html

75. In December of 1609 Galileo drew the Moon's phases as seen through the telescope, showing that the Moon's surface was rough and uneven. In January he discovered four moons revolving around Jupiter, and also found more stars than were visible with the naked eye. These discoveries were earthshaking, and Galileo quickly produced a little book, Sidereus Nuncius (The Sidereal Messenger), in which he described them.

76. This is according to Ed Hageman Hall's reckoning of Juet's locations, published in 1910.

77. Bacon, *Henry Hudson His Times and His Voyages*, p. 190. Quotation is not sourced.

78. Ronald Sanders, *Lost Tribes and Promised Lands; The Origins of American Racism*, (New York, Little, Brown/ Harper Perrennial, 1978), p.99.

79. Columbus' descriptions of the natives of Hispaniola, specifically the Taino (and not the Carib, which he detested), could have been said of the Munsee, Wappingers and Mohicans of the Hudson River Valley. "Then they came swimming to the ship's boats, where we now were, bringing us parrots and clews of cotton thread, as well as spears and many other things, and we took them in exchange for other things we gave them, like small glass beads and hawk-bells. In short, they gave as they received, all with the utmost pleasure." He later wrote, "They manifest great love towards all others in preference to themselves." Although Hudson's connections with the secretive Muskovy Company need further scrutiny, Columbus was a known slave trader with a slight Messianic complex who, though probably born a Jew, would dress himself in a Franciscan robe and give evasive answers whenever his past was questioned.

80. Op cit. *Lost Tribes and Promised Lands* p. 230.

81. Ibid. *Lost Tribes and Promised Lands* p. 233

82. This birth date is not well documented, but it is widely accepted, and no better date has come forward.

83. *Lost Tribes and Promised Lands* p. 239

84. (From Chadwick's Website) Events onboard, even troubles with the crew, were not necessarily recorded because they might make the captain look bad in the eyes of his sponsors....In 1625, Flemish geographer Jan de Laet published his Nieuwe Werelt, a history of the exploration of the New World. In it, he reprinted fragments of Hudson's own journal of 1609. The actual journal was lost to history when it was sold to an unknown buyer, along with other archives of the Dutch East India Company, at a public auction in 1821. De Laet also reprinted a map by Dutch cartographer, Hessel Gerritz, showing the route of Hudson's 1610-11 voyage, apparently received from Abacuck Prickett (one of the survivors). Gerritiz (or Gerritsz) also printed a tract about Hudson in 1613. There are a few brief, tantalizing references about Hudson in other documents, seldom more than a few lines each. All in all, the printed historical records of Hudson's voyages listed above are less than 100 pages, easily read in an hour. Modern readers can find the originals of these works in various forms online, or read many of them in Donald Johnson's 1995 book, *Charting the Sea of Darkness*. Later historians George Asher (1860), Llewelyn Powys (1907), John Meredith read (1866) and Thomas Janvier (1909) searched the records to uncover any reference to Henry Hudson. They found few additional documents: some references in company papers, some possible genealogical links with other Hudsons, and the Admiralty records of the trials of the surviving mutineers. The author of this site has found previously un-noted references to persons named Hudson online in the British archives at www.british-history.ac.uk. However, the relationship between these Hudsons and the explorer is unclear and still to be determined.In part, one of the reasons for the confusion is that spelling — even of family names — was seldom consistent in those days, and there are many examples where members of one family spelled their last names differently, and even where one person changed the spelling of his or her name in a lifetime. John Meredith Read lists several variant spellings, including Herdson, Heardson, Hodson, Hodgeson, Huddesdon, and Herdsone. Hudson must have learned his craft and skills by travelling with contemporary seafarers, probably British mariners and explorers (possibly even sailing with John Davis on one his voyages to the Arctic) or even in one of the fishing fleets that cross the Atlantic for the rich banks off Newfoundland. There was even a suggestion he had visited the east coast of America once before.

Like Frobisher before him, Hudson may have been in the company of a trading ship of the Muscovy Company. As a young man, Hudson may have even sailed on one of the English ships that faced and defeated the Spanish Armada in 1588, as were many English sailors. But no records of his early years have yet been uncovered.

85. Canada is a different story. Canadian Algonquins have always maintained a strong political presence and their society has produced many great leaders and artists.

86. Geroge H. Budke, ed. *Indian Deeds 1630 to 1748*, BCE – 88 of the Budke Collection, New York Public Library, Manuscripts and Archives Division, Fifth Avenue and 42 Street, NY NY 10018 by Library Association of Rockland County, 1975). p.144.

87. The use of tobacco for appeasing river spirits is mentioned in Kenneth Cohen's book *Honoring The Medicine*, (New York, NY, Ballantine, 2002), p. xxx. The expression "veins of our mother" is used at William Commanda's website, web.mac.circleofallnations.com.www.circleofallnations.com

88. Evan Pritchard, *Native New Yorkers*, Tulsa, San Francisco, Council Oak Books, 2002, revised edition, 2007, p. 47

89. New York State Museum, exhibit on New York City, June 4, 2008.

90. John W .De Forest, *History of the Indians of Connecticut*, p. 458-9.

Chapter Three
Hudson Out at Sea

91. There are various interpretations.

92. His locations during that first week as he traveled from what is now Delaware Bay to somewhere in what is New York is much disputed. I will offer the reader a reasonable reconstruction.

93. Nanticoke Language, (Bristol, Pa.: Evolution Press, 2004)p. 30. The word means "moon."

94. Joseph White Norwood, *The Tammany Legend* (Boston: Meador Publishing Company, 1938)pp. 118-119.

95. Donald Johnson, *Charting the Sea of Darkness* (Camden, Maine, International Marine, 1993), p. x (From introduction)

96. www.ianchadwick.com/hudson/hudson_overview.html

97. *Juet's Journal*, edited by John T. Cunningham (Newark, NJ: New Jersey Historical Society, 1959), p. 25.

98. From Dutch map.

99. P. 199, Joseph White Norwood, The Tammany Legend, (Boston,

Meador Publishing Company, 1938)

100. Much of this can be found in Daniel Brinton's *The Myths of the New World: A Treatise on the Symbolism and Mythology of the Red Race of America* (Boston, Ma: Longwood Publishing, 1879).

101. This case has been in and out of the Supreme Court for eighty years, and is still being disputed as of this writing.

102. Most sources are in Spanish, however Hunter College Library's Taino Cultural Center has a copy of a book in Spanish and English, published in Cuba; *Taino Pre-Columbian Art and Culture from the Caribbean*, (Havana, edited by Fatima Bercht,1997; El Barrio) which describes this god and retells some of the myths and legends associated with him.

103. William A. Douglass and Jon Bilbao, *Amerikanuak*, (Reno, Nv.: University of Nevada Press, 1975) p. 52.

104. It is unfounded to say that the Basque were fishing in Newfoundland by the 1470s. This idea is based on the much-disputed comment by Navarrete in his "The Basque Fishery," (p 47) to the same effect. In his critically acclaimed classic *History of Newfoundland*, Daniel Woodley Prowse states unequivocally that the Basque were confused, and that "Greenland… was mistaken for Labrador." (1895, p. 597) It is also incorrect to say that the yellow copper Hudson saw was from European sources, and that Native Americans were too primitive to be able to work with metals. This is in direct conflict with research done by Rafferty and Mann in their book *Smoking and Culture* (cited elsewhere) who found no similar metal pipes in Europe, and with New York State Museum's Curator of Mineralogy, Marian Lupulescu who traces yellow copper to nearby Ellenville, New York.

105. P. 54 *Amerikanuak*

106. If Henry had tried to navigate further in smaller boats it is possible he could have reached what is now Trenton, thirty miles north of Shackamaxon, where the Falls of the Delaware were located at that time. The falls were called Sunckheagan, which means the "head of the sea," and a village to the west carried the same name. This is similar to our English term "head of the tide," but should really be translated as the

"terminus" of the estuary, beyond which the tide cannot pass, a barrier to marine life and boats. It is intriguingly a feminine term for chief. Could it be that the Munsee thought of bodies of water, such as estuaries, as feminine, as did the Europeans of that era? It is likely, for rivers were, and still are referred to in every living Algonquin language as "the blood of our mother," the lifeblood of the earth itself. Could it be that the Algonquins saw the great estuary as a "womb" where life begins? It would harmonize well with the linguistic mélange at the root of the word "estuary" which crosses stars, springtime, chaos, estrus, Goddesses, and the east, in a mysterious way.

Although modest in height, no spring tide (?) could have risen above that falls at Trenton because of its position. Today's Route 13 traces a well-known "Indian Trade Route" that follows the Delaware Bay and River on its western side, and connects the southern tip of the Delmarva Peninsula with Trenton, New Jersey to the north. For the most part, it marked the inland edge of some of the east coast's marshiest wetlands, representing reliable year-round foot travel for humans and animals. Through Eastern Shore Maryland, it still follows the back of the ridge as mastodons must have done to avoid marshes.

Route 13 joins with route 1 (the Mid-Atlantic Rise Trail, and one of the first post roads) just below the Falls of the Delaware. Coastal/Estuarial Algonquins usually crossed rivers above waterfalls, although it is not always clear why. In most cases, the river bottom would be less muddy above and more muddy below, which would have been a factor for both the Delaware and the wild animals who preceded them. In the case of Pawtucketts like this one, (fresh water pouring into brackish or tidal water) the water above the falls would have always been drinkable. Let us remember that in 1000 AD the climate was unusually warm (Quimby) and the ocean level might have been higher, making the tidal water more brackish.

In this case, there were several crossings at Sunckheagan, mostly above the falls, one of which George Washington made famous in the winter of 1776 and January of 1777. There have been various islands of sand in different positions at different times near

that falls. It is hard to say if they were used as council fire islands, but it is probable. The western windows in the copola on today's State Capitol at Trenton provide a view of the falls, and on that earlier place of governance, (the probable council fire island spot, or a nearby equivalent) though not unobstructed. This is a pattern we find throughout the Eastern states and provinces, which some ascribe to Masonic tradition dating back to Fort Orange, as we shall see. William Richie's work indicates there was a large farming population in or near that region at the time.

Troy Falls, now Troy dam in Albany, New York, is an almost identical configuration to the Falls of the Delaware, and is also a Sunckheagan. There is an island, Schodack, which is larger, and there are a lot of crossings, two of them higher up at Green Island . Today's New York State Capitol does not have a copola, but high windows that see out to the direction of Schodack, and there between the windows are matching busts of Henry Hudson and Chief Joseph Brandt, both peering off into the distance.

Sunckheagan was the birthplace of Tedyuskung, a chief of great historical importance in both American and Delaware history, who considered himself half Munsee. He was the one whose demand for a good translator, someone well-versed in both Munsee Delaware and English, led to the discovery of a talented pen belonging to a young Quaker man named Charles Thompson. Teedyuskung and Thompson took certain corrupt British politicians head-on, and Thompson ended up as secretary to the Continental Convention and collaborator on the Declaration of Independence.

Trenton was the home of Teedyuskung's famous father, Captain Harris, whose grandfather would have been alive in 1609. Further research should be done to determine who Harris' grandfather was and whether he was a Munsee chief and at what side of the crossing. It is likely but not certain that he was a chief.

Beyond the Falls of the Delaware was the highly navigable waters of the upper Delaware, and Henry would have quickly found himself just south of Minisink Island, the Munsee capitol and "island of fire." Due to the shallowness of the water at Minisink, he would have had to anchor the main ship and proceed by row boat.

The wide, shallow bay that Hudson struggled to navigate was named after Lord De La Warr, first Governor (check) of the Virginia Colony, who never viewed the bay itself. It is interesting that the Native Americans that Hudson did meet are now often referred to, for better or worse, as "The Delaware," even though most of them would have never seen that river, or met Lord De La Warr. Today, anthropologists describe the cultures of the Wappingers, Munsee, Unami, Mohican, and Matouac as "Delawarian," as a way of categorizing them by their common traits, again after Lord De La Warr, who never met a Native American (check).

107. According to Donald Johnson.

108. There was a group in New Jersey called Sauwanew, either indicating the presence of Shawnee, or Sijanoy, a "shell bead people," See Hendrickson's map of 1616.

109. Donald Johnson writes, "Off Hereford Inlet, New Jersey." According to my maps, Hereford Inlet is 39 degrees 2 minutes, but from Juet's comment below about "the streams had deceived us," he may be right. Hereford Inlet runs north to south.

110. http://www.evolpub.com/cgi-bin/cgiwrap/crs/alrlexicon?lexicontype-dictionary&head 2/10/09

111. As mentioned, this is in the style of an Algonquin story-song, as no Navesink songs still exist. The chorus is made of vocables, words that express feeling rather than information, although igaton means "that is good" in Akansea language, written down by du Poisson in 1727) www.evolpub.com/cgi-bin/cgiwrap/crs/alrlexicon...

112. This would have been *peckamannak*, an inlet through the islands, which also sounds like *peckaminak*, the word for cranberries in Navasink.

113. The Block map of 1614, the Hendrickson map of 1614 and the Blau map of 1635 show Eyer Haven about 20 miles below the entrance to Barnegat Bay. However the shape of Barnegat Bay is different in each case. None show the mouth of Tom's River, a major inland feature.

114. From the oft-quoted *Place Names in New Jersey,* Touching Leaves/Nora Thompson Dean, as quoted in my *Introductory Guide to Lenape Indian Words*

and Phrases (Woodstock, NY., Resonance Communications, 2002) p. 62.

115. From *The Origin of New Jersey Place Names,* (Trenton, NJ: New Jersey Public Library Commission, State House Annex, Trenton, 7, New Jersey, May 1945), p. 19. This is available from the Ocean County Historical Society.

116. John T. Cunningham, *The Voyage of the Half Moon from 4 April to 7 November 1609,* Introduction by John Cunningham (Newark, NJ.: New Jersey Historical Society, 1959), p. 27.

117. My thoughts were inspired by a conversation with Greta Wagle at the New York Boat Show, January 21, 2008.

118. *The Origin of New Jersey Place Names,* (Trenton, NJ: New Jersey Public Library commission, State House Annex, Trenton, 7, New Jersey, May 1945), translates Barnegat as "gate at the end of barrens," page 7.

119. Julian Harris Salomon, *Indians of the Lower Hudson Region: The Munsee* (New York: Historical Society of Rockland, 1982) p.83.

120. The lower opening in the maps of Block, Hendrickson, and Blau is certainly Little Egg Harbor, and the next opening to the north is Barnegat Inlet, however the three maps disagree as to the shape of Barnegat Bay itself. The bay does not exist in Blau; in Block it heads north but is very short. in Hendrickson it turns into a river as it heads north, off the page, Hendrickson's map does not give us ten leagues north but does show a great stream, which might flow outwards to the sea. See article by Pauline S. Miller, "A New Discovery: The 1614/1616 Map of New Jersey by Surveyor Cornelius Hendricks." (Toms River, NJ: Ocean County Cultural and Heritage Commission, Vol 10 no 3, Fall 1988)

121. Assuming Cranberry Inlet's name was taken from the Navesink language, and assuming there were no cranberries there, (there are none there now) it stands to reason that the name was a play on words. As mentioned before, *peckamannak* is Algic for an inlet through the islands, whereas *peckiminak* is the word for cranberries in Navasink, from deLaet's "Sanhikan" list of 1633, Evolution Publishing.

122. Conversations with Ocean County historians at Historical Society Headquarters Hadley Avenue, Tom's River, NJ. The location of the channel includes Ortley Avenue and

6th Avenue of today's Seaside, NJ. Also, the book *Ocean County, Four Centuries in the Making,* by Polly Miller, p. 50.

123. *The Origins of New Jersey Place Names,* p. 19. It could also mean *Mete*=shallow or trout stream, *conk*= people of the place of.

124. Ibid.

125. *Match(oo)* =bears, in Munsee, *k*=plural, *us*=small.

126. *Origins of New Jersey Place Names,* p. 28.

127. The Raritan in this area is not a tributary as the name suggests, (the Tanracken River is a "tan" or tributary that runs into the Hudson, for example) but a primary estuary, and remains quite salty far inland. It should be called Rariteague in this section, and Raritan at the headwaters, which are not very dramatic.

128. This is generally translated "Fire Drill People," (see elsewhere) but has also been translated as "stone implement" people, assan=stone with hikan=implement.

129 . Karen Sivertson's doctoral thesis, *Babel on the Hudson.* Online.

130. Clinton A. Weslager, *The Delaware Indians, A History* (Princeton, NJ: Rutgers University Press, 1972, reprinted 1996), pp. 250-251. Elsewhere, on p. 43 he quotes Zeisberger as the source of the common misunderstanding about the confederacy.

131. Weslager, *The Delaware Indians,* 1972, p. 43, quoting John Heckewelder, 1820, *Account of the History, Manners and customs of the Indian Nation* (pub. 1876, reprinted, New York, Arno Press, 1971), 51-52.

132. Quoted in Weslager, 1972, p. 45, D.G. Brinton, *The Lenape and Their Legends,* (Philadelphia, Pa. 1885, reprinted Lewisburg, Pa.; Wennawoods Publishers, 1999) p. 36.

133. Ibid, p. 45.

134. Vera H.C. Chan, "Best Beware Thy Stingray," Yahoo Buzz, February 25, 2009. http://buzz.yahoo.com/buzzlog/92308/?fp=1

Chapter Four
The People of the Harbor

135. This was probably done immediately after the eclipse of the fourth fire, as seen by Captain John Smith.

136. Evan Pritchard, *Native New Yorkers,* pp 122, 123 in revised edition, generously provided by Chief Mark Peters (retired) of the Munsee band of Thames River, Ontario, Canada.

137. From a conversation December 16, 2008, with Gerald de Weerdt, Director of the Maritime Museum of Terschelling in the Netherlands (Het Behouden Huys) and former Director of the National Institute of Ship Archaeology in Lelystadt, the Netherlands. A nautical engineer and historic ship architect, Mr. de Weerdt is a recognized expert on 17th century Dutch shipbuilding. He is currently reconstructing the Onrust.

138. Ibid Gerald de Weerdt.

139. From a conversation with Gerald de Weerdt, December 16, 2008.

140. Edward Johnson, curator and science advisor to the Staten Island Museum, stated in a phone conversation of January 15, 2009, that at Seguine Point, ocean freighters navigate closest to shore.

141. From a sign posted at the display for the Onrust reconstruction; New York Boat Show, December 21, 2008.

142. I observed these cables being created at the New York Boat Show, on December 16, 2008 by Courtney Anderson, and gathered these details. Gerald de Weerdt described the making of pine tar at that same time.

143. The actual English term used in the handwritten 1849 document passed down to me and published in *Native New Yorkers,* was "great water fowl," but the similar term Great Floating Bird has also been used in the same context, and is immediately recognizable as an alternate translation.

144. Today there are no streams at Great Kills Harbor but there were five in 1609, hence the name. Only three would have been visible to Juet.

145. Nissequogue Marine Biologist Raymundo Rodriguez, conversation, June 2008, confirmed January 3, 2008.

146. Order: Rajiformes, Family: Myliobatidae, Genus: Manta, Species: M. birostris. According to *A Dictionary of Zoology* by Michael Allaby, (London: Oxford University Press, 1999), the manta is also called the "eagle ray," because of its ability to leap and glide on large wing-like pectoral fins.

147. Jack Sepkoski, "A compendium of fossil marine animal genera

(Chondrichthyes entry)" *Bulletins of American Paleontology* 364: p. 560. (2002)

148. Robin Kimmerer, interview May, 2008, Pace University, Pleasantville, NY. At Discovery Cove at Sea World, mantas and dolphins are placed in the same tanks.

149. The term "eagle ray" is used not only by Native North Americans but by indigenous people all over the world.

150. Nissequogue (related to Ray Wheeler, chief of the Nissequogue) Raymundo Rodriguez, telephone conversation June 16, 2008.

151. *Journal of the Museum of New Mexico* website, although one wonders what a "lion" is to a Peruvian. Published in: *El Palacio: Quarterly Journal of the Museum of New Mexico*, Vol. 85, No. 2, Summer 1979. Also on the web at http://www. peruvianwhistles. com/el-palacio.html.
Adoration for mantas does not seem to be limited to indigenous peoples; there has been a tendency lately for scientists to fall in love with manta rays, as exemplified by a recent headline in Deep Sea News www. scienceblogs.com/deepseanews/2008/07/ scientist_falls_in_love_with_m.php - 68k - Scientist Falls in Love with Manta Rays. The article of July 28, 2008 by Peter Etnoyer tells how scientist Andrea Marshall's life was changed by discovering a new species of Manta, and her newfound relationship with the creatures of the deep.

152. Katherine Berrin, with the Larco Museum; *The Spirit of Ancient Peru: Treasures from the Museo Arquelogicao Rafael Larco Herrera*. (New York: Thames and Hudson, 1997).

153. "Sacred Fish," by E.N. Anderson, Jr, *Man* (magazine) (1969 Royal Anthropological Institute of Great Britain and Ireland). pp.43-44.

154. Earnest Thompson Seton and Julia Seton, *The Gospel of the Redman* (Seton Village, Santa Fe, New Mexico, 1966,1937, 1963 Julia M. Seton), p. 12.

155. Reginald Pelham Bolton, *New York City in Indian Possession*, (New York, NY: Heye Foundation; Indian Notes and Monographs, Vol. 2 no. 7, 1920, reprinted 1975), p. 50. Shawcopoke also implies "a place in the south with shallow dark water."

156. Per conversation with Raymundo Rodriguez, June 7, 2008.

157. Bolton, *New York City in Indian Possession,* (Heye) p. 61, a word for the people of Aquehong, or Staten Island.

158. Alanson Skinner, "Staten Island," p. 21, quoting Wilson, "Prehistoric Art," Plate 52, opposite page 481, *Annual Report*, Smithsonian Institution, 1896.

159. The Grasmere Head possesses extremely high cheekbones of a type that seems typical of certain families of Munsee and Unami descendants, and some Wappingers. The eyes and forehead are similar, and the crescent eyebrows of the stone head resemble those of some Wappingers families today. I believe the face itself is an accurate portrait of an actual person. It was probably created by a native person, the same one who carved the similar head at Monmouth, New Jersey. I have collected a few photographs of Native Americans whose roots are in the New York City area and whose faces resemble the Grosmere Head, but don't have permission from their descendents.

The following article has been reprinted courtesy of Edward Johnson of the Staten Island Museum. "One of the most unusual Indian artifacts ever found on Staten Island was a stone head, unearthed by chance in 1884. The following account is by George F. Kunz, who presented the head at a meeting of the Natural Science Association of Staten Island on May 10, 1884: About one month ago my attention was called to a rumor in regard to the finding of a curious stone head on Staten Island, which I immediately investigated, and arrived at the following facts: About 30 feet east of the railroad, just above the fingerboard road, in Southfield, in a low swamp...A rustic basket worker, named James Clark, came upon the stone head while digging up the roots of a high huckleberry bush, at least ten years of age, growing at the edge of the swamp...When striking with his pick, at a depth of from 12 to 18 inches, he turned up the head - his pick striking and indenting the chin. It was at once thoroughly scrubbed and narrowly escaped painting by the enthusiastic finder and his friends... The spot where the head was found is so unfrequented, there being no house in the immediate vicinity, and the authenticity of its finding being duly attested, we are left to such conjecture as to its origin as the object itself suggests. The features are too well cut for a common off-hand piece of work by a stonemaker: the style is not Egyptian or Eastern; rendering it unlikely that it is part of an antiquity thrown away by some sailor; it is rather Mexican, and still more resembles Aztec work. This leads to the inference that it is probably of Indian origin..."

160. Per phone conversation with Edward Johnson, Staten Island Museum curator, naturalist, January 155, 2009.

161. Edward Johnson, January 15, 2009.

162. Edward Johnson, January 15, 2009.

163. Although Old Town is just over a mile from the beach, it is more than four miles from Great Kills by trail, and almost seven miles from Wolfes Pond Park where the tall oaks are today, plus another mile or so from where the Ambrose Channel hits the shoreline. These are not unlikely distances for native people to walk just to see a Great Floating Bird, but Princes Bay was in a different tribal territory.

164. State Capitol at Annapolis, MD, permanent exhibit, viewed by author in 2005.

165. From a confirmed source close to former Munseetown Chief Mark Peters. According to this source, a stump of a hemlock tree was brought into the meeting lodge and burned as a form of smudge. The smoke would fill up the lodge until nothing could be seen. When it dissipated, the lodge was pure and the meeting could begin.

166. This information concerning the dressing of skins is from a confirmed Munsee source close to former Munseetown Delaware Chief Mark Peters.

167. Wording in quotations provided by Brian Wilkes, former Eastern Band Cherokee sub-chief; conversation, March 14, 2009; Algonquin cultural norms known to author from lifelong contact with Mi'kmaq and other Eastern Algonquin groups.

168. Weatherford's book *Indian Givers* provides these and many other Native American terms for foods developed in the Americas. Juet never mentions sunflower seeds, but this too was a major source of protein for Native Americans at the time. Jack Weatherford, *Indian Givers:How the Indians of the Americas Transformed the World*

(New York, NY: Crown Publishers, 1988).

169. *History of Westchester County,* p.19

170. Wilbur L. Cross, "Foretaste," a foreword to Imogene Walcott's *The Yankee Cookbook* (Boston, Ma.:Coward-McCann, Inc. 1938), p. xiii. "At first the settlers depended most on Indian corn to keep them alive. From them has come delicious Johnnycake [his spelling] made of yellow or white cornmeal, which is still consumed all over New England, with Rhode Island at the head. Many other uses of Indian corn have been contrived such as hasty pudding, fried mush, hominy, and hulled corn, of which johnnycake and corn bread yet maintain their original prestige. The pleasant taste of many of these cornmeal dishes has been enhanced by a liberal flow of New England maple syrup, noted for its fine flavor." Elsewhere in the Yankee Cookbook, Sydney Wooldridge ("Sap's Risin'") states that "the manufacture of maple syrup is not a process, but a ritual—a ritual of mysticism that has all the appurtenances of paganism..." (p337)

171. The Yankee Cookbook, page 163.

172. Conversation with Gerald de Weerdt, December 16, 2008

173. Per Edward Johnson, Staten Island Museum, naturalist, curator, phone conversation, January 15, 2009. I use the term loamy soil to mean glacial outwash clay soil mixed lightly with sand, as described by Johnson. The same stretch featured a continuous strand of beach at the water's edge, which has now eroded to about fifty feet, and less in some places.

174. *History of Westchester County,* p 17.

175. Ibid.

176. Not a direct quote, but a synthesis of what is said in traditional circles.

177. From interview with Beulah Timothy, published in *Introductory Guide to Lenape Indian Words and Phrases,* page 28. I never asked her for a literal translation, but the term seems to break down as; "It is as hard as a rock to cut."

178. In John O'Meara's *Delaware-English, English-Delaware Dictionary* (Toronto, Canada: University of Toronto Press, 1996) On p. 528 there is the word asunaamiin, "hard maple tree." This word is apparently constructed of asun (stone) and aamihleew (to be knocked over) or aamsheew (cut and

knocked over) (p. 5) plus the –iin suffix.

179. Edward Johnson, curator and naturalist, Staten Island Museum, phone conversation, January 15, 2009. The information about maple competing with old growth and burn techniques is from Dan Atchison and also from an interview with Taro Ietaka of Cranberry Lake Preserve, in Westchester, NY.

180. *Charting the Sea of Darkness,* Donald Johnson, p. 116.

181. Audio recording provided by Bob Vedder.

182. Amy C. Schutt, *Peoples of the River Valleys, The Odyssey of the Delaware Indian* (Philadelphia, PA: University of Pennsylvania Press, 2007), p 1.

183. C.A. Weslager, *Dutch Explorers, Traders, and Settlers in the Delaware Valley, 1609-1664* (Philadelphia: University of Pennsylvania Press, 1961), 121-26; NEP, 18-19).

184. Lecture, Saturday March 22, 2008, Albany, NY, Susan M. Taffe, "The Delaware Stick Dance; An Adopted Haudenosaunee Social Dance Song." 2008 Algonquian People's Seminar, sponsored by the Native American Institute of the Hudson River Valley and the New York State Museum. [contact her directly for permission. She referenced the New York State Historical Society and the O'Reilly Papers and Henry Deerborn]

185. Touching Leaves Indian Crafts, Dewey, Oklahoma, 1991. http:// www.delawaretribeofindians.nsn.us/ social_dance.html January 22, 2009.

186. http://www.delawaretribeofindians. nsn.us/social_dance.html January 22, 2009.

187. Donald Johnson, *Charting the Sea of Darkness,* p. 116.

188. From a confirmed source close to former Munseetown Chief Mark Peters.

189. James Flowers, telephone conversation, Saturday, June 14, 2008.

190. "Since the late 17th century a mystery illness had been rife among the poor of Southern Europe. It began with skin rashes, followed by diarrhoea and vomiting, disruption to the central nervous system and finally death. Nobody knew that this was a disease called pellagra and even in the 19th century the scientific world believed the symptoms were caused by a lack of animal protein. It was not until the beginning of the 20th century that the cause of pellagra was found to be an almost exclusive diet of maize. Maize is low in the essential amino acids lysine and tryptophan. Lysine is important for bone growth and tryptophan is a precursor of niacin, which in turn releases essential vitamin B. The first successful treatments for pellagra consisted of administering brewer's yeast, which contains sufficient quantities of vitamin B.

Interestingly, this disease did not exist in the birthplace of maize, not even when the Spanish conquistadors forced the Indians to grow maize exclusively and destroyed their gardens. Today this puzzle has been solved: ancient knowledge about the right way to prepare maize did not cross the Atlantic along with the maize. In Europe the dry grains were ground, but the Indians softened the whole grains first, cooked them and then ground them. But their secret ingredient was ash, which they added to soften the husks and make the grains more digestible. By adding ash, in other words lime, the niacin in the maize is liberated and can take effect." http://www.gmo-safety.eu/en/maize/121.docu.html

191. Karen Olsen Bruhns and Karen E. Stothert, *Women in Ancient America,* (Norman, Oklahoma: University of Oklahoma Press, 1999), p. 81.

192. Colin G. Calloway, *One Vast Winter Count, The Native American West Before Lewis and Clark,* (Omaha,Nebraska: University of Nebraska Press, 2006), p. 96.

193. Colin G. Calloway, *One Vast Winter Count,* p. 97.

194. Linguistics seems to confirm the use of tulip trees as wood for dugout canoes.

195. http://www.umaine.edu/folklife/images/Newsletter/winter/winter04-05.pdf

196. William Ritchie, *The Archaeology of New York State,* page 270-272

197. Chadwick places Hudson near Coney Island. There were a number of tribes living near the beach who had been adopted by the Canarsie and may have been buffers for attack from the sea. Among them were the Mannahaning, whose territory stretched from today's Coney Island to Manhattan Beach. Manhattan Beach was named after

Mannahaning, which I will presume was really Man-nayan-ing which means "the island at the point place," referring to Coney Island. Behind them, in the area of Avenue X were the Mocung, and word implying muddy or swampy. To the east were the Massabarkem, in the territory now called Sheepshead Bay. To the east of them were the Shanscomacoocke, and beyond them the Hoopaninak.

The Narrioch people "at the point" may have started out at the northern tip of Staten Island, where Sailor's Snug Harbor is situated. Then they lived on Coney Island. Then they moved inland, mixing with Lenape speakers (possibly a Unami band?) becoming Nyack, as the Unami could not pronounce the R. There might have been a splitting off with the Mannahaning, "the island at the point place," or it could be that one is the place the other the people. Then they moved to what is now Bay Ridge. They were found there in early Dutch times as a distinct group at Bay Ridge. Later, during the Kieft War, they moved to the present town of Nyack, which bears their name.

198. One of the ancestral cultural groups of the Matouac are the Orient Point People, who reached a high level of sophistication just before 1000 BCE. They are best known for their "killed pots" and Orient Point fishtail projectiles. "Killed pots" are ceramics smashed during a burial ceremony so that the spirit of the pot would go to the spirit world with the deceased. The Mayans were widely involved in this practice at the same time. Their Orient Point fishtail projectile points, which are occasionally made of crystal, or local chert, seem to have had some magical significance to the Orient Point people. They were mainly used for hunting game, but it is also possible they used them as spear points for fishing spears, and given their location on the northern fin of Long Island (and near the reefs of Plum Island) they were probably spearing Atlantic salmon and mullets. Orient Point projectiles were also used as atlatl points, attached to a spear used in conjunction with a throwing device.

There are two types of Orient Point fishtail points. One shape resembles a wild, or natural male Atlantic Salmon, the other a mullet. It is possible that these people realized they needed a more hydrodynamic

point in order to spear fish underwater, and also realized that the shape of the fish was already an ideal hydrodynamic shape for the particular type of water it was swimming in. Although purely hypothetical, perhaps they put two and two together, and made the spear point so that it matched the fish. There is also more than a little shamanistic magic in knapping a quartz stone into the shape of the fish you are hunting. As at least one Algonquin elder used to say, "To catch a fish you have to think like a fish." Similar fishtail points soon appeared all over North America.

199. This particular example of division of labor is taken from Theresa O. Deming's 1938 juvenile work *Indians of the Wigwams; A Story of Indian Life.*

200. Charles C. Mann *1491,* p. 39.

201. I found New York City area archaeological trail maps in the archives at the Heye Foundation Musem of the American Indian at Bowling Green, noticed these trails and copied them

202. Most notably in *Current Perspectives in Northeastern Archeology; Essays in Honor of William A. Ritchie,* Edited by Robert E. Funk and Charles F. Hayes III. Research and Transactions of the New York State Archeological Association, Volume 17, No. 1, 1977. pp. 1-8

203. Kraft, *Current Perspectives* p. 5

204. Kraft, *Current Perspectives* p 7.

205. Kraft, *Current Perspectives* 1977, p. 5

206. Bruhns, Stothert, *Women in Ancient America,* (Norman, OK: University of Oklahoma Press, 1999), p. xlv

207. Bruhns, Stothert, *Women in Ancient America,* p.80

208. Judging from Bolton's writings.

209. *The Little Book of Native American Widsom,* compiled by Steve McFadden, (Rockport, Massachussetts: Element Books, 1994), p. 9.

210. *Smoking and Culture,* p. 74

211. *Smoking and Culture* p. 75.

212. James Flowers, telephone conversation, Saturday, June 14, 2008.

213. *History of Orange County* 1847 (Goshen, N.Y., Orange County Genealogical Society) p. 31.

214. Ed Johnson, curator of the Staten Island Museum, per

conversation January, 2009.

215. *History of Westchester County* p. 19. It follows quotations from Wassenares, so this may be the source.

216. *Indians Before Columbus, Twenty Thousand Years of North American History Revealed by Archaeology* (Chicago, Illinois: The University of Chicago Press, Paul S. Martin, George I. Quimby, Donald Collier), p. 40. One other major source was at the Coppermine River in northwestern Canada. All were worked to a considerable extent.

217. *Indians Before Columbus, Twenty Thousand Years of North American History Revealed by Archaeology*, (Chicago, Illinois: The University of Chicago Press, Paul S. Martin, George I. Quimby, Donald Collier), p. 44, 45.

218. *Indians Before Columbus*, p. 42.

219. Juan Javier Pescadore, *The New World Inside a Basque Village, 1550-1800*, internet.

220. Jennifer Higgins via internet.

221. Article, "Basque Whaling in Red Bay Labrador," by Jamie O'Leary. (Newfoundland, Canada, Bach Arts English Major, Memorial University of Newfoundland, 1997).

222. Rafferty and Mann, p. 91-92, *Smoking and Culture*.

223. Richard Veit and Charles A. Bello, chapter, "Neat and Artificial Pipes": Base Metal Trade Pipes of the Northeastern Indians. p. 185 (Ch. 7) of *Smoking and Culture; The Archaeology of Tobacco Pipes in Eastern North America*, by Sean Rafferty and Rob Mann.

224. Veit and Bello, *Smoking and Culture*, p. 188.

225. Sean Rafferty and Rob Mann, *Smoking and Culture* (Knoxville, TN: University of Tennessee Press, 2004), p. 194.

226. Douglas Hunter, *God's Mercie* p. 23. He suggests that as the truce with Spain had not been struck until the day after their departure, the crew were looking forward to engaging in piracy with Spanish ships in international waters as a bonus to their pay.

227. A long version of this prayer was published by the Center for Algonquin Culture as a wall hanging. This short excerpt was originally printed as a bookmark. It was created in cooperation with Unquechaug representatives, including Moon Hawk and his family.

228. Douglas Hunter, *God's Mercies*, p. 24.

229. I copied this deed by hand at the New York State Archives documents room in Albany, New York, (file GG6) The text is published in *Indian Deeds*, 1630 to 1748 by George H. Budke, p. 27, however there are three misspellings in his transcriptions of the names.

230. John Heckewelder, Thomas Jefferson, et al. *Early Fragments of Minsi* Delaware (Bristol, Pa.: Evolution Publishing, 2002) p. 12 These words reported by Cornelius Melyn in his testimony of 1659. Elsewhere, on page 60 we find the Manhattan word for friend nitap or nietap. In the same series the book Nanticoke Language uses the word wiit for good, page 24. Though unique, these words are clearly from the area of Manhattan. The words "keene, keene," are more unusual, however. The Unquechaug word bini for thank you seems to come closest. (Jefferson's list, bini, modified and corrected as binay, by several Long Island natives who wish to remain nameless.) The b to k substitution is not unheard of on Long Island.

231. Bolton, *New York City in Indian Possession* (New York, NY: Indian Notes and Monographs, Vol. 2 no 7, 1975) p. 92 (item 74).

232. Etaoquah, Mike Kelley, in correction of *Native New Yorkers* and the manuscript of this book, December, 2008.

233. Erik Baard, journalist and cofounder of New York Navigational Museum, per conversation, December 16, 2008. Some have stated that it was once called "Pawcatuck" and that this term means "Bear River," but that translation makes no sense. Pawkatuck would possibly describe Hell's Gate, "a churning spout of salty water in a channel that ebbs and flows," but that is an interpretive stretch.

234. Nissequogue Marine Biologist Raymundo Rodriguez, conversation June 155, 2008.

235. James Flowers, telephone conversation, Saturday, June 15, 2008.

236. Cornell University study, as conveyed to me by journalist Erik Baard.

237. The Yankee Cookbook, page 308-309.

238. From Bolton's map (inside back cover) in *New York City in Indian Possession* by R.P. Bolton (New York, NY, Museum of the

American Indian, Heye Foundation, 1975) included on Hudson Valley map CAC. 2007.

239. Bergen County Historical Society booklet, photo caption.

240. Per conversation with Courtney Anderson, December 16, 2008.

241. Coogan's Bluff at the mouth of the Harlem River, on the Manhattan side, is the former site of the Polo Grounds. It was at that stadium that Yankee Bobby Thompson hit the home run that felled their rivals, the Dodgers in 1951. This feat became known as "The Shot Heard Round the World."

242. Wampage has been described (at least in fiction) as a tall man, with "red dyed hair that looked like quills on top and a horsetail in the back, and he only wore a deerskin loincloth. His lean, tattooed body glistened with bear grease. Jonathan Kruk, "Anne Hutchinson (1643)" *Many Voices; True Tales from America's Past,* The National Storytelling Association, (Jonesborough, Tennessee, The National Storytelling Press, 1995), p. 5.

243. Bolton,1975 edition, *New York City in Indian Possession,* p36.

244. From conversations with the late Mike DiMico, circa 2003, a Renneiu speaker.

245. p. 16 *History of Westchester County.*

246. Ruttenber, xxx *Indians of Hudson's River,* Eastward of them, in Connecticut were the Sequins.

247. *History of Westchester County,* xxx

248. According to William Ritchie, in *Archaeology of New York State,* the village was in full swing by 1535.. Pins can mean "roots," in Unami, according to *Origins of Place Names in New Jersey,* p. 10.

249. There is a Solomon Pugsley mentioned in *History of Westchester County,* about the time of the Revolution, but his residence was unknown.

250. By coincidence or not, just at the end of the fifth fire of the Seven Fires Prophecies, three 56-year "star cycles" after Hudson's visit.

251. Bolton comments "...along Arthur Kill, or "Col," so often referred to in Dutch records." p. 59. *New York City in Indian Possession.*

252. Douglas Hunter, *God's Mercies: Rivalry, Betrayal and the Dream of Discovery;* (no city, Doubleday Canada, 2007) pp. 32-33

253. In modern Dutch the word for death is spelled "dood," but these letters are not pronounced as the English would.

254. Per conversation with Gerald de Weerdt, December 16, 2008.

255. Edgar Bacon states that it is not known for certain if this John was Henry Hudson's son, but that he had a son by that name, whereas Douglas Hunter, writing 100 years later, in *God's Mercies,* states with authority that John was his middle teenage son. (p.12)

256. Alanson Skinner, "Staten Island," *The Indians of Greater New York and the Lower Hudson Valley,* edited by Clark Wissler. (New York, Order of Trustees, American Museum of Natural History, September, 1609) p. 15. On page 13, he relates descriptions of several burials where the face is facing northwest.

257. The funeral proceedings are as described by Clinton A. Weslager in his book, *The Delaware Indian Westward Migration,* and also as described in *The Lewis Cass Material,* based on a questionnaire of 1821-22, pp. 99-100 of Weslager.

258. A Chippewa tradition (also Algonquins) see the strawberries as a temptation to distract the soul on its journey home, (see: Beverly Cox and Martin Jacobs, *Spirit of the Harvest* (New York: Stewart, Tabori, and Chang, 1991) page 55) but another tradition sees the berries as symbolic of the rewards of a good life, parallel to the "summer land" a popularized by Andrew Jackson Davis, or in the "happy hunting ground." I have combined both here.

Concerning singing like ravens, Alanson Skinner, "Staten Island," *The Indians of Greater New York and the Lower Hudson Valley,* edited by Clark Wissler. (New York, Order of Trustees, American Museum of Natural History, September, 1609) p. 51 "When they die they go to a place where they sing like the ravens; but this singing is entirely different from the singing of angels." Skinner, quoting DeVries, p. 164

259. Bacon p. 145 ... "a very childish proceeding." Bacon then writes, "Up to this time, no attack upon the vessel had been made or attempted. The Indians, who seem to have been impelled mainly by curiosity and a desire to barter, came without evil intentions and went without any difficulty,

even when their companions were detained by the Europeans. But now, having worked themselves to a pitch of suspicion for which their own ill-advised actions had given ample cause, the people of the Half Moon weighed and stood out towards the channel.."

260. Heckewelder 1818, quoted in Helen Hunt Jackson, *A Century of Dishonor* (Boston, Ma.: Roberts Brothers, 1885, reprinted Mineola, NY., Dover Pubs, 2003), p. 32.

261. Read Karen Sivertson's PhD thesis, *Babel on the Hudson,*online.

262. Dr. James Sullivan, ed.; *History of New York State, 1523-1927* (New York, NY: Lewis Historical Publishing Company, Inc., 1927), Volume 1, p. 140.

263. Dr. James Sullivan, ed., *History of New York State,* from T. Rasul Murray.

264. According to Johnson, in his book, *Charting the Sea of Darkness,* the shallows were actually a sand bank on the eastern shore of the Verrazzano Narrows, which is about two miles north of Coney Island, near Fort Hamilton. There is a beach there even today, along the shore parkway. If the narrows had as deep a channel in 1609 as it did in 1778, I find it hard to believe Hudson would have so much trouble finding it.

Chapter Five
People of the River

265. Helen Hunt Jackson, *A Century of Dishonor,* (Boston, Ma.: Roberts Brothers, 1885, reprinted Mineola, NY, Dover Pub. 2003) p. 32.

266. Chalres Goering interview, June 3, 2008

267. Alanson Skinner, "Staten Island," *The Indians of Greater New York and the Lower Hudson,* edited by Clark Wissler, p. 53.

268. Paul A. W. Wallace, *Indian Paths of Pennsylvania,* (Harrisburgh, Pa., Pennsylvania Historical and Museum Commission, 1998) p.21, 98, 99.

269. From Paxtun, the Tulpehoken Trail split, and continued southwest to Raystown via the Raystown Path and also northwest along the Warriors then along the Juniata Path. Wallace, p.77.

270. Answer to General Cass' Questions, p. 130 question #11, "What is the extreme point of longevity which they have ever

reached?" Answer: "Not over one hundred and forty years and that they say was a great many years ago." *The Delaware Indian Westward Migration,* (Wallingford, Pa. Middle Atlantic Press, 1978).

271. These prophecies and the timelines set forth within them are explained in detail in my book *Earth at the Crossroads,* (Woodstock, NY: Resonance Communications, 2005). This work is based in part on *The Mishomis Book,* by Eddie Benton Banaise, 1976. Stephen McFadden and William Commanda have also written about these prophecies, however the greater part of these teachings remain secret.

272. Eddie Benton Banaise, *The Mishomis Book, The Voice of the Ojibway* (Hayward, Wisconsin: Indian Country Communications, 1988), p. 89.

273. Jodi Kantor, "*Nation's Many Faces in Extended First Family*" (New York, NY: New York Times, January 20, 2009), p. 1, 17; Here is an excerpt: "For well over two centuries, the United States has been vastly more diverse than its ruling families. Now the Obama family has flipped that around, with a Technicolor cast that looks almost nothing like their overwhelmingly white, overwhelmingly Protestant predecessors in the role. The family that produced Barack and Michelle Obama is black and white and Asian, Christian, Muslim and Jewish. They speak English; Indonesian; French; Cantonese; German; Hebrew; African languages including Swahili, Luo and Igbo; and even a few phrases of Gullah, the Creole dialect of the South Carolina Lowcountry. Very few are wealthy, and some — like Sarah Obama, the stepgrandmother who only recently got electricity and running water in her metal-roofed shack — are quite poor."

274. C.A. Weslager, *The Delaware Indians, A History,* p. 105.

275. Donald Johnson, *Charting the Sea of Darkness,* p. 119.

276. This is only an esimate, or wild guess, as to the salinity levels in 1609. They are somewhat lower today.

277. Charles Goering mentioned this as a logical possibility. It is hard to think of a better explanation. Wednesday, June 3, 2008.

278. *Smoking and Culture,* Sean Rafferty and Rob Mann, pp. 191-193.

279. *Amerikanuak, Basques in the New World*, Reno, Nevada, University of Nevada Press, 1975, Willaim A. Douglass and Jon Bilbao.p. 55.

280. William Tompkins, *Indian Sign Language*, (Canada., by the author, 1931) republished (Mineola, NY, Dover Publications, Inc, 1969). On page 7, Lewis F. Hadley, a foremost authority on sign language, said in 1885 that there were still 110,000 sign-talking Indians in the United States. The nations he lists as using this same vocabulary are too numerous to mention here. In an interview of January 8, 2009, I asked former Algonquin chief William Commanda, 94 years old, if sign language was used when he was young. He said that when he was ten, sometimes elders would give an entire speech exclusively in sign language, without making a sound. He added that he does not see it being used very often any more.

281. Countless writers have commented that Henry Hudson must have communicated using some type of Native American sign language.

282. Map of "Wappinger Mohegan Indians" by Kurt Griesshaber, 1962, no address. Based on information from Ernest Miller, Clarence Red Bird and Calvin White Eagle.

283. Based on an article in *Maine Fisheries Review*, Clyde MacKenzie, Jr., from website, http://web.ebscohost.com/ehost/detail? vid=378bk=18hid=9&sid=7clb8106

284. Based on an article in *Maine Fisheries Review*, Clyde MacKenzie, Jr. Malpeques, Wellfleets, Cotuits, Narragansetts, New Havens, Saddle-rocks, Blue Points, Shrewsburys, Absecon Salts, Cape May Salts, Maurice Coves, Lynnhavens, Chincoteagues, Assateagues, Roanokes, Tangier Sounds, Apalachicolas, Barataria Bays, and Olympias were some of the other top oystering locations at the turn of the century.

285. Allan Keller, *Life Along the Hudson* (Tarrytown, NY: Sleepy Hollow Restoration, 1976), p. 15.

286. Bacon, *Henry Hudson*, p. 150.

287. Showed to me by David Moody, June 7, 2008, found below Maple Ridge, Ulster Park, NY. The shell of the pot was very thin for its size, and it seemed that the grout helped give it structural strength.

288. David DeVries, *Voyages from Holland to America AD 1632 to 1644* (New York, NY: New York Historical Society, 1857) p. 88. Entry of February 10.

289. Bacon p. 150.

290. Harry Hansen, *North of Manhattan: Persons and Places in Old Westchester* (New York, NY: Hastings House, 1950), p. 2.

291. Harry Hansen, *North of Manhattan*, (New York, Hastings House, 1950), p. 3.

292. R.P. Bolton, *New York City in Indian Possession* (New York, NY: Museum of the American Indian, Heye Foundation, 1975), p. 83.

293. Dr. John P. Hart has published a number of articles about how long ago beans were introduced to the New York area. Though bean remains found at Round Top (west of Binghamton) were originally dated to around AD1100, retesting has established a date of AD 1300 for the introduction of beans to the area. If true (and the evidence is now substantial) this means that the "Three Sisters" of the "Woodland Indians" were not triplets. See "The Age of Common Beans (Phaseolus vulgaris) in the Northeast United States," by John P. Hart and C. Margaret Carry (1999 Society for American Archaeology); http://www. nysm.nysed.gov/staff/details.cfm?staffID=37 Also see "Extending the Phytolith Evidence for Early Maize (Zea mays ssp.mays) and Squash (Cucurbita sp.) in Central New York," by John P. Hart, Hetty Jo Brumbach, and Robert Lusteck (Society for American Archaeology, 2007); In this article it is stated that, "*The results indicate that maize and squash were being used in New York by 2270 B.P. and 2945 B.P., respectively.*"This would place the introduction of maize roughly at about 270BCE and squash at about 945 BCE, although the words "present era" are based on the quirky rules of radiocarbon dating.

294. Will L. Clark, edited by Alvah P. French, *History of Westchester County, Volume One,* (New York, NY, Chicago, Ill.: Lewis Historical Publishing Company, Inc. 1925), p. 13.

295. According to the map by Michael Sullivan Smith, (Saugerties, NY: Hope Farm Press, 2008) the men were now sailing from 86th Street to Hastings on Hudson. (Hastings is the next town north of Yonkers.) Two and

a half leagues would be about six miles, and six plus "four miles" is ten. Most popular writers suggest Hudson arrived at Yonkers on the September 13, and Yonkers is twelve miles north of 96th, even farther north of 86th. Perhaps Juet was using Dutch miles, (three of our U.S. miles) and Hall's Leagues. Or perhaps they really were at Jeffreys' Point/Washington Heights, which is 179th Street. There is a high point of land to the east above Jeffry's Point, and a good place to make harbor. In fact, Edward Hagaman Hall has them stopping at Stryker's Bay, and then later at a point in the river between Inwood Park to the east and Englewood, New Jersey to the west. This makes sense as regards the high point of land.

296. Charles Goering, Vol. 18, no 2, May 2002 *MARC*: "De Nieu Nederlanse Marcurius" newsletter.

297. Harry Hansen, *Persons and Places in Old Westchester* (New York, NY: Hastings House, 1950), p. 3. There is no Algonkian word for fish that sounds like this, but the prefix *nii-* means "trap." (Ojibway) and *nii'ige* means "to set a trap." Hansen writes, "Saw Mill River is falling off the rocky ledge represented today by Warburton Street, tumbling past a group of rocks into what might be today's Main Street and then after executing a half circle to the north, flowing into the Hudson." p. 33.

298. Harry Hansen, *Persons and Places in Old Westchester*, p. 32.

299. Harry Hansen, *Persons and Places in Old Westchester*, p. v.

300. Kevin Wright, map, "Indigenous Place Names in North Eastern New Jersey" 1994. No address.

301. Edgar Bacon, *The Hudson River, From Ocean to Source*, (New York, NY: PG Putnam, and Son, 1907), p. 9.

302. Hansen, Ibid p 25.

303. Hansen, Ibid, page 33.

304. Bolton, *New York City in Indian Possession*, p. 122.

305. Karen Sivertson's doctoral thesis for Duke University, *Babel On The Hudson*, p.61

306. p. 16, *History of Westchester County*.

Chapter Six
People of the Waterfalls

307. Peggy Turco, *Walks and Rambles in Dutchess and Putnam Counties, A Guide to Ecology and History in Eastern Hudson Valley Parks*, (Woodstock, Vt.: Backcountry Publications,1990), p. 198.

308. *Complete Official Program, Ottawa Centenary August 16-21, 1926*, copied from original held by William Commanda, Kanata, Ontario, Canada on May 28, 2008.

309. Robin Hill-Chandler, a Munsee woman by descent and member of the Sand Hill Band of New Jersey, interviewed former chief Dr. Sam Beeler around Christmas of 2008, and sent a letter recounting this information about waterfalls.

310. Robin Hill-Chandler, a Munsee woman by descent and member of the Sand Hill Band of New Jersey, interviewed the man around Christmas of 2008, and sent a letter recounting this information about water falls.

311. One source for knowledge about aboriginal beliefs about sacred waterfalls is Mary Pat Fisher's classic textbook, *Living Religions*, now in its 6th edition, 2009, from Prentice Hall of Saddle River, New Jersey.

312. Robin Hill-Chandler, a Munsee woman by descent and member of the Sand Hill Band of New Jersey, interviewed the man around Christmas of 2008, and sent a letter recounting this information about waterfalls.

313. John William De Forest, *History of the Indians of Connecticut, From the Earliest Known Period to 1850*. Published with the sanction of the Connecticut Historical Society (Hartford, CT: W.J. Hammersley, 1853) p. 397-8, incorrectly quoting from John Warner Barber, History and Antiquity of New England, Worcester, Dorr, Howland & Co. 1841.

314. It is customary not to mix archaeological terms with linguistic terms. William Ritchie was a proponent of this approach, but did not always adhere to it. In *Native New Yorkers*, I stated the obvious and wrote that Ritchie's Clasons Point regions coincide exactly with Renneiu linguistic regions.. William Ritchie, on page 272 of *Archaeology of New York State*, writes, "The Clasons Point phase endured into historic times as proved by the presence of European

trade materials in the superior level of several sites. Historic records connect the cultural range with the territory of sundry members of the western Matouac on Long Island, with Wappinger groups on Manhattan Island, and northward, and perhaps with certain Delaware groups on northern Staten Island. Alanson Skinner assigned, probably correctly, the type of site to the Siwanoy. . . ."

On page 270, Richie quotes Smith to include the region between the Hudson and Housatonic Rivers north to the Hudson Highlands. This list encompasses all of the groups speaking Renneiu at first contact precisely, with no overlaps or omissions. I cannot imagine a scenario in which Clasons Point people were not speaking some form of Renneiu shortly after 1300 CE.

315. *Dutchess County*, (Poughkeepsie, NY: Dutchess County Historical Society, 1937), p. 6.

316. Daniel G. Brinton and James Hammond Trumbull both translated *maugh* as 'large," but this was recently corrected by Etaoquah/Mike Kelley as a superlative, meaning greatest, which makes more sense because *Kawatch* or *Kitche* is large.

317. For example, chief Ankerops original name was Kawach-Hikan, which he translated as "Great Sea." *Native New Yorkers,* (Tulsa, OK: Council Oak Books, revised edition 2007). p. 224.

318. Henry Cassidy, *Catharyna Brett; Protrait of a Colonial Businesswoman* (Poughkeepsie, NY: Dutchess County Historical Society YEARBOOK Volume 77, 1992). (Collections of the DCHS Volume 13), p. 37.

319. Ibid, page 38.

320. Eugene L. Armbruster, *The History of New England and New Netherlands* (New York, G. Quattlander, 1918)

321. *Dutchess County, 1937,* p. 6.

322. Cassidy spells it *Megriskar,* and says that a man named Sakoraghkigh was representing Megrsikar.

323. Mike D'Amico letter of December 7, 2008.

324. Will L. Clark, edited by Alvah P. French, *History of Westchester County, Volume One,* (New York, NY, Chicago, Ill.: Lewis Historical Publishing Company, Inc. 1925), p. 16.

325. *History of Westchester County,* p. 16.

326. *Voyages of David Pietersz DeVries,* p. 89.

327. The haul was on May 9, 2007, and the article dated May 11, 2007; I believe the clipping was from the Middletown Record. A so-called expert, in a letter of criticism to Columbia University Press, of July 1, 2008, concerning this ms, stated that "This is old and obsolete data...In the 1970s....conservationists convinced the court that this area was a major spawning area for striped bass....most biologists consider upriver areas from Norrie Point to Roger's Island as much more important striped bass spawning areas." I feel the 2007 catch helps to vindicate the hard work of the conservationists involved in protecting an excellent area for fishing, which was my original point.

328. Perhaps he was a descendant of Katonah, "Wild Wind," chief of the Kitchewan after whom the Croton River was named. In some spellings he is Kenoten, which is Munsee for Croton, or Kroatan, which is Wappingers for Katonah, which is Munsee. Chronomer may have been a misnomer.

329. Benson J. Lossing, *The Hudson, From the Wilderness to the Sea* (Troy, NY: H.B. Nims and CO. 1866, reprinted, Somersworth, NH: New Hampshire Publishing Co., 1972), p. 196-7.

330. *Voyages of David Pietersz deVreis,* p. 80.

331. Edgar Bacon, *The Hudson River,* p. 10.

332. "Tarwe-town, map of 1781," also see Harold L. Free's map of same period.

333. Will L. Clark, edited by Alvah P. French, *History of Westchester County, Volume One,* (New York, NY, Chicago, Ill.: Lewis Historical Publishing Company, Inc. 1925),p. 11.

334. Ibid p. 11.

335. I mentioned this in *Native New Yorkers,* second edition. The bear petraform was carefully studied and written about by Nick Schoumatoff.

336. Benson J. Lossing, *The Hudson, From The Wilderness to the Sea* (Troy, NY: H.B. Nims and CO. 1866, reprinted, Somersworth, NH: New Hampshire Publishing Co., 1972), pp. 208-9.

337. Reginald Pelham Bolton, *New York City in Indian Possession* (New York, NY, Museum of the American Indian, Heye Foundation, 1920, reprinted 1975) p.56, new edition.

338. E.M. Ruttenber, "The Valley of the Moodna in History," (Newburgh, NY: Historical Society of Newburgh Bay and the Highlands, 1901) p 59, 60. (Before Zuassaick Chapter DAR, March 30, 1901, and included in this Number of the papers of the Historical Society by Request.)

339. David Barkclay, "Balmville, From the First Settlement to 1860;" Historical Papers, No. VIII, (Newburgh, NY: Historical Society of Newburgh Bay and the Highlands, 1901), p 45-46.

340. Ibid p. 22.

341. According to Kurt Griesshaber's map of 1962, Gleneida Lake was also known as "Deep Lake" with a village situated on its western banks. Based on information from Ernest Miller, (E. Wolf Miller) Clarence Red Bird and Calvin White Eagle.

342. *Dutchess County*, p. 71

343. *Dutchess County*, p. 63

344. Scott Horecki, in an interview for "The Hudson Before Henry."

345. Thom Johnson and Barbara H Gottlock, *Bannerman Castle* (Bowie, MD: Heritage Publishing, 2006) p. 9.

346. As in Chief Monolaup ("an Island that has been plowed") translated in *Native New Yorkers*, based on Rich O'Meara's *Lenape Dictionary*.

347. Beulah Timothy, Munsee elder, quoted in *Native New Yorkers*.

348. *Introductory Guide to Micmac Words and Phrases*, p. 2 pronunciation guide, suffixes. Mi'kmaq is closely related to Lenape, both "L" type Algonquian languages.

349. Augustus H. Van Buren, *A History of Ulster County Under the Dominion of the Dutch* (New York, NY: J.C. and A.L. Fawcett, Inc. reprinted Kingston, NY) p. 143, "They were educated far beyond any other people in Europe."

350. Jesse Bruchac, interview, June 27[t], 2009, Saratoga Springs, NY, specifically in reference to Abenaki, however this grammatical rule has a distinctive Algonquin character and seems to have counterparts in other related languages.

351. Mel Johnson interview at George Washington State Historic Site, June, 2008

352. Oral tradition has Awissawa as the third grandson of Towaco, the first head of the Amorgarikakan family in the region; Addy Wright has recorded that Woodbury Creek was originally named after him.

353. Funk and Johnson 1964 incorporating Ritchie's 1958 studies.

354. Peggy Turco, *Walks and Rambles in Dutchess and Putnam Counties, A Guide to Ecology and History in Eastern Hudson Valley Parks*, (Woodstock, VT: Backcountry Publications, 1990), p. 133, writes, "Esopus, originally pronounced either SHO-pusor SO-pus, may be an archaic Munsee form of "creek." Such words include ship-O-shesh, ("little creek"), sip-O-sis, SOP-siw, and w-SO-psiw, the last means, "person from So-pus."...so an Esopus Indian would have simply meant a lowlander or river Indian."

355. *Voyages of David Pietersz DeVries*. Entry for May 27; There is a possibiliiy that by Esoopes he means Kingston, and by creek he means the Rondout, but this is less likely, as he arrives at Catskill the same day. p. 89.

356. Peggy Turco, in her book *Walks and Rambles in Dutchess and Putnam Counties*, writes, "Katzberg is roughly translated as 'the mountains of lynx and bobcat.' Somehow Katzkill, the Dutch name for the stream that flows through the Katzberg, got applied to the entire mountain range. Actually the Catskills are not mountains, in the sense of being shoved up, as were the Hudson highlands. They are stream deposits. When the air is clear, you can see the horizontal stripes on some of the Catskill slopes...." p. 108.

357. Peggy Turco, in *Walks and Rambles in Dutchess and Putnam Counties*, includes a diagram of these mountains as viewed from Clermont. P. 110.

358. *Calendar of State Papers, Col. Series, America and West Indies, 1675-1676*, also Addenda 1574-1675, no.48 quoted in Roy Harvey Pearce, *The Savages of America; A Study of the Indians, and the Idea of Civilization* (Baltimore, MD: Johns Hopkins Press,1953, rev. 1965) p. 6.

359. *The Savages of America*, Pearce, Frontpiece.

360. Charles Goering, Interview at State Archives in Albany, June of 2008.

361. *History of Westchester County*, p. 22.

362. Hall's report has Hudson sailing from Kykiut Hill, which means "a lookout" in Dutch. Johnson writes that the crew is enjoying a "view of Catskill Mountains, a very loving people."

363. *Dutchess County*, p. 15.

Chapter Seven
People of the Upper River

364. Funk and Johnson 1964. Published in *Recent Contributions to Hudson Valley Pre-history*, 1976.

365. Also confirmed by Vernon Benjamin. Funk and Johnston, 1964, published in *Recent Contributions to Hudson Valley Prehistory*, 1976; p. 7. Also called Rocky Point.

366. Per conversation, Marist College, February 21, 2009, in reference to Benjamin Meyer Brink, in "Old Ulster."

367. These important excavations are organized by Chris Lindner, but the account of the "crystal" projectile is provided by Native American author Barbara Three Crow.

368. Per conversation with Vernon Benjamin, Marist College, February 9, 2009.

369. Per conversation with Vernon Benjamin Marist College February 23, 2009.

370. These teachings were preserved by the late Twylah Nitch of the Seneca and passed on to me directly and through Valerie Brandt, her former assistant. I believe these are reflective of wider-spread teachings of the Northeast Woodland peoples, similar to what Hudson might have been told.

371. O'Meara's Dictionary for *pasquaw* and *nach-qua* separately (The town location may be from Parker; See Native New Yorkers xxx)

372. Michael Sullivan Smith also suggests that as 1609 was at the height of a "mini-Ice Age," the ocean levels might have been slightly lower than today. This would make the area around Smith's Landing even shallower than today.

373. Shirley Dunn, *The Mohicans and Their Land 1609-1730* (Fleischmanns, NY: Purple Mountain Press, 1994), p. 25.

374. The Mud Flats are near the mouth of Kinderhook Creek, but the town is far inland.

375. Edmund Bacon, p. 159.

376. According to *History of Westchester County*, Volume One, the entire Mohican territory was called Laaphawachking (p. 14) however, it is a place name near Hunter's Island, Laaphawachking. In Edmund Bacon's book, *The Hudson River, From Ocean to Source*, (New York, GP Putnam & Sons, 1907) p. 9, this name refers only to Westchester County, meaning "Place where beads are strung." *History of Westchester County* also states that Mohican means "Enchanted Wolf," (spelled Mohegan) and that the symbol was a wolf with its paw raised in a threatening manner (p.15). This needs further study.

377. Ruttenber, *Indian Tribes of Hudson's River to 1700, Volume One*, p. 63, quoting *Hubbard's Indian Wars*, pp. 94, 98, 188, Calahan and other sources.

378. Smith positions Hudson at Saugerties in the morning, traveling to Smith's Landing in the evening.

379. John W. Quinney, in *Wisconsin Historical Collections*, 1857-1858, p. 317, also reprinted in Shirley Dunn's *The Mohicans and Their Land, 1609-1730*, p. 13. See also John W. Quinney, Stockbridge Indian Chief, *Celebration of the Fourth of July, 1854* (Madison, Wisconsin, 1859).

380. Shirley Dunn, *The Mohicans and Their Land*, p. 14.

381. Dunn, p. 18, *NYCD, O'Callaghan and others, Documents Relating to the Colonial History of the State of New York* 6:881; NARR, Jameson, *Narratives of New Netherlands, 1609-1664*, p. 293.

382. Donald Johnson, *Charting the Sea of Darkness*, page 121.

383. "The Village of Thirty Centuries," a film by Beaver Creek Pictures, (Frederickton, New Brunswick, Canada: Northwest Passage Communications with the participation of the Red Bank First Nation, 1995.

384. *The Voyages and Explorations of Samuel de Champlain* (1604-1616), 2: 139-140, Champlain. Also cited in *The Mohican World*, Shirley Dunn, p. 17.

385. Evan Pritchard, *Earth at the Crossroads* (Woodstock, NY: Resonance Communications, 2005)

386. Benjamin Bussey Thatcher (1809-1840). I believe this was published in

his book, *Indian Biography*, (1833) p. 194.

387. *History of Westchester County*, p.19.

388. *The Yankee Cookbook*, page 107. It also acknowledges the native origins of the popular New England words sagiminity, samp, hominy, and nokehick which means a meal of parched corn.

389. *The Yankee Cookbook*, "Yankee Succotash Chowder." Mrs. James H. Prince, Auburn, Me., writes, "Boiling the cobs gives an interesting and unusual taste to the dish. The Indians boiled corn cobs with the succotash which they prepared." p. 17.

390. The Yankee Cookbook, page 174.

391. The making of mats by Delaware women was mentioned in Theresa O. Deming's *Indians of the Wigwams: A Story of Indian Life* (Chicago, Ill.: Junior Press Books, Albert Whiteman, 1938), but Bruhns and Stothert, *Women in Ancient America*, seems to agree.

392. Bruhns and Stothert, *Women in Ancient America*, see pages 152-153, 146-147.

393. John A. Strong, *The Algonquian Peoples of Long Island From Earliest Times to 1700* (Interlaken, NY: Empire State Books, Heart of the Lakes Publishing, 1997), p. 86.

394. Per conversation with Marian Lupulescu, New York State Museum.

395. Red ochre was a part of high spiritual ceremony for the ancestors of the Algonkian-speaking people for thousands of years. It is said to "make stronger" that which is painted with it. According to Manitouwiziwak (Algonquian) belief, it embodies the power of the Creator within it. In fact it has been found to have antibiotic properties. The Beothuks painted themselves with it even well into the contact period. When one Beothuk woman was forced to wash it off and live like a European, she died within a short time and it is suspected that her own immune system had adapted to the antibiotic, and could no longer resist infection from new diseases as carried by Europeans. In any case, it was highly sacred material for a burial, and such burial ceremonies were often performed in special places, what we might call "power spots" for lack of a better term.

396. *History of Westchester County*, p. 19.

397. Peggy Turco, *Walks and Rambles in Dutchess and Putnam Counties, A Guide to Ecology and History in Eastern Hudson Valley Parks* (Woodstock, VT: Backcountry Publications, 1990), p. 202.

398. Nancy Polk, "Horticulture: A Mountain Laurel by Any Other Name." *New York Times*, June 3, 2007.

399. Interview with "David," a Sand Hill Band member and elder and medicine man of Cherokee descent, around Christmas of 2008, by Robin Hill-Chandler, a Sand Hill member of Munsee descent.

400. Fred J. Alsop, III, *Birds of the Mid-Atlantic* (Washington, D.C., Smithsonian Handbook, 2002), p. 38.

401. A confirmed source close to former Munseetown Delaware Chief Mark Peters.

402. P. 38 Alsop mentions "Martha." The last known wild specimen of Passenger Pigeon was shot in 1898. (also Alsop) James Fennimore Cooper was the author of mis-named *The Last of the Mohicans*.

403. This can be surmised, as the common folk from around the world eat pigeon eggs. An Asian man shared his pigeon egg lunch with me on a bus while crossing the Malasian jungle northward to Thailand. As the chicken is not an indigenous bird, and raptor eggs were not eaten (at least not by Algonquins) the eggs of pigeons were probably the best available kind in the Hudson Valley in 1609.

404. *Encyclopedia Brittanica*, (New York, London, Chicago: Brittanica, vol 17, 1960 edition) pp. 920-1.

405. Alsop III, p 38.

406. *Encyclopedia Brittanica*, (New York, London, Chicago: Brittanica, 1960), vol 17, p 920-921.

407. *History of Westchester County*, p. 18.

408. *The Sacred, Ways of Knowledge, Sources of Life*, by Peggy V. Beck, Anna Lee Walters, (Tsaile, Arizona, Nia Francisco, Navajo Community College Press, 1996). P. 304-305.

409. From general observation of private feasting ceremonies among the Mi'kmaq.

410. Per telephone conversations with Les Hulcoop and Steven Hancock, Cornell Cooperative Extension, Dutchess and Columbia County offices respectively, on June 17, 2009.

411. Voyages of David Pietersz DeVries, p. 89.

412. Paul R. Huey, *Historical and*

Archeological Resources of Castleton Island State Park...(Peebles Island, Waterford, NY: New York State Office of Parks, Recreation and Historic Preservation Bureau of Historic Sites, May, 1997). p. 7.

413. This is also referred to in *The Mohican World*, Shirley Dunn, p. 16.

414. Huey, op cit, p. 12.

415. Huey, p. 31.

416. Huey, p 44.

417. Huey, p. 50.

418. *English-French, French-English Dictionary*, New York, NY: Barnes and Noble Books, Harper and Row, 1967 w/ Bancroft and Co. (Ltd) England)

419. Per conversation with Monique Renaud, October 11, 2007, however she maintains that it is a rare usage, and that the present tense form Je croisse is theoretical and never used. In addition, the term traverse is more commonly used when water is involved.

420. Oannes Pritzger was told that his first name is a geographical term in the Wabanaki group of dialects meaning "Where the wolf watches beaver," possibly from a high ridge. *Que* is most likely a part of speech (possibly meaning *from*) and the *thaw* ending is highly unusual. The *W* is probably *OO*, the suffix *ayoo* or *oo* indicating "it is." The *th* may be related to a council fire, *ti*, indicating "it is a high ridge from which one looks down onto the proceedings of the council fire at Schodack Island." This is an educated guess.

421. New York State Museum, Albany, NY: "Underneath the City," exhibit, October 11, 2007. One display spelled the name Joan, but this may have been Johan.

422. William Tompkins, *Universal Indian Sign Language of the Plains Indians of North America*, 1931 as republished, 1969, Dover Editions. page 144, "bad."

423. William Tompkins, *Universal Indian Sign Language of the Plains Indians of North America*, 1931 as republished 1969 Dover Editions. "peace."

424. Paul Huey, p. 11.

425. *History of Westchester County*, p. 19.

426. As stated in *History of Westchester County*, p. 19.

427. Interview with William Mameanskumw at the Kumic Center, Hull, Quebec, Canada, May 30, 2008.

428. Wendy Harris, from conversation June 26, 2001.

429. All from *Websters New World Dictionary* (New York, NY: Simon and Schuster, 1982).

430. Per conversation with Gerald de Weerdt, December, 2008)

431. Samuel W. Eager, Esq., *An Outline of the History of Orange County* (Newburgh, NY: T.S. Callahan; [marked S.T. Callahan on published book!) 1846-7) p. 32.

432. *Indian Deeds, 1630 to 1748,* Budke p. 26

433. Dehydrogenase helps break down alcohol, and is more prevalent in men than women and children, but those with type O blood, the ancient blood type most commonly found among Native Americans, may also be deficient in dehydrogenase.

434. John W. DeForest, *History of the Indians of Connecticut,* p. 478-479, quoting from the biography of Jonathan Trumbull.

435. Per discussion at the AMNH on Saturday, January 17, 2009.

436. Per conversation with a source close to Mark Peters, Munseetown Band, December 2008.

437. Paula Underwood, *Three Strands in the Braid,* (in collaboration with Rita Reynolds-Gibbs) (Anselmo, California: A Tribe of Two Press, 1984), p. 44.

438. When a wampum exchange rate was established a few years later, a white wampum bead was worth a "Stuyver" or a Dutch penny, a purple bead was worth three.

439. Although a "platter" was used in Algonquin tobacco ceremonies, the appearance of the "plate of venison" is problematic, in that this is usually associated with Mohawk ceremonies. In that this book focuses on the interplay between The Half Moon and Algonquin Culture, we present, for purposes of reconstruction, a scenario in which Mohicans are borrowing a Mohawk custom to honor Hudson. This would not be unusual. Although enemies with the Mohawk from time to time, the Algonquins had a great respect and admiration for their customs, stories, songs, and rituals, and often adopted them. In *Native New Yorkers*, I recount that Munsee chief Michtag Monolaup, in an English courtroom, gave

what was for all purposes, the Mohawk Condolence Speech, without citing sources.

440. Douglas Hunter, *God's Mercies*, xxx

441. Harry Sweet, *Where Hudson's Voyage Ended, An Inquiry*, 1909. p. 12. Further research is needed to determine that the castle or Indian Fort was already constructed in 1609. I believe it was. Huey and others dispute that such forts were made by the French.

442. New York State History Kiosk, rte 90 East

443. Harry Sweet, *Where Hudson's Voyage Ended*. p. 8.

444. Paul A.W. Wallace: *The White Roots of Peace: The Iroquois Book of Life*. Port Washington, NY: I.J. Friedman, 1968 (1946).

445. Theodore G. Corbett, *A Clash of Cultures on the Warpath of Nations, The Colonial Wars in the Hudson-Champlain Valley* (Fleishmanns, New York: Purple Mountain Press, 2002). p. 90.

Chapter Eight
The Return Trip

446. Bacon quotes a Dr. Asher, whose word he trusts. Asher says that "Hudson… always speaks kindly of the North American Indians." *Henry Hudson*, p. 147. We ourselves see that Juet rarely speaks of them kindly.

447. Marcus Brutus was the main character in "Julius Ceasar," written by Shakespeare nine years previous.

448. See *Native American Stories of the Sacred*, by Evan Pritchard, published by Skylight Paths Press, Woodstock, VT 2005.

449. This map appears as figure 9 in Paul R. Huey's essential work, *Historical and Archeological Resources of Castleton Island State Park*…(Peebles Island, Waterford, NY: New York State Office of Parks, Recreation and Historic Preservation Bureau of Historic Sites, May, 1997). Detail from the map of the Hudson River by William F. Link, published in 1878 (Link 1878).

450. Michael Sullivan Smith describes this entry as that of a journey from Hudson, NY to Saugerties, NY. Juet's comment "…and great stores of slate.." in the upcoming diary entry gives Smith's opinion considerable weight. However, there are several problems as mentioned.

451. Conversation with Marjan Lupulescu, February 4, 2009, Albany, New York, speaking on behalf of Dr. Kelly.

452. Shirley Dunn, *The Mohican World*, p. 16, quoting a New England minister. She quotes Daniel Denton as stating that they planted corn mainly at principle villages. According to fine historian Vernon Benjamin, a kernel of corn was found near the Roelof Jansen Kill dated to about AD 800, per conversation of February 19, 2009. See article by John P. Hart, Hetty Jo Brumbach, and Robert Lusteck, 2007. Maize was present in New York state about 270 BCE, but the Jansen Kill is exactly where Hudson would have seen it from the Half Moon.

453. DeVries, *Voyages of David Pietersz*, p. 89, entry for [April] 27.

454. Max Schrabish, "Rock Shelters," *The Indians of Greater New York and the Lower Hudson*, edited by Clark Wissler, anthropological Papers, Volume III, (New York, NY, American Museum of Natural History, Order of the Trustees, September, 1909, reprinted, AMS Press, 1975).

455. This is mentioned in *Native New Yorkers* as well.

456. The Smithsonian; The National Museum of Natural History Research Training Program website, 2006.

457. The Discovery Channel's program, "The Tyrolean Ice Man, Mummy from the Ice Age," 2000, and from the Smithsonian's National Museum of Natural History exhibit, 2006.

458. One can, for a much lower price, simply buy Vital Yew tea made from the Pacific Yew needles for about $11.50 a bottle. Charles L. Bolsinger and Annabelle E. Jaramillo, from their scholarly webpage, "The Pacific Yew." http://www.na.fs.fed.us/spfo/pubs/silvics_manual/volume_1/taxus/brevifolia.htm.

459. www.naturalremedies.com website; Readers are advised not to attempt to harvest their own yew tea. Stripping the bark is bad for this endangered tree, and the quantities of bark one would have to strip and boil from the eastern yew would contain proportionally higher quantities of toxins such as alkalins. However, having said that, the Munsee would burn the stump of the hemlock, a tree closely related to this

shrub, inside the meeting lodge until the smoke filled the lodge. When no one could see, the smoke was allowed to dissipate. When it was gone, the lodge was purified, and the meeting could commence. This from a confirmed Munsee source close to former Munseetown Chief Mark Peters. One wonders if the smoke from the bark of the stump would have anti-cancer and other healing qualities for the men just as the yew has for the women. Soaking, boiling, and burning are the three main ways that herbs become medicine for native peoples.

460. *Plantes Sauvages Comestibles, Guide D'identification Fleurbec* ; (Saint-Henri-de-Lévis, Quebec, Groupe Fleurbec, 1981) p. 33. (Fleurbec Auteur et Éditeur, National Library of Quebec. Translated by Monique Renaud.

461. If the place of the loving people were at Catskill then they are at Hudson.

462. Judging by the replica of the ship created by the New Netherland Museum, and comparing that to lunar maps for 1609, www.paulcarlisle.net.

463. City of Cohoes Hudson-Fulton Celebration, October 10 and 11, 1909; *Where Hudson's Voyage Ended, an Inquiry; Cohoes and the Origin of the Name* by Harry Montford Sweet, (Albany, New York: J.B. Lyon Company, 1909), p. 3. His discussions of the origins of the name Cohoes(p. 24-25) are lengthy and inconclusive. It is probably a mixture of Mohawk and Mohican. I feel it may be in reference to the white pine at Cohoes Falls in the story of the Peacemaker.

464. At DEC's *Hudson River Almanac*, page www.dec.ny.gov/lands/HudsonRiverAlmanac 26146.html, dated 3/24/06, Rich Guthrie comments on observing gulls and mergansers picking up young channel catfish and eating them near Catskill Point.

465. Michael Sullivan Smith writes "Saugerties to Esopus." Edward Hagaman Hall has the ship in the river between Turkey Point to the west and Tivoli Bay to the east. Johnson has Hudson in the vicinity of Red Hook.

466. It is true that the Sepasco Trail, now 308 went right to the Hudson shore, near where they must have fished, although there is now a cliff there. There is a marker at the Beekman Inn at the corner of 308 and Route 9 affixed to a boulder, which states,

"This site marks the crossing of the King's Highway and the Sepasco Indian Trail, later named the Ulster and Salisbury Turnpike, over which travelled the Connecticut pioneers to their new houses in western New York. 1922." If these settlers were headed towards western New York, they clearly crossed the Hudson at this point.

467. One of the first publications of the story was in the *New York Herald Tribune*, Sunday, February 9, 1896, and the name was spelled Van Horne. In that version of the story, his Wappingers name was White Feather. Turco spells it Van Horen.

468. Peggy Turco, *Walks and Rambles in Dutchess and Putnam Counties*, p. 182-183.

469. Ibid, p. 183.

470. www.Paulcarlisle.net

471. Peggy Turco, *Walks and Rambles in Dutchess and Putnam Counties, A Guide to Ecology and History in Eastern Hudson Valley Parks* (Woodstock, VT: Backcountry Publications, 1990), p. 132. We find a map showing the location of Cave Point at the foot of Esopus Meadows across from Vanderburgh Cove which is where Landsman's Kill empties into the Hudson.

472. Per conversation Courtney Anderson, December 16, 2008.

473. Per conversation Courtney Anderson December 16, 2008.

474. Funk, 1976 (1441-1445) Quoted in *Hudson Valley Regional Review*, (March 1992, Vol 9, no. 1).

475. Adapted from *Indians of the Lower Hudson Region; The Munsee*, by Julian Harris Salomon (NY: Rockland County Historical Society, 1982)p. 83.

476. *Dutchess County, American Guide Series* (Philadelphia, Pa.: The William Penn Association of Philadelphia, MCMXXXVII.1937), Frontpage. Sponsored by the Women's City and County Club of Dutchess County, NY .

477. Benton J. Lossing, *The Hudson, From the Wilderness to the Sea*, (Troy, NY: H.B.Nims, and Co, 1866, reprinted Somersworth, NH: New Hampshire Publishing, 1972), pp. 187-188.

478. Ruttenber, *Indian Tribes of Hudson's River to 1700*, p 84.

479. The term Mattawan is the proper name for the Wappingers between the

Mattawan (Fishkill) Creek and the Mahwenawasick (Wappingers) Creek to the north. This was confirmed by Lorraine Palmer MacAulay and members of the Beacon Historical Society, the Madam Brett Homestead and others in December, 2005. The Indians of the Long Reach (more closely associated with the Mohicans at contact) and the Mattawan were the northern-most nations of the Wappinger Confederacy.

480. The source, *Dutchess County* (p. 31) is unclear. It says this European-run ferry ran from Barnegat, Camelot station, and Milton.

481. Lossing, page 188.

482. *Dutchess County*, p. 14.

483. Most of Andrew Jackson Davis' books are still published by Kessinger Publishing, a UK company, found at www.kessinger. net. My summary biography is based on reading his autobiographies, in which there are many references to things "Indian."

484. Johannes DeLaet, *History of the New World*, (Leiden, The Netherlands: Bonaventure and Abraham Elseviers, 1625).

485. Interview with Courtney Anderson, December 22, 2008, Jacob Javits Center, New York, NY.

486. Interview with Courtney Anderson, December 22, 2008.

487. Putnam County Historical Society archives, news clippings, volume C, also volume F. p. 45 etc.

488. Benton J. Lossing, *The Hudson, From the Wilderness to the Sea*, p. 244.

489. *Dutchess County*, p.63; map, info from K. Hitt, Fishkill Historian.

490. Henry Cassidy, *Catharyna Brett; Protrait of a Colonial Businesswoman* (Poughkeepsie, NY: Dutchess County Historical Society YEARBOOK Volume 77, 1992). (Collections of the DCHS Volume 13) p. iii.

491. *Dutchess County*, p. 141.

492. *Catharyna Brett*, p. 73.

493. *Catharyna Brett*, p. 75.

494. *Catharyna Brett*, p. 36

495. Thomas Dongan document, transcribed Feb. 2004 by Lorraine Palmer MacAulay, from the original document owned by the Melzingah Chapter DAR, located at the Madam Brett homestead, Beacon, NY.

496. *Dutchess County*, p. 9.

497. Ibid.

498. Samuel W. Eager, Esq., *An Outline of the History of Orange County* (Newburgh, NY: S.T. [T.S. on published book!] Callahan; 1846-7) p. 619.

499. Charles E. Stickney, *A History of the Minisink Region...*(Middletown, NY: Coe Finch and I.F. Guiwits, 1867; reprinted Bowie, MD: Heritage Books, 1995), p. 18-19 (Ch. 2).

500. Funk and Johnson item 9, p. 10.

501. Arthur G. Adams, *The Hudson River Guide Book*, (New York, NY: Fordham University Press, 1996), p. 154.

502. Manna Jo Green, Clarkstown Town Hall Meeting, Thursday, April 30, 2009. See also http.www.radiation.org/spotlight/071112_IndianPont.html.

503. *The Hudson River Guide Book*, Arthur G. Adams, p. 156.

504. Many New Yorkers today are disgruntled with Indian Point Power Plant at or near this same location, and have staged many nonviolent protests against its unsafe practices. It is widely believed that old pipes are dissolving, releasing radioactive fluid into the Hudson River. The *Journal News* reported, on September 7, 2007, "Workers have discovered a pinhole sized leak in a conduit used to transfer spent fuel for the reactor to the containment pool at Indian Point 2." The unit was not shut down but switched to half power. (Brian Howard, *The Journal News*, September 7, 2007, Buchanan, NY: "Leak found in pipe at Indian Point.")

505. Many readers, upon reaching this point in the narrative, exclaim, "What was a cook doing with a sword?" Perhaps it was provided by Juet.

506. Michael Sullivan Smith correctly charts their course from Cornwall to Croton on Hudson, NY. This seems to be the case, but Smith and a majority of writers agree that the battle of the bandolier was at Indian Point.

507. Native Americans had already experienced the power of Spanish gunpowder on what is now United States soil, at St. Augustine, (Florida) and elsewhere.

508. This interpretation is from Kevin Wright's map. I believe that *quash* meant swift, referring to the creek

that descends to the lake there.

509. This is from Kevin Wright's map, but I have often heard it is from the Unami tappaan, for "a cold, dry place." (Russell)

510. Kevin Wright feels these are both derived from *schejawonge,* which he translates as "the side of a hill," but this seems to be Iroquoian speech.

511. Kevin Wright's map, *Uteneyik* means "villages." (similar to the suffix *–aten,* as used in Manahattan) The Dutch changed this to Ten Eck, after the famous family of settlers. The English then changed it to Teaneck.

512. Kevin Wright's map.

513. Kevin Wright's map, Also *Aquepuch.* Possibly from *wipochk,* a bushy place, a brush meadow. Other possible derivations listed do not resemble the original; *ukque-peck,* at the head of the bay or water; Now Overpeck Creek and Meadows.

514. Traditionally *Espan achtenne,* raccoon hill, Now North Bergen. *Espan* may literally mean "shoreside wanderer." Another word for raccoon means "He has half sized hands." The word for squirrel in Munsee, saqualindjaio, means "he has sticky hands."

515. From Kevin Wright's map. He feels the word *Weehawken* is derived from *weeqsha-achtenne,* a rocky point at the edge of a mountain. However, *Weehague* means "shellfish."

516. Kevin Wright's map, copyright 1994, available from the Bergen County Historical Society.

517. Kevin Wright translates *Sanhikan* as "flint striker," "fire maker." The Unami sources I've seen indicate they were not using flint, but used a bow drill to make fire, and that this is what the term referred to. He places them in a large area between Newark Bay and the Falls of the Delaware at Trenton. The early Dutch maps show them from the coast of the mainland on both sides of the Raritan, reaching far into the west, but Trenton was Munsee, at least at the time of Chief Harris, Teedyuskung's father, in the late 1600s. The Sanghigans were not Munsee.

518. Kevin Wright copyright 1994, available from the Bergen County Historical Society.

519. Kevin Wright's map. He says the term refers to people related to the Minisinks (Munsee) and Tappaans both,

who lived on Manhattan Island, but also at Bergen Neck, which is not an island.

520. Block's map of 1614 does not include these two "Manahattans," but Blaeu's famous map of 1635 does, and it is shown in Kevin Wright's map as well.

521. From Kevin Wright's map, from *Hopoakan echapink.*

522. According to Kevin Wright, the term derived from *awrasse-hannock.* The presence of R indicates a later influence, perhaps from the Matouac of Long Island.

523. According to Kevin Wright, from *Schahamuis,* crabs or crawfish. This refers to Meadow Creek, between Paulus Hook and Bergen, aka Jersey City Heights.

524. According to Kevin Wright, this is from *Pemapuchk,* rocks, part of Bayonne, New Jersey. Pema more often refers to turning aside or around.

525. Acording to Wright's map, from *Minihacking,* corn land. Near Constable's Hook.

526. From Wright's map, on the point of land, referring to a meadowed point that abutted the Hudson at Bayonne. Probably Nyacksink misspelled.

527. According to Wright's map, from *Pemapeek,* a body of water with no current. Secaucus, New Jersey.

528. According to Wright's map, *Sikakes* (*Secaucus*) derives from *assiskuju,* marshy ground. I believe that Secaucus comes from the same Algonquian root as "saco" as does the village of the same name in Secaucus, Massachusetts, and Saco, Maine, and other places, a spit of land where water comes out.

529. *The Mishomis Book,* by Eddie Benton Banaise, as quoted in *Earth At the Crossroads.*

530. Eddie Benton Banaise, *The Mishomis Book,* page 46, 47.

531. *New Jersey as a Colony and as a State, One of the Original Thirteen,* by Francis Bazley Lee, Associate Board of Editors William S. Stryker, LL.D.: William Nelson, A.M., Garret D. W. Vroom: Ernest C. Richardson, PH. D.; Volume One; (NY: The Publishing Society of New Jersey, New York, MDCCCCII, 1902, transcribed by Fred Kunchick, accessed via http://www.usgennet.org/usa/nj/state1/new_netherland. htm.

532. Daniel Atchinson, Lenape Trailside Museum, per phone

conversation January 9, 2009.

533. Per phone interview with Trao Ietaka, January 16, 2009.

534. A Munsee Delaware source close to former Munseetown Chief Mark Peters.

535. Daniel Atchison at the Lenape Trailside Museum spoke of the curative properties of maple syrup, in a more concentrated form, but the sugar becomes depleted in nutrients by cooking. Pace University workshop, March 26, 2008. In fact, 60 ml of Sleepy Mountain Maple syrup (a randomly selected brand from New Hampshire) contains 150 mg of potassium, and is 8% iron and 8% calcium.

According to Taro Ietaka, of Cranberry Lake Preserve in Westchester, NY, the maples did not compete well with old growth trees. They are highly flammable and would not survive slash and burn techniques of the Lenape as they created both farm land and "deer parks." During colonial times, colonists would have encouraged the growth of oak and chestnut which are good trees for lumber, and discouraged the maple which is poor lumber. The red maple is also called "swamp maple," as it was then relegated to marshy areas where oak and chestnut do not reproduce.

536. ICE (Indigenous Conference on the Environment), Ottawa, Ontario, Canada, January 3, 2007, panel.

537. Per conversation with Courtney Anderson, December 16, 2008.

538. Bacon, *Henry Hudson*, 133-137. He goes on to quote the Heckwelder version of the story in total, pp 138 -141, the best-known of all the versions.

539. There was no Harlem Channel until 1900, and no way to exit to the ocean except through the Verrazzano Narrows or through the Kill Van Kull and then the Arthur Kill thereafter. I believe they chose the western route, and nearly courted disaster. They had already passed through the Verrazzano Narrows and knew that it was very shallow in places.

540. See *Native New Yorkers*, appendix page 356. The translation is by Susan Tarrow and published in the 1970 Morgan Library edition of Lawrence Wroth's *The Voyages of Giovanni da Verrazzano 1524-1528*.

541. Douglas Hunter, *God's*

Mercies, p. 25-26.

542. Alanson Skinner, "Staten Island," 1909, p. 36-37.

543. Ibid, p. 37.

544. Douglas Hunter, *God's Mercies*, p. 25-26.

545. Ibid p. 26

546. Ibid.

547. Ibid.

548. Ibid p. 31-32, van Meteren's words.

549. 1609-1909, The Dutch in New Nethelands and the United States: The Netherlands Chamber of Commerce in America, 1909.

550. *Encylclopedia Brittanica,* "Dutch East India Company," vol. 17

551. Op Cit, *God's Mercies,* page 33-34.

552. Edgar Bacon, *Henry Hudson His Times and His Voyages*, p. 186.

553. Edgar Bacon, p. 201. This same Greene had watched over Hudson for his safety the night before, so Juet here is accusing an innocent man.

554. The best known of the East Main Cree villages is the Mistassini, but there are others. See *No Word For Time* for a brief listing.

555. September 12 was not only Hudson's but Demanon's birthday. September 11 is the last day of the Taino calendar.

Adams, Arthur G. *The Hudson River Guide Book*. New York: Fordham University Press, 1996.

Allaby, Michael. *A Dictionary of Zoology*. London: Oxford University Press, 1999.

Alsop, Fred J. III. *Birds of the Mid-Atlantic*. Washington, D.C.: Smithsonian Handbook, 2002.

Anderson, E.N. Jr,. "Sacred Fish." *Man* (magazine). Royal Anthropological Institute of Great Britain and Ireland, 1969.

Armbruster, Eugene L. *The History of New England and New Netherlands*. New York: G. Quattlander, 1918.

Atchinson, Daniel. Lenape Trailside Museum.

Bacon, Edgar Mayhew. *Henry Hudson His Times and His Voyages*. New York, NY: G.P. Putnam and Sons, Knickerbocker Press, 1907; reprinted Kessinger Publishers, London, UK, 2004.

Bacon, Edgar. *The Hudson River, From Ocean to Source*. New York: G.P. Putnam, and Son, 1907.

Banaise, Eddie Benton. *The Mishomis Book, The Voice of the Ojibway*. Minneapolis: Little Red Schoolhouse, 1976. Reprinted, Hayward, Wisconsin: Indian Country Communications, 1988.

Barkclay, David. "Balmville, From the First Settlement to 1860." Historical Papers, No. VIII, Newburgh, NY: Historical Society of Newburgh Bay and the Highlands, 1901.

Beach, Lewis. "Cornwall." Newburgh, NY: E.M. Ruttenber and Son, Printers, 1873.

Beck, Peggy V., Anna Lee Walters.*The Sacred, Ways of Knowledge, Sources of Life*. Tsaile, Arizona: Navajo Community College Press, 1977, 1996.

Bercht, Fatima. *Taino Pre-Columbian Art and Culture from the Caribbean*, El Barrio/ Havana: 1997.

Douglass, William A. and Jon Bilbao. *Amerikanuak*. Reno, Nevada: University of Nevada Press, 1975.

Bergen County Historical Society booklet.

Berrin, Katherine with the Larco Museum. *The Spirit of Ancient Peru: Treasures from the Museo Arquelogicao Rafael Larco Herrera*. New York: Thames and Hudson, 1997.

Bierhorst, John. *Mythology of the Lenape*. Tucson, Az.: University of Arizona Press, 1995.

Bockée Flint, Martha. *Early Long Island, A Colonial Study*. New York: G.P. Putnam's Sons, 1896.

Bolsinger, Charles L. and Annabelle E. Jaramillo. "The Pacific Yew."

Bolton, Reginald Pelham. *New York City in Indian Possession*. New York: Museum of the American Indian, Heye Foundation; Indian Notes and Monographs, Vol. 2 no. 7, 1920, reprinted 1975.

Boyer. *The Annals of Queen Anne's Reign* for 1710.

Brink, Benjamin Meyer. "Olde Ulster" Magazine (1905-1914).

Brink, Benjamin Meyer. *The Early History of Saugerties, 1660-1825*. Kingston, NY: R.W. Anderson and Son, 1902.

Brinton, Daniel G. *The Lenape and Their Legends*. Philadelphia: 1885. Reprinted Lewisburg, Pa.: Wennawoods Publishers, 1999.

Brinton, Daniel G. *The Myths of the New World: A Treatise on the Symbolism and Mythology of the Red Race of America*. Boston: Longwood Publishing, 1879.

Bruhns, Karen Olsen and Karen E. Stothert. *Women in Ancient America*. Norman, Oklahoma: University of Oklahoma Press, 1999.

Budke, George H. ed. *Indian Deeds 1630 to 1748*, BCE – 88 of the Budke Collection, reprinted New York Public Library, Manuscripts and Archives Division, Fifth Avenue and 42nd Street, New York: 10018; reprinted by Library Association of Rockland County, 1975.

Calendar of State Papers, Col. Series, America and West Indies, 1675-1676. Also Addenda

1574-1675, no.48 quoted in Roy Harvey Pearce. *The Savages of America; A Study of the Indians, and the Idea of Civilization.*

Calloway, Colin G. *One Vast Winter Count, The Native American West Before Lewis and Clark.* Omaha: University of Nebraska Press, 2006.

Cassidy, Henry. *Catharyna Brett; Portrait of a Colonial Businesswoman.* Poughkeepsie, NY: Dutchess County Historical Society Yearbook. Volume 77, 1992. Collections of the DCHS, Volume 13.

Chadwick, Ian. *Legends and Oral Histories.*

Champlain, Samuel de. *Voyages and Explorations of Samuel de Champlain* (1604-1616). 2: 139-140.

Chan, Vera H.C. "Best Beware Thy Stingray." Yahoo Buzz, February 25, 2009. http://buzz.yahoo.com/buzzlog/92308/?fp=1.

Clark, Will L. edited by Alvah P. French. *History of Westchester County, Volume One.* New York, Chicago: Lewis Historical Publishing Company, Inc. 1925.

Cohen, Kenneth. *Honoring The Medicine.* New York: Ballantine, 2002.

Commanda, William. *United Nations Statement, November 22nd, 1993.*

Commanda, William with Romola Trebilcock. www.circleofallnations.ca.

Commanda, William with Romola Trebilcock. *Learning From a Kindergarden Dropout.*

Corbett, Theodore G. *A Clash of Cultures on the Warpath of Nations, The Colonial Wars in the Hudson-Champlain Valley.* Fleishmanns, New York: Purple Mountain Press, 2002.

Cox, Beverly and Martin Jacobs. *Spirit of the Harvest.* New York: Stewart, Tabori, and Chang, Publishers, 1991.

Cross, Wilbur L. "Foretaste," a foreword to Imogene Walcott's *The Yankee Cookbook.* Boston:Coward-McCann, Inc., 1938.

Cunningham, John T. *Juet's Journal, The Voyage of the Half Moon from 4 April to 7 November 1609, Introduction by John Cunningham.* Newark: New Jersey Historical Society, 1959.

Dean, Nora Thompson/Touching Leaves. *Place Names in New Jersey.*

De Forest, John William. *History of the Indians of Connecticut, From the Earliest Known Period to 1850.* Hartford: Connecticut Historical Society, W.J. Hammersley, 1853.

DeLaet, Johannes. "Sanhikan" list of 1633. Bristol, Pa.: Evolution Publishing. 2006, 2nd ed. From *A Vocabulary of New Jersey Delaware,* James Madison (papers).

Deming, Theresa O. *Indians of the Wigwams: A Story of Indian Life.* Chicago: Junior Press Books, Albert Whiteman, Publisher, 1938.

Desmarquets. *Memoires pour server a l'histoire de Dieppe.* Paris: 1785. i 100, as noted in Fiske, *The Dutch and the Quaker Colonies in America,* New York: Houghton Mifflin Co.,1899, 1927.

DeVries, David. *Voyages from Holland to America AD, 1632 to 1644.* New York: New York Historical Society, 1857.

Discovery Channel. "The Tyrolean Ice Man, Mummy from the Ice Age," 2000.

Douglass, William A. and Jon Bilbao. *Amerikanuak, Basques in the New World.* Reno, Nevada: University of Nevada Press, 1975.

Dunn, Shirley. *The Mohicans and Their Land 1609-1730.* Fleischmanns, NY: Purple Mountain Press, 1994.

Dutchess County Historical Society. *Dutchess County, Poughkeepsie, NY: 1937. American Guide Series* Philadelphia: The William Penn Association of Philadelphia, MCMXXXVII.1937. Sponsored by the Women's City and County Club of Dutchess County, NY.

Eager, Samuel W. Esq. *An Outline of the History of Orange County.* Newburgh, NY: T.S. Callahan; [marked S.T. Callahan on published book) 1846-7.

Encyclopedia Brittanica, New York, London, Chicago: Brittanica, 1960.

English-French, French-English Dictionary. New York: Barnes and Noble Books, Harper and Row, 1967. w/Bancroft and Co. (Ltd) England.

Etnoyer, Peter. "Deep Sea News." July 28, 2008.

Eusebii chronicon. Paris: 1512. Folio 172, quoted on page 59 of Fiske, *The Dutch and* the *Quaker Colonies in America.*

Murray, William Vans, Daniel G. Brinton. Nanticoke Language, Bristol, Pa.: Evolution Press, 2004/2005.

Fiske, John *The Dutch and the Quaker Colonies in America,* Vol. 1, New York: Houghton Mifflin Co. 1899, 1927, renewed by Ethel F. Fisk.

Fisher, Mary Pat *Living Religions.* 6th edition, Saddle River, N.J.: Prentice Hall, 2009.

Fitch, John G., Esquire of Montiville, letter, dated the sixth of November, 1849. Biography of Jonathan Trumbull. Quoted in DeForest, John W. *History of the Indians of Connecticut.*

Funk, Bob. *Tivoli Bays as a Middle-Scale Setting for Cultural Ecological Research;* Anthropological Survey, New York State Museum, Albany, NY, 1976. Quoted in *Hudson Valley Regional Review,* March 1992, Vol 9, no. 1.

Funk, Robert E. and Charles F. Hayes III, Ed. *Current Perspectives in Northeastern Archeology; Essays in Honor of William A. Ritchie,* Edited by Research and Transactions of the New York State Archeological Association, Volume 17, No. 1, 1977.

Funk, Robert and Johnson, Melvin 1964. Published in *Recent Contributions to Hudson Valley Pre-history,* 1976.

Goering, Charles Vol. 18, no 2, May 2002 MARC: "De Nieu Nederlanse Marcurius" newsletter.

Hansen, Harry *Persons and Places in Old Westchester* New York: Hastings House, 1950.

Groupe Fleurbec, *Plantes Sauvages Comestibles, Guide D'identification Fleurbec* Saint-Henri-de-Lévis, Quebec, Groupe Fleurbec, 1981. (Fleurbec Auteur et Éditeur, National Library of Quebec.

Hansen, Harry. *North of Manhattan: Persons and Places in Old Westchester* New York: Hastings House, 1950.

Hart, John P. and C. Margaret Carry. "The Age of Common Beans (Phaseolus vulgaris) in the Northeast United States," (1999 Society for American Archaeology); http://www.nysm.nysed.gov/staff/details. cfm?staffID=37.

Hart, John P. and Hetty Jo Brumbach, and Robert Lusteck. "Extending the Phytolith Evidence for Early Maize (Zea mays ssp. mays) and Squash (Cucurbita sp.) in Central New York," Society for American Archaeology, 2007.

Heckewelder, John; Thomas Jefferson, et al. *Early Fragments of Minsi Delaware.* Bristol, Pa.: Evolution Publishing, 2002.

Heckewelder, John. *Account of the History, Manners and customs of the Indian Nation* 1820, pub. 1876, reprinted, New York: Arno Press, 1971.

Hill-Chandler, Robin.

History of Orange County. Goshen, N.Y.: Orange County Genealogical Society, 1847.

Howard, Brian. "Leak found in pipe at Indian Point." Buchanan, NY. *The Journal News,* September 7, 2007.

Hubbard, William. *The History of the Indian Wars in New England.* 2 volumes. Boston: Samuel Drake, 1845.

Huey, Paul R. *Historical and Archeological Resources of Castleton Island State Park* Peebles Island, Waterford, NY: New York State Office of Parks, Recreation and Historic Preservation Bureau of Historic Sites, May, 1997.

Hunter, Douglas. *God's Mercies, Rivalry, Betrayal and the Dream of Discovery;* Doubleday Canada, a division of Random House of Canada, Ltd. 2007.

Irving, Washington. *Knickerbocker's History of New York,* New York, NY: Capricorn Books, 1965.

Jackson, Helen Hunt. *A Century of Dishonor.* Boston: Roberts Brothers, 1885. Reprinted, Mineola, NY: Dover Pubs, 2003.

Jameson, J.F., *Narratives of New Netherlands, 1609-1664.*New York: Charles Scribner's Sons, 1909.

Johnson, Donald. *Charting the Sea of Darkness.* Camden, Maine: International Marine, 1993.

Johnson, Thom and Barbara H Gottlock. *Bannerman Castle.* Bowie, MD: Heritage Publishing, 2006.

Journal of the Museum of New Mexico website *El Palacio: Quarterly Journal of the Museum of*

New Mexico, Vol. 85, No. 2, Summer 1979.

Kantor, Jodi "Nation's Many Faces in Extended First Family," New York, NY: *New York Times*, January 20, 2009.

Keller, Allan *Life Along the Hudson*, Tarrytown, NY: Sleepy Hollow Restoration, 1976.

Kessinger Publications www.kessinger.net.

Kraft, Herbert. *The Lenape: Archaeology, History, and Ethnography*. Newark, NJ: New Jersey Historical Society, 1986.

Kruk, Jonathan. "Anne Hutchinson (1643)" *Many Voices; True Tales from America's Past*, The National Storytelling Association, Jonesborough, Tennessee: The National Storytelling Press, 1995.

Lee, Francis Bazley. *New Jersey as a Colony and as a State, One of the Original Thirteen.* Associate Board of Editors William S. Stryker, LL.D.: William Nelson, A.M., Garret D. W. Vroom: Ernest C. Richardson, Ph.D.; Volume One; New York: The Publishing Society of New Jersey, New York, MDCCCCII, 1902, transcribed by Fred Kunchick, accessed via http://www.usgennet.org/usa/nj/state1/new_netherland.htm.

Lossing, Benson J. *The Hudson, From the Wilderness to the Sea*. Troy, NY: H.B. Nims and CO. 1866. Reprinted, Somersworth, NH: New Hampshire Publishing Co., 1972.

Lupulescu, Marian New York State Museum.

MacAulay, Lorraine Palmer. Beacon Historical Society; Madam Brett Homestead/Museum Melzingah Chapter DAR, Beacon, NY.

MacKenzie, Clyde, Jr., *Maine Fisheries Review*, from website, http://web.ebscohost.com/ehost/detail?vid=378bk=18hid=9&sid=7cl b8106.

Mameanskumw, William, interview with author, May, 2008.

Mann, Charles C. *1491: New Revelations of the Americas Before Columbus*. New York: Vintage Books, 2006.

Martin, Paul S. with George I. Quimby, Donald Collier. *Indians Before Columbus, Twenty Thousand Years of North American History Revealed by Archaeology*. Chicago: The University of Chicago Press.

McFadden, Steve. *The Little Book of Native American Wisdom*. Rockport, Massachussetts: Element Books, 1994.

Miller, Pauline S. "A New Discovery: The 1614/1616 Map of New Jersey by Surveyor Hendricks." Cornelius Toms River, NJ: Ocean County Cultural and Heritage Commission, (Fall, 1988): Vol. 10 no 3.

Miller, Pauline S. *Ocean County, Four Centuries in the Making*. Ocean County Historical Society, Headquarters, Hadley Avenue, Tom's River, NJ. 2008.

Munsee Nation, letter of 1849 to President Zachary Taylor.

Murphy, Henry C. *Henry Hudson in Holland*. New York: Burt Franklin,1972.

Navarrete "The Basque Fishery."

Norwood, Joseph White. *The Tammany Legend*. Boston: Meador Publishing Company, 1938.

O'Callaghan and others, Documents Relating to the Colonial History of the State of New York 6:881; NYCD.

O'Leary, Jamie. "Basque Whaling in Red Bay Labrador." Newfoundland, Canada: Bach Arts English Major, Memorial University of Newfoundland, 1997.

O'Meara, John. *Delaware-English, English-Delaware Dictionary*. Toronto: University of Toronto Press, 1996.

Origin of New Jersey Place Names The, Trenton, NJ: New Jersey Public Library Commission, State House Annex, Trenton, 7, New Jersey, May 1945.

Ottawa Centenary: The Complete Official Program, August 16-21, 1926.

Pearce, Roy Harvey. *The Savages of America; A Study of the Indians, and the Idea of Civilization*. Baltimore: Johns Hopkins Press, 1953, rev. 1965.

Pescadore, Juan Javier. *The New World Inside a Basque Village, 1550-1800*.Internet.

Polk, Nancy. "Horticulture: A Mountain Laurel by Any Other Name." *New York Times*, June 3, 2007.

Pritchard, Evan. *Earth at the Crossroads*. Woodstock, NY: Resonance Communications, 2005.

Pritchard, Evan. *Introductory Guide to Lenape Indian Words and Phrases.* Woodstock, NY. Resonance Communications, 2000.

Pritchard, Evan. *Introductory Guide to Micmac Words and Phrases.* Woodstock, NY. Resonance Communications, 1990.

Pritchard, Evan. *Native American Stories of the Sacred.* Woodstock, Vt. Skylight Paths Press, 2005.

Pritchard, Evan. *Native New Yorkers, The Legacy of the Algonquin People of New York.* Tulsa: Council Oak Books, 2001, revised 2006.

Pritchard, Evan. *No Word For Time, The Way of the Algonquin People.* Tulsa,: Council Oak Books, 1997, 2001.

Prowse, Daniel Woodley. *History of Newfoundland.*

Purchas, Samuel *Henry Hudson's Voyage,* from *Purchas' Pilgrimes,* a facsimile, New York: Google Books, no date.

Quinney, John W. in *Wisconsin Historical Collections,* 1857-1858.

Quinney, John W., Stockbridge Indian Chief, *Celebration of the Fourth of July, 1854* Madison, Wisconsin, 1859.

Rafferty, Sean and Rob Mann. *Smoking and Culture.* Knoxville: University of Tennessee Press, 2004.

Ritchie, Robert C. *The Duke's Province.* Chapel Hill, NC: University of North Carolina Press, 1977.

Ritchie, William A. *Archaeology of New York State.* Fleischmanns, NY: Purple Mountain Press, 1994.

Ruttenber, E.M. *Indian Tribes of Hudson's River, 1700-1850.* Albany: J. Munsell, 1872. Reprinted, Saugerties, NY: Hope Farm Press and Book Shop, 1992.

Ruttenber, E.M. "The Valley of the Moodna in History." Newburgh, NY: Historical Society of Newburgh Bay and the Highlands, 1901. p 59, 60. (Before Zuassaick Chapter DAR, March 30, 1901, and included in this number of the papers of the Historical Society by request.

Salomon, Julian Harris. *Indians of the Lower Hudson Region: The Munsee.* New York: Historical Society of Rockland, 1982.

Sanders, Ronald. *Lost Tribes and Promised Lands: The Origins of American Racism.* New York: Little, Brown/Harper Perrennial, 1978.

Schutt, Amy C. *Peoples of the River Valleys, The Odyssey of the Delaware Indian.* Philadelphia: University of Pennsylvania Press, 2007.

Sepkoski, Jack. "A compendium of fossil marine animal genera (Chondrichthyes entry)." *Bulletins of American Paleontology.*

Seton, Earnest Thompson and Julia Seton. *The Gospel of the Redman.* Santa Fe, New Mexico: Seton Village, 1966,1937. Renewed, 1963 Julia M. Seton.

Sivertson, Karen. *Babel On the Hudson.* Doctoral thesis for Duke University History Department, 2007.

Skinner, Alanson. "Staten Island," *The Indians of Greater New York and the Lower Hudson Valley,* edited by Clark Wissler. New York: Order of Trustees, American Museum of Natural History, September, 1809.

Skinner, Alanson. "Staten Island," quoting Thomas Wilson, "Prehistoric Art," Plate 52, opposite page 481, *Annual Report,* Smithsonian Institution, 1896.

Smith, John. "True Relation" entered for publication at the Stationer's Hall on August 13, 1608. American Scenic and Historic Preservation Society's Fifteenth Annual Report, J.B. Lyon Company, 1910, Submitted to the Legislature of New York, April 19, 1910.

Smithsonian: The National Museum of Natural History Research Training Program website, 2006.

Smithsonian: The National Museum of Natural History exhibit, 2006, The Tyrolean Ice Man.

Sullivan, Dr. James, ed.: *History of New York State, 1523-1927,* Volume 1. New York: Lewis Historical Publishing Company, Inc., 1927.

Stickney, Charles E. *A History of the Minisink Region.* Middletown, NY: Coe Finch and I.F. Guiwits, 1867; reprinted Bowie, MD: Heritage Books, 1995.

Strong, John A. *The Algonquian Peoples of Long Island From Earliest Times to 1700.*

Interlaken, NY: Empire State Books, Heart of the Lakes Publishing, 1997.

Sweet, Harry Montford. "*Where Hudson's Voyage Ended, an Inquiry;* Cohoes and the Origin of the Name." City of Cohoes Hudson-Fulton Celebration, October 10 and 11, 1909. Albany, New York: J.B. Lyon Company, 1909.

Thatcher, Benjamin Bussey (1809-1840). *Indian Biography or an historical account of those individuals who have been distinguished....* New York: Harper and Brothers, 1848.

Tompkins, William. *Universal Indian Sign Language of the Plains Indians of North America.* Canada, 1931. Republished, *Indian Sign Language.* Mineola, NY: Dover Editions, 1969.

Turco, Peggy. *Walks and Rambles in Dutchess and Putnam Counties, A Guide to Ecology and History in Eastern Hudson Valley Parks.* Woodstock, Vt.: Backcountry Publications, 1990.

Underwood, Paula. *Three Strands in the Braid* (in collaboration with Rita Reynolds-Gibbs). Anselmo, California: A Tribe of Two Press, 1984.

Van Buren, Augustus H. *A History of Ulster County Under the Dominion of the Dutch.* New York: J.C. and A.L. Fawcett, Inc. Reprinted Kingston, NY. 1923.

Vedder, Robert. *Journeys into Indian Country.* "The Village of Thirty Centuries." Frederickton, New Brunswick, Canada: Beaver Creek Pictures, Northwest Passage Communications with the participation of the Red Bank First Nation.

Virginia.; *Sir Thomas Gates, Governor.; His services and death.'Preface', Calendar of State Papers Colonial, America and West Indies: 1675-1676 and Addenda 1574-1674, volume 9* (1893), pp. V-LVIII. URL: *http://www.british-history.ac.uk/report.aspx?compid=70022.*

Walcott, Imogene. *The Yankee Cookbook.* Boston:Coward-McCann, Inc., 1938.

Wallace, Paul A. W. *Indian Paths of Pennsylvania.* Harrisburgh: Pennsylvania Historical and Museum Commission, 1998.

Weatherford, Jack. *Indian Givers: How the Indians of the Americas Transformed the World.* New York: Crown Publishers, 1988.

Weslager, C.A. *Dutch Explorers, Traders, and Settlers in the Delaware Valley, 1609-1664.* Philadelphia: University of Pennsylvania Press, 1961.

Weslager, Clinton A. *The Delaware Indian Westward Migration* Wallingford, Pa.: Middle Atlantic Press, 1978.

Weslager, Clinton A. *The Delaware Indians, A History.* New Brunswick, NJ: Rutgers University Press, 1972.

Wilson, Freda F. II. prolegomeno al romanzo Manituana. Pubblicato nell'Aprile 2006.A bibliography of sources for "The Four Kings" at the University of Toronto Press Journals Vol. 16, No 3/1935 266-275.

Wroth, Lawrence *The Voyages of Giovanni da Verrazzano 1524-1528.*

Zeisberger, David.*Essay of a Delaware-Indian and English Spelling-Book for the use of the schools of the Christian Indians on Muskingum River,* Henry Miller, publisher 1776. Reprinted by Arthur W. McGraw, 1991 (ISBN 1-56651-007-4).

http://crystalinks.com/galileo.html.

http://solar-center.stanford.edu/AO/bighorn.html.

www.british-history.ac.uk.

www.delawaretribeofindians.nsn.us/social_dance.html.

www.gmo-safety.eu/en/maize/121.docu.html.

www.ianchadwick.com/hudson/.

www.naturalremedies.com.

www.paulcarlisle.net. (lunar maps).

www.peruvianwhistles.com/el-palacio.html.

www.scienceblogs.com/deepseanews/2008/07/scientist_falls_in_love_with_m.php - 68k - .

Scientist Falls in Love with Manta Rays. The article of July 28, 2008.

www.umaine.edu/folklife/images/Newsletter/winter/winter04-05.pdf.

Other Sources

Anderson, Courtney. Interview, December 2008, New York:

Beeler, Dr. Sam.

Benjamin, Vernon.

Brandt, Valerie (Rainbow Weaver).

De Weerdt, Gerald. Director of the Maritime Museum of Terschelling in the Netherlands (Het Behouden Huys) and former Director of the National Institute of Ship Archaeology in Lelystadt, the Netherlands. Interview, December 2008.

Du Poisson. www.evolpub.com.

Flowers, James, native botanist.

Free, Harold L. map of Tarrytown.

Galilei, Galileo Sidreus Nuncius (*The Sidereal Messenger*).

Goering, Charles, New Netherlands Project. Albany: New York State Library.

Harris, Wendy.

Hart, John P. with Hetty Jo Brumbach, Robert Lusteck, 2007.

Griesshaber, Kurt. Map, "Wappinger Mohegan Indians." Based on information from Ernest Miller, (E. Wolf Miller). Clarence Red Bird and Calvin White Eagle, 1962.

Horecki, Scott.

Huguenot Historical Society, New Paltz, Erik Roth, Director.

ICE (Indigenous Conference on the Environment), Ottawa, Ontario, Canada.

Ietaka, Taro Cranberry Lake Preserve, in Westchester, NY. New York State Parks and Recreation.

Johnson, Edward, curator and science advisor to the Staten Island Museum.

Johnson, Melvin, PhD, June, 2008, interview at George Washington State Historic Site, Newburgh, NY.

Kelly, William, New York State Museum, Albany, NY.

Kimmerer, Robin. interview May, 2008, Pace University, Pleasantville, NY.

Lindner, Chris. Bard College, Annandale on Hudson, New York.

Miller, Pauline S., The Great Sedges.

Moody, David.

New Netherlands Project.

New York State Museum.

Nitch, Twylah.

Onrust Reconstruction. New York Boat Show, Jacob Javitz Center, New York, 2008.

Peters, Chief Mark, former Munsee Chief at Munseetown, Ontario.

Renaud, Monique.

Smith, Michael Sullivan. Map, Saugerties, NY: Hope Farm Press, 2008.

Taffe, Susan M. Lecture, "The Delaware Stick Dance; An Adopted Haudenosaunee Social Dance Song." 2008 Algonquian People's Seminar, sponsored by the Native American Institute of the Hudson River Valley and the New York State Museum. Saturday March 22, 2008, Albany, NY. [She referenced the New York State Historical Society and the O'Reilly Papers and Henry Deerborn.]

Tarwe-town, map of 1781.

Three Crow, Barbara.

Timothy, Beulah Munsee elder.

Touching Leaves Indian Crafts, Dewey, Oklahoma, 1991.

"Underneath the City," exhibit, October 11, 2007. New York State Museum, Albany, NY.

Veit, Richard and Charles A. Bello. Chapter, "Neat and Artificial Pipes: Base Metal Trade Pipes of the Northeastern Indians." (Ch. 7) of *Smoking and Culture; The Archaeology of Tobacco Pipes in Eastern North America,* by Sean Rafferty and Rob Mann.

Wilkes, Brian, former Eastern Band Cherokee sub-chief.

Wright, Kevin. Map, "Indigenous Place Names in North Eastern New Jersey." 1994.

Index

EVAN PRITCHARD, of Mi'kmaq (Algonquin) and Celtic-American descent, is the author of many critically acclaimed books including *Native New Yorkers*, (Council Oak), *No Word for Time* (Council Oak), and *Native American Stories of the Sacred* (Skylight Paths). He is currently adjunct professor of Native American Studies at Pace University (Pleasantville) and Vassar College in Poughkeepsie, New York. He also teaches writing in the English department at Poughkeepsie's Marist College, and World Religion at Pace University. Pritchard lectures frequently around the Eastern United States and in Canada where he has been working with elder William Commanda for many years. Pritchard is the director of the Center for Algonquin Culture in Pine Hill, New York.